P9-DEW-362

American Indian Places

AMERICAN INDIAN PLACES

A Historical Guidebook

FRANCES H. KENNEDY
Editor and Principal Contributor

HOUGHTON MIFFLIN COMPANY
BOSTON NEW YORK
2008

For information about permission to reproduce selections from
this book, write to Permissions, Houghton Mifflin Company,
215 Park Avenue South, New York, New York 10003.

www.houghtonmifflinbooks.com

Library of Congress Cataloging-in-Publication Data
American Indian places : a historical guidebook / Frances H.
Kennedy editor and principal contributor.
p. cm.
ISBN-13: 978–0–395–63336–6
ISBN-10: 0–395–63336–2
1. Indians of North America — Antiquities — Guidebooks. 2. Indians
of North America — History — Guidebooks. 3. Historic sites — United
States — Guidebooks. 4. Sacred places — United States — Guidebooks.
5. United States — Antiquities — Guidebooks. I. Kennedy, Frances H.
E77.9.A44 2008   973.04'97 — dc22   2008013750

Book design by Victoria Hartman
Section maps by Neal Etre
Unicoi Turnpike map, p. 115, by Brett H. Riggs

Printed in the United States of America

DOC 10 9 8 7 6 5 4 3 2 1

This book is dedicated
to all American Indians,
and its proceeds to
the National Museum of
the American Indian

Contents

✦ SECTION THREE

✦ SECTION FOUR

✦ SECTION FIVE

To the Reader

American Indian Places presents 366 places that are significant to American Indians. Each place is open to the public and provides information about that significance. The book does not include places that became significant after 1900. Because so many voices speak through the book, it is more than place-based history. The Native voices share their emotional and cultural responses to the places and provide insights into what they mean to Native people. Many of the Native authors also tell about their people today. The non-Native voices provide archaeological and historical information about the cultures that these places embody. Thanks to all of these voices, *American Indian Places* has become a way to learn about Indian peoples and cultures from a perspective grounded in the places they revere.

The places are organized in five geographic sections, determined by the homelands and subsequent movements of the peoples for whom the places are significant. Within each section, the places are presented in rough chronological order according to the period of their most intense significance. If the significance of a place is not limited to a specific time, the place is presented after one that is nearby geographically.

The places are numbered continuously throughout the book, and each place is followed by the abbreviation of the state name, to facilitate locating them on the section maps.

People who know and revere the places wrote essays on 229 of them. I wrote the short entries for 137 of the places, with the generous assistance of people who know them well (any errors are my own). As place-based history, this book cannot, by its very nature, tell about American Indians as comprehensively as books such as the *Encyclopedia of North American Indians* or *The People: A History of Native America*. So the book begins with three essays that provide an overview of the history of American Indians prior to 1900. Additional essays throughout the text provide general information about Native peoples.

In About the Contributors, the author of each essay has written about his or her work and publications. The publications cited there and in the Further Reading sections at the end of most essays are listed in the Bibliography for readers who want to learn more about the places and people discussed in the book. The Web site of the Tribal Archive, Library, and Museum Directory is a useful source of information about American Indian collections; see http://www

.statemuseum.arizona.edu/frame/index.asp?doc =/aip/leadershipgrant/directory/tlam_directory _03_2005.pdf.

The royalties from the book will go to the National Museum of the American Indian in Washington, D.C. I am very grateful to the Dodge Jones Foundation, the Fund of the Four Directions, and the Weyerhaeuser Family Foundation for grants toward the research expenses of the book.

It has been a great pleasure to edit *American Indian Places* and to learn from the 279 people who wrote the essays. Without them there would be no book. I am very grateful to them. My thanks also to the hundreds of other authorities whom I consulted about these places. They were generous in guiding my research and providing information. There are too many names to list or thank individually, but my gratitude to them is profound. We could include only a few photographs of the places; many thanks to the photographers and to the people at public agencies who contributed them. I thank my friend Rick West for his wise counsel over the years it took to complete this book. I am grateful to Harry Foster, the book's editor at Houghton Mifflin from the beginning until his death in 2007, and to Will Vincent, Lisa White, Peg Anderson, and Liz Duvall, who guided it wisely to publication. My thanks, as always, to Roger Kennedy, who helped and cheered and was with me on the great adventure in learning that is now this book.

Frances H. Kennedy
Washington, D.C.
September 2007

American Indian Places

The National Museum of the American Indian: A Native Place in Washington, D.C.

W. RICHARD WEST, JR.

ON SEPTEMBER 21, 2004, the Smithsonian Institution's National Museum of the American Indian opened on the National Mall in Washington, D.C., resoundingly establishing a Native place in the political center of the nation's capital. Its significance as place is both literal and metaphorical.

As metaphor, the opening of this centerpiece building of the museum transcended, in profound ways, the very boundaries of the occasion. The 25,000 to 30,000 Native people who gathered for the occasion were commemorating much more than the opening of a museum. This international institution of living cultures of the Americas is more than just a new jewel in the illustrious crown of the Smithsonian, America's renowned national cultural institution. The museum's establishment at the head of the National Mall marked a turning point in the consciousness of the Americas regarding the centrality of Native peoples to the shared cultural heritage of all who call themselves Americans.

The National Museum of the American Indian is also quite literally a Native place in many ways. Planned over the course of a decade in direct consultation and collaboration with the Native peoples of the Americas, the physical place and, perhaps more important, its spirit derive directly from the substance and sensibilities of the first citizens of the Americas.

The tangible aspects of the building and its surrounding ecohabitat offer compelling evidence of a thoroughly Native impact. The presence of wetlands, native plants indigenous to the original site, and flowing water that greets and ushers visitors into the building — all signal arrival in a very different place. The building — with its sweeping curvilinear and organic form, its earth-colored Kasota limestone cladding, its embrace of natural light in interior spaces, and its visually permeable skin joining inside and outside — emphasizes architectural accents and themes that directly reflect the institution's collaborative enterprise with Indian Country.

It is the intangible, however, that makes the National Museum of the American Indian a Native place rather than simply a physical space. The museum is about the long continuum through time of Native cultures, peoples, and communities. It embraces and empowers the capacity of Native peoples to represent and interpret themselves to all who visit and learn. This spirit, this combination of the tangible and the intangible, is what makes the Smithsonian's National Museum of the American Indian a powerful and important Native place of the twenty-first century.

Places of the First Americans

DAVID J. MELTZER

ALTHOUGH ARCHAEOLOGISTS HAVE NOT yet pinpointed just how long ago the first people came to America, we are certain they were here during the waning millennia of the Ice Age. These intrepid colonizers witnessed the retreating but still vast glaciers that once buried much of Canada and the northern reaches of the United States under ice. They experienced climates and environments far different from those of today — cooler overall, wetter in some places, drier in others. And they must have gazed across a landscape teeming with a zoo of giant mammals (megafauna) — among them the mammoth, giant ground sloth, and saber-toothed cat — all soon to go extinct.

The earliest archaeologically secure evidence of this pioneering human presence in North America — the Paleoindians — is the Clovis culture, first discovered in the 1930s at an ancient spring-fed pond on the southern High Plains near the New Mexico town of the same name. Although the site was for decades a commercial gravel quarry, it is preserved today as Blackwater Draw Locality 1. There, 11,300 years ago, Clovis people preyed upon large game, such as mammoth and bison, and small, including turtles; it is likely, although the evidence is meager, that they gathered plants as well. Clovis groups

ranged widely and dispersed across much of the continent at archaeologically breathtaking speed. Their signature artifacts — large fluted projectile points — have been found in all corners of the continent. Oddly enough, Clovis points have never been found in Siberia, their presumed ancestral homeland, suggesting that they were invented in America. Routinely depicted as big-game hunters, Clovis groups were almost certainly capable of bringing down a mammoth on the plains or, if the occasion demanded, a mastodon — the elephant denizen of the eastern forests — as can be seen at Mastodon State Historic Site in Missouri. And yet here and elsewhere other animals (turtles again!) and plants were also on the menu. Clovis groups showed great flexibility in adapting to the different resources available in many different landscapes.

Those habitats were changing. As the Ice Age came to a close, climates warmed, plants and animals shuffled about the landscape in response, and the Pleistocene megafauna — thirty-five genera in all — went extinct. But in loss there is opportunity, and on the Great Plains of North America, bison (buffalo), which had long shared the grassland with megafaunal grazers, suddenly found themselves in nearly sole possession of this vast area. Their numbers skyrocketed, and later Paleoindians, known by their signature Folsom points (fluted also, but more finely made), initiated what would become a 10,000-year plains tradition of bison hunting. At a bend of Yellowhouse Draw in Lubbock Lake Landmark in Texas, there is an extraordinary archaeological record of bison hunting from Folsom times to the historic period. At nearby Caprock Canyons State Park, the special relationship between Folsom-age people and bison can be seen in the reconstruction of the discovery of carefully stacked bison jaws and skulls. Bison were taken during the best of times and the worst of times: even in the midst of a 2,000-year-long drought (starting about 7,500 years ago), groups came to places such as Blackwater and Lubbock Lake to hunt the bison that remained, to dig wells to reach fallen water tables, and to gather drought-resistant plants.

The mainstay of life on the plains — the bison — was scarce in other regions, and later Archaic-age human foragers in those places depended on a wide range of animals and plants. The people who lived in the eastern forests gathered a cornucopia of plants and hunted deer, cottontail rabbit, and turkey. Those on the East Coast gathered shellfish in abundance and created large shell mounds and middens. In these forests and in the southwestern deserts, Archaic groups collected an array of wild plant foods, including some that would over time become domesticated, including native squashes and gourds, sumpweed, amaranth, chenopods, and sunflowers. In time these indigenous species were replaced by the great triumvirate of domestic plants brought north from Mesoamerica: corn, beans, and squash. These are the plants that the descendants of Ice Age colonizers provided to the next wave of New World colonizers — those who disembarked from European ships.

FURTHER READING: *Search for the First Americans,* by David J. Meltzer

Indian-White Relations in North America Before 1776

NEAL SALISBURY

THE COLONIZATION OF North America by Europeans decisively altered the histories of the continent's Native peoples. But the scope and impact of these changes varied enormously from one place to another and from one period to another.

When Europeans began arriving in North America, they encountered a land characterized by both continuity and change. For more than ten thousand years, kin-based communities had developed myriad ways of living off the land, of exchanging goods, and otherwise interacting with one another, and of expressing themselves spiritually and aesthetically. This diversity was reflected in their societies, which ranged from small, mobile bands of a few dozen hunter-gatherers in the Great Basin to Mississippian temple-mound centers in the Southeast with thousands of inhabitants.

Indians in some areas were experiencing particularly pronounced changes during the fifteenth and sixteenth centuries. Inhabitants of Chaco Canyon, Mesa Verde, and other Ancestral Pueblo centers in the Southwest had dispersed in the face of drought and political upheaval after the thirteenth century. Their descendants settled in pueblos on the Rio Grande and elsewhere and by the sixteenth century had begun

trading with newly arrived Athabaskan-speaking Apaches and Navajos. In the Mississippi Valley, Cahokia and several other urban trade centers had collapsed in the thirteenth and fourteenth centuries, sending refugees in all directions and significantly reorienting exchange networks and alliances. Elsewhere in the eastern woodlands, a pattern of gradually increasing, intensifying conflict between communities was linked to the pressure of growing populations on resources and to competition for control of exchange networks.

The earliest contacts between Native Americans and Europeans began after the late tenth century as Norse settlers from Iceland established several settlements among Thule Eskimos in Greenland and, briefly, one among Beothuk Indians in Newfoundland. At first the newcomers exchanged metal tools and woolen cloth for animal pelts and ivory. But trade disputes, intensified if not caused by Norse attitudes of superiority, increasingly led to violence. Facing hostile Natives and a gradually cooling climate, the Norse withdrew from America by the fifteenth century.

The Norse departure coincided with the beginning of more sustained European expansion. From the 1490s to the 1590s, Europeans, by various means, spread themselves, their material goods, and their microbes over the eastern subarctic coast, most of the eastern woodlands, and portions of the southwestern interior and the California coast. In the Northeast, some fishermen and whalers gradually turned to specialized trading of glass, cloth, and metal goods for beaver and other furs. Observing Native norms of reciprocity, they succeeded where efforts to kidnap or dominate Indians failed. By the 1580s French traders returned regularly to clients on the Northeast Coast and in the St. Lawrence Valley. In the Southeast, initial Spanish efforts by Ponce de León, Narváez, de Soto, and others, as well as a chain of Jesuit missions on the Atlantic coast, failed because of Indian distrust and resentment. Expeditions from Mexico to the Southwest, led by Fray Marcos de Niza and Coronado, alienated Pueblos and other Native peoples. As a result of all these encounters, many Indians were drawn toward European goods, but their attitudes toward newcomers themselves depended greatly on previous experiences. European diseases proved especially virulent in the Southeast, where they undermined most Mississippian temple-mound centers.

During the early seventeenth century, Europeans made use of alliances and instabilities created by themselves and their predecessors to establish permanent colonies. English colonizers in New England and the Chesapeake took advantage of population losses from epidemics to establish themselves, as did the Spanish in renewing the expansion of Florida. Heavy Spanish levies on Pueblo corn in New Mexico caused Apaches and Navajos to raid the Pueblos for what they had formerly obtained by trade, forcing the Pueblos to rely on the Spanish for protection. The English and the Spanish did not hesitate to use force to subdue Natives they considered subjects. On the St. Lawrence, the exclusion by the Montagnais and the Hurons of the Five Nations Iroquois from direct contact with French traders generated a fierce rivalry.

Upon founding New France in 1608, the French aligned themselves with the Montagnais and Hurons, both to garner the thick pelts of the Canadian interior and to protect these Indians from the Iroquois. In response, the latter began trading with the new colony of New Netherland at its headquarters on the Hudson River.

For the remainder of the century, relations between Natives and colonizers varied enormously from one area to another as groups sought to survive and flourish in a rapidly changing colonial milieu. The influx of settlers in several Atlantic coastal colonies led to violent conflicts over land in New England, New Netherland, and the Chesapeake. Native resentment against Franciscan missionaries and secular authorities led to several revolts by Indians against Spanish rule in Florida and to the massive Pueblo Revolt in New Mexico, in which the Spanish were driven entirely from the region for twelve years (1680–1692).

During the same period, Indian-white relations in the northeastern interior centered on the struggle for control of trade on the St. Lawrence and the Great Lakes. During the 1630s both the Iroquois and the Indian allies of New France suffered losses of population in the face of epidemics and depletions of beaver due to overhunting. Amply supplied with Dutch guns and ammunition, the Iroquois escalated their raids in the 1640s and 1650s into the "Beaver Wars," in which the Five Nations destroyed the Hurons, Petuns, Neutrals, and Eries as political entities and adopted captives and refugees from these nations into their own ranks. Thereafter the Iroquois drove Algonquian-speaking peoples out of their homelands in the eastern Great Lakes, the Michigan Peninsula, and the Ohio Valley. Many of the refugees clustered in the western Great Lakes, where interethnic villages emerged to trade and ally with the French.

The Iroquois were weakened after 1664, when New Netherland was seized by the English. As France moved to arm its Indian allies to the north and as anti-Iroquois sentiment crystallized among eastern Indians from Canada to the Chesapeake, the Iroquois were obliged to subordinate their strategic goals to those of New York and the English empire. They helped defeat anti-English Indians in King Philip's War in New England (1675–76) and then joined the colony of New York in a series of "Covenant Chain" treaties, giving them a role in overseeing subject Indians in several seaboard colonies. In the 1680s they launched a new round of wars against New France's western allies. After these conflicts merged in 1689 with the Anglo-French conflict known as King William's War, growing numbers of Iroquois found the English alliances less than effective in protecting them from devastating attacks. The growth of neutralist and pro-French sentiment finally led the Five Nations to sign treaties of peace and neutrality, known as the Grand Settlement, with both France and England in 1701.

In the meantime, the founding of Charleston in 1670 stimulated the rapid expansion of English trade and settlement in the Southeast. English traders supplied guns to Indians in exchange for deerskins and for captives sold as slaves, mostly to the West Indies. France's establishment of Louisiana in 1699 provided the Choctaws with a source of arms for resisting slave raids by Creeks and Chickasaws, but the Spanish in Florida were less inclined to distribute guns to Timucua, Guale, and Apalachee subjects, who frequently rebelled against Spanish rule. As a result, these peoples were the principal victims of the Indian slave trade. English abuses of their own allies finally led to a large-scale uprising by the Yamasees, supported by the Creeks and Catawbas, in 1715. Only the support of the Cherokees, who had suffered frequently at the hands of the Creeks, enabled the English to crush the Yamasees. Thereafter the Creeks, following the pattern of the Iroquois, pursued a policy of neutrality toward England, France, and Spain.

Indian life west of the Mississippi River also changed decisively during the late seventeenth and early eighteenth centuries, but along very different lines. Although the Spanish formally reconquered New Mexico after the Pueblo Revolt, their dependence on Pueblo support for defending New Mexico obliged them to rule with a lighter hand. In particular, the Franciscans were obliged to tolerate Native religions. The colony also abolished the forced labor system known as the *encomienda.*

During the Spanish absence, Navajos captured many horses and sheep left behind and moved toward a more sedentary way of life based on herding. The Apaches focused more strictly on horses to improve their mobility during raids on the Spanish and on the Pueblos. Navajos and Apaches also traded horses to neighboring peoples, including Utes and Shoshones, some of whom moved on to the southern Great Plains and became known as Comanches. Meanwhile, French traders in Canada and Louisiana extended their activities to the plains, often arming Indians in the process. The effect was to stimulate conflicts over hunting territory in which some Indians were forced from their homelands, such as the Lakota Sioux by bands of Ojibwas (Anishinabes). By midcentury many Plains peoples had incorporated guns and horses into their material and ceremonial lives. Some, such as the Pawnees, Mandans, Arikaras, and Hidatsas, retained their farming, village-oriented ways. Others, such as the Lakota Sioux, Cheyennes, Arapahos, Crows, and Comanches, developed more nomadic ways of life based on the movements of bison herds.

In eastern North America, the rapid growth of the British empire and its settler population was transforming Indian-white relations. Well before the middle of the eighteenth century, settlers occupied most lands east of the Appalachians, forcing peoples like the Housatonics of Massachusetts and the Catawbas of South Carolina to accommodate themselves to a white majority and producing extensive losses of land and autonomy. Others, such as the Delawares of Pennsylvania and the Tuscaroras of North Carolina, were forced from their homelands entirely. Most Delawares fled west toward the Ohio Valley, after the Pennsylvania government and the Iroquois used a fraudulent treaty as a basis for evicting them, while the Iroquoian-speaking Tuscaroras, driven out by force, found refuge as the sixth nation of the Iroquois Confederacy. Even the powerful Creeks were pressured into ceding land to the new colony of Georgia in 1733. (The process was largely, but not exclusively, English; in Louisiana, the French turned on their erstwhile Natchez allies in order to gain land for expanded tobacco production.)

English colonial expansion led to intensified Anglo-French imperial competition. By the late 1740s speculators in Virginia and Pennsylvania were eyeing the upper Ohio Valley as an area for future settlement. The region was inhabited by various Indian peoples, many of them refugees, who were nominally allied with the French but generally sought to remain independent of French, English, and Iroquois influence. Although they resented French efforts to exert more direct control over them, the Shawnees, Delawares, and other Indians were even more alarmed by British intentions. On July 9, 1755, they ambushed General Edward Braddock as his regular troops attempted to seize France's Fort Duquesne; then, along with the Cherokees to the south, they attacked frontier settlements that were encroaching on Indian lands. But in 1758, fearing that the French had gained too great an advantage, the Shawnees, Delawares, and Iroquois agreed, in the Treaty of Easton, to support the English. Within a year, the British and their Indian allies had driven the French from Ohio, and in 1760 they seized New France. In the meantime British troops invaded Cherokee country, burning homes and crops and forcing the Cherokees to surrender in 1761.

The totality of the British victory and the withdrawal of the French from their posts on the Ohio and the Great Lakes stunned Indians in the area accustomed to "playing off" the two powers. Their astonishment turned to anger when the British commander, Sir Jeffrey Amherst, ordered a cessation of presents to allied Indians. Many Natives heeded the message of Neolin, the "Delaware Prophet," who urged a rejection of all contact with Europeans and their goods as the means of restoring Indian autonomy and abundance. Others seized on rumors that the French would return if the Indians began an uprising against the British. In 1763 Indians mounted a series of loosely coordinated assaults on the British posts, since termed "Pontiac's War" after a prominent Ottawa participant. Amherst approved the presentation of smallpox-infested blankets to peace-seeking Indians at Fort Pitt, but the uprising was otherwise settled amicably when the British promised to protect the Indians from settler incursions. By the Proclamation of 1763, Britain established a line along the Appalachian crest, west of which Indians retained title to all lands not freely ceded and from which squatters, outlaws, and unauthorized traders were banned.

British efforts to enforce the new policies foundered on colonial resistance to the policies themselves, to the taxes imposed by the British to finance them, and to the prerogatives claimed by Crown and Parliament vis-à-vis the colonies. The encroachment of settlers on Indian lands continued, and in 1768, financially strapped Britain returned control of trade to the individual colonies. In the same year the British and Iroquois, in the Treaty of Fort Stanwix, ceded Shawnee, Delaware, and Cherokee lands in Ohio without those nations' consent. Tensions remained high along the frontier until the outbreak of the American Revolution. As war approached, the minority of Indians who were already subjects of colonial governments supported the rebels. Most others lined up with the British or sought to remain neutral, hoping thereby to maximize their political sovereignty and cultural integrity in a world radically altered during the preceding three centuries.

Excerpted from the *Encyclopedia of North American Indians*, edited by Frederick E. Hoxie.

FURTHER READING: *New Worlds for All: Indians, Europeans, and the Remaking of Early America*, by Colin G. Calloway

Indian-White Relations in the United States 1776–1900

R. DAVID EDMUNDS

BETWEEN 1776 AND 1900, relations between American Indians and the non-Indian majority in the United States were characterized by a growing imbalance of power between the two peoples and by considerable misunderstanding. In the postrevolutionary period most Native American peoples, while cognizant of the growing political and military power of the new United States, remained politically autonomous. Most tribes east of the Mississippi River were economically dependent upon trade with outsiders, but they maintained considerable political control over their lives. As the nineteenth century progressed, however, Indians became first economically more dependent on, and then politically subjugated by, white men and their governments. Meanwhile, federal programs designed to acculturate and assimilate Indian people into white society generally failed.

During the American Revolution most of the trans-Appalachian tribes supported the British. In the South, American military campaigns generally defeated the Creeks and Cherokees, but in the North the tribesmen carried the war to Kentucky, and by 1783 tribes such as the Shawnees remained on the offensive. Yet after the Treaty of Paris (1783) the Americans treated all tribes as defeated enemies and attempted to dictate policies to them. In the South, Alexander McGillivray centralized power within the Creek Confederacy, and by negotiating a series of diplomatic agreements between Spain, the federal government, and the state of Georgia, he shrewdly, if temporarily, maintained Creek autonomy. North of the Ohio River the federal government claimed ownership of most tribal lands, and when the Indians refused to recognize that claim, federal officials entered into a series of spurious treaties disavowed by most of the tribes. When Indians resisted white settlement north of the Ohio, federal officials dispatched two expeditions — one led by Josiah Harmar (1790), the other by Arthur St. Clair (1791) — against tribal villages along the Maumee watershed, but the tribesmen defeated both armies. Only in 1794, after Anthony Wayne's victory at Fallen Timbers, did the northern tribes sign the Treaty of Greenville, relinquishing their claims to most of Ohio.

Following the Treaty of Greenville, federal officials championed a "civilization program" designed to acculturate Indian people and transform them into small yeoman farmers. During the 1790s Congress passed the Indian Intercourse Acts, a series of laws designed to regulate trade and land transactions, codify legal relationships between Indians and whites, and provide goods and services that would facilitate the government's "civilization" program. Thomas Jefferson was particularly interested in promoting such programs, and during his administration such activity increased.

The programs generally were unsuccessful. Among the southern tribes some mixed bloods who embraced acculturation and established farms and plantations were praised by their agents, but elsewhere the programs floundered. With few exceptions, more traditional tribespeople resented ethnocentric efforts to transform them into carbon copies of white men. Meanwhile the fur trade declined, alcoholism increased, and Indians were repeatedly subjected to racial discrimination and injustice. Socioeconomic conditions among the tribes deteriorated, and tribes were forced to cede additional lands for dwindling annuity payments. In response, many turned to the nativistic teachings of the Shawnee Prophet (Tenskwatawa) and his brother Tecumseh, who offered both a religious deliverance and a unified political front against any further land cessions. During the War of 1812 warriors loyal to Tecumseh joined with the British, while hostile Creeks fought both their kinsmen and the United States. When the war ended, Tecumseh had been killed and the anti-American warriors had been defeated.

In the postwar decade the pace of acculturation accelerated. The Bureau of Indian Affairs (BIA) was founded in 1824, and mixed-blood leaders among the southern tribes joined with Protestant missionaries to advocate Christianity, representative government, statutory laws, literacy, and plantation agriculture. North of the Ohio many mixed-blood leaders, modeling themselves after the Creole French, pursued careers as entrepreneurs. After the election of Andrew Jackson, Congress passed the Indian Removal Act (1830), which was designed to

remove the eastern tribes to the trans-Mississippi West.

Most of the tribes preferred to remain in their homelands. Warfare erupted in 1832 when Black Hawk led a large group of Sauks and Foxes back to Illinois, from which they had been forced to remove to Iowa; the Seminoles fought a protracted guerrilla campaign (the Second Seminole War), which lasted from 1835 to 1842, before part of the tribe was removed to Indian Territory. The Cherokees fought removal in the federal court system, but when the U.S. Supreme Court ruled in their favor (*Worcester* v. *Georgia*, 1832), Jackson ignored the decision and refused to protect the tribe from the state of Georgia. During the 1830s most of the tribes were removed to the West. These forced emigrations, often mismanaged and poorly financed, were disastrous for the Indians. Although some tribes arrived in Kansas or Oklahoma relatively unscathed, others suffered hardship and death. Historians argue over the final figures, but the Cherokees, for example, lost between 2,000 and 4,000 people from a total population of 16,000.

In the West the removed tribes encountered opposition from Indians indigenous to the region (for example, the Osages, Pawnees, and Dakotas), but after an initial period, most endured and some flourished. In Kansas, Potawatomi entrepreneurs sold food, livestock, and fodder to white travelers en route to Colorado and California, while the Cherokees, Creeks, Choctaws, Chickasaws, and Seminoles — a group known as the Five Southern Tribes — reestablished farms, plantations, schools, and tribal governments in eastern Oklahoma.

The Plains tribes fared less well. Their initial distance from white settlement and reliance upon the bison herds provided them with some political and economic autonomy, but during the late 1840s growing numbers of white Americans crossed their territories en route to Oregon and California. Although the popular media have emphasized unfriendly encounters between the

Plains tribes and wagon trains, such confrontations rarely occurred. Sometimes Indians stole horses or pilfered camp equipment, but more often warriors served as guides for wagon trains or traded game for flour, sugar, or other staples. Yet in order to minimize conflict, federal officials decided to concentrate the Plains tribes in areas that were well away from the emigrant trails. In 1851 they met with the northern Plains tribes at Fort Laramie, where most of those tribes agreed to remain north of the Platte River. In 1853 at Fort Atkinson, Kansas, the Comanches, Kiowas, and Apaches promised to stay south of the Arkansas. At times both Indians and whites violated the agreements, which became totally ineffective once the discovery of gold in Colorado and Montana in the late 1850s brought white miners into the area in unprecedented numbers.

During the Civil War the Five Southern Tribes split into pro-Northern and pro-Confederate factions. In most cases these divisions reflected old quarrels from the removal era more than political allegiance to either the North or the South, but the resulting conflict devastated the Cherokees and Creeks, where old animosities sparked particularly bitter warfare. When the conflict ended, federal officials used the pretense of disloyalty to seize lands from the Creeks and Cherokees for use as new reservations for tribes previously residing in other states and territories. Meanwhile, in Minnesota, the Eastern Dakotas rose in retribution for the government's inability to meet past treaty obligations (1862) but were defeated, and thirty-eight of their number were hanged at the largest public mass execution in American history. In Colorado, over 150 peaceful Cheyennes were massacred by militia at Sand Creek (1864), while in the Southwest, James Carleton campaigned against the Apaches and Navajos, sending members from both tribes to a bleak reservation at Bosque Redondo (1863) in eastern New Mexico. Finally, as the Civil War waned,

federal officials violated the 1851 Treaty of Fort Laramie and constructed forts to protect the Bozeman Trail, a road that carried miners across Wyoming's Powder River country to the goldfields. Red Cloud led a successful Sioux resistance, then signed the Second Treaty of Fort Laramie (1868), a document in which the Sioux and other northern Plains tribes agreed to remain within well-defined borders in exchange for federal promises to protect both the tribes and their territories.

The Second Treaty of Fort Laramie foreshadowed President Ulysses Grant's "Peace Policy," which began in the 1870s. Influenced by reformers, Grant appointed a board of commissioners to oversee Indian policy and then assigned different Indian agencies to various religious denominations. Responding to charges of corruption, he replaced career bureaucrats with religious leaders and other reformers. Although the latter were motivated by high ideals, they often lacked experience, and after 1880 the policy was abandoned.

Ironically, the Peace Policy years also witnessed the last of the "Indian wars," which pitted soldiers against tribesmen who resisted confinement to reservations. Confrontations occurred between the government and the Modocs (1873), the Nez Perces (1877), and the Utes (1879), but the most notable clashes took place on the northern plains and in Arizona. In 1874, after gold was discovered in the Dakota Territory's Black Hills, miners invaded the region and the Sioux struck back, killing prospectors. Since the army could not keep miners from the Black Hills, federal officials violated the Second Fort Laramie Treaty, seizing the hills and demanding that all Sioux relocate onto new reservations. When several bands refused, military expeditions were dispatched, and on June 25, 1876, George A. Custer and 225 soldiers were defeated and killed at the battle of the Little Bighorn. Within six months most of the Sioux were forced onto reservations. In the Southwest,

Victorio, Nana, and Geronimo led an Apache resistance that extended from 1874 until 1886, when Geronimo finally surrendered.

The final two decades of the nineteenth century marked the nadir of Native American existence. Confined to reservation lands that whites considered undesirable, many Indian people existed through the acceptance of annuity payments or demeaning food rations. Although the Five Southern Tribes and a few other tribal governments still exercised some control over their constituents, most Indians were stripped of political power by military forces and federal bureaucrats. Some participated in government-sponsored agricultural programs, but most reservations were ill suited to farming. Continuing a policy of mandatory acculturation, the BIA urged tribespeople to adopt white dress, economic skills, and domestic institutions and to speak English. Indian parents were forced to enroll their children in distant boarding schools, where the students were forbidden to speak their Native languages and were taught to disdain their tribal heritage. Federal agents supported Christian missionary efforts but outlawed traditional religious practices, including dances, ball games, and other ceremonies. Meanwhile, tuberculosis, trachoma, and other communicable diseases ravaged the reservations. By 1900 the Native American population in the United States had fallen to 237,196, the lowest figure ever reported in any recorded census.

In response, Indian people again turned to religion. Although some of the tribal religions, particularly in the Southwest, persisted, others were overshadowed by newer, more syncretic beliefs. The peyote faith, long a tradition among the Lipan Apaches, emerged among the tribes of southwestern Oklahoma. Combining traditional beliefs with Christianity, the "Peyote Road" offered Indian people a religious manifestation of pan-Indian identity, but it was opposed by the BIA and missionaries. In the Northwest, revivalistic leaders such as Smohalla (1870s), Taivibo

(1870s), and John Slocum (1880s) paved the way for Wovoka, a Paiute holy man whose vision in 1889 initiated the Ghost Dance, a ceremony promising that both the Indians' dead relatives and the bison would return to a world free of white men. The new faith spread to the northern plains, where it found willing converts among the Sioux, a people devastated by their reservation experiences. Tragically, the conversion of the Western Sioux threatened both the military and local Indian agents. In December 1890 American troops surrounded a party of Ghost Dancers led by Big Foot, and a scuffle led to the Battle of Wounded Knee, in which more than 150 Indians and 29 soldiers were killed.

Convinced that the reservations contributed to the Indians' "lack of progress," reformers such as Carl Schurz, Helen Hunt Jackson, and participants at the Lake Mohonk Conference (a meeting of religious and humanitarian leaders in New York State) petitioned Congress to abolish the reservation system. In response Congress passed the General Allotment Act in 1887, which instructed the BIA, upon the president's recommendation, to divide reservations into 160-acre plots, which would be assigned to individual Indians. The reformers believed that such legislation would provide each Indian with a small farm, strengthen the Indians' commitment to private property, and force Indian people to leave their communal tribal villages. Unfortunately, the act also was supported by special-interest groups that wished to gain access to reservation lands, since the surplus land left after allotment would be sold to white settlers. To prevent fraud, individual allotments supposedly would be held in trust by the government for twenty-five years, after which Indians would receive the allotments in fee simple.

Indian people overwhelmingly opposed allotment, but federal officials began to divide their lands anyway, concentrating first on those reservations that held good agricultural land. Although the Five Southern Tribes, the Osages, and a few other groups initially were exempt from allotment, other legislation soon made them eligible. Meanwhile, additional legislation altered the size of the allotments and limited the safeguards on eligibility so that the actual administration of the allotment process was rampant with fraud. In 1887, prior to the act's passage, Indian people owned approximately 138 million acres. In 1934, when allotment finally ceased, they held only 48 million acres, half of which was either desert or semidesert. Obviously, by 1900 Indian people could look back over a "century of dishonor" and looked forward to an uncertain future.

Excerpted from the *Encyclopedia of North American Indians,* edited by Frederick E. Hoxie.

FURTHER READING: *The People: A History of Native America,* by R. David Edmunds, Frederick E. Hoxie, and Neal Salisbury

SECTION ONE

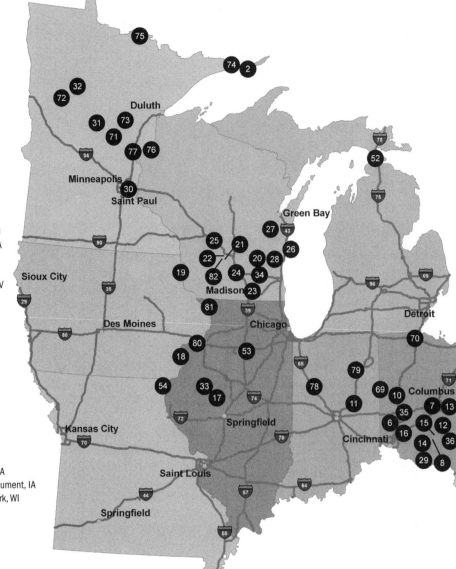

1. Flint Ridge, OH
2. Isle Royale National Park, MI
3. Rock House Reservation, MA
4. Grave Creek Mound Historic
   Site, WV
5. South Charleston Mound, WV
6. Miamisburg Mound, OH
7. Shrum Mound, OH
8. Story Mound, OH
9. Conus Mound, OH
10. Piqua Historical Area, OH
11. Mounds State Park, IN
12. Hopewell Culture National
    Historical Park, OH
13. Newark Earthworks, OH
14. Fort Hill, OH
15. Seip Mound, OH
16. Fort Ancient, OH
17. Rockwell Mound Park, IL
18. Toolesboro Indian Mounds, IA
19. Effigy Mounds National Monument, IA
20. Nitschke Mounds County Park, WI
21. Man Mound County Park, WI
22. Devil's Lake State Park, WI
23. Panther Intaglio, WI
24. Mendota State Hospital, WI
25. Indian Mounds Park, WI
26. Sheboygan Indian Mound County Park, WI
27. High Cliff State Park, WI
28. Lizard Mound County Park, WI
29. Serpent Mound, OH
30. Indian Mounds Park, MN
31. Gull Lake Recreation Area, MN
32. Itasca State Park, MN
33. Dickson Mounds Museum, IL
34. Aztalan State Park, WI
35. SunWatch Indian Village/Archaeologica l Park, OH
36. Leo Petroglyph, OH
37. Whaleback Shell Midden State Historic Site, ME
38. Colonial Pemaquid State Historic Site, ME

39. Maquam Wildlife Management Area, VT
40. Mashantucket Pequot Museum and Research Center, CT
41. Acadia National Park, ME
42. St. Croix Island International Historic Site, ME
43. Cape Cod National Seashore, MA
44. The Cliffs of Aquinnah, MA
45. Mohawk Trail State Forest, MA
46. Deerfield, MA
47. Plimoth Plantation, MA

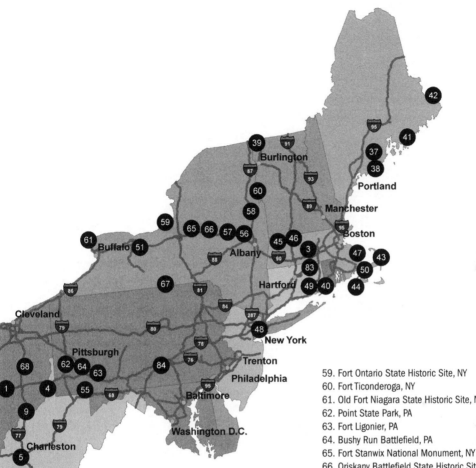

59. Fort Ontario State Historic Site, NY
60. Fort Ticonderoga, NY
61. Old Fort Niagara State Historic Site, NY
62. Point State Park, PA
63. Fort Ligonier, PA
64. Bushy Run Battlefield, PA
65. Fort Stanwix National Monument, NY
66. Oriskany Battlefield State Historic Site, NY
67. Newtown Battlefield State Park, NY
68. Schoenbrunn Village, OH
69. Fort Recovery, OH
70. Fallen Timbers Battlefield and Fort Miamis National
    Historic Site, OH
71. Mille Lacs Kathio State Park, MN
72. Tamarac National Wildlife Refuge, MN
73. Rice Lake National Wildlife Refuge, MN
74. Grand Portage National Monument, MN
75. Voyageurs National Park, MN
76. Folle Avoine Historical Park, WI
77. North West Company Fur Post, MN
78. Tippecanoe Battlefield and Prophetstown State Park, IN
79. Forks of the Wabash Historic Park, IN
80. Black Hawk State Historic Site, IL
81. Apple River Fort State Historic Site, IL
82. Battle of Wisconsin Heights, WI
83. Tantiusques, MA
84. Carlisle Indian Industrial School, PA

48. Historic Battery Park and the Smithsonian
    National Museum of the American Indian's
    George Gustav Heye Center, NY
49. Fort Shantok, CT
50. Old Indian Meetinghouse, MA
51. Ganondagan State Historic Site, NY
52. Marquette Mission Park and Mackinac
    State Historic Parks, MI
53. Starved Rock State Park, IL
54. Iliniwek Village State Historic Site, MO
55. Fort Necessity National Battlefield, PA
56. Old Fort Johnson, NY
57. Johnson Hall State Historic Site, NY
58. Lake George Battlefield Park, NY

1. Flint Ridge, OH

Off I-70 on Rte. 668, north of Brownsville

Museum

About 10,000 years ago people began quarrying flint in a five-square-mile area here. They shaped the flint into knives, projectile points, and other tools, which were traded so widely that they have been found from the Atlantic coast to western Missouri.

2. Isle Royale National Park, MI: The Minong Mine

Caven Clark and Tim Cochrane

By ferry from Houghton and Copper Harbor, MI, and from Grand Portage, MN

People began mining copper at Isle Royale National Park possibly as early as 4500 B.C. The copper is in the Keweenawan geologic formation and is also a component of the glacial drift concentrated by water action along the shorelines and in riverbeds to the south of the formation. Much of the mining was along the Minong Ridge, which the early people — and more recently the Ojibwe — reached by canoeing into McCargoe Cove. They left hundreds of pit and fissure mines as well as the cobble hammerstones used to separate the nearly pure copper from the basalt bedrock. They used cold-hammering techniques to make spear points, gaffs, hooks, awls, and other tools. More recent people made smaller objects, including knives and beads. They traded or exchanged copper as far as the Ohio Valley and Illinois, where it was fabricated into highly ornamented objects. The Ojibwe revered copper and associated it with the underwater being Mishebeshu, the Long-Tailed Underwater Panther, to which offerings were made for safe canoe passages across the lakes. The Ojibwe also used copper tablets to record clan genealogies.

Rumors and legends of an island made of copper in Lake Superior attracted French, English, and, later, American explorers, but the Indians kept secret the locations of large boulders of pure copper. After they lost control of the copper sites, Ojibwe worked as miners and fishermen on Isle Royale. Minong (the beautiful place in Ojibwe) continues to be important to Grand Portage and Canadian Ojibwe living along the north shore of Lake Superior.

FURTHER READING: "A Risky Business: Late Woodland Copper Mining on Lake Superior," by Caven P. Clark and Susan R. Martin, in *The Cultural Landscape of Prehistoric Mines*, edited by Peter Topping and Mark Lynott

3. Rock House Reservation, MA

On Rte. 9, east of Ware

Glaciers carved this rock shelter, which people used as a winter camp from as early as 8000 B.C. until about the 1600s.

Early Mound Builders

BRADLEY T. LEPPER

❖ The fertile valleys of the Ohio River and its many tributaries were home to people known for their prodigious and intricate earthen mounds and enclosures. A cascade of their innovations began to appear in the Ohio Valley by about 800 B.C., when hunting and gathering peoples began to settle in small villages. Their more sedentary way of life was supported by the earliest domesticated plants in this region, including squash, sunflower, maygrass, knotweed, and goosefoot. These early farmers made the region's first pottery vessels and used them to store or cook their harvested crops. They also acquired exotic materials such as copper and marine shells to make ornaments and ritual objects.

One of the most distinctive of these early farming cultures was the Adena, named by archaeologists after the estate of former Ohio governor Thomas Worthington, the location of a renowned burial mound. In the early 1900s archaeologists excavated the mound before it was leveled for cultivation. The most spectacular artifact found in the Adena mound was a marvelous cylindrical pipe sculpted in the form of a man, perhaps a shaman, wearing a decorated loincloth and a feather bustle. (It is now in the Ohio Historical Center.) The Adena culture was centered in southern Ohio, southern Indiana, northern Kentucky, and West Virginia from about 800 B.C. to A.D. 100. The people lived in small, dispersed villages, and the mounds may have been ceremonial hubs connecting networks of neighboring people. Two of the most impressive burial mounds are the Grave Creek and Miamisburg mounds, whereas the Story and Shrum mounds are perhaps more typical in size. Mounds State Park is one of the best-preserved Adena earthwork centers. (The Adena mounds are places numbered 4 through 11.)

4. Grave Creek Mound Historic Site, WV

801 Jefferson Ave., Moundsville

Delf Norona Museum

This mound, built between about 250 and 150 B.C., was 69 feet high and 295 feet in diameter when measured in 1838.

5. South Charleston Mound, WV

In Staunton Park off U.S. 60 on Seventh Ave., South Charleston

This mound is 35 feet high and 175 feet in diameter.

6. Miamisburg Mound, OH

Off I-75 at exit 44; off Rte. 725 on Mound Ave., south of Miamisburg

This conical burial mound on a bluff above the Great Miami River is 877 feet in circumference and was once more than 70 feet high.

7. Shrum Mound, OH

In Campbell Park on McKinley Ave. south of Trabue Rd., Columbus

This conical burial mound is about 20 feet high and 100 feet in diameter.

8. Story Mound, OH

On Delano St. off Allen Ave., Chillicothe

This burial mound is about 20 feet high and 95 feet in diameter.

9. Conus Mound, OH

Mound Cemetery at Fifth and Scammell sts., Marietta

This burial mound is about 30 feet high.

10. Piqua Historical Area, OH

9845 North Hardin Rd., northwest of Piqua

Museum

This small circular earthwork is on a farm that was the home of John Johnston, the U.S. Indian agent for western Ohio between 1812 and 1829.

11. Mounds State Park, IN

On Rte. 232, east of Anderson

Visitor center

The Great Mound is the largest of the ten Adena earthworks in the park. It was built about 160 B.C. and has locations for astronomical observations, including sunset at the summer and winter solstices.

Between 100 B.C. and A.D. 400 in southern Ohio, an explosion of art, architecture, and ritual reverberated across eastern North America. Archaeologists named it the Hopewell culture after the Hopewell farm near Chillicothe, which encompassed a marvelously rich series of mounds and elaborate enclosures. Hopewell mounds generally mark the location of large wooden buildings, sometimes referred to as charnel houses but probably more analogous to the Big Houses used for ceremonial gatherings by many tribes, including the Delaware and the Creek. The Hopewell may have used these timber structures for a variety of social and ritual purposes, including burial of the dead, before they dismantled the small buildings and buried them beneath mounded earth. Another Big House might then have been built nearby to serve the needs of the next generation. Mound City Group in Hopewell Culture National Historical Park is an enclosure surrounding more than twenty mounds, varying in shape and size, which may represent successive Big Houses used by the surrounding communities and then buried beneath the commemorative mounds.

Hopewell villages were not much larger than Adena settlements, but their sphere of influence was more extensive. Hopewell artisans worked in materials gathered from the ends of their world, including mica from the Carolinas and obsidian from the Rocky Mountains, in addition to copper and seashells. The most extraordinary achievements of the people of the Hopewell culture were the huge earthen enclosures that framed their places of ceremony. Many people must have participated in their construction, and the enormous spaces they enclose could have accommodated vast congregations. At Fort Ancient in southern Ohio, 3.5 miles of embankments wind their way around a mesalike hilltop. The Newark Earthworks include a series of gigantic enclosures built in the shapes of circles, squares, and an octagon. These were connected by parallel-walled roads in ways that suggest highly ritualized movement through this labyrinthine geometry. One set of parallel walls extended more than 10 miles to the southwest in a straight line aimed at another center of Hopewell earthworks, now the Hopewell Culture National Historical Park, more than 60 miles away. The great earthworks may have been pilgrimage centers to which visitors traveled along these sacred roads. The monumental architecture that is one of the hallmarks of the Hopewell culture depended upon close cooperation among dozens of villages. It is not known what force held these coalitions together or why they came apart in the fifth century, giving rise to more regionally diverse cultures. (The Hopewell mounds are numbered 12 through 18.)

12. Hopewell Culture National Historical Park, OH

Off Rte. 104, north of Chillicothe

Visitor center

The earthwork sites are Mound City Group, Hopeton Earthworks, and portions of High Bank Works, Hopewell Mound Group, and Seip Earthworks. At Mound City an enclosure surrounds twenty-three burial mounds. The exhibits include fine examples of Hopewell artistry, including a bird-shaped copper cutout.

13. Newark Earthworks, OH

99 Cooper Ave., Newark

Earthworks once covered more than 4 square miles between the tributaries of the Licking River. The Great Circle Earthworks cover 26 acres and are about 1,200 feet in diameter and 8 to 14 feet high. A mound inside the circle marks the site of a Hopewell Big House. The Octagon Earthworks encloses 50 acres and is connected by parallel walls to a circular embankment that encloses 20 acres. The walls of the octagon are aligned to moonrises and moonsets marking the 18.6-year

lunar cycle. The 50-foot-long earthwork in the Wright Earthworks is the only remaining side of a large, square enclosure. Another segment preserves part of the parallel walls that connected the square with another earthwork.

14. Fort Hill, OH

Off Rte. 41 on Fort Hill Rd., south of Cynthiana

Museum

The 6- to 15-foot wall of earth and stone — 1.5 miles long — encloses about 40 acres of the hilltop.

15. Seip Mound, OH

On U.S. 50, east of Bainbridge

The burial mound is 240 feet long, 130 feet wide, and 30 feet high.

16. Fort Ancient, OH

Rte. 350, southeast of Lebanon

Museum

The earth and stone walls on a bluff above the Little Miami River are 4 to 25 feet high and about 18,000 feet long. People of the Hopewell culture built them between about 1 B.C. and A.D. 400. The people of the later Fort Ancient culture (circa A.D. 1000–1650) built a village within the walls. They were a regionally distinctive group of settled farmers who lived in central and southern Ohio as well as in neighboring parts of Kentucky and Indiana. They cultivated maize, beans, and squash and frequently surrounded their villages with a palisade or an earthen wall or ditch, suggesting the need for defense. In the later phases of Fort Ancient, there is evidence for the increasing adoption of ideas derived from the Mississippian civilizations to the west and south, such as Cahokia and Moundville.

17. Rockwell Mound Park, IL

Orange and Franklin sts., Havana

The date of the 2-acre mound is about A.D. 200; it is 14 feet high.

18. Toolesboro Indian Mounds, IA

On Rte. 99, Toolesboro

Education center

The seven burial mounds are on a bluff near the confluence of the Iowa and Mississippi rivers.

FURTHER READING: *People of the Mounds: Ohio's Hopewell Culture*, by Bradley T. Lepper

Effigy Mound Builders

ROBERT A. BIRMINGHAM

❖ Between about A.D. 700 and 1100, the people who lived in the present-day upper Midwest sculpted the landscape into thousands of shapes that to our eyes include birds, animals, and people. Most of the effigy mounds are between 75 and 700 feet long, but the largest recorded is a bird with a wingspan of ¼ mile. Effigy mound forms and their landscapes provide important clues to their meaning. Some, but not all, of the mounds were places of interment, suggesting that their purpose transcended mortuary ritual. Birds are common on higher elevations. There are bears on slopes and waterbirds and long-tailed "water spirits" near water. The geographic distribution of the mounds and the location and arrangement of mound groups suggest a direct relationship between ideology and landscape, and between the supernatural and the natural world. The mound groups vary in size from a few mounds to several hundred, and most are near lakes, rivers, or streams. Some include round or rectangular earthen enclosures, perhaps creating ceremonial areas.

Archaeological evidence suggests that the effigy mound groups were ceremonial centers where fairly mobile people gathered from over a broad area. These people hunted, collected wild foods, and probably kept small gardens. Effigy mound building diminished as the shift to corn agriculture consolidated the communities. By 1200, as the people formed more sedentary farming villages in several densely occupied areas, they stopped building mounds and ceremonial earthworks. A new culture emerged, called Oneota by archaeologists. Some scholars believe that these people are the ancestors of the Ho-Chunk (Winnebago) and related Chiwere Sioux–speaking nations: Ioway, Missouria, and Otoe. There are links between effigy mound symbolism and the traditional beliefs and clan structure of some American Indian peoples today, such as the Ho-Chunk/Winnebago. (These effigy mounds are numbered 19 through 28.)

19. Effigy Mounds National Monument, IA

On Rte. 76, north of Marquette

Visitor center

Of the more than two hundred mounds in the monument along the Mississippi River, thirty-one are bird and bear effigy mounds. The climate, geology, plants, and animals sustained the remarkable people who formed the mounds — some of which are burial mounds — beginning more than 2,500 years ago.

20. Nitschke Mounds County Park, WI

Off Rte. 26 on County Rd. E, south of Burnett

The forty-six effigy, conical, and linear mounds along a drumlin include "water spirit" effigy mounds. The major springs at the base of the drumlin are the only source of water in the area.

21. Man Mound County Park, WI

On Man Mound Rd., northeast of Baraboo

The effigy mound is in the shape of a huge walking man.

22. Devil's Lake State Park, WI: Mounds

Off Rte. 159, south of Baraboo

The four effigy mounds are near the lake.

23. Panther Intaglio, WI

On Rte. 106, west of Fort Atkinson

Early people scooped out a 125-foot-long intaglio near the Rock River.

24. Mendota State Hospital, WI: Mounds

Troy Dr., Madison

Visitors must check in at the administration building

The large conical and effigy mounds are on the hospital grounds.

25. Indian Mounds Park, WI

Off U.S. 12, south of New Lisbon

There are conical, linear, compound or chain, and effigy mounds in the park, some of which have been restored.

26. Sheboygan Indian Mound County Park, WI

South 9th St., Sheboygan

There are sixteen restored conical and effigy mounds.

27. High Cliff State Park, WI: Mounds

On Lake Winnebago off Rte. 55, Sherwood

There are conical and effigy mounds in the park.

28. Lizard Mound County Park, WI

Off Rte. 144 and County Rd. A, northeast of West Bend

Some of the twenty-nine mounds have been restored.

FURTHER READING: *Indian Mounds of Wisconsin,* by Robert A. Birmingham and Leslie Eisenberg

29. Serpent Mound, OH

3850 Rte. 73, northwest of Peebles

Museum

The 1,348-foot-long mound is in the shape of an uncoiling snake. Its head is aligned with the setting sun on the summer solstice, and other solar alignments have been suggested for the serpent's coils. Recent radiocarbon dates for charcoal from two layers of the mound range from A.D. 1025 to 1215. If accurate, these dates indicate that the people of the Fort Ancient culture, farmers who lived in the area, built the mound. One of their villages is nearby. It is not known if there were cultural connections between these people and those who built the effigy mounds of the Upper Midwest.

30. Indian Mounds Park, MN

Mounds Blvd. along the Mississippi River, St. Paul

People have hunted, gathered, and lived on the bluff above the river since about 10,000 years ago. Mound-building people built burial mounds here, six of which remain. They and more recent American Indians lived in villages along the river.

31. Gull Lake Recreation Area, MN: Mounds

Off Rte. 371, northwest of Brainard

Interpretive center

The people who lived in the area between about 800 B.C. and A.D. 900 built burial mounds.

32. Itasca State Park, MN

Off U.S. 71, north of Park Rapids

Jacob V. Brower Visitor Center

About 8,000 years ago people killed bison by driving them into bogs about 6 miles south of today's headwaters of the Mississippi River. Sometime about 1,000 years ago, people built a village and burial mounds near the headwaters.

33. Dickson Mounds Museum, IL

10956 N. Dickson Mounds Rd., Lewistown

On the grounds of the archaeological museum are the Dickson Mounds, a burial ground from about A.D. 1000 to 1250; the Myer-Dickson Site, a Mississippian village; the Eveland Village Site, which may have been the ceremonial center for villages in the area about A.D. 1100; the Ogden-Fettie Site, where people of the Hopewell culture built more than thirty mounds; the Pond Camp Site of about 50 B.C.; and the Dickson Camp Site of about 150 B.C.

34. Aztalan State Park, WI

South of I-94 on County Rd. Q, southeast of Lake Mills

Farmers built their first village here between A.D. 800 and 900. Mississippian people came north after about 1000 and built a village that had platform mounds surrounded by a timber and clay wall on the west bank of the Crawfish River. Two of the three mounds and segments of the wall have been reconstructed. The people left between 1200 and 1300.

35. SunWatch Indian Village/Archaeological Park, OH

Off I-75 at exit 51 to West River Rd., Dayton

Interpretive center

About A.D. 1200, people of the Fort Ancient culture built a village in concentric circles: a center pole was surrounded by a plaza, then a ring of burials, another ring of storage and trash pits, and another of ceremonial and other houses. A stockade encircled the village. After farming along the Great Miami River for about fifteen to twenty years, the villagers left. The reconstruction includes five lath, daub, and thatch buildings, the center post complex from which they made astronomical alignments, part of the stockade, and a native garden with crops typical of those grown by the villagers.

36. Leo Petroglyph, OH

Northwest of Jackson, in Leo

The Fort Ancient people who lived in this area between about A.D. 1000 and 1650 carved thirty-seven petroglyphs into the sandstone on the edge of the ravine.

Eastern North America

DANIEL K. RICHTER

❖ For many people, North America east of the Mississippi hardly seems part of Indian country at all. Populated in the historical imagination by a handful of characters blended more from myth and literary invention than from hard evidence — Pocahontas, Squanto, Tamanend, and Natty Bumppo's sidekick, Chingachgook — the East seems frozen in a time of dramatic discoveries by explorers, first Thanksgivings, chance encounters in the woods, and occasional bursts of bloody interracial violence. But perhaps most profoundly, the East seems a landscape where Indians are a phenomenon of the distant past, a landscape where for centuries no Native People have dwelled, where somehow, right from the first chapter of the story, the race was doomed on a practically empty continent that waited patiently for Europeans to put it to good use. Significantly, the characters who populate this imaginary Eastern Indian past are almost always solitary individuals rather than members of vibrant communities. In *The Last of the Mohicans,* James Fenimore Cooper had Chingachgook speak for them all: "Where are the blossoms of those summers! — fallen, one by one; so all of my family departed, each in his turn, to the land of spirits. I am on the hilltop and must go down into the valley; and when Uncas follows in my footsteps there will no longer be any of the blood of the Sagamores, for my boy is the last of the Mohicans."

Of course these images of solitary Indians on an empty landscape tell us far more about the comforting myths of European conquerors than about historical reality. The name by which Pocahontas knew her corner of that landscape on Chesapeake Bay, after all, was Tsenacomoco, "the densely inhabited land." Exact statistics will never be known, but in 1492 the land east of the Mississippi was probably home to well over 2 million people, most of whom spoke one of the many diverse languages that comprised five great mutually unintelligible linguistic families. The southeastern interior belonged to speakers of Muskogean languages, whose descendants would be known as Creeks, Choctaws, and Chickasaws. Siouan languages dominated the southern Piedmont from the present-day Carolinas at least as far north as Virginia. Iroquoian speakers — divided for many centuries between a southern group, consisting of ancestors of the Cherokees and Tuscaroras in present-day Georgia, Tennessee, and North Carolina, and a northern group, including the Iroquois, Hurons, Susquehannocks, and others encircling Lakes Erie and Ontario — occupied most of the East's midsection. Surrounding them in a vast inverted V — from the Ohio River through much of present-day Canada and down the coast to the Chesapeake — were speakers of the Algonquian languages. Each of these linguistic groupings had even less in common than did the Germanic and Romance language families of Europe, and each contained several related but mutually unintelligible languages further diversified into countless local dialects. Nearly everywhere, agricultural villages composed of a few dozen to a few thousand people were the norm; these might be linked in loose regional confederacies or short-lived, more tightly centralized polities, but for the most part each community was independent of the others.

Still, for all its decentralized diversity, and the inevitable hostilities that resulted, eastern Indian country was deeply interconnected. Routes of trade and communication, most of them millennia old and following the great river systems, crossed the continent. The goods that moved along them were, for the most part, few and rare — rarer and perhaps more valuable than the gold and spices that Western Europeans of the same era traveled the world to acquire. Some closely neighboring peoples might exchange crucial resources, such as corn for meat or fish, and some at slightly greater distances may have controlled access to particularly valuable quarries that provided the raw materials for stone tools or weapons. But long-distance exchanges centered on exotic substances such as marine shells and beads made from them, chunks of rare minerals such as mica, and pieces of copper cold-worked into various forms. Such items, found at archaeological sites deep in the continental interior — shell beads from the mid-Atlantic and Gulf coasts, copper from the Great Lakes region, quartz from the Rocky Mountains — attest to the existence of trade. The fact that exotic goods are most often found in cemeteries and burial mounds suggests that their primary value was believed to be spiritual rather than utilitarian or, rather, that their utility rested on concerns deeper than mere food, drink, and shelter.

Later Indian stories that describe such items as gifts from "underwater grandfathers" or spirit beings further suggest both their rarity and their great significance to those who acquired them. That they were described as gifts rather than commodities also suggests something about how such goods moved along the ancient communication routes; they probably passed from hand to hand in small-scale reciprocal exchanges rather than through the marketplace behavior that Europeans would recognize as trade. Nonetheless, reciprocity did not necessarily imply equality, and the exchanges often confirmed differential access to power, spiritual as well as political. Underwater grandfathers had more power than those on whom they bestowed their gifts, and so did the intermediary figures who in turn gave the gifts to others. Leaders enhanced, if they did not acquire, their status by access to tribute and control of exotic commodities. They displayed their lofty status by wearing rare, spiritually charged goods such as copper or shell on their bodies and by claiming titles such as *mananatowick* (paramount chief), which shares a common Algonquian linguistic root with *manitou* (spiritual power).

Much of the interconnected countryside in which these leaders and their followers lived would, indeed, have appeared to our eyes empty of human inhabitants, for each village required extensive hunting and fishing territories to supplement the people's agricultural diet. Men spent weeks, perhaps months, on end traversing these territories, pursuing game, conducting diplomacy, and waging war, leaving the villages a realm controlled by women much of the time. But no one would have mistaken those villages — packed with the large communal houses of kin groups traced through the female line, surrounded by the acres of corn, bean, and squash fields that the women cultivated, often surrounded by heavy palisaded fortifications that protected them from enemies — as anything other than a "densely inhabited land." Iroquoian villages of what is today upstate New York, for instance, sheltered on average about 200 people per acre in the early seventeenth century, a concentration no city in the United States would match even in its most crowded wards until well into the nineteenth century.

During the seventeenth century, the numbers of eastern Natives shrank rapidly as European colonists unwittingly brought with them epidemic diseases to which Indians had no immunity. Still, as late as 1700, the colonizers' population barely exceeded 250,000, and the colonists were confined almost exclusively to coastal and riverine enclaves, most very near the Atlantic seaboard. By 1750 the population balance had shifted decisively, with Europeans and their enslaved African work force exploding to nearly 1.25 million and the Native population probably shrinking to less than 250,000. Nonetheless, the vast area between the Appalachians and the scattered French outposts on the Mississippi remained almost entirely in Indian hands. It would take until the eve of U.S. independence for the number of Euro-Americans and African Americans to exceed 2 million and return the total population of the East to the level it probably sustained in 1492. And it would take until nearly 1820 for the United States to gain hegemony between the mountains and the Mississippi.

Eastern North America, then, was not a new world but an old one, the product of millennia of Native experience and centuries of interaction between colonizers and colonized. The localism, the patterns of long-distance exchange, the connections between reciprocity and power, the rivalries that existed between diverse Native communities — all shaped early American history in profound ways. Thus, try as nineteenth-century mythologizers like Daniel Webster might to imagine the "descendants of New England ancestors, living, free and happy, in regions which scarce sixty years ago were tracts of unpenetrated forests," reminders that the United States grew up in, and was molded by, Indian country were everywhere those forests used to be. What the citizens of the new nation could not obliterate, they appropriated to their own purposes, dressing as "Mohawks" to throw tea into Boston Harbor, preserving Algonquian and Muskogean place names on real estate maps, modeling fraternal organizations and athletic mascots after what they wanted Indian people to be, creating *Last of the Mohicans* characters to die with obligingly noble inevitability. In their darker moments, white Americans might even admit (and in their worst moments celebrate) that their nation's prosperity was based on the expropriation of Native land or that its participatory politics rested on racial exclusion — for all these admissions still envisioned a continent on which, either gloriously or tragically, European "civilization" and Indian "savagery" could never coexist.

Thus conflict with stereotyped Indians could — indeed had to — become central to the American story, but flesh-and-blood Indian people and the histories they made for themselves and for the colonizers during the long years of European colonization in the East could not. As white Americans wrote their nation's past, their greatest erasure of all was of memories of Indians who had made their own histories on the land and who had adapted and changed in accordance with their own histories and traditions rather than Euro-American scripts — and who have indeed survived into the present in Maine, Massachusetts, New York, Virginia, Wisconsin, and countless places where renewed claims to land and political autonomy accompanied the rise of the gleaming casinos most non-Natives now see as the only incongruous markers of people long presumed to have disappeared. The human stories behind the survival of these Indian communities — and the ways in which those stories shaped the history of the continent — could find no place in the mythology of a nation born in an empty land of vanishing Chingachgooks, where Indian country, if it still existed at all, lay somewhere west of the Mississippi.

FURTHER READING: *Facing East from Indian Country: A Native History of Early America,* by Daniel K. Richter, from which this was drawn with permission from Harvard University Press.

37. Whaleback Shell Midden State Historic Site, ME

On U.S. 1, Damariscotta

Walking trail

Whaleback shell midden and the larger Glidden midden (visible across the Damariscotta River) grew as American Indians discarded oyster shells and other food debris, primarily fish bones, between about 200 B.C. and A.D. 1000. Most of Whaleback was hauled away in 1886 and 1887 to be used as an additive for chicken feed, but isolated mounds remain. Glidden borders the river for about 150 feet and is about 30 feet high and 75 feet wide.

38. Colonial Pemaquid State Historic Site, ME

Arthur Spiess, Bonnie Newsom, and Leon Cranmer

West of Rte. 130, off Huddle Rd., Bristol

Museum

The Mi'kmaq word *pemaquid* means "far out it rests" or "long point" and is the name for the peninsula, the rocky headland, and the protected harbor. People of a series of Archaic and Woodland cultures lived here beginning about 2500 B.C. After about A.D. 1400, there was a major village on the peninsula where the people hunted and fished and grew corn and beans. They used a portage across the peninsula to avoid the dangers of paddling their birchbark canoes around it. To date, Pemaquid is the farthest northeast site that has charred corn and bean remains, thus marking the boundary between mixed farming and pure hunting-fishing-gathering economies in northeastern North America. When the Europeans arrived in 1605–1607, there was a Wabanaki village where about 250 people lived in about fifty dwellings. In 1605 George Waymouth, an English explorer sent to gather information for future English settlement, kidnapped five villagers and took them to England. When two, Tehanedo (or Tahanada) and Amoret (Samoset), were returned to their homeland, they played an influential role in the relationships between their people and the growing number of Europeans. Tehanedo later met other English explorers on the Maine coast, including Captain John Smith in 1614. Samoset visited the Plymouth colony in Massachusetts in its early months and conversed at length with Governor Bradford. Early archaeological excavations and the construction of utility lines disturbed several Indian burials, some with European copper trade goods, dating to the 1500s or early 1600s. These remains, now repatriated, documented the site of the village and provided a silent clue to the fate of the village. Between 1615 and 1621, war and epidemics decimated much of the coastal Indian population from Massachusetts to southwestern Maine, leaving relatively few survivors to deal with European settlement.

The peninsula was a landmark for European mariners sailing the coastline, and by 1610 European fishermen were using the harbor at Pemaquid. The English established a village and trading post on the peninsula after 1630 and traded European manufactured goods such as metal pots, axes, and glass beads for fur and hides. In 1635 the French began a settlement at Pentagoet in Acadia, 40 miles to the northeast. Pemaquid's strategic location resulted in colonial wars and cultural upheaval for the American Indians. Between 1676 and 1696, when French, Indian, and English forces battled for control of the peninsula, the settlement was destroyed and refortified several times.

FURTHER READING: *The Forts of Pemaquid, Maine: An Archaeological and Historical Study,* by Helen Camp and Robert Bradley

39. Maquam Wildlife Management Area, VT: The Grandma Lampman Site

Lisa Brooks and Louise Lampman Larivee

Off Rte. 78, northwest of Swanton

Visitor center

"Grandma Lampman's" has long been a significant site and gathering place within the Abenaki village of Missisquoi, or Mazipskoik (place of flint), located on the northeast shore of Betowbagw (the lake between), or Lake Champlain, where the Missisquoi River flows into one of the largest bodies of water in New England. The village was a refuge for Abenaki and other Algonquian families during the Anglo-Abenaki wars, during which Greylock, also known as Wawanolet, launched raids on the colonial settlements in Massachusetts and southern Vermont/

New Hampshire. Even after American settlement took hold in northern Vermont, many Missisquoi families remained in the marshes of the delta. They lived by fishing in the bay, gathering berries and medicinal plants, and hunting and trapping the abundant game animals. During the late 1800s John Lampman married Martha Morits, and they built a small house and barn in the marsh area known as Maquam. Families came together here, camping during the summer and making trips into the village to sell their surplus gatherings. Always there was dancing, singing, and storytelling at Grandma Lampman's. Here families were sustained.

Then, in the mid-twentieth century, the Missisquoi Wildlife Refuge was established, and many of Grandma Lampman's descendants were forced from their homes. While families continued to hunt, fish, and gather in the refuge, they were no longer allowed to live there. As development along the lakeshore increased, the families' reliance on the adjacent area known as "Grandma Lampman's" increased. In the 1990s, when a developer threatened to turn Maquam into a housing development, Grandma Lampman's great-grandchildren fought back, asserting their claims to their homelands as critical for cultural survival and subsistence. After a long battle in the state's administrative bureaucracy, the courts, and the public sphere, Grandma Lampman's was protected as the Maquam Wildlife Management Area, with the Lampman family as its primary caretakers. The state and federal officials who manage the refuge and the wildlife area are now working more closely with the Abenaki to recover and tell the history of Missisquoi and its importance to the present and future of the community.

My name is Louise Lampman Larivee. I am the daughter of Chief Leonard Lampman and the great-granddaughter of "Grandma Lampman." She was an Abenaki herbalist and medicine woman who lived and raised her children and grandchildren in the ancient village of Missisquoi. This area was always known for the Native values the elders taught the children from one generation to the next. Protecting this land was important. It was sacred and spiritual to my family and others. It took three years to protect this site. Today, a plaque on the site of her home honors the memory of one very special Abenaki woman.

FURTHER READING: *The Western Abenaki of Vermont,* by Colin Calloway

40. Mashantucket Pequot Museum and Research Center, CT: Recreated Sixteenth-Century Pequot Village and Site of a Seventeenth-Century Fortified Village

Theresa Hayward Bell and Jack Campisi

110 Pequot Trail, Mashantucket

Native peoples have hunted, fished, and farmed in southeastern Connecticut for about 10,000 years. About 500 years ago, the ancestors of the Pequot lived in inland villages during the winter and along the coast of Long Island Sound in the summer, farming and harvesting from the rich abundance of forest and ocean. Today the Mashantucket Pequot Tribal Nation, informed by the limited archaeological evidence and the journals of the first Europeans who visited, traded, and settled in the region, has reconstructed a mid-sixteenth-century village in its museum and research center. Visitors can see the activities of a summer's day: women and children chasing rapacious crows from the ripening corn, women dressing game and making pottery, men fishing in an estuary near the village, and a couple building a round house, or *wetu.* Throughout the village are *wetus* of varying sizes, some covered with mats and others with bark from elm trees. In the palisaded section of the village is a long *wetu* used for tribal meetings and ceremonies. The village is set in a grove of American chestnut trees. In one corner of the village a man is emerging from a sweathouse; in the village's center a child sleeps in a *wetu* while a little boy on the roof hides from his dog, their only domesticated animal. A woman in mourning speaks to the sachem. Nearby men are playing a game of chance called *hubbub*. Other women are cooking meals and tending their children, while an elder is teaching a boy to make arrows.

The village shows a subtle transition from the time before the Europeans to the growing impact of traders and later settlers, evident in the palisaded section of the village. There are many trade items as well as aspects of traditional culture, such as the curing efforts of a *pawwaw*. A family sits outside its *wetu,* making wampum with European metal tools, which have replaced the stone drills used before contact. Two types of wampum are manufactured: white wampum, most commonly made from the columellas of whelk shells (*Buccinum undatum*), and purple or black wampum, made from quahog shells (*Mercenaria mercenaria*). The latter were broken into pieces or cores approximately 5.5 millimeters in length, drilled, and then made cylindrical. Pequot and other Native people in the Northeast used wampum in social and ceremonial settings, as gifts, to honor the dead, as decoration, and to cement friendships and alliances, but never as money. That use came with European colonization because of the scarcity of hard currency in the colonies.

Wampum readily fit into the evolving trade with Europeans, and the Pequot were soon caught up in the trade networks. The English and Dutch demand for the beads was great, leading to a conflict for control of the Connecticut and Hudson river valleys. The English won and soon settled into areas within the Pequot sphere of influence. In 1636 warfare broke out between the English and the Pequot. The following spring, the English and their Mohegan and Narragansett allies attacked a Pequot village, killing most of the inhabitants. The war against the Pequot continued until the fall of 1638, when a treaty made at Hartford gave the English all of the Pequot land, forbade the use of the Pequot name, sold many Pequots into slavery, and gave a number of them to the Narragansetts and Mohegans. It is from this latter group that the modern-day Mashantucket Pequot Nation derives.

West of the museum is the only known site of an intact fortified village in southern New England. It was the home of Mashantucket Pequots at the time of King Philip's War. The palisade — 190 feet by 170 feet — that protected it combined European military design of a bastion at each corner with the Native type of entrance on the south side.

FURTHER READING: *The Pequots in Southern New England: The Fall and Rise of an American Indian Nation,* edited by Laurence M. Hauptman and James D. Wherry

41. Acadia National Park, ME: Asticou's Island Domain

Bunny McBride and Harald E. L. Prins

Mount Desert Island

Visitor centers and Cadillac Summit Center

Centered on Mount Desert Island, Acadia National Park is in the homeland of the Wabanaki (Dawnland) peoples — Algonquian-speaking Native Americans living where the light of dawn first touches the continent. In the early 1600s the island and its surrounding archipelago formed part of a tribal territory used by a community of hunters, fishers, and gatherers headed by Chief Asticou, whose domain included the coastal lands between Schoodic Peninsula and

Blue Hill Neck. This was "the eastern door" of Mawooshen, the large coastal alliance of more than twenty Wabanaki villages spread out between Schoodic and Cape Neddick (York). The Wabanaki called the island Pemetic, referring to its "range of mountains." Visible from Cadillac Mountain, the highest point on this seaboard, are ancient canoe routes along which the Wabanaki paddled, following nature's seasonally shifting storehouse of food, medicine, and the raw materials for their clothing, shelter, boats, and weapons. The ocean and its shores provided shellfish (especially clams), sea mammals (especially seals), and seasonal multitudes of water birds. Moose, deer, bear, and smaller mammals thrived in the coastal woodlands. Vital to the Wabanaki diet were freshwater fish — eel, trout, and bass — and those that lived in both fresh and saltwater, such as sturgeon and salmon. Expressing a spiritual kinship with a natural environment that met their every need, Wabanakis spoke of *manitou* (spirit power), a mysterious life force that enlivened all of nature.

Near Southwest Harbor on Somes Sound, the only fjord on North America's eastern seaboard, is Fernald Point — an open sweep of land frequented by generations of Wabanaki, beginning at least 3,000 years ago. Here, in 1613, French Jesuits established the St. Sauveur mission with the approval of Chief Asticou, whose seasonal village lay across the sound above Northeast Harbor. Within a few months an English privateer from Jamestown, Virginia, destroyed this mission — delivering the opening salvo in what became 150 years of colonial competition and warfare. Seeking protection from English invaders and Iroquois raiders, Wabanaki groups established the Wabanaki Confederacy (an intertribal alliance that replaced and was more far-reaching than Mawooshen) and allied themselves with the French. In 1713 the French Crown officially gave up its colonial claims to the Maine coast but continued aiding the Wabanaki for another

fifty years. The confederacy, which supported the American Revolution against Great Britain, remained a political and military force until that war's end in 1783, when the new border between Canada and the United States divided Wabanaki lands. Relegated to small reservations or to squatter status on their ancestral lands, the Wabanaki struggled to survive and adapt to the dramatic changes forced upon them. Many relied on age-old artisan skills for subsistence, making utility baskets and other wares for white settlers. In the mid-nineteenth century they began crafting fancy wood-splint and sweetgrass baskets as well as birchbark boxes and canoes to sell to summer residents and tourists.

In 1970 Wabanaki tribes jointly founded T.R.I.B.E. (Teaching and Research in Bicultural Education) in Bar Harbor, a school for Native students to learn about, appreciate, and hold on to cultural traditions. Two years later they filed a lawsuit laying claim to ancestral lands in Maine. The claim, settled out of court in 1981, was followed by another settlement in 1991, totaling $82.5 million, much of it earmarked for the purchase of 305,000 acres of trust land. Today there are four federally recognized, reservation-based Wabanaki tribes in Maine: the Penobscot Nation on Indian Island, the Passamaquoddy Tribe at Pleasant Point and Indian Township, the Houlton Band of Maliseet Indians in Houlton, and the Aroostook Band of Micmacs in Presque Isle. They come to Mount Desert Island to attend the annual Native American festival and to market their crafts. Many collaborate with Bar Harbor's Abbe Museum (founded in 1928 to "fix indelibly" the Wabanaki presence in the minds of visitors to Acadia National Park). The Wabanaki work with the Abbe, the National Park Service, and the Friends of Acadia to protect the homeland of their ancestors, who struck a balance with the natural environment in ways that preserved the splendor of this place for thousands of years. The deep roots of Wabanaki culture in this region are still evident in shell middens and petroglyphs, Glooskap myths and legends, and the names of places and geographic features.

FURTHER READING: *Asticou's Island Domain: Waba- naki Peoples at Mount Desert Island 1600–2000,* by Harald E. L. Prins and Bunny McBride

42. St. Croix Island International Historic Site, ME

Donald G. Soctomah

On U.S. 1, south of Calais

National Park Service Ranger Station

Interpretive trail (Wonessonuk) and island (Mehtonuwekoss)

Headquarters: Acadia National Park on Mt. Desert Island

Passamaquoddy people have lived on the land between today's Maine and New Brunswick, Canada, since time immemorial — in harmony with nature and with a spiritual bond to the land and the water. The stories our ancestors passed down to us show a strong connection with the environment in order to survive. They lived in small, rounded wigwams made of poles and hoops covered with birchbark, cattail mats, and balsam fir branches to protect them from the harsh winter climate. The Passamaquoddy moved with the seasons to fish and to hunt por- poise and caribou. St. Croix Island was a place to store food for protection from the wolves and the giant black bears.

In 1604 the French came to establish a per- manent colony and control the fur trade. The Native people welcomed them and helped them through difficult times, but that meeting forever changed the lives of the Passamaquoddy. This first contact determined the relationship of the French to the Native people across North Amer- ica. More than 90 percent of Native people died from European diseases, and others were killed when they went into battle with the French against the English. The Wabanaki Confederacy was made up of five Algonquian tribes along the East Coast: the Abenaki, the Penobscot, the Maliseet, the Passamaquoddy, and the Mi'kmaq. Each tribe had its own leaders, but the tribes worked together until the confederation dis- banded in 1862. In the 1980s the Wabanaki Con- federacy was revived, and there are now annual ceremonies in the villages of the five tribes.

Over the years, some Wabanaki leaders jour- neyed to France, including Chief Assacombuit, who was honored for his loyal services to the Crown, but Passamaquoddy people just wanted to be left alone and not pulled into the Euro- pean battles. After 400 years of contact with the Europeans, the Passamaquoddy language is still spoken, and the traditions live on, showing the strength and endurance of the Passamaquoddy people, who live in two communities in Maine — Pleasant Point and Indian Township — and one in New Brunswick — St. Andrews. The in- terpretive trail, constructed in 2004, is dedicated to the meeting of two worlds 400 years ago and to the continued survival of the Passama- quoddy. Along the trail are interpretive panels and six life-size bronze statues, two depicting Passamaquoddy and four depicting members of the French expedition. The name of the trail is Wonessonuk, which means "wind in the cove." It is said that when the wind blows you can still hear the drums beating.

FURTHER READING: *Unsettled Past, Unsettled Future: The Story of Maine Indians,* by Neil Rolde

43. Cape Cod National Seashore, MA: The Nauset Area

Francis P. McManamon

Headquarters: South Wellfleet

Province Lands Visitor Center, Salt Pond Visitor Center, Fort Hill Trail, Nauset Marsh Trail, High Head Trail

People have lived in the Nauset Harbor area, now in the Cape Cod National Seashore, since at least 4000 B.C. The view from the top of Fort Hill, overlooking the modern marsh, takes in all of Nauset Harbor, with its steep shorelines and extensive marsh divided by natural channels. Beyond it are the breakers of the Atlantic Ocean. Nauset Beach, a barrier beach with a narrow natural entrance, protects the tidal lagoon. Radiocarbon dating and research on the shellfish and other faunal remains from ancient shell middens suggest that by at least 1,000 years ago people lived near Nauset Marsh year-round. Concentrations of ancient sites around the marsh indicate past residences and activities in the Coast Guard Beach, Salt Pond, and Fort Hill areas. Recent excavations and analysis have recovered a site from about 1,000–2,000 years ago. The Carns site was probably a winter encampment where a small group — fewer than fifty people — lived, collecting wild plants and game from a nearby freshwater wetland. The people also left camps and villages in other parts of Cape Cod, such as the High Head area.

By the time of historical contact with Europeans, the settlements around Nauset Marsh were extensive. The first written account of the Indians at Nauset Harbor was by Samuel de Champlain, who sailed in on July 21, 1605, and saw "a bay with wigwams bordering it all around." He went ashore with some of the crew: "Before reaching [the Indians'] wigwams, [we] entered a field planted with Indian corn . . . [which] was in flower, and some five and a half feet in height. . . . We saw Brazilian beans, many

edible squashes . . . tobacco, and roots which they cultivate." He also described the round wigwams covered by a thatch made of reeds and the people's clothing, woven from grasses, hemp, and animal skins. Unfortunately, the visit to Nauset ended after four days with a fight between the French and the Indians in which one Frenchman was killed. When he returned the next year, Champlain recorded that about 150 people were living around Nauset Harbor and about 500–600 in the area of present-day Chatham. After 1620 English colonists from the settlement at Plymouth visited Nauset many times to trade and buy food. Along with the trade goods, these contacts spread European diseases, to which the Indians had no immunity. Many of the Nauset Indians died, and the population declined drastically. In 1639 about half of the English from Plymouth relocated to the Nauset area, settling the town that is now Eastham.

FURTHER READING: *The Archaeology of New England,* by Dean R. Snow

44. The Cliffs of Aquinnah, MA: We Belong Where We Are From

Donald A. Widdiss

Aquinnah, Martha's Vineyard

Aquinnah Wampanoag people live in the place where they have always been. Here is a small part of the telling of our story. We understand that our people came to be through the actual changing of the earth by forces that have brought power to the place we call home: 3,300 acres of land and water that is called the town of Aquinnah in the Commonwealth of Massachusetts.

Approximately 13,500 years ago the great glacier moved inexorably through today's Cape Cod. The mile-high wall of ice creaked to a stop in today's Vineyard Sound, leaving a 100-square-mile piece of the earth rising from the sea 5 miles off the coast of Cape Cod; it is known as Martha's Vineyard, or Noepe (land amid the waters). The pressure of millions of tons of earth and ice moving south formed the western end of the island into three glacial moraines, culminating in the Gay Head (Aquinnah) cliffs. The natural forces of nature had formed clay predominately of the four sacred colors; red, yellow, white, and black. This clay helps tell the story of our relationship to each other by being of the earth formed by the process that created Aquinnah.

Our stories come from the oral tradition of our people, who traditionally use metaphor and mnemonic devices to pass on our history so that future generations know where we came from and where we belong. Our legends tell of a giant being, Moshup, who lived in this place and provided for the people. The voices tell us that he created the surrounding land and waters and passed on a prophecy that we would see the coming of people from another place who might not have the same respect for the land that the people from Aquinnah had as their inherent nature. Sadly, the truth of this prophecy is manifest in present-day ecological and legal conditions, which affect the ability of all indigenous people to sustain themselves, not just the Aquinnah Wampanoag. Aquinnah is the metaphor of our existence. The natural world has given Aquinnah power. It provides a place for our people where the voices of our ancestors speak to us. We cannot separate our people from the land because it is a sacred place. We belong where we are from.

The eleven-member Tribal Council promotes self-sufficiency and self-determination on behalf of tribal members and provides resources to preserve the almost 500 acres of tribal trust land for future generations.

FURTHER READING: *Spirit of the New England Tribes: Indian History and Folklore, 1620–1984,* by William Simmons

45. Mohawk Trail State Forest, MA: The Mohawk Trail

Robert T. Leverett

On Rte. 2, west of Charlemont

Visitor center

The Mohawk Trail was the shortest route across the Berkshire highlands for American Indians, including the Mahican and the Mohawk of New York and the New England tribes, traveling between the Connecticut River and the Hudson for trade and in raiding parties. During King Philip's War the rebel Indians went west along the trail to the area around Albany, seeking support from the Iroquois, but they were attacked by Mohawks. After the war, New England Natives traveled west over the trail and settled in Schaghticoke, New York, near its end. In 1745 the Massachusetts colonists built a fort on the trail in North Adams to stop French and Indian raiders from Canada. In 1754 a new road between Deerfield and Albany, which came to be known as the Albany Road, replaced the trail, which it followed for short stretches; Route 2 follows the trail/road in only a few places in Charlemont and Shelburne. The state forest protects 1.5 miles of the trail in the ancient forest on the crest of the Todd-Clark Ridge, which rises prominently 1,000 feet above the Deerfield Valley. Along the trail are the remains of an encampment at the confluence of the Cold and Deerfield rivers, where Indians caught the Atlantic salmon that spawned here. In 1997 the forest was the meeting ground for the Narragansett and the Mohawk from the Kahnawake Reserve, who gathered to reestablish their historical bonds of friendship. The state forest honors both individual Indians and Indian nations with named groves of white pines, the state's tallest tree, including the Jani Grove, which honors the late president of the Friends of the Mohawk Trail State Forest, Jani Leverett, who was of Cherokee and Choctaw lineage.

46. Deerfield, MA

Evan Haefeli and Kevin Sweeney

Deerfield

Deerfield, a place that the English later saw as a frontier or boundary, was, in fact, an ancient intersection known as Pocumtuck. Its residents traded with other Native peoples up and down the Connecticut River and east and west over what is now called the Mohawk Trail. Foods such as maize, cultivated by women; deer and bear, hunted by men; and fish, taken at the nearby falls at Peskeompscut, sustained the community. During the 1600s, as in earlier centuries, great changes followed the trade routes into Pocumtuck. First came deadly diseases, then English traders. Shortly before settlers arrived in Pocumtuck in the later 1660s, its Native peoples had dispersed after a devastating attack by the Iroquois. The survivors moved south to join neighboring communities or north to find refuge with the French in Canada. After King Philip's War (1675–1677), the Pocumtuck and Sokoki still in the area headed north or moved west to settle along the Hudson under the protection of their erstwhile foes, the Mohawk of the Iroquois League. Still, some of these people returned to trade with the English residents of Deerfield, and some settled for several years in what is today South Deerfield. Others contested English possession of their homeland. When war returned in the 1690s, they joined French and Native raiders operating out of Canada.

Many of the Natives who joined the famous 1704 raid on Deerfield were continuing a contest that had started in the 1670s. On February 29, 1704, 48 French and 200 to 250 Native allies surprised Deerfield's 275 inhabitants and 20 garrison soldiers. Among the Native attackers were Christian Indians from villages in New France, such as the St. Francis Abenakis, many of whom spoke English and had been driven from their homelands by the Iroquois and the

English in the 1660s and 1670s. The raiders killed 50 residents and took 112 men, women, and children captive. Still, the English put up more of a fight than is suggested by the much later designation of the attack as the Deerfield Massacre. They killed 11 raiders and wounded at least 22. Some of those taken prisoner remained with the Iroquois of the Mountain or the Mohawk at Kahnawake, and some of the latter had descendants who lived at St. Francis.

Instead of ending Native ties to the place, the 1704 raid actually reinforced old ones and forged new ones. The dominant account has been *The Redeemed Captive*, written by Deerfield's minister, John Williams, one of those taken prisoner and held until November 1706. Twelve years later, one of his two Indian captors visited him in Deerfield. Other captors also visited their former captives. These reunions of old enemies were as characteristic of the colonial New England frontier as their violent meetings during the raid. Visits continued into the 1830s, when St. Francis Abenakis came to the place that they called Williamscook, the place of their Williams ancestors.

FURTHER READING: *Captors and Captives: The 1704 French and Indian Raid on Deerfield,* by Evan Haefeli and Kevin Sweeney

47. Plimoth Plantation, MA: The Wampanoag Homesite

Linda Coombs

Off Rte. 3 at exit 4, Plymouth

The Wampanoag Homesite, part of the Wampanoag Indigenous Program (WIP) of Plimoth Plantation, represents the home of Hobbamock, who came to live in Patuxet after the Pilgrims landed in 1620 and renamed the area Plimoth. Hobbamock was a highly trusted counselor to the Pokanoket Wampanoag sachem, or chief, Ousemequin. (Pokanoket is now Bristol and Warren,

Rhode Island.) Better known by his title, Massasoit, Ousemequin sent Hobbamock to be a liaison between the English settlers and the Wampanoag. The Homesite includes two bark-covered homes, a round house covered with cattail reed mats, and two corn-mound gardens. Nearby, next to the Eel River, is an area where dugout canoes are made and launched. There is also a bark-covered smokehouse, hide tanning racks, and drying racks for food and reeds.

The Native staff, most of whom are from the Wampanoag Nation, interpret history, culture, and contemporary events from a Native perspective for museum visitors. The living history at the Homesite also gives staff the opportunity to learn the seventeenth-century arts, skills, and technologies of our ancestors, many of which WIP has reclaimed during its thirty-five-year history. Staff members recreate all the artifacts and buildings in the exhibit and demonstrate skills including house construction, gardening, cooking, sewing and clothing decoration, boat construction, weaving of cattail and bulrush mats, baskets, and bags, pottery making, and the making of burl bowls and spoons, as well as bone, stone, metal, and wood implements.

Although it is not the actual place where Hobbamock lived, the Homesite is very special, being a place where people came every year for millennia to plant corn and fish. It is very gratifying to be in the same place doing the same things that our ancestors did. It is also a place of great sadness. In the early seventeeth century, prior to 1620, Wampanoag and other Native men were kidnapped and sold into slavery or exhibited as novelties in Europe. Between 1616 and 1618, a devastating plague decimated more than half of the Wampanoag and other nations along the coast. Today the Wampanoag number approximately 4,000 people. The two largest communities are Mashpee on Cape Cod and Aquinnah on Martha's Vineyard. Both are governed by Tribal Councils and are federally recognized tribes. Several other Wampanoag communities also exist throughout our original homeland.

FURTHER READING: *Spirit of the New England Tribes: Indian History and Folklore, 1620–1984,* by William S. Simmons

48. Historic Battery Park and the Smithsonian National Museum of the American Indian's George Gustav Heye Center, NY

John Haworth

Bowling Green and Battery Park, New York

Battery Park and the Heye Center were part of the homeland of Lenape-speaking people — members of a confederacy of tribes that populated the area from eastern Connecticut to central New Jersey — when Europeans arrived. The present-day name of Manhattan comes from their word *mannahata*, which means hilly island. Mohawks as well as Mahicans and other Algonquians lived and traded in the region.

In 1624 the Dutch established New Amsterdam here, the seaport of their New Netherland colony, and, according to a contemporary Dutch report, bought Manhattan for sixty Dutch guilders' worth of goods, described in legend as trinkets and beads. In the park across the street from the museum is a monument to the Native American trade with the Dutch. This trade foreshadowed the treaties in which American Indians lost their homelands and also the trade networks that had grown up between them and Europeans. Jutting out into New York Harbor, lower Manhattan was a trade center, as it is today. It seems appropriate that the Heye Center, which celebrates and honors American Indian cultures, is in the renovated 1907 U.S. Custom House, considering the significance of trade to the Indians who lived here. Their trade route north was the Wiechquaekeck Trail, an old Algonquian trade route that began at today's park and continued north along the Hudson River.

Today part of the trail is the famous avenue Broadway. There were conflicts between the Europeans and the Indians as well as trading partnerships. Wall Street, five blocks north of the museum, was named after a barricade built by the Dutch to protect their settlements from the Indians.

As Manhattan expanded skyward during the twentieth century, Mohawk ironworkers from the Kahnawake Reserve came here to build bridges and skyscrapers and, after September 11, 2001, to help dismantle the wreckage at Ground Zero. By 2000, New York City had the largest urban Indian population of any city in the country, more than 87,000 people who describe themselves as American Indians or Alaskan Natives.

FURTHER READING: *New Tribe New York: The Urban Vision Quest*, edited by Gerald McMaster

49. Fort Shantok, CT

Melissa Tantaquidgeon Zobel

Fort Shantok Rd., Uncasville

Here lie the ruins of the fortified village Shantok, home of the famed Mohegan Indian sachem Uncas, who lived from 1598 until 1683. The site, bordered by the Thames River and two steep embankments, was chosen because it was easily defensible — an important factor in the ongoing battles from 1643 until 1657 with the nearby Narragansett tribe. The conflicts, provoked by colonial efforts to divide and conquer the Natives, resulted in the execution by the Mohegan of the Narragansett sachem Miantonomo. Uncas's alliance with the Connecticut colonists against the nearby Pequot and Narragansett tribes earned him the nickname "Friend of the English." He led the Mohegans as allies of the colony in both the Pequot Massacre of 1637 and King Philip's War of 1675.

Today there is a sacred grove of red cedars on the site of Uncas's village. It was once surrounded by rows of posts, protecting the wigwams in the village. The people grew corn, hunted deer, and gathered clams and oysters. Crushed *apunihag* (oyster shells) are reminders of the shellfish beds and the modern Mohegan aquaculture project, which continues that tradition. Shantokware pottery, which features motifs of women and corn, reflects the traditional matriarchal Mohegan society. Nearby the tribe maintains its ancient burial ground. The older graves face southwest, the direction that, our Mohegan stories tell us, is the place of origin for both the tribe and corn.

Because of the sacred nature of Shantok, the ancient Wigwam Festival, the annual tribal Thanksgiving for the corn harvest, is held in the cedar grove on the third weekend in August. Nearby are a Mohegan Veterans Monument; a boulder dedicated to Fidelia Fielding, the last speaker of the Mohegan language; the Leffingwell Memorial, which honors those who aided the Mohegan during the Narragansett siege; Tantaquidgeon Pond, named for Chief Harold Tantaquidgeon; Fielding Falls; Samuel Uncas's eighteenth-century gravestone, repatriated from the Slater Museum; and the One Hundred Giant Steps, constructed by the Mohegan chiefs Burrill Fielding (Matahga) and Courtland Fowler (Little Hatchet). The state of Connecticut converted Shantok into a state park in 1926. After the Mohegan tribe was federally recognized in 1994, the tribe purchased it from the state.

Today the Mohegan tribe is a thriving community of nearly 1,800 members, many of whom live in New London County. The tribe is governed by a nine-member Tribal Council, which oversees most legislative matters, and a seven-member Council of Elders, which offers judicial and cultural oversight. The tribe owns and operates the Mohegan Sun Casino, an entertainment, meeting, shopping, and gaming destination with a hotel and spa. It also operates Mohegan Sun at Pocono Downs, a casino in Pennsylvania, and the Tantaquidgeon Indian Museum, the oldest Indian-owned and operated museum in the United States.

FURTHER READING: *The Lasting of the Mohegans: The Story of the Wolf People,* by Melissa Jayne Fawcett

50. Old Indian Meetinghouse, MA

John A. Peters, Jr.

Rte. 130, Mashpee

Not so long ago, about 1657, there was a place along the shores of Santuit Pond in Mashpee where Richard Bourne preached the Gospel. Much had happened since the Pilgrims came in 1620. Other colonials had followed, displacing the Wampanoag from their lands and increasing the tensions between the cultures. With concern for the plight of the Indians, the Society for the Propagation of the Gospel to the Indians was founded by a group of Englishmen. In 1684 the Old Indian Meetinghouse was founded by Shearjashub Bourne as part of the English efforts to Christianize the Wampanoag. In 1741 it was moved to its present location and expanded. The Old Indian Meetinghouse has been in some respects a shield, ensuring our survival of the conquest of America. This very old building is surrounded by the graves of our people and has within its walls the spirits of our ancestors, with accounts of many confessions, lessons, discussions, and prayers to the Great Spirit.

In spite of all that has happened, we, the Mashpee Wampanoag, continue to take on all challenges to our existence, and we are thankful that the Old Indian Meetinghouse has assisted us on our path. For nearly four centuries it was often led by Mashpee ministers and always managed by tribal members. In the 1830s, when a local minister tried to take control away from the tribe and local residents illegally tried to cut wood on tribal lands, the tribe revolted against local authority and fought to keep control of its lands. Even after the Commonwealth of Massa-chusetts abolished the tribal reservation and divided the commonly held land and sold off part of it, the tribe kept control of the Old Indian Meetinghouse. When the renovations begun in 2006 are completed, its historic significance will be showcased for the public, and it will be used by our community for the spiritual and cultural purposes it has always served. Although we struggle to make ends meet, we commit to those that came before us to take responsibility for this sacred historic Indian place. And as we, "the Mashpee Wampanoag, People of the First Light," continue on our journey in pursuit of our destiny, a new path has been placed before us. On May 17, 2007, the Department of the Interior acknowledged the Mashpee tribe as a sovereign entity. We give thanks to all our relations for keeping us on the path, and we pray that we have the strength and wisdom to carry on our responsibility for the generations to come.

FURTHER READING: *Son of Mashpee: Reflections of Chief Flying Eagle, A Wampanoag,* by Earl H. Mills, Sr., and Alicja Mann

51. Ganondagan State Historic Site, NY: Ganondagan, the Town of Peace

G. Peter Jemison and Michael J. Galban

1488 Rte. 444, south of Victor

Visitor center/museum

The Five Nations of the Haudenosaunee, the Iroquois Confederacy — the Seneca, Cayuga, Onondaga, Oneida, and Mohawk — were united more than 1,000 years ago by a message of peace. Since the Tuscarora joined them in 1722, they have been known as the Six Nations. Ganondagan, the site of the capital of the Seneca Nation from 1655 until 1687, was the center of Seneca culture and governance; more than 3,000 people lived there in 150 longhouses. The Seneca were and remain Keepers of the Western

Door of the Confederacy, with the Cayuga, On-ondaga, and Oneida to the east. The Mohawk remain Keepers of the Eastern Door. The Tuscarora live on the Niagara escarpment above Lewiston, not far from Niagara Falls. The Seneca grew corn and could store hundreds of thousands of bushels in their huge, fortified granary on top of Fort Hill, which could also serve as a refuge for the people when they were attacked. They trapped beaver and traded furs in the market centers at Albany and Montreal. In 1683 a Seneca could trade five beaver pelts for a common French gun or one pelt for two hundred sewing needles. They also traded furs for axes, wool, kettles, iron tools, and finished European clothing, such as shirts and coats. The Seneca at Ganondagan were well-informed consumers, clever businessmen, expert agrarians, practiced politicians, proficient orators, and skilled warriors.

In 1687 a French force led by the Marquis de Denonville burned the town and the cornfields. Today Ganondagan is a center for the preservation of Haudenosaunee culture. The seventeenth-century Seneca bark longhouse was reproduced from drawings of historic longhouses, oral history, and a longhouse excavated during the 1960s. It was built — as longhouses have been built for 300 years — by many hands, starting in the spring when the bark is best peeled, while the sap is up in the trees, when the earth is soft for setting poles, and when the forest floor is clear of underbrush, making it easier to harvest the poles. The bark longhouse is a portal to the past, with its hickory-bark lashings over a cedar and hickory framework enclosed in long-lasting elm bark. It is furnished with hundreds of accurate reproductions of clothing, tools, games, and blankets from the time period. Almost every aspect of Seneca life is reflected in its interior. It is so effective that our new obstacle is convincing children that no one actually lives there today.

There are four trails on the site. The Earth Is Our Mother Trail has signs that identify twenty-nine trees and plants, giving their names in Seneca, Latin, and English, and explaining their uses within Seneca tradition. Three other trails tell more about the Seneca: the Trail of Peace, the Fort Hill Granary Trail, and the Great Brook Trail.

Today the Seneca Nation of Indians is flourishing. Great efforts are being made to preserve our language and our way of life. In contrast, we have opened two casinos to provide employment and an economy to support our infrastructure. The Tonawanda Band of Seneca has chosen to avoid gaming and retain its chiefs and their titles.

FURTHER READING: *War Against the Seneca: The French Expedition of 1687*, by John Mohawk

King Philip's War

JAMES D. DRAKE

❖ In the decades before King Philip's War, the inhabitants of New England did not foresee a future in which English colonists would inevitably expand and Native Peoples would retreat. Before New England was torn apart by war in 1675, it rested upon a delicate balance of power wherein the various English and Indian polities had consciously linked their futures. Though the English and the Indians had retained distinct cultural identities, divisions within each group had led to an intricate web of rivalries and loyalties among the region's colonies and tribes. This biracial society grew out of efforts to preserve cultural identity in a rapidly changing world. Well before the English began establishing colonies, the growth of New England's Indian population had led to greater reliance on maize, to competition for land, and to political centralization. Epidemics scoured the region in 1619, but two groups, the Pequot and the Narragansett, escaped their devastation. Because of this, and because these groups controlled wampum, the highly valued shell beads used by the Iroquois and New England's Algonquian for ceremonial purposes, they were the most powerful Indian groups when the English began settling in 1620.

The Pequot War in 1637 represented a successful effort by the English and their Indian allies to reduce the Pequot's power and their control of wampum. Following the brutal defeat of the Pequot, the Mohegan rose to prominence in what is now Connecticut and closely allied themselves with that colony's English settlers. To counter this alliance, the Narragansett established ties with the Algonquians near the Connecticut River, the Iroquois near the Hudson, and the English in Rhode Island. To keep from becoming isolated, the Wampanoag, mostly within Plymouth Colony, forged an alliance with their English neighbors, as did many of the Indians in Massachusetts. The Wampanoag, under the leadership of Metacom, commonly known as King Philip, thought that their relationship with Plymouth was one of mutual protection. By the 1670s, however, they saw clear signs that their ties to the colony would not protect their land base against English encroachment. Making this failure seem all the more stark, rival Christian Indians in Massachusetts seemed to be holding on to their land and even making inroads into Plymouth. When Plymouth colonists executed two Wampanoags in June 1675 for the alleged murder of a Christian Indian from Massachusetts, Wampanoags retaliated by attacking and killing several settlers in Swansea, effectively severing their ties to the colony.

What began as a minor skirmish in Plymouth escalated over the next six months into a civil war that affected all of New England. The chaos of King Philip's War made people grope for clear dividing lines where none existed. Even among the Wampanoag, loyalties were torn. The female leaders of two bands, Awashunkes and Wetamoo, simultaneously faced divided followers and intensive lobbying efforts from both English and Indian leaders to come down on their side. These two women had risen to power partly by navigating political minefields, but the pressures of King Philip's War were unprecedented. Following a strategy of self-preservation, Awashunkes initially joined Metacom, only to switch sides later when the tide of war favored the English and their Indian allies. Wetamoo wavered initially, joined Metacom, and then found herself fighting against her family and followers who had abandoned her. With communities divided, it was not easy to decide who was friend and who was foe, and cultural differences, misunderstandings, and outright paranoia eventually lured most Indians and English into the conflict. The early success of the rebel Indians allied with the Wampanoag led the English to be suspicious of all Indians, even Christians. In October 1675 Massachusetts removed loyal Indians who had been living in missionary communities, or "praying towns," to Deer Island in Boston Harbor, where they suffered through the winter with inadequate food and shelter.

The colonies of Connecticut, Massachusetts, and Plymouth then accused the powerful Narragansett, who had professed neutrality along with the colony of Rhode Island, of harboring rebel Wampanoags. English forces, together with Mohegan and Pequot allies, staged a devastating and lopsided preemptive strike against a Narragansett stronghold on December 19, 1675. Following the Great Swamp Fight, as it came to be known, it became impossible for either the Narragansett or Rhode Island to remain neutral, and all major groups within New England became embroiled in the war. Knowing that they were not safe anywhere in New England, rebel Indians sought winter refuge among the Mohawks near the Hudson River. Rather than play host, however, the Mohawks attacked these Indians, dramatically aiding the New England colonists. This rebuff, along with the colonists' gradual acceptance of many Indians' assistance and the adoption of their tactics, eventually led to the defeat of Philip's forces. Though they managed successful raids through the spring of 1676, by the summer their resolve had weakened. Realizing that the English would accept nothing less than complete victory, many Indians surrendered or fled the region entirely. On August 12, 1676, a Christian Indian fighting alongside English forces struck one of the final blows, shooting Philip near his home on Mount Hope peninsula.

In just fourteen months King Philip's War transformed New England society. While the English population remained stable, the Indians suffered a demographic collapse, depriving them of the political clout to shape the future significantly. And though much of our culture today has English origins, we should not forget the hybrid nature of early New England and its role in sowing the seeds of our republic.

FURTHER READING: *King Philip's War: Civil War in New England, 1675–1676,* by James D. Drake

The Fur Trade

WILLIAM R. SWAGERTY

❖ Since Paleolithic times, people have valued animal furs as well as their relationships with the furbearers who give up their lives to provide clothing and shelter. When the animals were harvested in moderation, a symbiosis between people and furbearers kept the animal species abundant and people warm and dry. Furs were a part of the vast trade networks among American Indians. Tribes traded regularly with those who spoke the same language and gathered with other tribes at certain times and places. Very old places where furs regularly crossed tribal bound-

aries include Cahokia in Illinois, the Mandan and Arikara villages on the Missouri River, and the Pecos and Zuni Pueblos in the Southwest. Well into historic times, the largest trade center in North America was The Dalles on the Columbia River in the Pacific Northwest. Each summer Cayuse, Umatilla, Nez Perce, and other eastern Plateau tribes brought in hides, furs, antlers, and other by-products of the hunt and joined peoples from as far away as the Northwest Coast and California to socialize, gamble, and trade for salmon, fresh and smoked, as well as for exotic goods such as baskets, hats, and shell money (primarily dentalium shells) from coastal tribes. By 1800 European objects included sailors' caps, coats, knives, and trade beads, which came up the Columbia River system into The Dalles' trade network.

The first European-Indian fur trade began when European cod fishermen in the North Atlantic started trading cloth, metal, and glass beads for sable, mink, otter, and ermine. By 1550 the French were trading with coastal Algonquians for marten and deerskins. By the seventeenth century the European demand for beaver hats and the Indians' desire for blankets, kettles, hatchets, knives, guns, and decorative objects were so great that intertribal tensions erupted over the hunting grounds for fur-bearing animals. Traditional rivalries among tribes escalated into wars of attrition and near-genocide, especially in the Northeast, where the Iroquois nearly wiped out the Huron in a series of destructive wars during the seventeenth century.

Rivalries increased between the London-based Hudson's Bay Company (HBC) and the French in Montreal, who sent explorers, missionaries, and independent licensed traders into unmapped lands. For the next century, the English and the French vied for Native allegiance and trade, and the French initially succeeded. By 1680 there were about 800 French traders gathering furs, building posts at strategic sites, and marrying Indian women. One of these important gathering places was Michilimackinac on Mackinac Island, a crossroads in the Great Lakes region that served as a vortex for Indians and whites traveling by land and by water from the 1670s into the late eighteenth century. Another was Sault Ste. Marie, at the falls on Saint Marys River, between Lake Superior and Lake Huron, where the Jesuits established a mission in 1655. Before 1763 the French had acquired the major share of furs harvested in North America by mixing national policy with free enterprise and friendly relations with Indians. But even with the majority of Indians on their side, the French lost the continent to the English. Four intercolonial wars between 1689 and 1763 enveloped every Indian nation of the Northeast in European disagreements over monarchial succession, colonization rights, and the guarantee of supplies of North American staples, especially beaver. The immediate losers in these struggles were the American Indian allies of the French. The victory of England over France was confirmed by the Treaty of Paris in 1763.

Unlike the French, who considered diplomatic and imperial costs along with their business strategies, the Hudson's Bay Company focused on profits. Their competitors were the North West Company (NWC), based in Montreal, and New England traders, who operated mainly offshore. From the late 1770s through the War of 1812, the NWC moved deep into the North American interior and on to the Pacific coast, mapping the land, building posts, and securing Indian friendships by including them in their operations. For the next forty-seven years, the two companies clashed, each trying to drive out the other. Beginning in the 1780s, the NWC used Grand Portage on Lake Superior as its major transfer point along the Voyageurs' Highway, 1,300 miles from Montreal and another 1,700 miles from the Athabaska country in present-day western Canada. At its peak in the 1790s, more than 100 tons of trade goods and furs were exchanged here during the summer. In 1821 the

HBC and the NWC merged into one giant corporation, retaining the name Hudson's Bay Company. Their main competition continued to be the American Fur Company, founded by John Jacob Astor in 1808, with three departments by 1823: the Northern Department, based at Mackinac, which contested the British for Indian allegiance long after the War of 1812 ended; the Detroit Department, which traded south into Indiana and Ohio; and the Western Department, headquartered in Saint Louis, made possible by cooperation with old French families who had a near-monopoly on the fur trade of the lower Missouri region. The company expanded and built Fort Union in 1829 at the confluence of the Missouri and Yellowstone rivers, built Fort Pierre in 1832 on the central Missouri, and purchased Fort Laramie in 1835 from the smaller St. Louis firm of Sublette and Campbell. Smaller posts such as Fort Clark (1835) were built at logical intervals between posts where Indian villages already existed.

Native peoples continued to cooperate and never rebelled en masse. The reasons for this uneasy but workable interregnum are complex, but they include the fact that most Indians were not politically unified and preferred to maintain local sovereignty. Also, most Native kin networks included French, English, and Scottish outsiders through intermarriage. Of great importance was the Indians' increasing dependence on trade goods, especially cutting and skinning tools, blankets, and guns. The most deleterious of white introductions was alcohol. Many companies claimed that they controlled the flow of liquor into Indian Country, but in reality none succeeded, mostly because of the whites' intemperate use of alcohol. Many Indian groups came to expect liquor as a present before trade; brandy and furs became inseparable early in the East Coast trade and remained so as the trade expanded westward. Many Indian tribes were also decimated by European diseases, including measles, mumps, influenza, and smallpox. Although few Indians worked directly as wage earners for companies, they continued to be the major procurers of furs on their own lands. Whites who trapped on their own did so at their peril. Most tribes had sanctions by species, gender, and season in which animals could be harvested. White trappers scoured many regions of North America indiscriminately, diminishing the resource base and forcing confrontation. No place exemplifies this pattern better than the Rocky Mountains, where mountain men worked in military-style brigades, undermining traditional Native economies and suffering many fatalities in the process of avoiding Native middlemen traders. Places such as Bent's Fort (1833–1849) and Fort Vasquez (1835–1842) served whites well but did not incorporate American Indians except on their periphery. Some fur posts were authorized to distribute annuity goods prescribed by treaties between the U.S. government and Indian tribes.

By the 1840s raccoon was the dominant trade fur in the Old Northwest. In the West buffalo were hunted for their outer hair, or robe, which was used in rugs and clothes, and for their hide, which was made into industrial conveyor belts. By 1900 the buffalo, which once numbered about 60 million, were almost exterminated by hunters killing them for tongues, horns, and hides — and to deny them to the Plains Indians. While whites profited, Indians were left hungry and angry and rallied in wars and religious movements that sought a return to the days when whites were few and buffalo plentiful.

The HBC withdrew from the United States in 1870. The remaining companies diversified in response to the increased settlement of the West, selling the hardware and general merchandise that the settlers needed. The Indians who had been economic and social liaisons between the fur company traders and distant Indians had no place in the new economy. Indian and métis (mixed-blood) wives of white fur-trade personnel were especially marginalized when the goodwill of their people was no longer essential. Furs

are still big business in both Canada and the United States, and full-time trappers — Indian and white — still work in remote places, but fur farms, environmental laws, and changes in public attitudes about wildlife have helped revive the ethic embraced long ago by Native peoples.

FURTHER READING: *Exploring the Fur Trade Routes of North America,* by Barbara Huck

52. Marquette Mission Park and Mackinac State Historic Parks, MI

George L. Cornell

Marquette Mission Park and Museum of Ojibwa Culture: 500 North State St., St. Ignace

Mackinac State Historic Parks: off I-75 at exit 339, Mackinaw City

The Great Lakes area known as Mackinac includes Mackinac Island and the Straits of Mackinac, five miles of open water where Lakes Michigan and Huron meet. The two Michigan peninsulas are north and south of the straits. The Ojibwa and the Ottawa called the straits Pequod-e-nong (headlands or bluff, a rounding of land), referring to the northern point of land on the southern peninsula. The straits region and, particularly, Mackinac Island are prominent in the beliefs and history of the Anishinaabe — the Ojibwa, the Ottawa, and the Potawatomi — the People of the Three Fires. Historically, the region was called Michilimackinac (pronounced Mackinaw), from the Ojibwa words *michi* (large or big) and *mi-ki-nok* (turtle). Some say that the name for Mackinac Island, Great Turtle, came from the shape of the island. Others believe that the island is central to the Anishinaabe migration stories about entering the Great Lakes and finding a new home after their long and arduous journey from the "Great Salt Sea" to the east.

Father Jacques Marquette established a Jesuit mission on Mackinac Island in 1671 and moved it the next year to the present site of St. Ignace on the north shore of the straits. The French built Fort de Buade near the mission in 1683, and in 1701 Sieur Cadillac moved the fort to Detroit. Fort Michilimackinac was constructed at Pe-quod-e-nong in 1715 and became important in the fur trade and in regional commerce. In 1761, during the Seven Years' War, the British took control of the fort and held it until June 1763. During Pontiac's War, the Ojibwa and allied tribes staged a ball game near the walls of the fort as a distraction, which made it possible for them to attack the fort and capture it. The British regained the fort, then abandoned it and built Fort Mackinac on Mackinac Island in 1781. The British surrendered that new stronghold to the Americans at the end of the American Revolution, recaptured it during the War of 1812, and held it until 1815.

Marquette Mission Park is on the site of Marquette's original mission to the local Native populations, which included Hurons who had relocated from east of Lake Huron during the Beaver Wars with the Iroquois. A reconstructed Huron longhouse on the site commemorates Marquette's work with these refugee groups. Colonial Michilimackinac, operated by the Mackinac State Historic Parks, was designated a National Historic Landmark in 1960. The restored Fort Michilimackinac, in Mackinaw City, is one of the premier early French archaeological sites in North America and provides excellent interpretative history to visitors.

Mackinac Island is a place of enchantment and intrigue, commerce and historical conflict. We hope that when you visit the island you will go to the bluffs at sunrise and watch as the sun brings new life to the day. Perhaps you might offer some tobacco to the spirits of the Native people who have journeyed through this place and, as you look out over the waters, open your heart to the Creation. Then decide for yourself why this island was sacred to the Anishinaabe — and travel on in peace.

FURTHER READING: *People of the Three Fires,* by G. L. Cornell, J. A. Clifton, and J. M. McClurken

53. Starved Rock State Park, IL: Starved Rock

Mark Walczynski

Off Rte. 178, Utica

Visitor center

Standing like an impregnable fortress on the south shore of the Illinois River is the 125-foot-high sandstone bluff known as Starved Rock. Native Americans began living in the area about 10,000 years ago. By 1673 the Kaskaskia, a subtribe of the Illinois Alliance, were living in a village about a mile upstream from the rock. By 1675 other Illinois subtribes, including the Peoria and the Tamaroa, had moved to the Kaskaskia village for protection against their enemies, the Iroquois. By 1679 there were about 8,000 people in the village. The Illinois grew corn, beans, and squash in the fertile land along the river, hunted game in the woods and on the plains, caught fish in the river, and utilized timber for firewood and dugout canoes. Their homelands had everything the Illinois needed to live, and live well.

The Illinois were the magnet that drew the French to the area. During much of the year they lived in their large village, which the Jesuit and Recollet missionaries saw as an opportunity to try to convert them to Catholicism. In September 1680, after most of the villagers had dispersed for the winter hunt, the Iroquois attacked the Kaskaskia village and drove all of the Illinois bands out of present-day Illinois. The French explorer La Salle built Fort St. Louis on the Rock in 1683 and persuaded the Miami, Shawnee, and other tribes to move into the nearby Illinois Valley. Trade was conducted at the fort, which was a symbol of French influence and a place where tribes were safe from Iroquois war parties. The Illinois, including many of the numerous subtribes, returned to Kaskaskia — which became known as the Grand Village of the Illinois — and maintained good relations with the French between 1683 and 1691. After depleting the area's resources, the Illinois abandoned the village in the fall of 1691 and moved to the Lake Peoria area.

In 1712 members of another Illinois subtribe, the Peoria, returned and lived below the Rock on today's Plum Island. By 1722 the remaining Peoria had joined these Rock Peoria for protection against marauding Fox warriors. The Rock got the name Starved Rock as a result of a Fox attack, led by the aging war chief Ouashala, on the Peoria village. The Fox drove the Peoria to the summit of the Rock. Besieged by their enemies and with no way to escape, the Peorias' only hope was to convince Ouashala to urge his warriors to end the siege. After much persuasion, they succeeded. Soon after the siege ended, the Peoria abandoned the Rock again and settled in the camps of other Illinois along the Mississippi in southern Illinois. By 1730 the Fox were no longer a threat to the Illinois, so the Peoria and some members of the Cahokia subtribe returned to Starved Rock. By 1752 they had left the villages there forever and had moved downstream to the Peoria area and then to the Mississippi River.

FURTHER READING: *The Time of the French in the Heart of North America 1673–1818*, by Charles J. Balesi.

54. Iliniwek Village State Historic Site, MO

Off Rte. 27, northeast of Wayland

Trail to the site of a longhouse

Beginning about 1640, a subtribe of the Illinois, the Peoria, lived in a village on the high sand terrace in the Des Moines River floodplain. Louis Jolliet and Father Jacques Marquette visited the village in 1673 and estimated that there were about 300 houses and a population of about 8,000. Some may have left their village in 1677 and moved to the Kaskaskia village near Starved Rock to seek protection from the Iroquois; if so, they returned after Iroquois burned Kaskaskia in 1680. They ceded their land in treaties between 1808 and 1832 and were forced to move first to Kansas and then to Oklahoma. Their descendants are the Peoria Indian Tribe of Oklahoma with tribal headquarters in Miami, Oklahoma.

The Seven Years' War

FRED ANDERSON

❖ The Seven Years' War in America, also called the French and Indian War, was a great conflict between the empires of Britain and France over control of the eastern half of North America. Native Americans, acting as allies, enemies, negotiators, and neutrals, critically shaped the war's outcome. This vast conflict began in North America but eventually saw battles fought in Europe, the Caribbean, West Africa, the Indian subcontinent, and the Philippines, as well as on the Atlantic and Indian oceans. That so titanic a struggle originated in competition over control of the Ohio Valley reflected the growing importance of North America to Britain and France. The war decisively shaped American history, as well as the histories of Europe and the Atlantic world in general. It also marked a decisive turning point in wars between Indians and whites, establishing patterns of conflict that would persist through the 1880s.

In the mid-eighteenth century the Ohio Country was of increasing importance to both the French and the British. The French wanted an arc of settlements and Indian alliances that swept from the Gulf of St. Lawrence to the Mississippi Delta. The British feared a French cordon to the west that would preclude new settlements west of the Appalachian Mountains. When in 1754 the French built Fort Duquesne at the Forks of the Ohio — that is, the confluence of the Monongahela and Allegheny rivers — Governor Robert Dinwiddie of Virginia sent twenty-one-year-old Lieutenant Colonel George Washington, in command of a small, inadequately supplied regiment, to dislodge them and defend Virginia's claim to the Ohio Country.

On May 27, 1754, Washington was in southwestern Pennsylvania near the modern town of Farmington, awaiting the arrival of supplies and reinforcements that would enable him to march against Fort Duquesne. Around sunset, a courier arrived from the Seneca "Half King" Tanaghrisson, who represented Iroquois interests in the Ohio Country, with a warning: a French force was camped in the woods seven miles away. Its mission, apparently, was to reconnoiter Washington's position. That night Washington led a detachment to the French camp; the following morning, together with the Half King and perhaps a dozen warriors, he attacked. The skirmish ended with the massacre of thirteen French soldiers; Tanaghrisson himself tomahawked the commander, Ensign Joseph Coulon de Villiers de Jumonville, as a means of cementing an alliance between the Virginians and himself.

This act of mass murder in a wilderness glen was the first military encounter of the Seven Years' War, and it left Washington's men terribly exposed to French retribution. In June, Washington's men completed a hasty defensive position, Fort Necessity, while waiting for the reinforcements that would enable them to advance against Fort Duquesne. Tanaghrisson, meanwhile, failed to convince the Ohio Indians — Delawares, Shawnees, Mingo Seneca, and a variety of smaller refugee groups — to fight alongside the British and expel the French from the Forks. They had good reasons not to cooperate: the French were mili-

tarily powerful and supported by large numbers of Indians from Detroit and the Great Lakes; moreover, unlike the land-hungry British, who clearly intended to establish farm settlements in the interior, the French generally preferred trade and alliance to colonization. On July 3 the French and Indian allies — including Shawnee, Delaware, and Mingo warriors from the Ohio villages, as well as Ottawas, Mississaugas, Nipissings, Algonkins, and mission Indians from the St. Lawrence reserves — attacked Fort Necessity, forced Washington to surrender, burned the fort, and returned to Fort Duquesne. Washington and his men returned, humiliated, to Virginia. By the end of October Tanaghrisson was dead, and the Iroquois League had recognized French predominance at the Forks by establishing amicable diplomatic contacts at Montreal.

Within a year both the French and the British Empire had sent reinforcements and commanders across the Atlantic to defend frontiers and, if need be, to prosecute offensive warfare in North America. In June 1755 the new British commander, Major General Edward Braddock, marched slowly toward Fort Duquesne. Only Scarouady (Tanaghrisson's successor as Half King) and seven other Mingo warriors accompanied him as scouts. Braddock had alienated the Ohio Indians, who after a year of dealing with the French at the Forks were willing to explore the possibilities of a change in sides, when the Delaware chief, Shingas, asked him the only question that mattered to the Ohio Indians — "What he intended to do with the land if he Could drive the French and their Indians away?" Braddock summoned all his considerable reserves of arrogance and replied, "No Savage Should Inherit the Land." On July 9 the French and their Indian allies — mainly Mingo, Delaware, Shawnee, Ottawa, Mississauga, Wyandot, and Potawatomi warriors — attacked Braddock's approaching column about eight miles from the Forks, mortally wounded Braddock, and won a quick victory.

The importance of Indian allies during a war

in the wilderness was lost on Braddock, as it had earlier been lost on Washington and other provincials who, like him, were deeply interested in land speculation and therefore prone to see Indians as obstacles to their plans for the future. By contrast, the French understood the importance of Indian alliances and used them to foil virtually every Anglo-American military initiative for the next three years. Thus on a strategic level the collapse of Braddock's force foretold much about the war's cultural dimensions. During the war, people of very different cultures met in encounters that defined the character of American history for decades to come. The British whom the young provincials met challenged many of their inherited preconceptions about the relations among men — which they assumed were contractual and voluntary but which British officers regarded as founded on status and deference that could, if necessary, be enforced by coercion. In the postwar period these provincials became landowners and community leaders; twenty years later many would stake their own and their sons' lives on the independence of the United States of America.

For the Ohio Indians as much as for the settlers in the backcountry, Braddock's defeat marked a point of no return. After Iroquois diplomats assured the French of their neutrality between the French and the English, the Ohio Indians "agreed To Come out with the French and their Indians in Parties to Destroy the English Settlements." In the fall of 1755 French and Indian war parties took captives, plunder, and scalps throughout the Virginia and Pennsylvania backcountry. With few soldiers to protect it, the frontier simply collapsed. Refugees flooded east across the mountains in numbers so great that officers trying to join Washington in the Shenandoah Valley complained that they could barely force their way over the Blue Ridge to reach his headquarters at Winchester.

The first battle north of the Pennsylvania–

Virginia frontier took place on September 8, 1755, when William Johnson, a wealthy trader from the Mohawk Valley, in command of a provincial force and 200 Mohawk warriors, defeated French soldiers, Canadian Abenakis, and Caughnawaga Mohawks at the southern end of Lake George. Johnson was wounded, and the French commander, Baron Armand de Dieskau, was captured. Following the battle the French retreated northward and built Fort Carillon on the promontory of Ticonderoga, where the waters of Lake George drain into Lake Champlain. Johnson began the construction of Fort William Henry at the south end of Lake George to protect the British presence on the lakes and to guard the supply road to Fort Edward, Saratoga, and Albany.

The following March, William Shirley, the governor of Massachusetts, who had succeeded Braddock as Britain's commander in chief, was recalled to England. Thomas Pownall was named royal governor of Massachusetts, and John Campbell, the earl of Loudoun, was dispatched to America as commander in chief and governor of Virginia. In May, Louis-Joseph, marquis de Montcalm-Gozon de Saint-Véran, arrived to replace Baron Dieskau as commander of the French regular forces in Canada. During the next two years Montcalm's forces were victorious, but he could not hide his metropolitan contempt for his Indian allies and the Canadians whom he had been sent to defend; eventually he succeeded in permanently alienating both, with disastrous effects. Meanwhile Lord Loudoun's prickly and pompous manner provoked bitter disputes with the colonial assemblies. To understand how and why the Anglo-Americans failed to take advantage of their vastly superior numbers and resources and to see the reasons for Montcalm's abandonment of strategies of proven merit is to begin to grasp the decisive influence of cultural factors in the war.

British policy complicated cooperation with

the provincials because it made all provincial officers junior to all regular officers and made all provincials serving with regulars subject to British martial law and discipline. Virginia was more concerned about a slave revolt and allocated 55 percent of its military appropriation to the militia, which controlled the slaves, and only 45 percent to the Virginia Regiment, which defended the frontier. Pennsylvania, whose Quaker heritage had prevented the formation of a militia until the war was well under way, was essentially defenseless in the face of French and Indian attacks, which eventually reached to within 70 miles of Philadelphia. Only the northern colonies — particularly Massachusetts and Connecticut — remained dependable as sources of men and money for the war effort, but even these grew steadily more disenchanted with the imperious Loudoun and less and less willing to appropriate the troops and resources he demanded of them. The result was a series of defeats for British arms, in a context of growing friction between the provincial assemblies and metropolitan authorities.

In August 1756 Montcalm's 3,000-man force, including 250 Indians from six nations, from the Abenaki of upper New England to the Menominee from the western shore of Lake Michigan, defeated the British at Fort Oswego and took the entire garrison prisoner. Montcalm could not keep his promise of safe conduct to Montreal for the prisoners. His Indian allies had received presents and provisions but no pay and expected what previous French commanders had accorded them for their services: plunder, trophies, and captives. In an afternoon of violence they killed between 30 and 100 soldiers and took what they had expected: supplies from the forts and captives, some of whom Montcalm later ransomed.

The next French victory came in August 1757, when Montcalm attacked Fort William Henry with 6,000 French and Canadians and about 2,000 Indians. These included Ottawa from upper Lake Michigan country, Ojibwe (Chippewa and Mississauga) from the shores of Lake Superior, Menominee and Potawatami from lower Michigan, Winnebago from Wisconsin, Sauk and Fox from farther west, Miami and Delaware from the Ohio Country, and even a few Iowa from beyond the Mississippi; among the Canadian Indians (largely Catholic converts) who participated in the siege were Nipissing, Abenaki, Caughnawaga, Huron-Petun, Malecite, and Micmac warriors. Lieutenant Colonel George Monro, in command of about 2,000 men, accepted Montcalm's offer of surrender with the honors of war and capitulated after six days. The terms of the surrender stipulated that he and his force would be allowed to withdraw to Albany with their personal property, arms, and colors. It was a perfectly honorable, conventional ending to a siege conducted according to European professional military standards, but it outraged Montcalm's Indian allies, who believed that they had earned both captives and plunder by their service. In response to this perceived betrayal by their French "father," the Indians launched a brief but terrifying massacre, killing about 185 men, women, and children from the surrendered garrison and taking perhaps 300 to 500 more captive. Montcalm, who believed himself dishonored by this "savage" violation of the surrender terms, ransomed all but about 200 of the captives and retreated to Fort Carillon.

Montcalm had alienated the Indians by seeking to command them as auxiliaries rather than negotiating for their cooperation as allies. The results of the battle were critical. Indian warriors never again flocked from the interior to fight with the French. Those who returned to their villages disgusted by Montcalm's behavior learned too late that the prisoners and the loot they brought with them had been infected with smallpox, beginning a massive epidemic throughout the Great Lakes basin and beyond.

Finally, the "massacre of Fort William Henry," blown out of all proportion by the New Englanders who had witnessed it, fanned provincial hatred of Catholics and Indians and set the stage for further atrocities as the war progressed.

All the while, the Virginia-Pennsylvania frontier reeled under Indian attacks launched from Fort Duquesne and the Native villages of the Ohio Country. Loudoun ordered Colonel John Stanwix and a battalion to Pennsylvania and gave him authority over Washington and the understrength regiment of Virginia provincials who were to defend Virginia's chain of eighteen forts along a 350-mile frontier. Washington, who could man only seven of these posts, was forced to rely on militia units for the bulk of frontier defense, an expedient that left the region largely open to French and Indian raids. The result was the abandonment of virtually all settlements not immediately under the protection of a fort.

At about this time a remarkable Philadelphia merchant, Israel Pemberton, emerged as the leader of a Quaker peace society, the Friendly Association for Regaining and Preserving Peace with the Indians by Pacific Measures, and opened a dialogue between the Delaware of the Susquehanna Valley, led by Teedyuscung, and the government of Pennsylvania. The chief sought the admission from the Penn family that the Walking Purchase of 1737 had been a fraud. In compensation he demanded that 2.5 million acres of the Wyoming Valley and adjoining lands be set aside as a perpetual reservation for the Indians of the Susquehanna region. The power of the Penns and the Iroquois (who had been complicit in the fraudulent purchase) ultimately doomed the prospect of creating that great reserve, but for the time being the peace effort continued, with Teedyuscung establishing contacts with the western Delawares on the Ohio and inviting them to contemplate abandoning the French alliance.

In late 1757, William Pitt, who had emerged in Parliament as the greatest war leader England would see before Sir Winston Churchill, named General Sir John Ligonier, a general of prodigious administrative talents, to head the British army. Pitt ordered the navy to prevent France from resupplying their forces in North America, and in March 1758 he relieved Lord Loudoun of command, replacing him with Major General James Abercromby. At the same moment, Pitt reversed the policy of subordinating provincial officers to those of lower rank in the regular army and offered subsidies to assist the colonial assemblies in the war effort against France. He asked for the colonists' help rather than compelling it, and he treated them as allies rather than subordinates. Pitt's changes undercut the emerging pattern of resistance to imperial authority in New England. Within a month the American colonial assemblies had voted to raise 23,000 provincials for the coming campaign.

Ligonier knew that Abercromby had a reputation for indolence and indecision but had confidence in the men under him — a notably talented group that included generals Jeffrey Amherst, James Wolfe, John Forbes, and George Augustus, Viscount Howe — to lead the nearly 50,000 Anglo-American troops who would be employed in the expeditions of 1758. Montcalm had about half as many men to oppose them; he had, moreover, lost most of his Indian allies, even as Canada had experienced harvest failures that left the country and its defenders critically short of food supplies. Even so, Montcalm and about 3,500 French regulars fought off an attack by nearly 16,000 British and provincial troops under Abercromby. In the preliminary fighting, Lord Howe, an officer idolized by redcoats and provincials alike, was killed. When Abercromby ordered an assault on the defensive lines Montcalm hastily constructed outside the walls of Fort Carillon on July 8, 1758, the British suffered their worst defeat of the war, with 551 killed and nearly 1,350 wounded. Montcalm's forces, by contrast, suffered only 377 casualties.

Brigadier General John Forbes, meanwhile,

led his forces in a slow, carefully planned and well-provisioned march toward Fort Duquesne, building the road and fortifications as they advanced. Forbes understood the strategic importance of the Indians as allies and worked with Teedyuscung and Pemberton to develop contact with the Ohio Indians. When the French could not get the Delaware to fight Forbes's approaching force, which included George Washington's 1st Virginia Regiment, they burned the fort and fled on November 23, 1758. Pitt replaced Abercromby with Amherst, a competent administrator. Forbes died in March 1759. His lasting legacy was Forbes Road, from Philadelphia to the Ohio Valley.

As Forbes systematically advanced on Fort Duquesne, more than 500 Indians from thirteen nations attended a great congress at Easton. The Six Nations of the Iroquois League sent many representatives to reassert its dominance over its tributary peoples, including those of the Ohio Country. Teedyuscung, having made peace between his eastern Delaware and the British and having delivered the western Delaware to the peace table, had lost his negotiating position and found himself marginalized. His response was to stay drunk for most of the time the Treaty of Easton was being negotiated, an unfortunate decision that strengthened the Iroquois position that he was unfit to lead. There was no action to void the Walking Purchase or to provide the Delaware with Wyoming Valley land, but the Iroquois regained dominance over the eastern Delaware. The Ohio Delaware, represented by Pisquetomen, were free to negotiate with the Pennsylvania government on their own and agreed to peace on the condition that whites would not establish permanent settlements in the Ohio Country after the war. Four years later, in a hearing before Sir William Johnson, Teedyuscung signed a release on the land in return for £600 in goods and cash.

Between 1754 and 1758, George Washington, a man of unshakable physical courage, had grown into a competent military officer and administrator. He had learned what Forbes knew: that an army need not win battles to gain its ultimate goal; tactical defeats could be compensated for by retaining discipline, lines of communication, and fortified supply depots, and by staying on the field longer than the enemy. He had also learned, as few other provincial and regular officers did in the course of the war, how critical Indian allies were to success in a wilderness conflict. Unlike many of his contemporaries, he emerged from the war not as a confirmed Indian hater but as a man convinced that negotiation was to be preferred in every instance to making war on Native peoples, who could inflict terrible damage on colonists ignorant of forest warfare. In December 1757 he returned to Virginia and resigned his commission as colonel of the 1st Virginia Regiment. He was elected to the House of Burgesses, married Martha Dandridge Custis, and took up a role as one of the rising leaders of Virginia's planter elite.

British subsidies made it possible for 17,000 provincials to join the 1759 expeditions against Canada led by Jeffrey Amherst and James Wolfe. Of these, Georgia, the Carolinas, and Maryland raised none, and Virginia's only regiment was ordered to secure the Forks while its militia was to protect the settlers who were moving beyond the Blue Ridge. Pennsylvania feared a Virginia hegemony at Pittsburgh and raised 3,000 troops commanded by Forbes's successor, Brigadier General John Stanwix, to improve Forbes Road, refortify the Forks, and restore a vigorous trade to keep the Ohio Indians from trading with the French. The competition between Virginia and Pennsylvania was complicated by land speculators who were also traders and Indian diplomats, such as George Croghan, Sir William Johnson's deputy agent. And the Indians' greatest fear was becoming a reality: white settlers were moving in, and the British were building Fort Pitt, a huge pentagonal fort at the confluence of the Monongahela and the Allegheny that could house 1,000 men and dominate the region strategically in ways that the much smaller Fort Duquesne had been unable to do.

The shift in advantage to the British and Anglo-Americans encouraged the Six Nations to reconsider the posture of neutrality they had assumed at the end of 1755 and to throw their weight onto the scales with the power that looked most likely to succeed. Thus Brigadier General John Prideaux's Niagara expedition was strengthened on June 27 by Sir William Johnson and 1,000 Iroquois warriors who joined it at Oswego. The Grand Council seems to have decided that by helping the British to defeat the French and to maintain their hegemony at the Forks, they could increase their influence over the Ohio Indians, whose resistance to Iroquois control was developing a powerful religious dimension. Because of the Iroquois presence, the Niagara Senecas decided not to fight with the French. The French surrender of Fort Niagara meant that no supplies could reach their forts and trading posts on the upper Great Lakes, from Detroit to Michilimackinac and beyond. A second result was the loss of most of their remaining Indian allies.

The final French losses of 1759 included Fort Carillon at Ticonderoga and Fort St. Frédéric at Crown Point in July and Quebec in September. The following year Amherst delivered the coup de grace to French resistance by taking Montreal with a three-pronged campaign in which forces converged on the city from the west, east, and south. He did not fully realize that the Iroquois warriors and diplomats who accompanied two of these three expeditions were largely responsible for detaching the remaining Canadian Indians from their alliance with New France; hence he never understood the degree to which he owed the comparatively bloodless final victory over Canada's defenders in 1760 to Native allies. Amherst, who in fact understood Indian people little better than Braddock had, proceeded to reverse the policies that William Johnson had

employed with great success, including diplomatic gift-giving and generous subsidies to any Indians who were willing to enter the war as Britain's allies. This reversal of policy, driven by the need to economize, eventually resulted in the catastrophic breakdown of Anglo-Indian relations in the pan-Indian movement that the British would know as Pontiac's War (1763–64).

To the south, the British built forts in Cherokee country to be both trading posts and fortified bases for troops. Their trade ended in the summer of 1758, when the Cherokees returned from the Forbes campaign to find that white settlers had poached their game and diminished both their food supply and their trade in deerskins. Warfare followed. The Creeks saw their interests advanced by isolating the Cherokees. The British regulars who came in 1760 burned five of the Lower Towns; the Cherokees retreated to the Middle Towns and held out there until the following year. In 1761 a better-organized British expedition penetrated the mountains and devastated the Middle Towns, leaving 4,000 Cherokees homeless, with little food and no ammunition, and no choice but to withdraw as refugees to the Overhill towns, which were ill prepared to support them. The chief whom the English knew as Little Carpenter, Attakullakulla, negotiated a peace treaty that brought an end to the war. The Cherokee War and Amherst's reforms together thus gave the Indians of postwar America what they had never had before: a common grievance and tangible evidence that the English would not hesitate to threaten their way of life.

By 1761 many settlers, including provincial veterans, were moving into the backwoods, particularly near the forts, where Amherst and other commanders encouraged them to settle and grow food to support the local garrisons. Most backwoods settlement, however, was out of the officials' control. The settlers aggravated relations with the Indians, putting conflicting pressures upon the officials in charge of maintaining the forts and preventing trans-Appalachian settlement, in accord with the Easton Treaty of 1758. All this was massively complicated by the postwar revival of land speculation. While Governor Francis Fauquier of Virginia and Colonel Henry Bouquet at Fort Pitt tried to stop the invasion of Indian lands, Governor Benning Wentworth of New Hampshire encouraged settlement on more than 3 million acres in what is now Vermont. The Susquehanna Company's attempts to settle the Wyoming Valley of Pennsylvania triggered fighting with the local Indians following the murder of Teedyuscung, who died in April 1763 when arsonists set his cabin afire as he slept within. Teedyuscung's sons and their fellow warriors took their revenge on the white settlers, inaugurating the long and bloody duel over the ownership of the Wyoming Valley that would continue, off and on, through the War of Independence.

The Indians came to understand that British promises, made at the Treaty of Easton, to refrain from settlement west of the mountains after the war were lies. The war between empires ended with the final Treaty of Paris in February 1763, but war resumed in the interior of America as Native warriors launched the great pan-Indian movement called Pontiac's War. This massive uprising, an Indian victory in the sense that it forced the British to reverse Amherst's economizing reforms and renew their promises of settlement restriction in the West, should have taught the British that their imperial power ultimately depended on the consent of the governed. That lesson in humility, unfortunately, was lost on British ministers blinded by the incredible worldwide scope of their victory over France. Their subsequent attempts to impose reforms on their own colonists, beginning in 1764 and 1765, would encourage the growth of another resistance movement, as unexpected as Pontiac's War — a movement that within a dozen years would lay Britain's continent-bestriding empire in ashes and raise in its ruins a new and more successful empire: the United States of America.

FURTHER READING: *Crucible of War: The Seven Years' War and the Fate of Empire in British North America,* by Fred Anderson, from which this was excerpted with permission from Random House Inc.

55. Fort Necessity National Battlefield, PA

On Rte. 40, the National Road, east of Uniontown

Fort Necessity/National Road Interpretive and Education Center

On May 28, 1754, the first military action in the Seven Years' War ended in the massacre of French soldiers, including their commander, Ensign Joseph Coulon de Villiers de Jumonville, by George Washington's Virginia regiment and their Seneca allies. The site is the Jumonville Glen unit of the National Battlefield. On July 3 the French and their Indian allies attacked Washington, who no longer had Indian allies, in his small stockade, Fort Necessity. They forced him to surrender and burned the fort. Washington agreed to the surrender terms, which allowed his force to leave with honor if the English would not return to the Ohio Country for one year.

Fort Johnson, Johnson Hall, and the Anglo-Mohawk Alliance

KIRK DAVIS SWINEHART

❖ Throughout the eighteenth century, Britain profited from an alliance with the Mohawk Indians of central New York, who once lived in the valley that bears their name. Hundreds of Mohawk warriors died fighting for the Crown; hundreds more were maimed. Initially, the Mohawk allied themselves with Britain against France in wars waged for control of North America — a seventy-five-year struggle culminating in France's defeat during the Seven Years' War. In what proved a disastrous move, the Mohawk also fought for Britain during the American Revolution.

Behind the Mohawk alliance with Britain stood Sir William Johnson (1715–1774), an Anglo-Irish émigré, Indian trader, land speculator, hero of the Seven Years' War, and the Crown's charismatic superintendent of Indian affairs north of the Ohio River. As Indian superintendent, Johnson was charged with maintaining peaceable relations among three entities often at cross-purposes: the Crown, a rapidly growing settler population, and a kaleidoscopic, often hostile array of Indians. Broadly defined, his Indian Department held responsibility for negotiating treaties and land sales on the Crown's behalf, for regulating trade between Indians and whites, for settling their disputes, and, when necessary, for enlisting Iroquois warriors to defend British colonial interests. Aided by Mohawk forces, Johnson defeated French troops under Jean-Armand, baron de Dieskau, at the Battle of Lake George in 1755, for which he received a baronetcy and his commission as Indian superintendent.

Although Johnson brought an admirable humanity to his office, he nevertheless used his royal appointment to accumulate several hundred thousand acres and to provide cronies with lucrative sinecures. Between 1749 and his death, Johnson built two houses in the Mohawk Valley; both were famously hospitable domestic empires within the British Empire. At Fort Johnson (1749) and at Johnson Hall (1763), he entertained powerful guests from throughout the realm as well as thousands of Native people, who traveled from as far south as the Carolinas and from as far north as Nova Scotia. As the Crown's foremost (if unofficial) embassies for negotiating with Native peoples in North America, Fort Johnson and Johnson Hall introduced them to an expanding repertoire of British goods and rituals, such as billiards and tea drinking.

At the end of the Seven Years' War in 1763, Johnson left Fort Johnson, hoping to create at his Johnson Hall estate a feudal manor where tradesmen and farmers would live under his benevolent rule. Johnson Hall became the seat of a dynasty more commonly associated with British India than with British North America. Together with his Mohawk common-law wife, Gonwatsijayenni, or Molly Brant, Johnson presided over a large, racially mixed, and seldom harmonious family that had accrued fantastic wealth by administering nearly all aspects of Britain's dealings with the Indians. Born around 1736, Molly Brant has been harder to know — and generally less well known — than her famous younger brother, Joseph. But in ways only now coming to light, Molly Brant exerted tremendous influence over Johnson and his political maneuverings. Indeed, after his death in 1774, it was her frequent exhorting that kept many Iroquois peoples on the side of George III during the American Revolution of 1775–1783. Friends and enemies alike recalled her as a magnetic speaker and fierce guardian of her family's material interests.

The house she shared with Johnson was a marvel. What awaited visitors behind Johnson Hall's Georgian-style façade was a spectacle of life peculiar to this margin of the empire. White observers often had trouble describing the house. Upon its walls and scattered across its horizontal surfaces were English silver and ceramics as well as tomahawks and moccasins. Although described by many white visitors as an oddity, Johnson Hall had enormous symbolic significance for the Iroquois, who kept a council fire there and came for political counsel as well as material support. There might be 700 Natives there at any given time, and sometimes as many as 900. As the house was being finished, Pontiac's War (1763–1764) erupted in the Ohio Country, a violent reaction against severe cutbacks imposed on Johnson's Indian Department after the Seven Years' War. What began as a monument to Johnson's success became at times a refugee camp for Indians disenfranchised by the closure of British military forts, which had provided them with what they needed to survive. Indians came in vast numbers to protest against settlers crossing the Ohio River in violation of the Proclamation of 1763, which forbade white settlement west of the Appalachian Mountains.

Despite criticism from London, Johnson persisted in his old ways, providing costly handouts of clothing, food, medicine, tools, and weapons. For Johnson, as for the Indians, lavish displays of hospitality — nearly always at crushing expense to the Crown and sometimes to Johnson himself — were the bedrock of diplomacy. In July 1764, for example, Johnson received and entertained about 2,000 warriors at Fort Niagara, where he negotiated peace with western Indians previously at war with Britain. The cost of the gathering ran to an estimated £138,000, an astronomical sum for the day. In the years leading up to Johnson's death in 1774, the Crown and the increasingly disgruntled North American colonists became unwilling to bear such expenses.

Johnson is easily caricatured as a ruthless man of empire, but the record of everyday life at his two famous houses provides a more complicated portrait. Shaped for many years by Johnson's hospitality at Fort Johnson and Johnson Hall, the Anglo-Mohawk alliance owed more to both houses than is generally acknowledged.

56. Old Fort Johnson, NY

At Rtes. 5 and 67, Fort Johnson

57. Johnson Hall State Historic Site, NY

Hall Ave., Johnstown

FURTHER READING: *The Ordeal of the Longhouse: The Peoples of the Iroquois League in the Era of European Colonization,* by Daniel K. Richter

58. Lake George Battlefield Park, NY

Off Fort George Rd., Lake George

On September 8, 1755, William Johnson's expedition against the French at Crown Point on Lake Champlain included about 1,000 provincials and 200 Mohawk warriors led by Chief Hendrick. They advanced into a trap set by the French forces, commanded by Baron Jean-Armand, baron de Dieskau, which included about 700 Abenaki and Caughnawaga Mohawk who lived in Canada. The chief and 30 Mohawks were killed, Johnson was wounded, and Dieskau was wounded and captured. The battle ended the expedition.

59. Fort Ontario State Historic Site, NY

Fourth St., Oswego

Museum/visitor center

On August 11, 1756, the Marquis de Montcalm attacked Fort Ontario, a wooden stockade that was one of the British defenses at Oswego, with a 3,000-man force that included about 250 American Indians. The French destroyed the fort and defeated the British. The restoration is the star-shaped fort of 1868–1872.

60. Fort Ticonderoga, NY: Ticonderoga in Indian Eyes

Wes (Red Hawk) Dikeman and Nicholas Westbrook

Off Rte. 74, Ticonderoga

For more than 250 years Fort Ticonderoga has stood on a limestone peninsula dominating the ancient strategic portage that links Lake Champlain with Lake George. This is the central portage of a principal natural water highway from the interior of the North American continent, around the Appalachian Mountains, and into the Atlantic Ocean. Looking north from their homelands, the Iroquoian Mohawk called this place Ticonderoga (the junction of two waterways). Looking south from the eastern shore of Lake Champlain and the St. Lawrence Valley, the Western Abenaki people called it Tsitôtegwihlá (the place where the waterway forks and continues). People have been in the area for about 10,000 years. By 1569 it was where the territory of the Mocosa, the Mohawk, began and was contested ground at the intersection of Mohawk, Abenaki, and Mahican homelands.

During the seventeenth century, Ticonderoga was on the strategic frontier between the expanding efforts by the French, Dutch, and English to dominate the fur trade and the Indian peoples essential to that trade. Native people developed a steady but unsanctioned smuggling trade along the north–south waterway linking Montreal in French Canada and Orange/Albany on the Hudson River, using the portage at Ticonderoga. For the next century and a half, forces surged back and forth past Ticonderoga, repeatedly fortifying the place during the shifting tides of commerce and war. Each contingent included major Indian participation (typically a third to half of the force): Mohawk and Schaghticoke accompanied the English and Dutch raiders, and Algonquin, Huron, Mohawk, and Abenaki allied with the French.

The construction by the French of Fort Carillon at Ticonderoga, begun at the opening of the Seven Years' War in 1755, was the result of the French commander's failure to understand war in the wilderness and the strength of Native kinship ties even in the face of political and military alliances. Native nations negotiated independently to maximize their own diplomatic and economic integrity while they attempted to establish strategic alliances, which wavered with the fortunes of war. From Fort Carillon, Indians and Canadians assisted French regulars by scouting British strength at the south end of Lake George, raiding deep into British territory, and occasionally helping to meet their food requirements by hunting. In the summer of 1757, the Marquis de Montcalm's force, assembled to drive the British from the Ticonderoga strategic waterway, included 1,800 Indians belonging to seventeen nations from thirty-nine communities, some as far away as the *pays d'en haut,* the upper Great Lakes basin. Native forces briefly aligned with Montcalm and the Great Onontio (King Louis XV via his viceroy, the governor general) to attack Fort William Henry and to pursue their opportunities for plunder, captives, and the prospect of holding at bay the land-hungry Anglais. The Indian coalition that came together in July 1757 at Ticonderoga was perhaps the most geographically and culturally diverse gathering of peoples in North America recorded until that time. Montcalm defeated the British when they attacked the fort in July 1758. A generation later, the fort was again the site of warfare. It was attacked four times early in the American Revolution, and both the British and the Americans sought alliances with the Indian tribes.

In 1820 William Ferris Pell began to preserve the fort, and Indians continued to make winter camps below the fort near the pavilion during the next decade. Through its museum, Fort Ticonderoga continues to educate visitors about its significance to American Indians.

FURTHER READING: *Fort Ticonderoga: Key to the Continent*, by Edward P. Hamilton (Introduction by Nicholas Westbrook)

61. Old Fort Niagara State Historic Site, NY

Robert Moses Parkway, 15 miles north of Niagara Falls in Youngstown

The French established their first fort at the mouth of the Niagara River in 1679. In 1726 they received permission from the Iroquois to build a limestone building surrounded by a wooden stockade on a bluff above Lake Ontario. They described it as a trading post and a House of Peace, but it also enabled them to control access to the Great Lakes and to the fur-trade route to the West. After the Seven Years' War began, the French replaced the stockade with earthworks. In July 1759 Brigadier General John Prideaux's large Niagara expedition, which included about 1,000 Iroquois warriors, forced the French to surrender the fort after a nineteen-day siege. In September 1763 about 300 warriors, mostly Geneseos Senecas and possibly Ottawas and Chippewas, attacked and destroyed a British wagon convoy at Devil's Hole, south of Fort Niagara. They frequently attacked the nine-mile portage around Niagara Falls, disrupting the delivery of supplies to Detroit. In July 1764 Sir William Johnson held a successful peace conference at the fort, attended by more than 2,000 warriors from nineteen nations. After General John Sullivan's victory at Newtown in August 1779, his army destroyed Iroquois villages. Thousands of Iroquois fled to Fort Niagara, where the British did not have adequate provisions for so many, and hundreds starved to death.

62. Point State Park, PA

Commonwealth Place, Pittsburgh

Fort Pitt Museum

The Ohio River is formed by the confluence of the Monongahela and Allegheny rivers at a place known as the Forks. The French built Fort Duquesne here in 1754 as part of their chain of forts and trading posts between Canada and Louisiana. As a result of raids by the French and their Delaware, Mingo, and Shawnee allies in the Virginia-Pennsylvania backcountry, most settlers had fled east by the end of 1755. After the French lost their Indian allies in 1758, they burned the fort and left. The next year the British built Fort Pitt, a huge pentagonal fort, and occupied it until 1772. The blockhouse is the oldest remaining building; the museum is in a reproduction of one of the bastions. Pontiac's War began in May 1763 with the attack and siege of Fort Detroit, led by the Ottawa war leader Pontiac. A force of Shawnee, Delaware, Mingo, Wyandot, Ottawa, and Miami warriors held Fort Pitt under siege. In late June the Delaware met with Captain Simeon Ecuyer at Fort Pitt to advise him to evacuate before their attack. He refused and gave them gifts, including blankets from the smallpox hospital. In October 1775 the Americans held a treaty council at Fort Pitt, where the Indians agreed that the Ohio River was the boundary between their territory and the whites', and Cornstalk, the leader of the Maquachake division of the Shawnees, called for peace. By the time a second council was held a year later, so many American settlers and land speculators had moved onto Shawnee lands in Kentucky that Cornstalk sent a message to Congress in which he stated, "That was our hunting Country & you have taken it from us. This is what sits heavy upon our Hearts."

63. Fort Ligonier, PA

At the intersection of U.S. 30 and Rte. 711, Ligonier

Museum

The fort is on a hilltop in the Laurel Highlands near the site of the village of Loyalhanna, where the Delaware lived from the 1720s until the 1740s. The fort is a restoration and reconstruction of the one built in 1758 by General John Forbes on his advance to Fort Duquesne. His army included British and provincial troops and Cherokees led by Attakullakulla (Little Carpenter). During Pontiac's War in 1763, a Delaware, Mingo, and Shawnee force attacked the fort and placed it under a quasi-siege until Colonel Henry Bouquet's force arrived on its march to Bushy Run. The fort was decommissioned in 1766.

64. Bushy Run Battlefield, PA

West of PA Rte. 66, turnpike exit 8 on Rte. 993, Jeannette

Visitor center

In July 1763 Colonel Henry Bouquet's British forces moved slowly out the Forbes Road toward Fort Pitt. On August 5 they marched into the trap set by the Shawnee, Delaware, Mingo, Wyandot, Ottawa, and Miami warriors in the forested country near Bushy Run Creek, twenty-five miles from Fort Pitt. The next day the British fought their way out but suffered 110 casualties. In late October, after Pontiac learned of the Treaty of Paris, he lifted his siege of Detroit and withdrew to the Maumee River. He was killed in 1769.

American Indians and the American Revolution

COLIN G. CALLOWAY

❖ The national mythology of the United States accords Indians a minimal and negative role in the story of the Revolution: they chose the wrong side and they lost. Their contribution to the outcome of the Revolution was therefore negligible, and their treatment after the Revolution justified. Because many Indians sided with the British, they have, from the Declaration of Independence onward, been portrayed as allies of tyranny and enemies of liberty. Yet Indian people in revolutionary America, whether they sided with rebels, redcoats, neither, or both, were doing pretty much the same thing as the American colonists: fighting for their freedom in tumultuous times. The Revolution was an anticolonial war of liberation for Indian peoples, too, but the threat to their freedom often came from colonial neighbors rather than distant capitals, and their colonial experience did not end with American independence.

We cannot tell the full story of revolutionary America without including American Indians, and we cannot begin to grasp the reality of the Revolution for Indian people without shifting our focus to where Indians lived and to Indian communities. Any broadly brushed treatment of Indian involvement and experiences is likely to obscure and distort local diversity; only by looking at different groups and communities can one get a sense of the range of experiences of Indian peoples in these times. Indian villages, as much as New England towns, were communities living in and responding to revolutionary conditions, although getting at their story is, of course, much more difficult.

For Indian people in eastern North America, the entire century was an age of revolution, a pivotal era in which, as James Merrell wrote, "the balance tipped irrevocably away from the Indian." In some ways the Revolution only intensified familiar pressures on Indian lives and lands. The Indians' "War of Independence" was well under way before 1775, was waged on many fronts — economic, cultural, political, and military — and continued long after 1783.

War was nothing new in Indian country in the eighteenth century, but the Revolution generated new sources of conflict and new levels of violence that destroyed much of the world Indians and non-Indians had created there. As elsewhere in North America, old structures, traditional patterns of behavior, and long-standing alliances broke down in a climate of tumult and change. Religious ferment and dissension split Indian congregations and communities as well as white ones. Dissident groups challenged established authority in Indian country as well as in colonial society. Refugees from war and hunger choked forts and villages. By the end of the Revolution, Shawnees from Ohio were living in Missouri, New England Indians were living among the Oneidas in New York, and there were two Iroquois leagues: one in New York, the other on the Grand River in Ontario. Stockbridge Indians from Massachusetts, who had been loyal allies of the Crown in earlier wars against the French, now turned away from the king and made common cause with the rebels, defying the authority of their Mohawk "fathers" in doing so. In the meantime their home community underwent final transformation into a white man's town. Abenaki Indians who had been driven north and suffered bitter losses at the hands of New Hampshire rangers in the Seven Years' War now returned south and served alongside the rangers in defense of the Connecticut Valley, while their relatives who remained at Odanak evaded British recruitment efforts. Delaware and Shawnee chiefs who counseled moderation found themselves swept aside by the current of events in the Ohio Valley. Young Cherokee war-

riors challenged the authority of older chiefs and joined hands with militants from the north. Alliances that cut across old tribal lines became the norm. Seminole communities in northern Florida asserted autonomy from the parent Creek confederacy and engaged in their own version of "nation building." Chickasaw headmen who had been steadfast in loyalty to Britain throughout the century found that by 1783 they needed to develop new foreign policies to preserve their independence in a region now coveted by both Spaniards and Americans. When Indian chiefs told the Spanish governor of St. Louis in 1784 that the American Revolution constituted "the greatest blow that could have been dealt us," they made it clear that the important point about the Revolution was the flood of American settlers it unleashed onto their lands.

In the end, white Americans excluded Indians from the republican society that the Revolution created. Despite their absence from much of the historical literature, Indian people were everywhere in colonial America. In 1775 Indian nations, despite intrusive and disruptive pressures unleashed by European contact, still controlled most of America west of the Appalachians. In 1783, when Britain transferred that territory to the new United States, most of it was still in Indian hands, but a new era had begun. The American revolutionaries who fought for freedom from the British Empire in the East also fought to create an empire of their own in the West. Contention over Indian land was an old story by 1775, but the Revolution elevated acquisition of Indian lands to a national policy. The new nation, born of a bloody revolution and committed to expansion, could not tolerate America as Indian country. Increasingly, Americans viewed the future as one without Indians. The Revolution both created a new society and provided justification for excluding Indians from it.

The agony of the American Revolution for American Indians was lost as the winners constructed a national mythology that simplified what had been a complex contest in Indian Country, blamed Indians for the bloodletting, and justified subsequent assaults on Indian lands and cultures. In the aftermath of the Revolution, new social orders were created and new ideologies developed to explain which groups of people were included and excluded, and why. In the long run, the legacy the war produced in the minds of non-Indians proved almost as devastating to Indian peoples as the burned towns, fractured communities, and shattered lives of the war itself.

The Declaration of Independence depicted Indians as savage allies of a tyrannical monarch, who "endeavored to bring on the inhabitants of our frontiers, the merciless Indian savages, whose known rule of warfare is an undistinguished destruction of all ages, sexes, and conditions." Embodied in the document that marked the nation's birth, the image of Indians as vicious enemies of liberty became entrenched in the minds of generations of white Americans. However, Benjamin Franklin admitted in 1787 that "almost every War between the Indians and Whites has been occasion'd by some Injustice of the latter towards the former." William Apess, a Pequot, bitterly understood that "the Revolution which enshrined republican principles in the American commonwealth, also excluded African Americans and Native Americans from their reach." Referring to the guardian system reinstituted by Massachusetts, placing Indian settlements under the authority of state-appointed overseers, he wrote, "The whites were no sooner free themselves, than they enslaved the poor Indians." The new republic needed African labor, and it excluded African Americans from its definition of "free and equal" on the basis of supposed racial inferiority. The new republic needed Indian land and excluded Native Americans on the basis of supposed savagery.

American Indians could not expect to be ac-

cepted in a nation that denied the fruits of an egalitarian revolution to so many of its citizens and that lived with the contradiction of slavery in a society built on principles of freedom. Native Americans had been heavily dependent on, and interdependent with, colonial society and economy before the Revolution. But as Indian land became the key to national, state, and individual wealth, the new republic was less interested in their dependence than in their absence. The United States looked forward to a future without Indians. The Indians' participation in the Revolution guaranteed their exclusion from the new world born out of the Revolution; their determination to survive as Indians guaranteed their ultimate extinction. Artistic depictions of Indian people showed them retreating westward, suffused in the heavy imagery of setting suns, as they faded from history.

Fortunately for us all, Indian people had other ideas.

Excerpted from *The American Revolution in Indian Country*, by Colin G. Calloway, reprinted with the permission of Cambridge University Press

Fort Stanwix, Oriskany Battlefield, and Newtown Battlefield

JOHN C. MOHAWK

❖ In 1768 at Fort Stanwix, Sir William Johnson negotiated a treaty between the British government and the Haudenosaunee, the Iroquois Confederacy. It established a Line of Property that was farther west than the 1763 Proclamation line, opening Kentucky and the Ohio Country to white settlement. The Cherokee, the

Shawnee, and the Delaware — who were not parties to the treaty — continued to try to drive squatters from their lands.

At the outbreak of the American Revolution the Haudenosaunee adopted an official position of neutrality. That ended in August 1777. As the British and Tory army marched toward Fort Stanwix, officials met with Indians and invited them to join the battle. When an American rescue force, which included sixty Oneida warriors, approached the fort, the British, the Tories, and their Indian allies — Senecas and Mohawks commanded by Joseph Brant — led by Sir John Johnson and Colonel John Butler attacked at Oriskany. It was the first time in memory that Haudenosaunee warriors had fought other members of the confederacy on the battlefield.

Two years later, the battle at Newtown in the Clinton-Sullivan Campaign, one of the largest military operations during the war, was designed to eliminate the Haudenosaunee as a military force. General John Sullivan commanded about 4,500 soldiers. The Indians and the Tories, a force about one third as large, retreated after a short battle, and Sullivan burned their villages and their cornfields. The following year, Indian fighters ravaged the frontiers, depopulating whole farming areas and causing hardships. The Haudenosaunee's effectiveness at this kind of warfare served to harden white attitudes toward Indians, which continued for many years after the war.

The second Fort Stanwix treaty was signed in 1784 at the end of the American Revolution. The Americans claimed that the British surrender amounted to their conquest of all Indian lands, an assertion the Indians vigorously denied. The treaty was concluded with warriors who did not have the authority to sign treaties. The ceded lands in Ohio belonged to Mingo, Shawnee, Delaware, and other Indians. American settlers began pouring into the Ohio region, resulting in the Indian wars of the 1780s and

1790s and further losses of the tribes' homelands.

Both Fort Stanwix treaties centered on taking land from the Indians. The Anglo-Americans took it through cessions, wars, land sales, frauds, swindles, and politics. When land transactions were clearly illegal, the Haudenosaunee had no viable way to seek justice. The courts were closed to Indian nations except in cases where the state legislature or the federal government gave the nations permission to sue. This state of affairs lasted until a Supreme Court decision in 1974. The individual Iroquois nations and the confederacy have sought justice but have never been very successful in petitioning the government or in courts. In recent years the Supreme Court has stated that Indian nations waited too long to bring claims. Today Haudenosaunee live on eight reservations in New York and on reserves in Quebec, Ontario, Wisconsin, and Oklahoma.

65. Fort Stanwix National Monument, NY

Off Erie Blvd. at James and Park sts., Rome

Visitor center

The British built the fort in 1758 to protect the short portage between the waterways that connect the Atlantic Ocean with the Great Lakes. They left in 1763 after the Seven Years' War.

66. Oriskany Battlefield State Historic Site, NY

On Rte. 69, northwest of Oriskany

Visitor center

The battle at Oriskany was on August 6, 1777.

67. Newtown Battlefield State Park, NY

Off Rte. 17, southeast of Elmira

The battle at Newtown was on August 29, 1779.

FURTHER READING: *Divided Ground: Indians, Settlers, and the Northern Borderland of the American Revolution,* by Alan Taylor

Under Treaty Oaks: Lingering Shadows of Unfinished Business

RENNARD STRICKLAND

❖ As a young Indian boy in the 1890s, Thomas Gilcrease attended tribal schools in his Muskogee (Creek) Nation. Years later, as a respected oil man, the Creek millionaire founded a great institution to house the documents, artifacts, and paintings he had assembled to tell the story of his Native ancestors and the colonizers who forever changed life on the North American continent. Today, among the treasures in the Gilcrease Museum in Tulsa is a monumental painting, *William Penn's Treaty with the Indians,* by the great early American artist Benjamin West. Perhaps the painting is so stark, so shocking, and so meaningful because it is unfinished.

West's subject matter is an Indian tribe negotiating a treaty with the white commissioners for Indian affairs. It is a scene that was repeated hundreds of times, from Maine (whose state treaties were held invalid in the last quarter of the twentieth century) to California (where many treaties were never ratified). As the empires of the European colonists and the fledgling United States moved west, it was treaties that most often opened the way. In West's painting, red men and white men are gathered under great spreading oaks, outlining the content of their treaty. West's unfinished canvas proclaims that the business of Indian-white relations remains unfinished. Today these treaties help establish the interrelated rights and duties of Indian tribes and the citizens of the United States. Historic eighteenth- and nineteenth-century treaties, hammered out under such great oaks, remain the pledged word of the American people just as much as the Constitution itself. Indeed, these treaties are sacred documents of our secular society. The Supreme Court justice Hugo Black reminded the American people of the importance of treaty obligations in his classic dissent in the Tuscarora Power case. "Great Nations, like Great Men," Black concluded, "keep their word."

Across Tulsa from the museum, on the high ground above the Arkansas River, stands the historic Muskogee (Creek) Council Oak. This mighty tree, under which the tribe conducted their government, is a reminder of the sovereignty of all the Indian nations that negotiated the hundreds of treaties. Almost from the moment of the Indian nations' initial contact with the European nations, their relationships were articulated by treaties. International law as well as the political, economic, and military powers of the Native peoples dictated the use of treaties as the form for agreements and governance. The United States conducted much of its historic Indian policy through such agreements. The new nation's treaties date from the peace agreements signed soon after the Revolution at Fort Stanwix (1784) until 1871, when Congress prohibited treaties with Indian nations. Even then the treaties already signed continued to have the full force of law, and to this day they remain a major source of federal Indian law and policy.

Nonetheless, as Felix Cohen (the father of the study of modern Indian law) concluded, "The legal force of Indian treaties has not assured their enforcement." It is a historic fact that the United States failed to fulfill the terms of most treaties and was even less willing to prevent states or individuals from violating treaty provisions. Indian treaty making and enforcement is one of the darkest chapters in American history. Many treaties were ignored; some were negotiated with minority groups of tribal members; the Senate refused to ratify others; bribery and threats were commonplace in treaty negotiations; there were translation difficulties, differences in cultural values, and fraudulent misrepresentation; and misreading and misunderstanding often kept tribes from comprehending the provisions of the treaties.

At the beginning of the treaty era, the Europeans had few options, because the balance of power often rested with the Native people. Early negotiations were genuinely about issues of mutual power and interest. Without the treaty concessions of the independent tribal governments, the European powers and the struggling American colonies faced starvation, extermination, or military defeat. By the end of the War of 1812, that had changed; power had shifted, and the tribes' alternatives were now so severely limited that the United States was positioned to dictate rather than negotiate the terms of treaty agreements. The purpose of these treaties was generally to strip tribes of whatever power and land they had managed to retain. And yet many significant contemporary rights of Indian tribes and obligations of the federal government grew out of this treaty process.

The clauses of treaties vary significantly, from the concession of millions of acres of land to supplying scissors and other "instruments of civilization." The primary focus of treaties was resource distribution, ranging from occupancy of land to limitations on hunting and fishing rights. Other significant treaty provisions addressed jurisdiction over intruders and criminals, services such as health care and education, protection of tribal self-governance, and even the rights of tribal representation in the United States Congress. Federal courts have long acknowledged that domestic Indian treaties are similar in power to international agreements between nation-states. "To compensate for the disadvantage at which the treaty-making process placed the tribes," Ninth Circuit Judge William C. Canby, Jr., noted, "the Supreme Court has fashioned rules of construction sympathetic to Indian interest." Courts must interpret treaties as the Indian negotiators understood them and resolve conflicts and ambiguities in favor of the Indians by looking beyond the written words to the entire historical experience.

Students of American history write of "the theatre of the treaty." They describe formal rituals associated with treaty negotiations and enactment, symbolized by wampum belts, ceremonial pipes, peace medals, elaborately decorated land patents, and formally signed and sealed documents. Even into the twenty-first century, virtually all tribes remember the sites, scenes, sounds, and promises of their treaties. For some, such as the Cherokee with the Treaty of New Echota (1835), the hostility, which led to assassination and tribal civil war, survives to this day. Other tribes, such as the Lakota, want strict enforcement and the return of treaty lands. Despite having been awarded money damages that now amount (with interest) to $1 billion for the loss of their treaty-protected homelands in the Black Hills, the Lakota have refused to accept a penny of this money, instead holding out for the return of their historic lands. Plains tribes (the Kiowa, Cheyenne, Arapaho, and Comanche) forced to settle on reservations after the Treaty of Medicine Lodge (1867) continue to feel, as Chief Ten Bears protested, that "these things . . . were not sweet like sugar, but bitter like gourds."

Perhaps the primary examples of forced treaty negotiations and surviving rights are the Northwest fishing agreements known as the Stevens Treaties, signed in the 1850s. By the middle of the twentieth century, tribal members in Washington and Oregon and Indian civil rights advocates began a campaign to enforce treaty fishing rights growing from these treaties. One hundred and fifty years after these treaties were forced on the fishing tribes of the Pacific Northwest, the courts have used them to guarantee the signatory tribes the right to take fish in the "usual and customary" places "in common with all citizens of the Territory." The courts have found, based on these treaties, that Indians are entitled to half of the harvestable fish. This finding has produced a renewed resource and a growing spirit of cooperation that has enhanced the fish harvest for all.

Stored in the rare book vaults of the Gilcrease Museum, the National Archives, the Library of Congress, and universities, as well as in tribal headquarters, are yellowing handwritten and government-printed copies of hundreds of treaties of the American settlement experience. These treaties are full of broken promises, unfulfilled dreams, and continuing rights and obligations — the bargained-for agreements of nations both white and red. As Benjamin West's painting reminds us, this is America's unfinished historical business — a business that casts a dark shadow of hypocrisy over the nation's present-day crusade to bring liberty and human rights to other nations around the world.

FURTHER READING: *American Indian Treaties: The History of a Political Anomaly,* by Francis Paul Prucha

68. Schoenbrunn Village, OH

Jay Miller

On Rte. 250, southeast of New Philadelphia

Visitor center

The years at Schoenbrunn, 1772–1777, were happy and prosperous for the Unami and Munsee Delaware, despite the tribe's forced westward migrations far away from the Delaware (Len-

ape) homelands along the Atlantic coast and their namesake river. After making stops across Pennsylvania, the Delaware congregated in Ohio along the Muskingum (then called Tuscarawas) River. Each of their three clans (Wolf, Turkey, and Turtle) lived separately, near their capital, led by an aged Turtle chief known as Netawatwas, or Newcomer. Christian missionaries were unwelcome in Ohio with one exception. To advance their tribal consolidation efforts, the Delaware chiefs' council invited their Moravian convert kin to settle nearby. The Moravian Church, based in Bethlehem, Pennsylvania, had long sponsored missions among the Mahican of the Hudson River Valley and the Delaware across Pennsylvania. Moravian tenets included pacifism as well as education and literacy, so that converts had personal access to the Bible. Most Moravians were multilingual, and they used native languages throughout their worldwide missions.

A lovely spring (*schoenbrunn* in German, *welhik thuppeek* in Delaware) twenty miles from the Delaware capital was selected as the site of the first mission, occupied by the Delaware converts. Gnadenhutten (Grace Huts), ten miles away, became the mission for resettled Mahicans. Surrounded by a fence to keep out livestock, drunks, and enemies, Schoenbrunn had two wide streets forming a T, generous family lots, and, at the center, a church and school, which introduced the first all-American textbook. Nearby were large pastures and fields, as well as God's Acre, the cemetery for the baptized. Today the reconstructed village includes seventeen log buildings, period gardens, field plantings, nature preserves, a visitor center, and a museum.

David Zeisberger (1721–1808), the lead missionary, was advised by a council of elder converts. He lived at Schoenbrunn and kept its official diary, documenting Delaware life. While Americans were educating only rich young men, the Moravian school was coeducational. Native converts were drawn to the consensual ways of the Moravians — a religion of the "heart," not the "head" — whose watchwords are "In essentials unity, in non-essentials liberty, in all things charity."

National Helpers, often long-married couples, were wise converts who guided the missions and organized work teams. Older widowed converts, who enjoyed this neat, calm, and ordered life, continued to be respected leaders of their families and clans. Their kin, over time, were drawn into mission activities but were on probation until they passed religious and emotional tests for full acceptance. Several clan chiefs converted, giving up their authority in exchange for a better (calmer) life, but then converts were given full status in the Delaware national council and their roles as chiefs were restored. The Killbucks, grandsons of Netawatwas, became strong Moravians. A century later, the Reverend John Kilbuck was a founder of the 1885 mission among Alaskan Yup'ik Eskimos, which still thrives.

Native life became tragic during the American Revolution when British agents and their Munsee allies escorted the converts, without food or warm clothing, to northern Ohio and sent the missionaries to Detroit. One hundred suffering Moravians were allowed to go back for cached supplies and standing crops. At Gnadenhutten on March 8, 1782, they were methodically massacred by American militia, who plundered $18,000 in property. In 1792 the British gave Moravian survivors a tract in Ontario, where they settled Fairfield (Moraviantown) until it was destroyed by American forces in the 1813 Battle of the Thames. They relocated across the river. Outraged by the 1782 massacre of faithful pacifists, the U.S. Congress in 1785 granted Moravians three town sites. In 1798 Zeisberger led Ontario Moravians back to Ohio and founded the Goshen mission near Schoenbrunn, where he died in 1808. From Ohio most Munsee removed to Ontario, while Unami struggled westward through Indiana, Missouri, and Kansas before staying in Oklahoma, where their governments remain.

FURTHER READING: *The Moravian Mission Diaries of David Zeisberger 1772–1781,* edited by Herman Wellenreuther and Carola Wessel

69. Fort Recovery, OH

One Fort Site St., Fort Recovery

Museum

In late 1791 Chief Little Turtle led the Miami against about 2,000 soldiers commanded by General Arthur St. Clair and won a major victory here along the Wabash River. The fort built in 1793 on the site of the battle protected General Anthony Wayne's force from an attack on June 30, 1794, led by Miami chief Little Turtle and Shawnee chief Blue Jacket. Two blockhouses with a connecting stockade have been reconstructed.

70. Fallen Timbers Battlefield and Fort Miamis National Historic Site, OH

Donald R. Rettig, Jr., and G. Michael Pratt

Near intersection of U.S. 24 and Rte. 23, Maumee

In 1790 and 1791 the allied American Indian tribes of the Old Northwest Territory, led by the Miami chief Little Turtle, Shawnee chief Blue Jacket, Delaware chief Buckongahelas, Wyandot chief Tarhe, and Ottawa chief Little Otter, were successful in defeating two large American forces. On August 20, 1794, the tribes made their last attempt to hold on to their lands north of the Ohio River, the boundary promised them during the Revolution. By then General "Mad"

Anthony Wayne, a Revolutionary War hero, had revitalized the Legion of the United States. Between 900 and 1,200 American Indians and Canadian militia attacked Wayne's force — about 1,600 regulars and 1,500 Kentucky militia — in an area where timbers had been felled by a tornado years before. The Native forces surged early, but the strong Legion advance ended the battle. The British, several miles away inside the recently constructed Fort Miamis, refused to assist their American Indian allies and turned them away from the fort. Wayne returned victorious down the Maumee River and ordered the burning of the Indians' villages and their vast cornfields. The defeat, the battle deaths, the abandonment by the British, and the destruction of their homes and food supplies were devastating for the allied nations.

The battle led to the Treaty of Greenville of 1795, in which the United States took nearly three quarters of the future state of Ohio, leaving only the northwest corner for the Ohio tribes. This treaty opened the area to white settlement and led to the federal government's control of much of the Old Northwest Territory, ensuring the development of the future states of Indiana, Michigan, Illinois, and Wisconsin. The British abandoned Fort Miamis in 1796. In 1995 archaeologists found the site of the battle, which led to a public effort to preserve the site as a National Park Service affiliate.

FURTHER READING: *President Washington's Indian War: The Struggle for the Old Northwest, 1790–95,* by Wiley Sword

71. Mille Lacs Kathio State Park, MN

Off U.S. 169 on County Rd. 26, northwest of Onamia

Interpretive center

People began living in this area about 9,000 years ago and were making copper tools on Petaga Point about 3,500 years ago. There are a number of village sites in the park, including one where people lived between about A.D. 500–1600 and another where Mdewakanton Dakota lived in the 1500s and 1600s. They moved south and west in the 1700s, and the Ojibwe moved into the Mille Lacs area.

Manoominike: Making Wild Rice

WINONA LADUKE

❖ *Manoomin* (wild rice) is a gift to the Ojibwe from the Creator and is used in our daily lives, our ceremonies, and our thanksgiving feasts. It feeds the body and the soul and continues a generations-old tradition for the people of the lakes and rivers of the North. Our harvesting practices continue to this day as we travel across our lakes and rivers, harvesting the rice in canoes with sticks, and parching it in the many local rice mills in the Great Lakes region. Our traditional harvesting methods have ensured the continuation and sustainability of our way of life. *Manoomin* tastes like the lakes and rivers of our region, which today is the only place in the world where this grain grows naturally. This area, the genetic center of our wild rice, holds an amazing array of biodiversity. A domesticated version of our rice is now being cultivated in rice paddies, some in Minnesota but most in California. Today our rice is threatened by both genetic engineering and patenting.

Visitors to the Tamarac National Wildlife Refuge near Rochert, Minnesota, can see old ricing sites and, in the fall, ricers on the lakes of the North Country. The people ricing today recall their ancestors on the same lakes, feeling the peace that comes from being out on the water.

In the mill there is the sweet smell of rice parching as it moves through the ancient machines. The local producers process the rice carefully, and it emerges shiny, dark green, and brown. The rice tastes like a lake, and that taste cannot be replicated.

FURTHER READING: *Wild Rice and the Ojibway People,* by Thomas Vennum

72. Tamarac National Wildlife Refuge, MN: Ricing Sites

North of Rochert

There are ricing sites and maple sugaring sites in the refuge.

73. Rice Lake National Wildlife Refuge, MN: Ricing Sites

On Rte. 65, south of McGregor

The Dakota and, more recently, the Ojibwe have gathered wild rice here for hundreds of years.

74. Grand Portage National Monument, MN

Norman Deschampe

Off Rte. 61 within the Grand Portage Indian Reservation, Grand Portage

Grand Portage Heritage Center

There are many remarkable places in our homeland. Grand Portage — Gitchi-Onigaming in the Anishinaabe language — is one of these places. It is the ancient footpath around the falls and rapids on the Pigeon River, linking water routes to the Atlantic and Pacific Oceans, to Hudson Bay, and to the Gulf of Mexico. Copper from Isle Royale and furs from the area were traded in all directions. From the 1780s on, there were fur-trading posts on the portage. It also became a

new route for European and American exploration. Using Grand Portage as an anchor point, Alexander MacKenzie was the first white man to cross the continent. And, like the better-known Lewis and Clark expedition, MacKenzie used Native American guides to find the route and to communicate with First Nation peoples along the way.

The Grand Portage Ojibwe have many stories about these places, such as Partridge Falls of the Pigeon River. As a small boy I learned about hunting moose from my dad. From our small boat, my dad shot a moose in the river above the falls. I thought we would lose him, but my dad told me, no, it would sink first, then swell up and rise to the surface. It did! But then we had to negotiate the current and shallows. We tied the moose to the side of the boat and ran with the current, using the river to guide us. In the darkness we pulled the moose ashore above the roar and mist of the falls. We had made it!

Today this area is in the reservation's "preservation zone" to protect it for our descendants. Pigeon Point, which juts out into Lake Superior, is also in the zone. A narrows on Pigeon Point was a small crossing place for families canoeing on the lake. In rough seas or heavy fog they would pull in here, portage across, and resume their travels once conditions improved. We call this place the narrows, and it, along with the upper Pigeon River, is an important place to us. They are not as well known as Ma-ni-do Gee-zhi-gance, the Little Cedar Spirit Tree, or the restored fur-trading post of the national monument, which is within the Grand Portage Reservation. All of these places are important to us. Our memories are lodged in these places, as is our future.

FURTHER READING: *The Grand Portage Story,* by Carolyn Gilman

75. Voyageurs National Park, MN

Rose Berens

Off U.S. 53, east of International Falls

Visitor centers

Voyageurs National Park, 218,000 acres of water and pristine shoreline encompassing four major interconnected lakes along the U.S.-Canadian border, is part of the Canadian Shield, which has some of the oldest exposed rock in the world. The area was home to four bands of Bois Forte Ojibwe from the early 1700s through 1941, when they moved away after the state required the children to attend school on the Nett Lake Reservation. The Bois Forte Band still owns a small parcel of land in the park.

In the seventeenth century, French fur traders gave the name Bois Forte — which means "strong wood" — to the Ojibwe of today's northeastern Minnesota and southwestern Ontario, recognizing the hardiness of the people who lived, and continue to live, in this challenging environment. The Bois Forte lived in harmony with the land and water, picking blueberries, trapping beavers, harvesting wild rice, netting fish, and snaring sturgeon, among other seasonal activities. The plants and animals provided food as well as clothing and shelter. They traded with trappers, French fur traders, and voyageurs who used the interconnected waterways. The voyageurs brought guns, kettles, fabric, beads, and other goods to trade with the Bois Forte, mostly for beaver pelts. In the 1866 treaty the Bois Forte Ojibwe surrendered their legal hold on this land but were able to continue living here for more than fifty years. While the Bois Forte have seen many changes — the great white pine forests are gone, and there are many more people and fewer animals — the band has endured and has preserved our ancient traditions, including harvesting wild rice, tapping maple trees, and picking berries. Weaving everything together is the sense of community, expressed in our gatherings and celebrations, in powwows and sacred ceremonies.

Voyageurs National Park continues to be a place held in reverence by the Ojibwe people known as Bois Forte. The land, the lakes, the trees, the animals, and the sky are part of our culture, our language, and our traditions. This land, which once was our home, is now our history.

FURTHER READING: *History of the Ojibwe People,* by William W. Warren

76. Folle Avoine Historical Park, WI

Off Rte. 35 on County Rd. U, between Webster and Danbury

Visitor center

In 1802 both the North West Company and the XY Company built trading posts, about 100 feet apart, along the Yellow River. For two winters they traded with the Ojibwe — mostly beaver for textiles and metal tools. The park has reconstructed four cabins typical of the period on the sites of the trading posts and has recreated Indian camps representing the seasonal travels of the Ojibwe, including a ricing camp and a sugaring camp.

77. North West Company Fur Post, MN

Off I-35 at exit 169, Pine City

Visitor center, open May 1 through October 31

In 1804–5 the North West Company traded with the Ojibwe. Their post has been reconstructed and an Ojibwe camp site recreated.

78. Tippecanoe Battlefield and Prophetstown State Park, IN

Stephen Warren

The battlefield is in Battle Ground; the park is nearby on State Rd. 225, West Lafayette

Museum; Historic Prophetstown

Between 1808 and 1811 more than 800 American Indians from the Eastern Woodlands, including Shawnee, Kickapoo, Ho-Chunk, Wyandot, Sac, Mesquaki (Fox), Ojibwe, and Potawatomi, among others, founded a pan-Indian village along the north bank of the Wabash below the mouth of the Tippecanoe River. Main Poc, a Potawatomi warrior, helped the Shawnee holy man Tenskwatawa (the Prophet) choose the site for the village, named Prophetstown. The site of the village is now in Prophetstown State Park. At its height it featured 200 bark-sided wickiups organized in neat lanes. Reflecting its importance as a cross-cultural oasis for Woodland Indians, the village also included a large frame council house (a replica is in Historic Prophetstown) as well as a cabin called the "house of the stranger." Below the village, Native women raised corn, beans, squash, and pumpkins on more than 100 acres of the Wabash floodplain. Between 1805 and 1807, this multiethnic confederacy had settled at Greenville, Ohio, but a host of Indian and non-Indian opponents had forced the group to relocate.

Accessible by canoe as well as by an extensive trail system, the village was ideally located for coordinating resistance to the American expansion. Soon after its founding, Native people from great distances were drawn to Tenskwatawa's message of reform, which included stopping the alcohol trade, alcohol abuse, domestic violence, and skin hunting. They hoped for the general revitalization of American Indian cultures. By all accounts, those who lived at Prophetstown created a well-ordered community. Others were drawn to Tenskwatawa's brother, Tecumseh, and his eloquent defense of Indian lands. The 1795 Treaty of Greenville, which ceded most of Ohio to the United States, fueled the pan-Indian resistance movement in that region. The treaty also foreshadowed a series of devastating land cessions, such as the September 1809 Treaty of Fort Wayne, which ceded 3 million acres in Indiana and Illinois. These continuing land cessions, coupled with Tenskwatawa's powerful vision of reform, added to the resistance movement. Nevertheless, many American Indians opposed Tenskwatawa's revitalization movement. After more than a century of resistance, large numbers of Miami, Delaware, Shawnee, and Wyandots chose to find a way to live alongside their former enemies.

The territorial governor of Indiana, William Henry Harrison, faced the challenge of destroying Prophetstown. On September 26, 1811, Harrison, in command of 1,000 men, left Vincennes to attack the town. It was an opportune moment for the confrontation, because Tecumseh had left Prophetstown in search of supporters among the southern tribes. He had advised Tenskwatawa to avoid open conflict with Harrison while he was away, but many of their adherents refused to follow this advice. After a brief parlay on November 6, 1811, White Loon, a Wyandot-Shawnee warrior, and Stone Eater, a Kickapoo, with 600 to 700 warriors, led a predawn attack on Harrison's encampment. Harrison won the two-hour-long battle with losses of 62 killed and 126 wounded; approximately 30 warriors lay dead on the battlefield. Harrison's men destroyed the village in the days after the battle, but Indian resistance did not recede until Tecumseh was killed fighting with his British allies in the War of 1812 at the Battle of the Thames in Canada on October 5, 1813. The site of the battle is in Tippecanoe Battlefield.

FURTHER READING: *The Shawnee and Their Neighbors, 1795–1870,* by Stephen Warren

79. Forks of the Wabash Historic Park, IN: *alikalakonci wiipicahkionki* (Beyond the Place of Flint)

George Ironstrack and Scott M. Shoemaker

At intersection of U.S. 24 and Rte. 9, west of Huntington

wiipicahkionki — the Forks of the Wabash or, more literally, the flint place — has long been an important site of beginnings for the *mihtohseeniaki* (human beings), also known as the *myaamiaki* (downstream people) or the Miami, the indigenous people of present-day Indiana, Ohio, Illinois, and Michigan. The heart of their homelands, *myaamionki,* was and continues to be the *waapaahšiki siipiiwi* — the Wabash River. Along this river and its many tributaries the *mihtohseeniaki* have maintained a distinct culture and numerous communities since time immemorial.

The flint place illustrates its uniqueness in that it provided a useful resource, flint, for the people's daily and ceremonial activities and for trade. Numerous shallow pits remain as reminders of the labor they invested in extracting the flint. They traded it along an overland portage that began at the *taawaawa siipiiwi* — Maumee River — and ended at the Forks, where they could enter the Wabash River and paddle to either the St. Lawrence or the Mississippi. Rivers were the means through which the *mihtohseeniaki* connected with other people, animals, and other-than-human beings. It was at places such as the Forks that they maintained these relationships. In the 1700s they easily incorporated Europeans into these expansive networks, but with increased American encroachment in the early 1800s, the Forks changed from being an important place of trade to a major point of negotiation.

In the 1830s and 1840s the Forks became a place where treaties were negotiated between the *mihtohseeniaki* (Miami) and the United States.

Through these treaties their leaders sought to maintain their way of life, but the U.S. government forced them to relinquish ever-larger areas of their heartlands. These negotiations also produced the most tangible reminder of a Miami presence at the Forks — the Chief's House. Treaty houses such as the Chief's House were built not as external examples of a leader's wealth but as places to host negotiations and bring people together in order to maintain the community. The treaties negotiated in 1834 and 1840 coincided with momentous changes in the story of the flint place. The Americans altered the surrounding landscape by dredging canals, draining wetlands, and farming, using Euro-American practices. On the surface, it appears to be a *mihtohseeniaki* place no longer. But memory and interaction persist, and the *mihtohseeniaki* still visit. In 1996 *mihtohseeniaki* peoples gathered here to sign another agreement, one that laid out a plan for them to work together to renew and revitalize their language. Those who still visit the flint place live throughout the United States. However, the three largest centers of population — northeastern Oklahoma, eastern Kansas, and northern Indiana — reflect a shared past of removals, dislocations, and resistance. These geographic centers continue to form *myaamionki* — core places where the *mihtohseeniaki* live and maintain interconnected communities.

FURTHER READING: *Atlas of Great Lakes Indian History,* by Helen Hornbeck Tanner and Miklos Pinther

The Black Hawk War

MICHAEL SHERFY

❖ Beginning in the early 1700s, the Sauk people and their relatives the Mesquakie (Fox) lived in today's northern Illinois, eastern Iowa, and southwestern Wisconsin. Their lives centered on Saukenuk, a large village at the confluence of the Rock and Mississippi rivers, where they farmed during the spring and summer before dispersing to hunt during the winter. In 1804 a Sauk delegation that did not include any significant chiefs went to St. Louis to secure the release of an imprisoned kinsman. Not only were they unsuccessful in their mission, they signed a treaty with William Henry Harrison — without sanction or approval from the leaders of their tribe — that provided an annuity of $1,000 per year in exchange for 3.7 million acres — all of the Sauk lands east of the Mississippi and portions west of the river.

Although the Sauk were understandably upset, the treaty did not affect them for decades. Aside from the mining country around Galena, their territory had little to offer that could not be found elsewhere, and few settlers in Illinois pushed north of Springfield. In 1830, however, settlers came to Saukenuk — where nearly 6,000 Native Americans were living — attracted by the fertile soil and proximity to the rivers. The 1804 treaty had authorized American officials to order the Sauk to abandon their village and move west. Most Sauk and Mesquakie eventually left their homeland, but Black Hawk and the "British Band" refused. Black Hawk possessed no formal authority, but he was renowned for his martial prowess. He became the leader of a faction of Sauk, Mesquakie, and Kickapoo refugees who maintained close ties to the British in Canada. Against the advice of most leaders of the Sauk and Mesquakie nations, Black Hawk led his band, including elders, women, and children, east across the Mississippi in 1832. He assumed that he would be supported by tribes such as the Winnebago and Potawatomi who still lived in Illinois. However, the rumors of his invasion led to panic in the region. The army dispatched units from St. Louis, and bellicose militias mustered and rushed to the scene.

Finding himself without allies, Black Hawk attempted to parley with Major Isaiah Stillman's militia, but they fired on Black Hawk's white flag. When the militia followed the retreating Indians, they were ambushed by Black Hawk's warriors. This began a decentralized conflict between small parties of warriors skirmishing with isolated Americans, both military and civilian, while Black Hawk, pursued by a plodding, disease-ridden American army, tried to lead his followers to safety. They fled into Wisconsin and on July 21 fought one major battle before being caught near the Bad Axe River between the Mississippi River and the army. A massacre followed. No more than 300 of the 1,000 who "invaded" Illinois rejoined their families in Iowa Territory that winter. Black Hawk survived, wrote an autobiography, and — while a prisoner of war guarded by the U.S. Army — became a celebrity during a tour of the United States in 1833. He was released that October and retired with his family. Tensions within the Sauk Nation took many years to heal, and Black Hawk, who died in 1838, was never again a leader of his people. His people were repeatedly displaced after his death. Today the headquarters of the Sac and Fox Nation is in Stroud, Oklahoma; that of the Sac and Fox Tribe of Missouri is in Reserve, Kansas; and that of the Sac and Fox Tribe of the Mississippi in Iowa are in Tama, Iowa.

80. Black Hawk State Historic Site, IL

1510 Forty-sixth Ave., Rock Island

Hauberg Indian Museum

The historic site is adjacent to the site of the village of Saukenuk, which was covered long ago by development. The nature preserve along the river offers glimpses into the area's appearance when Saukenuk was a thriving village. The Hauberg Indian Museum documents Sauk and Mesquakie life in the area from 1750 to 1830.

81. Apple River Fort State Historic Site, IL

311 E. Myrtle St., Elizabeth

Interpretive center

Galena was founded in 1826 and became one of Illinois's largest towns as lead miners and farmers settled the area. When they heard of the battle between Black Hawk and Major Isaiah Stillman on May 14, 1832, residents of this settlement 15 miles from Galena built a (now restored) block fort for protection. Black Hawk attacked it unsuccessfully on June 24, 1832.

82. Battle of Wisconsin Heights, WI

On Rte. 78 at Wisconsin Historical Society marker, southeast of Sauk City

On July 21, 1832, the British Band suffered heavy losses in the only major battle of the Black Hawk War.

FURTHER READING: *Black Hawk: An Autobiography*, edited by Donald Jackson

83. Tantiusques, MA

J. Edward Hood

Off I-84 at exit 1; right on Mashapaug Rd.; right on Leadmine Rd., Sturbridge

Tan-tas-qua or *Tantiusques* is the Nipmuck Indian name for the area (today part of Sturbridge) where they mined graphite from a natural deposit and made decorative and body paint. Near the old graphite mine, which continued to be worked by Euro-Americans during the nineteenth century, is a cellar hole and a barn foundation, the remains of a nineteenth-century farm. As the site of an abandoned farm, it is one of many. But this one bears witness to a part of New England history too little known: the lives of an intermarried family of American Indians

and free African Americans. The farm was the home of Robert E. and Diantha Crowd from 1842 to 1860. Robert Crowd was of Punkapog and African American descent. His wife was also both African American and American Indian. Intermarriage was not unusual in the late eighteenth century and for most of the nineteenth century in southern New England. Robert and Diantha Crowd's descendants are very aware and proud of the achievements of their ancestors during an age of profound racism and economic disadvantage for people of color.

FURTHER READING: *Bodies Politic: Negotiating Race in the American North, 1730–1830*, by John W. Sweet

American Indian Boarding Schools

BRENDA J. CHILD

❖ American Indian education has a unique history in the United States. Beginning in the late nineteenth century, policymakers and reformers interested in the "Indian problem" created unusual institutions for the purpose of separating Indian children from their Native backgrounds and families. Boarding school advocates argued that the institutions were designed for "cultural assimilation" and "progress," but the policy coincided with an era of intense interest in lands owned by tribal people. During the fifty-year period that boarding schools were the primary means of educating Indians, millions of acres of tribal lands passed out of Indian ownership, and the total tribal land base was reduced by some 85 percent. The history of the boarding schools cannot be understood apart from the land policies that dominated federal policy toward American Indian tribes from 1887, when the General

Allotment Act was passed, until 1934, when the allotment of Indian reservations ended. The purpose of a segregated system of Indian education in off-reservation boarding schools was to indoctrinate Indian children with American values in a setting where they would speak the English language, begin to practice Christianity, and learn a vocation that would enable them to be productive but second-class citizens in the mainstream of American society. Boarding school graduates would have no need for a tribal homeland.

The first government boarding school was established in a former army barracks in Carlisle, Pennsylvania, in 1879. Indian children and youths from a number of tribes in the western states were recruited to Carlisle, as were the children of Apache prisoners of war. Students were photographed as they arrived at school in tribal dress and braids, then later as they adopted uniforms and new haircuts. The photographs popularized for the American public the concept that Indians would be easily "civilized" and culturally transformed through their boarding school education. Carlisle was well known for its vocationally oriented curriculum, including the "outing program," which placed young Indian boys and girls in local farms and homes to work as laborers and domestic servants. By the turn of the century, twenty-five other residential schools operated in fifteen states, with Carlisle as the model.

American Indian students and their families responded in complex and creative ways to the boarding school agenda. Some students thrived, while others languished in homesickness and melancholy. In the first decades, the expectation was that students would stay at school for a term of four years before returning home. Students resisted school life and such impossible expectations by running away. Parents and guardians worried about their distant children and hated the rules that called for lengthy periods of separation. As one Ojibwe mother complained to her daughter's school superintendent, "It seems it would be much easier to get her out of prison than out of your school."

Schools were poorly funded, and as a consequence the students' diet and health and the quality of education were persistent problems for Indian families during the boarding school era. The health of students was neglected, and tuberculosis and trachoma were epidemic in the government schools. Hundreds of boarding school students died. Today the cemeteries on the grounds of the former boarding schools at Carlisle and Haskell, in Lawrence, Kansas, testify to the worst aspects of the assimilation policy. By the 1930s the exploitation of tribal lands was beginning to subside. During the years of the "Indian New Deal," a new generation of reformers and policymakers turned away from the boarding school model and advocated public school education for American Indians.

FURTHER READING: *Boarding School Seasons: American Indian Families, 1900–1940,* by Brenda J. Child

84. Carlisle Indian Industrial School, PA

Carlisle Barracks

A walking tour of the exterior of buildings is available at www.carlisleindianschool.org, "Maps"

The Indian Industrial School operated from 1879 to 1917. Carlisle's influential founder, Richard Henry Pratt, a former army officer, devised the "civilization" program that other federal boarding schools used as a model. This program, with half-days in academic training and the remainder in industrial training for boys and in domestic arts for girls, formed the standard Indian boarding school curriculum. Carlisle's student population included children from nearly every American Indian nation. Its famous student Jim Thorpe was an Olympic athlete who founded an all-Indian professional football team.

Reformers

FREDERICK E. HOXIE

❖ From the outset of the European invasion of North American, critics on both sides of the Atlantic pressed the newcomers to alter both their cultural attitudes and their formal policies toward the Native peoples. These reformers called on their contemporaries to view American Indians as fellow human beings and to deal with them peacefully. In the colonial era, these ideas emanated from religious people who based their arguments on Christian theology; in the nineteenth and twentieth centuries, these ideas had a more secular cast. Particularly in the United States, these later reformers stressed the practical advantages of peaceful relations with the tribes (wars, after all, are very expensive) and reminded politicians that democratic societies should use justice, rather than expediency, as the standard for social relations.

In the English colonies the call for reform often came from dissenting clerics, such as Roger Williams, who wrote *Christenings Make No Christians* in 1645, a plea for peaceful diplomacy and tolerance. The Quakers who settled in William Penn's Pennsylvania colony in 1685 extended their policy of nonviolence to the tribes. They insisted on purchasing land for settlement and pledged to deal honorably with their Indian neighbors. Reformers in the eighteenth century included David Brainerd in New England and Samuel Kirkland, who lived and worked with the Oneidas and Tuscaroras in New York.

At the end of the eighteenth century, the new American government's empty treasury and lofty self-image combined to produce a modest and practical approach to Indian affairs. Henry Knox, George Washington's secretary of war, pointed out the ruinous financial and human cost of military campaigns against the tribes opposing American expansion in the West and urged the president to negotiate equitable treaties with them. His recommendations were followed initially, but as increasing numbers of settlers moved west and new states in the Mississippi Valley entered the Union, a populist cry for removal slowly undermined the government's commitment to treaties and negotiation. Opponents of this new tide (which included the members of the American Board of Commissioners for Foreign Missions and the Whig opponents of President Andrew Jackson) argued that Indian and white communities could coexist peacefully, but they had little influence until midcentury, when two Indian commissioners, Luke Lea and George Manypenny, managed to create "reservations" in the West as alternatives to removal or warfare.

In 1869 Congress created the Board of Indian Commissioners, led by William Welsh, to investigate corruption in the Indian Office. It created a cadre of national reform leaders who founded the Boston Indian Citizenship Committee, the Women's National Indian Association, and, in 1882, the Indian Rights Association. In 1883 Albert Smiley, a Quaker, chaired the first annual Lake Mohonk Conference of the Friends of the Indian, which brought together religious leaders, civil reformers, women's groups, and writers.

However, by 1900 new laws and humanitarian rhetoric had produced little besides pious handwringing; dispossession continued without interruption. The Indians' aggressive neighbors had used the reformers' policy of peace to buy up Native resources and silently divide tribal communities into scattered constellations of individuals whose circumscribed economic and political power could not threaten non-Indians. To oppose this trend, a new generation of reformers arose in the first decades of the twentieth century. Modern reformers argued that Indian people *as a group* shared certain common interests and that *all* Native American tribes should have a say in the shaping of their futures.

Two groups were vital to this new defense of

tribal rights. First, English-speaking Indians, including Charles Eastman, Carlos Montezuma, and Gertrude Simmons Bonnin, stepped forward to criticize white "civilization" and celebrate their tribal past. They founded the Society of American Indians in 1911 and, in 1944, the National Congress of American Indians. The second group of reformers consisted of social scientists and their political supporters who argued that there was no single definition of culture or civilization. The anthropologist Franz Boas held that cultures should not be arranged in an imaginary pecking order with Europeans at the top and tribal people at the bottom. He and his students produced detailed studies of American Indians that revealed the complexity of their lifeways, their ancient origins, and their ability to adapt to new circumstances. As commissioner of Indian affairs between 1933 and 1945, John Collier brought both of these groups into discussions of policy. He recruited Indians into the Bureau of Indian Affairs in small but unprecedented numbers, and he drew on social science experts for advice. After World War II the number of Indian advocacy organizations proliferated. These included the National Indian Youth Council, the American Indian Movement, the National Tribal Chairmen's Association, the Council on Energy Resource Tribes, and the National Indian Education Association.

By 2000, reform no longer depended on non-Indian idealism or religious fervor. Leading reformers were Native people themselves, and their ideas rested on a concern for tribal interests and aspirations as well as a concern for equity in a multiethnic, democratic society. At the same time, however, supporters of reform continued to advocate peaceful and mutually respectful relations between Native Americans and those who had immigrated to North America.

Excerpted from *Encyclopedia of North American Indians,* ed. Frederick E. Hoxie

FURTHER READING: *The Great Father: The United States Government and the American Indians,* by Francis Paul Prucha

SECTION TWO

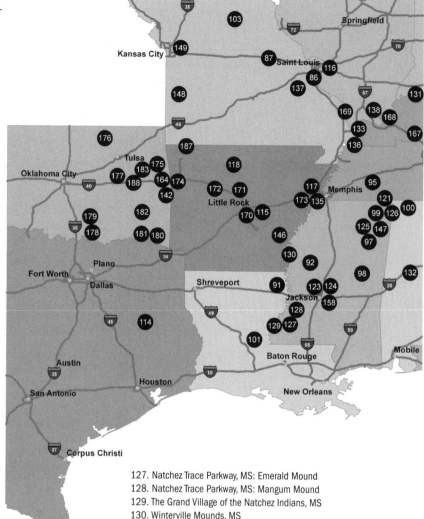

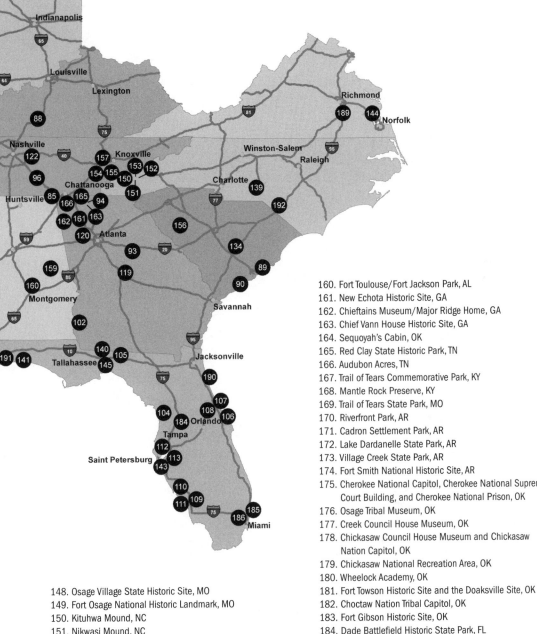

160. Fort Toulouse/Fort Jackson Park, AL
161. New Echota Historic Site, GA
162. Chieftains Museum/Major Ridge Home, GA
163. Chief Vann House Historic Site, GA
164. Sequoyah's Cabin, OK
165. Red Clay State Historic Park, TN
166. Audubon Acres, TN
167. Trail of Tears Commemorative Park, KY
168. Mantle Rock Preserve, KY
169. Trail of Tears State Park, MO
170. Riverfront Park, AR
171. Cadron Settlement Park, AR
172. Lake Dardanelle State Park, AR
173. Village Creek State Park, AR
174. Fort Smith National Historic Site, AR
175. Cherokee National Capitol, Cherokee National Supreme Court Building, and Cherokee National Prison, OK
176. Osage Tribal Museum, OK
177. Creek Council House Museum, OK
178. Chickasaw Council House Museum and Chickasaw Nation Capitol, OK
179. Chickasaw National Recreation Area, OK
180. Wheelock Academy, OK
181. Fort Towson Historic Site and the Doaksville Site, OK
182. Choctaw Nation Tribal Capitol, OK
183. Fort Gibson Historic Site, OK
184. Dade Battlefield Historic State Park, FL
185. Tree Tops Park, FL
186. Ah-Tah-Thi-Ki Museum and Living Village, FL
187. Pea Ridge National Military Park, AR
188. Battle of Honey Springs Historic Site, OK
189. Petersburg National Battlefield, VA
190. Castillo de San Marcos National Monument, FL
191. Gulf Islands National Seashore, FL
192. University of North Carolina at Pembroke, NC

148. Osage Village State Historic Site, MO
149. Fort Osage National Historic Landmark, MO
150. Kituhwa Mound, NC
151. Nikwasi Mound, NC
152. Oconaluftee Indian Village, NC
153. Great Smoky Mountains National Park, NC
154. Unicoi Turnpike Trail, GA, NC, and TN
155. Chota Memorial, TN
156. Ninety Six National Historic Site, SC
157. Fort Loudoun State Historic Area, TN
158. Natchez Trace Parkway, MS: Choctaw Agency
159. Horseshoe Bend National Military Park, AL

Sacred Places and Visitor Protocols

Suzan Shown Harjo

❖ Native sacred places are naturally formed churches where Native people go to pray, to sing, to dance, for the good day, the precious earth, the blessing waters, the sweet air, and a peaceful life for all living beings. These landscapes and waterways can be as strong as rock or as delicate as the blossoms of the medicine plants that grow there. Many of these ancient places are threatened by modern development, pollution, and recreation activities, and efforts are being made to save and reclaim them. Native people are also looking for ways to preserve and protect those places that are not endangered now but could be in the future.

Most Native sacred places are not known to the general public and are not included in this book. Only those places where the public is welcome are discussed here, but some areas of these public sites are sacred places, too. Visitors should be aware that Native ceremonies at public and nonpublic places are carried out privately. If you happen upon a ceremony at one of these places, the respectful, polite, and right thing to do is to leave the people alone, for they are at prayer.

People leave remembrances in sacred places to honor relatives, events, passages, or the way the places were created. Some places embody the health and well-being of a whole people or the entire world. Others stand for a single person and a journey through life. Any disturbance of these sacred formations or objects interrupts the intended course and can cause great turmoil for families, clans, societies, and nations. The best advice for the public at these places may be found in the Cheyenne instruction "Walk gently through life." This means one should behave in a fitting manner and not disturb or remove anything. The protocols for Native sacred and historic places are the same as the unwritten rules for guests at a monument, cemetery, royal garden, or grand palace. Just as it would be defiling to walk away with a chunk of the Wailing Wall or a mosaic from a mosque at Mecca or to draw on the walls of the Sistine Chapel, proper decorum in Native places is to leave everything where and how you find it and not leave behind anything you brought in with you.

In most of the places in this book, private and public activities coexist. The National Museum of the American Indian is such a place. It is a place for all people to expand their knowledge and understanding about the Native peoples of this quarter of Mother Earth. It also has elements that are sacred to Native people. Thousands of Native people from throughout the hemisphere consecrated the museum on its spectacular opening day. The air was rich with the smell of cedar, sage, and sweetgrass smoke. People shook shells, blew conchs, beat drums, dressed in their grandparents' finest, and danced with sacred objects that are meant to be a part of grand occasions. Every person brought the spirits of countless ancestors and myriad generations to come. The National Mall and the museum were filled with the memories of those who made it possible for Native peoples to be there that day and for there to be a Native museum facing the sun as it rises every day. A pair of bald eagles, one female and one male, joined the already amazing procession at midday. They soared high in the clear sky, then descended in widening circles as the last of the Native delegations took their seats for the opening ceremonies. A single eagle returned before sunset and circled the portion of the National Mall where an indigenous religious ceremony was being conducted.

Visitors to these special places can enjoy their glorious landscapes or architecture even without knowing every detail of their origins or exactly why they may be considered sacred ground.

85. Russell Cave National Monument, AL

3729 County Rd. 98, Bridgeport

Gilbert H. Grosvenor Visitor Center and Museum

About 10,000 years ago, and possibly earlier, people began to use Russell Cave and other rock shelters during the fall and winter as part of their seasonal travels. As populations increased, they used the cave more frequently and stayed longer, storing large quantities of nuts in pits dug into the floor of the cave. When they began to make pottery, they used their vessels to store and cook food. After about A.D. 500 they used the cave less frequently, probably as a winter hunting camp.

86. Mastodon State Historic Site, MO

1050 Museum Dr., Imperial

Museum

Perhaps as early as the late Pleistocene Epoch, people hunted here, just west of the Mississippi River. In 1979 scientists found a Clovis spear point in direct association with the bones of a mastodon.

87. Graham Cave State Park, MO

217 Hwy. TT, Montgomery City

Visitor center

The first people who used this rock shelter in the hills above the Loutre River, about 8000 B.C. (10,000 radiocarbon years B.P.), had to face the challenges of rapid environmental change resulting from the retreat of the glaciers. The remarkable discoveries in the cave show that people used it almost continuously until about A.D. 1200. Near the cave is an interpretive shelter with exhibits. In 1961 the cave was the first archaeological site in the nation to be designated a National Historic Landmark.

88. Mammoth Cave National Park, KY

Off I-65, Cave City

Visitor center

The people known as Paleoindians and the later Archaic people hunted animals and gathered plants in the area of Mammoth Cave. For about 1,000 years, beginning about 1000 B.C., people mined the cave for minerals, probably for pigments and for medicines as well as for trade. They grew squash, sunflowers, sumpweed, maygrass, and chenopodium. Between about A.D. 500 and 900, they began hunting with bows and arrows and living in larger villages. They began growing corn sometime between A.D. 900 and 1000. After the Europeans arrived, the American Indians were caught up in their competition for control of the area, which resulted in the tragic loss of lives from warfare as well as from diseases. By the time settlers arrived, the survivors had moved out of the area. Mammoth Cave is in the longest known cave system in the world: explorers have mapped more than 365 miles of cave passages.

89. Francis Marion National Forest, SC: Sewee Shell Ring

5821 U.S. 17 North, Awendaw

Sewee Visitor and Environmental Education Center

Between about 5,000 and 3,000 years ago, the people who lived along the coast from South Carolina to Florida built circular shell rings. Many authorities think that this ring of oyster shells, 250 feet across and 10 feet tall, was built by people who lived here seasonally, although some may have lived here year-round. Its extent and height suggest that it might have been built for ceremonies. Some of the earliest pottery made in North America — Thom's Creek pottery — was found here. Nearby, coastal people left a midden — consisting almost entirely

of clamshells — which was carbon-dated to A.D. 1450. The Sewee Shell Mound Interpretive Trail leads to the ring and to the midden.

90. Edisto Beach State Park, SC

Off U.S. 17 on Rte. 174, Edisto Island

Interpretive center

The people who gathered shellfish in this area built a large shell mound, now eroded by the creek. The pottery suggests that they built it between about 3,500 and 3,800 years ago.

91. Poverty Point State Historic Site, LA

Jon L. Gibson

On Rte. 577, northeast of Epps

Visitor center

Poverty Point is a large Archaic settlement created by a determined people who carried nearly 1 million cubic yards of basket-loaded dirt to build its giant earthworks. They constructed a C-shaped enclosure by raising six concentric embankments around a 37-acre open area. Five aisles radiated through the embankments like the spokes of a giant wheel. They also built mounds, including two massive cruciform structures, as well as three smaller platform mounds and a conical tumulus. The architecture had both practical and sacred purposes, serving as foundations for domestic activities and public services as well as offering magical protection and cosmic origin memorials. Poverty Point, named for the nineteenth-century plantation built on the ancient grounds, had its heyday between 1700 and 1350 B.C., a momentous time globally. It was the time of Hammurabi's Babylonian Empire, the Minoan civilization, Stonehenge, the Shang dynasty, Queen Nefertiti, and the boy-king Tutankhaten.

The Archaic people who built the earthworks were bound by the technology of that time, but their other creations were as unique as their mounds. They cooked in earth ovens, controlling cooking time and temperature with variously shaped hand-molded clay objects. Their soft, untempered, and fiber-tempered ceramics were the earliest pottery containers made in the Lower Mississippi Valley. They made many chipped-stone tools, including projectile points, adzes, celts, hoes, and small blade tools, as well as ground and polished stone tools: plummets, gorgets, and spear-thrower weights. The objects that set Poverty Point people apart were their ornaments and fetishes. They fashioned beads, bangles, and pendants in many geometric and zoomorphic shapes, including their unusual in-the-round owl effigy pendants and bird-head cutouts. They brought in exotic rocks, some from more than 1,000 miles away. More than a third of today's United States fell within their exchange network. The Arkansas, Ohio, Tennessee, and Mississippi rivers were probably the main trade routes. Exchange seems to have been conducted for both political and practical purposes, since materials were made into all kinds of objects and got into everyone's hands.

The few animal-food remains recovered from the Poverty Point site included primarily fish and mud turtles and, rarely, land mammals. Plant foods included acorns, hickory nuts, pecans, walnuts, persimmons, lotus, cattails, and grapes. No cultivated plants were grown, and the squash seeds and rinds recovered were from an inedible wild species. Since their foods show that their domestic economy was based on fishing and gathering, Poverty Point is particularly intriguing. For fishers and gatherers to settle down, build earthworks rivaling the largest ever constructed by later farming peoples, and operate an exchange network as wide as any that ever existed in the heartland is unusual in human development and a special moment in American prehistory.

FURTHER READING: *The Ancient Mounds of Poverty Point, Place of Rings,* by Jon L. Gibson

92. Jaketown Site, MS

On Hwy. 7, north of Belzoni

Visitors may view the mounds only from the side of the highway.

Fourteen mounds once stood here. During Poverty Point times, people built eight mounds in an arc shape. Later people constructed six mounds along the bank of Wasp Lake; there is no certainty about the age of these mounds, but the pottery found here dates from about 300 B.C. to A.D. 1300. Except for the two rectangular, flat-topped mounds, they are now barely evident because of years of plowing.

93. Rock Eagle, GA

Off Rte. 441, between Madison and Eatonton

Between about 1000 B.C. and A.D. 1000, people gathered quartz rocks to create a bird-shaped effigy mound that is 120 feet from head to tail with a wingspread of 102 feet. The soil under the bird is in layers of different colors and consistencies.

94. Fort Mountain State Park, GA

Off Rte. 52, east of Chatsworth

Between about 500 B.C. and A.D. 500, people built a stone wall 855 feet long on the highest part of the mountain.

95. Pinson Mounds State Archaeological Park, TN

Robert C. Mainfort, Jr.

Off U.S. 45 on Ozier Rd., Pinson

Interpretive center, archaeological laboratory, walking trails

The largest Middle Woodland period (circa 100 B.C.–A.D. 400) site in the Southeast, Pinson Mounds, in western Tennessee, includes at least twelve mounds, an earthen geometric enclosure, and associated short-term habitation areas within about 400 acres. Among the five large rectangular mounds, the 72-foot-high Sauls Mound is the second tallest earthen mound in eastern North America. (Monks Mound at Cahokia is the tallest.) The people built Ozier Mound, a 33-foot ramped earthwork, in at least six stages and covered each summit with pale yellow sand. They constructed the uppermost summit during the first century A.D., making it the oldest dated flat-topped mound in North America. In it were specimens of mica and copper and microblades of nonlocal cherts.

Most of the earthworks at Pinson Mounds were not burial mounds, but the partial excavation of one of a pair of large, intersecting burial mounds revealed a complex construction sequence, including a flat-topped primary mound capped with multicolored layers of sand and clay. At the base of the mound, which was dated to about A.D. 100, four log and/or fabric-covered tombs were excavated. In one tomb were the remains of eight women, some wearing fiber headdresses decorated with copper ornaments, accompanied by freshwater pearl beads and thousands of beads made from *Marginella* shells. Some of the ceramics from Pinson are stylistically attributable to Georgia, to the Tennessee River Valley, and to the Mobile Bay area, suggesting that people living hundreds of miles away may have visited here.

FURTHER READING: *The Woodland Southeast*, edited by David G. Anderson and Robert C. Mainfort, Jr.

96. Old Stone Fort State Archaeological Park, TN

Off U.S. 41, north of Manchester

Visitor center

Between about 50 B.C. and A.D. 400, people built a large ceremonial center with extensive earthworks at the confluence of the Duck River and Little Duck River. The earthen wall encloses a 52-acre plain.

97. Natchez Trace Parkway, MS: Bynum Mounds

Natchez Trace Parkway at milepost 232.4, Houston

Between about 100 B.C. and A.D. 100, the people who lived in a village in the area built six burial mounds, four of which were destroyed by road construction and plowing. The two remaining are dome-shaped.

98. Nanih Waiya, MS

Kenneth H. Carleton

Off State Hwy. 21 on County Rd. 393/Mound Rd., northeast of Philadelphia

Nanih Waiya, the "Mother Mound" of the Choctaw Indians, is a large ceremonial mound on Nanih Waiya Creek, a beautiful cypress swamp. *Nanih* means hill, and *Waiya* means slanting or stooping. The earthen mound is about 25 feet high, 218 feet long, and 140 feet wide. Nearby are the remains of a smaller burial mound and Nanih Waiya Cave. There were several smaller mounds and a 10-foot-high earthwork that partially enclosed the area until plowing destroyed them in the nineteenth and twentieth centuries.

Native Americans constructed the mound between A.D. 1 and 300 and had probably left the area by 900. Since at least the 1700s the Choctaw have venerated this place as the central location of their origin stories. In their migration story, the ancestors of the Choctaw and the Chickasaw moved from the west, following a prophet. They traveled for a very long time and came to Nanih Waiya, which the signs told the prophet was their new home. The people settled and split into two groups, known today as the Choctaw and the Chickasaw. In the creation story the One Above brings forth the ancestors of the Choctaw from a dark underworld place through a passage in the mound. In another version of this story, the ancestors of the Choctaw come from the underworld through Nanih Waiya Cave. During the eighteenth and early nineteenth centuries, offerings were occasionally taken to the mound and placed in a large hole on the top. Today Nanih Waiya is a small park owned by the Mississippi Band of Choctaw Indians along the edges of a well-preserved cypress swamp. It offers much to visitors through its prehistoric and historical presence and its scenic beauty.

FURTHER READING: "Nanih Waiya (22WI500): An Historical and Archaeological Overview," by Kenneth H. Carleton, in *Mississippi Archaeology*

99. Natchez Trace Parkway, MS: Pharr Mounds

Natchez Trace Parkway at milepost 286.7, Tupelo

The people who lived in villages in the area between about A.D. 1 and 200 may have been the builders of a large, 85-acre ceremonial area with eight burial mounds. This is also the site of a later stockaded village built by Mississippian people.

100. Indian Mound, AL

South Court St., Florence

Museum

Sometime between about A.D. 100 and 500, people built a large mound that is 39 feet high and about 52 by 121 feet across the top.

101. Marksville State Historic Site, LA

837 M. L. King Dr., Marksville

Museum

By about the first century A.D. the influence of the Hopewell culture had extended to the people of this area, called the Marksville culture. These people began living in larger villages, building conical burial mounds, and making pottery that was similar to that of the Hopewell. Six mounds, both conical and flat-topped, are partially enclosed by a low, 3- to 7-foot earthwork about 3,300 feet long that is open on the Old River bluff side. The two openings in the earthwork suggest that it defined a ceremonial area rather than being used for defense. Some of the mounds within and outside the enclosure may have been built earlier and some later. Many ceremonial centers in this area were used again and again over the centuries.

102. Kolomoki Mounds Historic Park, GA

Thomas J. Pluckhahn

Off U.S. 27, north of Blakely

Museum

Between about A.D. 350 and 750, people lived here in a ring-shaped village of small houses around a central plaza. This may have been the largest community of its day in the Southeast, with an estimated population of several hundred people. They built eight earthen mounds now protected within the park. The largest, Mound A, is a flat-topped pyramid nearly 60 feet tall. Across from it is Mound D, a large burial mound in the center of the plaza. There were once several more mounds encircled by a low earthen embankment, but these were destroyed in the 1900s. Research suggests that most of the mounds were used for ceremonies rather than as residences for elites. The people hunted, gathered wild plants from the surrounding forests and swamps, and grew corn and squash. Their decorated pottery is known by archaeologists as Swift Creek and Weeden Island ceramics. Examples of their artistry, often in the shape of animals, can be seen in the park museum.

Kolomoki is one of the most important but, until recently, least understood mound groups in the southeastern United States. Because of the number and size of the mounds, archaeologists had thought that later Mississippian people had built them sometime after A.D. 1000. Mississippians were known for their monumental earthworks, particularly flat-topped mounds. Research during the last decade has enabled us to recognize the remarkable accomplishments of the people who lived here between the fourth and eighth centuries.

FURTHER READING: *Kolomoki: Settlement, Ceremony, and Status in the Deep South, A.D. 350 to 750,* by Thomas J. Pluckhahn

103. Thousand Hills State Park, MO: Images on Stone

Carol Diaz-Granados

Off Rte. 6 on Rte. 157, west of Kirksville

American Indians created images on stone — petroglyphs — by carving or pecking them into dolomite, limestone, sandstone, or granite. There are petroglyphs all across Missouri, with a concentration in the southeast. There are also pictographs painted on stone. The explorers

Meriwether Lewis and William Clark recorded seeing pictographs in Missouri in May and June 1804. Between about A.D. 400 and 900, when this was a ceremonial site, people carved petroglyphs — especially birds, a deer on each of two boulders, other animals, and a turtle — on lowlying boulders. They are protected by a rustic building. Between about A.D. 1000 and 1450, later people carved hundreds of petroglyphs on dolomite outcrops in a glade in Washington State Park.

FURTHER READING: *The Petroglyphs and Pictographs of Missouri,* by Carol Diaz-Granados and James R. Duncan

Florida's Native American Heritage

JERALD T. MILANICH

❖ The remains of the mounds and villages of the American Indians who once lived in Florida can still be seen at Crystal River, Safety Harbor, Lake Jackson, and Pineland. They offer testimony to a Native American heritage spanning thousands of years; the tens of thousands of sites destroyed during the past century and a half are great losses to our nation.

The earliest Florida Indians, called Paleoindians, were hunter-gatherers who came to the area about 14,000 years ago, near the end of the Great Ice Age. The climate was drier then, sea levels were several hundred feet lower, and Florida's landmass was about twice as large as it is today. By 7500 B.C., with a wetter and slightly warmer climate, the Paleoindians began a more settled existence. These people are known as the Archaic Indians. They lived along Florida's coasts, on the St. Johns River, and near other freshwater sources where they could fish and gather shellfish. Sometime before 2000 B.C. they learned to make fired-clay pottery vessels. By 500 B.C. they were making different styles of pottery in different areas, enabling modern archaeologists to differentiate among regional cultures. The names of those cultures are often taken from modern landmarks where the cultures were first studied.

The people of the St. Johns culture of the St. Johns River drainage and the adjacent Atlantic coast north of Cape Canaveral are associated with numerous shell mounds and middens, including Turtle Mound in Canaveral National Seashore. They hunted, fished, collected wild plants, and may also have had small gardens. After A.D. 750 they began to grow corn and squash, and their agricultural way of life continued into the sixteenth century when their descendants, the Timucua Indians, watched the first Europeans come ashore.

People of the Deptford culture and the later Weeden Island culture lived throughout the central and northern peninsular Gulf coast. They built the mounds and middens in the Crystal River Archaeological State Park and established trade ties with Indians living north of Florida. After A.D. 1000 their descendants, people of the Safety Harbor culture, built villages and mounds around Tampa Bay, including the Safety Harbor Mound and the Madira Bickel Mound. The sixteenth-century Uzita, Mocoso, Pohoy, and Tocobaga Indians were Safety Harbor people. Other north Florida cultures contemporary with Safety Harbor include the Alachua and Suwannee Valley cultures, associated with the Potano and northern Timucua Indians, respectively.

The Apalachee were associated with the post–A.D. 1000 Fort Walton culture of northwest Florida, a Mississippian culture like those of the interior Southeast. The Apalachee were Florida's premier farmers and relied heavily on corn. Fort Walton societies maintained a complex hierarchical political system to support their dense populations and dependence on agriculture. Chiefs and their families ruled towns featuring multiple mounds and plazas. The best known is in Lake Jackson Archaeological State Park.

Among the other regional cultures in south Florida were the Caloosahatchee culture, ancestors of the Calusa Indians, who left the shell mounds in the J. N. "Ding" Darling National Wildlife Refuge and the Pineland Site Complex, the Glades culture of the Everglades and southeast Florida, and the Belle Glade culture of the Lake Okeechobee Basin.

The first documented contact by Europeans with the Florida Indians was in 1513, when Juan Ponce de León sailed down the Atlantic coast and into Biscayne Bay, home of the Tequesta Indians, and then up the Gulf coast to the territory of the Calusa Indians. Other explorers followed, including Pánfilo de Nárvaez in 1528, who landed on the coast north of modern St. Petersburg, and Hernando de Soto in 1539, who headed from Tampa Bay to an Apalachee Indian town near modern Tallahassee. Their attempts to settle Florida were not successful. In 1564 the French under René de Laudonnière built Fort Caroline (reproduced in the Fort Caroline National Memorial on the south bank of the St. Johns River east of modern Jacksonville). The next year Pedro Menéndez de Avilés ousted them and established St. Augustine. These invasions brought great changes to the Florida Indians, who tried to deal with the problems forced upon them, but colonialism was too harsh. By the early eighteenth century, warfare, enslavement, diseases, and poor health had caused massive loss of life. When Spain relinquished her Florida colony to Great Britain in 1763, few Florida Indians remained, and most were living in refugee villages far from their homelands.

Today many Indians live in Florida, including the Miccosukee and the Seminole, descendants of Creek Indians who migrated into the state in the eighteenth and early nineteenth centuries.

Despite efforts by the United States between the 1830s and the 1850s to remove them, the Miccosukee and the Seminole persevered. By the 2000 census, 52,541 people in Florida identified themselves as American Indians. Their proud heritage, a heritage shared by all of us, remains written on the land.

FURTHER READING: *Florida's Indians from Ancient Times to the Present*, by Jerald T. Milanich

104. Crystal River Archaeological State Park, FL

3400 N. Museum Point, Crystal River

Museum

People lived here, several miles from the Gulf of Mexico, from a few hundred years B.C. until sometime after A.D. 900. Those who built the earliest part of the larger burial mound later added a surrounding platform and enclosed it with a circular embankment. People of the Weeden Island culture added to it between about A.D. 300 and 400. The park also includes shell middens, flat-topped shell mounds, a second burial mound, and a large temple mound. The variety of styles of pottery and other decorated objects of mica, copper, greenstone, and quartz in the museum's exhibit point to Crystal River as an important ceremonial center with connections to other parts of the Southeast and Midwest. It was designated a National Historic Landmark in 1990.

105. Letchworth-Love Mounds Archaeological State Park, FL

Off U.S. 90, west of Monticello

Between about A.D. 200 and 900, people built a large platform mound, nearly 300 feet wide and 46 feet high, and smaller mounds, five of which have been identified. On the large mound are a ramp, winglike platforms on two sides, a secondary mound summit or apron in the rear, and a truncated pryamidal mound summit. Artifacts found on the site document the presence of people here beginning with late Paleoindians and continuing through Seminoles.

106. Canaveral National Seashore, FL: Seminole Rest and Turtle Mound

Seminole Rest: on River Rd., north of Halifax Avenue, Oak Hill; Turtle Mound: on Rte. A1A, south of New Smyrna Beach

People of the St. Johns culture harvested and dried clams and built a 7-acre clamshell mound, called Seminole Rest, between about 500 B.C. and A.D. 800. Their descendants built Turtle Mound, an oyster-shell mound, now about 40 feet high, next to Mosquito Lagoon between about A.D. 800 and 1400. The Surruque Indians lived in the area in the sixteenth century. The mound was such a prominent landmark that it was used as a navigation point by early Spanish sailors.

107. Green Mound State Archaeological Site, FL

Off Rte. A1A, Ponce Inlet

People of the St. Johns culture built a very large mound, mostly of oyster shells, after about A.D. 800.

108. Hontoon Island State Park, FL

Off Rte. 44, southwest of DeLand; accessible only by boat

People of the St. Johns culture built four mounds, mostly of snail shells.

Three Places in the Domain of the Calusa

WILLIAM H. MARQUARDT

❖ The Calusa once ruled all of south Florida from an island in Estero Bay now known as Mound Key. When Spaniards arrived in the 1500s, scores of Indian villages many miles away were paying tribute to the Calusa chief in the form of mats, hides, feathers, foods, and captives. Calusa artists engraved, carved, and painted, producing some of the best-known Native American art. Their spiritual beliefs were unshakable, even though Spanish missionaries tried to convert them to Christianity. They built enormous mounds of shell and sand as well as large communal houses and elaborate temples. They traveled far by canoe and engineered canals that connected their villages. Remarkably, they accomplished all this without being farmers. The Calusa succeeded and ultimately prevailed in south Florida principally because of their prowess in fishing the rich inshore estuaries known today as Charlotte Harbor, Pine Island Sound, Estero Bay, and the Ten Thousand Islands. Devastated by disease, warfare, and slavery, the Calusa disappeared from Florida in the mid-1700s.

109. Mound Key Archaeological State Park, FL

Mound Key is accessible by boat from Koreshan State Historic Site, U.S. 41 and Corkscrew Rd., Estero

The park conveys the richness of Calusa society and the bountiful environment that sustained it. Surrounded by breathtaking mangrove forests, ancient shell mounds rise more than 30 feet above sea level. The highest point for many miles around, the 100-acre island is nearly all artificial, the result of almost 2,000 years of human activity. The first settlers arrived about

A.D. 100 to benefit from the plentiful fish and oysters of Estero Bay. As the years went by, the discarded shells piled up, and the island grew higher. The Indian people reworked and recycled their leftover shells, building mounds, platforms, and ridges and excavating canals and water courts. By the 1500s, the town was known as Calos, the capital of the Calusa Nation, where more than 1,000 people lived. Juan Ponce de León landed near Calos in 1513, and in 1566 Pedro Menéndez de Avilés met here with the Calusa chief, Caalus.

110. Pineland Site Complex, FL

13810 Waterfront Dr., Pineland

Randell Research Center

The Calusa Heritage Trail winds past mounds and canals where people lived for 2,000 years, the Calusa from about A.D. 100 to 1710. They built mounds, the tallest of which was more than 30 feet high, and a 2.5-mile-long canal that began at Pineland. There are interpretive signs along the trail and observation platforms atop the highest mounds.

111. J. N. "Ding" Darling National Wildlife Refuge, FL: Mound

Periwinkle Way to Palm Ridge Rd., Sanibel Island

Visitor center

The refuge is a 6,000-acre preserve of wetlands, sea-grass beds, mud flats, mangrove islands, and interior freshwater habitats. The large sand and shell mound is thought to have been associated with ceremonies of the Calusa, who lived on Sanibel Island from about 1200 to the 1600s.

FURTHER READING: *The Calusa and Their Legacy: South Florida People and Their Environments,* by Darcie A. MacMahon and William H. Marquardt

112. Safety Harbor Mound Site, FL

Philippe Park, Safety Harbor

Tocobaga, the village of the Safety Harbor culture, was similar to others around Tampa Bay between about A.D. 1000 and 1600, consisting of a few timber houses covered with palm leaves and a house on a high mound for the chief. Beyond the mound are shell middens and a burial mound. Here in 1567 Chief Tocobaga and twenty-nine vassal chiefs met Pedro Menéndez de Avilés, the governor of Spanish Florida, whose attempts to establish a Spanish garrison failed. Because of European diseases and warfare, the Native people in the Tampa Bay area did not survive past the early eighteenth century.

113. Madira Bickel Mound State Archaeological Site, FL

Off U.S. 19 on Bayshore Dr., Palmetto

Between about A.D. 300 and 400, people of the Weeden Island culture built a burial mound, which they and later people used until the late 1400s. Nearby the people of the Safety Harbor culture built a temple mound with a ramp leading to the top.

114. Caddoan Mounds State Historic Site, TX: A Sacred Site

Cecile Elkins Carter

On Rte. 21, southwest of Alto

Interpretive center

For Caddo people today, this is a sacred place — a place where *kee-o-nah wah'-wah ha-e-may'-chee*, the Old People, built great monuments of earth to honor the Creator and to hold the graves of the revered ones. This was the home of the most sophisticated prehistoric civilization in

Texas — the Caddo Indians — for 500 years, beginning late in the eighth century. Their reasons for moving from their homeland north and east along Red River to settle a new southwestern frontier community are a mystery. Their reasons for leaving about 1250 are equally puzzling.

Walking the trail that winds past the three large, grass-covered mounds is a stirring experience. The great earthen mounds are the visible remains of the once-thriving Caddo community. Two are ceremonial mounds, platforms for special houses used for the performance of certain rites or the residence of a spiritual leader. The third mound is a cemetery formed early in the history of the community. It grew to a height of 20 feet as generations of villagers labored to dig and fill individual basketloads of fresh soil, which were carried and spread to cap and cover the graves of the exceptionally venerated individuals they buried there. Outside the area of the mounds and the plaza they surround, the remains of the extensive village inhabited by most of the populace lie unseen beneath flat prairie land. The people of the village grew corn, gathered wild plants, and used bows and arrows to hunt game. They lived in beehive-shaped structures made of poles and thatch that were about 25 feet in diameter.

Decades of archeological investigation have revealed much about the structure of the mounds. Thousands of artifacts have been recovered and analyzed. Displays in the interpretive center include exquisite Caddo pottery, beautifully shaped arrow points, shell necklaces, and copper ornaments. Caddo people see these as hallowed objects taken from their ancestors' graves. The Caddo feeling that graves should never be disturbed is deep. Members of the Caddo Nation in Oklahoma leave the park with mixed emotions: sadness that sacred ground has been disturbed; hesitant appreciation for scientific investigation and scholarly interpretation that gives everyone an opportunity to learn some of the history of their people; and gratitude that the park respects, protects, and cares for a place where the Old Ones lived and died.

The old Caddo Nation dominated a vast territory in adjoining sections of Texas, Louisiana, Arkansas, and Oklahoma for more than 1,000 years, but by the early 1840s they were made virtually homeless by the flood of immigrants. In 1855 they were given a reserve on the Brazos River, but in 1859, threatened with annihilation by anti-Indian agitators, they agreed to move to permanently assigned land in Indian Territory. Protected by U.S. cavalry, they were led to the bank of the Washita River in present-day Caddo County, Oklahoma. Today, 5,056 direct descendants are members of the federally recognized Caddo Indian Nation, governed by an elected council and chairperson. Most live within a 60-mile radius of the Caddo Nation headquarters, where administrative offices, the Caddo Heritage Museum, a senior citizens center, a Head Start School, and traditional dance grounds are located, east of Binger. The ancient Caddo culture — embedded in stories, songs, dances, social traditions, and ceremonies perpetuated by our Caddo ancestors — is kept alive and passed on to the next generation by the present generation of Caddos.

FURTHER READING: *Caddo Indians: Where We Come From*, by Cecile Elkins Carter

115. Toltec Mounds Archaeological State Park, AR

Off U.S. 165 on Rte. 386, southeast of Scott

Interpretive center

Between about A.D. 700 and 1000, political and religious leaders lived here. There are eighteen mounds, most of which were low and flat-topped, protected by a ditch and an earthen embankment on three sides and a lake on the fourth. Eleven of the mounds surround a rectangular open space. Some may have had buildings on them, and several were built to align with the sun on the horizon at the summer solstice and the equinoxes.

Mississippian: A Way of Life

STEPHEN WILLIAMS

❖ The term "Mississippian" refers to the culture and way of life of the farmers who lived in large towns and villages in the eastern United States from about A.D. 1000 until about 1600. These settled agriculturalists farmed the rich bottomlands of the great Mississippi River basin. Their successful way of life — blending the older patterns of hunting, fishing, and gathering in the bountiful eastern woodlands with intensive field agriculture (including corn) — provided a strong base for population growth. New patterns of village life, social and religious practices, and interaction accompanied the change to agriculture. The Mississippians lived in thatched houses with peaked roofs and clay-plastered walls and often protected their larger villages with wooden stockades. Some of the people lived in small hamlets near the surrounding fields.

The people in the villages and hamlets were usually under the political influence of a major town, where a principal chief held ceremonial and economic power. Their rich ceremonial life was conducted in impressive temples on large earthen platform mounds set around a plaza. The plaza was also the site of ceremonies and probably of games such as chunkey, which involved throwing special poles at a rolling stone, and stickball, which was similar to lacrosse. In addition to hunting, fishing, gathering, and farming, the Mississippians created remarkable works in pottery, stone, shell, and copper. They were the first to add freshwater shells to clay to strengthen their pottery and the first to add handles to pottery vessels. Despite the huge variety of languages spoken, they reached out to other groups across the whole eastern half of the country through extensive trade and a shared system of religious and ceremonial symbolism. The distinctive and identifiable work of local and regional craftspeople has been found throughout the East. Elaborate objects of ceremonial art, including stone sculptures, are among their most remarkable accomplishments.

Mississippian societies were still flourishing when Spanish explorers encountered them in the 1540s. Not all of their meetings were peaceful. The Spaniards had armor, horses, and firepower, but the Mississippians could shoot arrows faster than the Spaniards could reload their muskets, and their arrows could pierce chain mail. They did not, however, have defenses against the European diseases, which by 1700 had decimated them. The lasting achievements of these extraordinary people are their great ceremonial mound centers, including Cahokia, Moundville, Ocmulgee, Spiro, Etowah, Winterville, and Emerald Mound.

FURTHER READING: *Fantastic Archaeology,* by Stephen Williams

116. Cahokia Mounds State Historic Site, IL

John E. Kelly

30 Ramey St., Collinsville

Interpretive center

Centrally located on the North American continent, Cahokia is the largest Mississippian mound center, covering nearly 6 square miles and including 105 earthen monuments, of which more than half were rectangular, truncated earthen pyramids and platform mounds. For 200 years the City of the Sun, the largest urban center north of Mexico, was the ritual, so-

cial, and political capital of the culture we call Mississippian. Perhaps as many as 50,000 people lived here and in mound centers and in hundreds of smaller communities up and down the central Mississippi River Valley. They were the largest and most powerful population along the Mississippi from the Gulf of Mexico to the Great Lakes, and they traded both raw materials and prized goods. The size and the number of mounds provide important insights into the organizational skills of its leaders and the human labor involved.

People lived at the site of Cahokia beginning in the late 900s. They began to remodel the ridge-and-swale landscape, and by about 1050 they had created four extensive 15- to 50-acre plazas surrounding a mound that was oriented to the cardinal directions. The mound is now known as Monks Mound from the Trappist monks who lived here in the early nineteenth century. In the early 1100s, when Cahokia was at its peak, the people expanded the site and enlarged its monumental architecture. In addition to the truncated earthen pyramids, many of which were topped with large wooden buildings, they completed Monks Mound to a height of 100 feet, covering 16 acres, and constructed an 8,600-square-foot building on the summit. At the north end of the West Plaza they built a series of large, 75- to 100-foot-square wooden enclosures. Post pits aligned to the four cardinal directions marked the center of this plaza. A half-mile west of Monks Mound were circular "woodhenges" 300 feet in diameter. These exceptional monuments were important measuring devices not only to mark the solstices and equinoxes but also to accentuate the continuous nature of life.

Toward the end of the twelfth century, people began to leave Cahokia and the region as other Mississippian centers throughout the midcontinent began to grow. The smaller population at Cahokia enclosed the sacred core of Monks Mound and the Grand Plaza with a 2-mile-long stockade built with about 20,000 wooden posts. They created new mounds and a large plaza outside the stockade to the east. More people left Cahokia in the thirteenth century, and by the fourteenth century most people had probably abandoned the region. Many Cahokian researchers now regard the Dhegihan-speaking people, such as the Osage, as the probable descendants of the people who once lived here.

FURTHER READING: *Cahokia: Mirror of the Cosmos,* by Sally A. Kitt Chappell

radiocarbon dates suggest that it was from a tree that was cut down between 1515 and 1663, it may be the remains of a cross erected after de Soto preached Christianity to the Casqui people. Ongoing research will help determine if it is the location of Casqui and what happened to the people who lived here after the Spaniards left.

FURTHER READING: "Mississippian Research at Parkin Archeological State Park," by Jeffrey M. Mitchem, in *Proceedings of the 14th Mid-South Archaeological Conference*

117. Parkin Archaeological State Park, AR

Jeffery M. Mitchem

On Rte. 184, north of U.S. 64, Parkin

Visitor information center

From about A.D. 1000 to 1600 this park was a 17-acre Mississippian village on the St. Francis River. The people built a two-tiered platform mound about 20 feet high and surrounded the village with a moat about 85 feet wide and 7 feet deep. They also constructed a sturdy stockade wall with bastions (or guardhouses) along the inside edge of the moat. They grew corn, beans, squash, and sunflowers, collected nuts, fruits, and seeds, hunted deer, and fished. They were skilled potters, and some of their effigy pots tell us about their physical appearance, such as their having tattoos on their faces and bodies. Some of the vessels are on display in the visitor information center.

The accounts of Hernando de Soto's expedition in 1541 include a visit to a village they called Casqui, where the expedition received a friendly welcome. The descriptions in the accounts match characteristics of the Parkin site. The brass bells and lead bullets that researchers have found at Parkin are additional evidence of de Soto's visit. In 1966 part of a large wooden post was found on top of the mound. Since the

118. Buffalo National River, AR: Rockhouse Cave and Cobb Cave

11 miles north of Marshall

Visitor center

People used the two bluff shelters seasonally. They used Rockhouse Cave beginning about 4,000 years ago, and Cobb between about A.D. 1100 and 1400.

119. Ocmulgee National Monument, GA

Alfred Berryhill and Blue Clark

Off I-16 at exit 2 on Coliseum Dr. to Emery Hwy., Macon

Visitor center/museum

People have lived in the area that includes the national monument for about 12,000 years, as documented by the projectile points and pottery that they left behind. In the Muscogee (or Creek) oral tradition, the mother towns of Cusseta and Coweta were settled along the Chattahoochee River west of here — the first stop in their migration — and were ancestral to the Muscogee and a part of the formation of the later sixty-town Muscogee Confederacy. Between A.D. 900 and 1200, in the Macon Plateau area of the national monument, people known as Mississippians built a great ceremonial center called Ocmulgee, which means bubbling water — *vkmorke* — in the Hitchiti dialect of the Muskoghean language. There are seven mounds, the tallest of which is 55 feet high. There is also an original earthen lodge floor with seats and a bird effigy, protected by a modern covering. These people traded, made pottery, raised crops, hunted, and fished; they left by about 1200.

Sometime between 1300 and 1600, people built a ceremonial site protected by a stockade about 2 miles to the south in the swamps of the Ocmulgee River. Known today as Lamar, it has a plaza and two mounds, one of which is 20 feet tall and has a spiral ramp that ascends counter-clockwise to its summit.

At the end of the seventeenth century, British traders from Charleston established a trading post at Ocmulgee near a Muscogee town. They called the Indians who lived along the Ocmulgee River Ochese Creeks, then shortened it to Creeks. Warfare and the diseases brought by Europeans had decimated the population by the early eighteenth century. After the 1715 Yamassee War, the Muscogees at Ocmulgee moved west to the Chattahoochee and Flint rivers. This group became known as the Lower Creeks. Those who lived along the Coosa and Tallapoosa rivers became known as the Upper Creeks. In 1805 the Creeks signed a treaty with the United States, giving up their lands between the Oconee and Ocmulgee rivers except for the 3-by-5-mile area known as Ocmulgee Old Fields.

Today the Muscogee (Creek) Nation cultural preservation staff works effectively as a partner with the Ocmulgee National Monument personnel. Like many other prehistoric sites in the path of roads and development, the area known as Ocmulgee Old Fields — which was the first Traditional Cultural Property designated east of the Mississippi River — has suffered from intrusions. The Muscogee (Creek) Nation continues to work to protect their most sacred original heartland.

FURTHER READING: *Ocmulgee Archaeology, 1936– 1986,* edited by David J. Hally

120. Etowah Indian Mounds Historic Site, GA

Adam King

Off Rte. 113/61 to Indian Mounds Rd., Cartersville

Museum

Etowah began about A.D. 1000 as the modest capital of an ancient chiefdom. By about 1200 the people had left. When they returned fifty years later, they built the dominant Mississippian center in the region, with large platform mounds arranged around open plazas and a ditch and stockade complex to fortify them. One of the six mounds was more than 64 feet high. They buried important people in the center's burial mound with a spectacular array of art objects. Still considered sacred by Native Americans, these objects stand as a testament to the richness of their religious and artistic traditions.

If current interpretations are correct, the fortifications built at Etowah did not keep the people safe. Sometime after 1250, they left once again. The burned stockade suggests that the cause was an armed attack. By the time people returned to Etowah about 1350, the center of power in the region had shifted to the north. Etowah was just another town in a larger chiefdom called Coosa, which was described by Hernando de Soto, who traveled through it in 1540. Today Etowah is important to the Creek and the Cherokee. Ancestors of the Creek built Etowah, and it was part of the Cherokee homelands from the seventeenth century until they were forced along the Trail of Tears. Like the objects found at Etowah, the site itself is a sacred part of their history.

FURTHER READING: *Etowah: The Political History of a Chiefdom Capital,* by Adam King

121. Shiloh National Military Park, TN: Mississippian Mound Group

David G. Anderson and Paul D. Welch

Off Hwy. 22, Shiloh

Visitor center, interpretive walking trail

For more than a century one of the most beautiful and well-preserved Indian mound groups in the southeastern United States has been protected within Shiloh National Military Park. Nestled between two steep ravines in a tranquil oak-hickory forest on a high bluff overlooking the Tennessee River, the mound group covers almost 40 acres. Between about A.D. 1000 and 1300 this political and ceremonial center of a powerful Mississippian society dominated the region. Eight large temple and burial mounds enclose a central plaza, the place of ceremonies and sporting events as well as daily life. The people built residences for chiefs and temples atop the larger flat-topped mounds. Some of the more rounded mounds were the burial places of high-status individuals. Beyond the plaza are more than 100 smaller mounds on which houses once stood. The center was a place of safety in times of war and was once briefly encircled by a stockade.

The Tennessee River is eroding the largest mound, prompting recent stabilization efforts and archaeological excavations, which have revealed that the mound was constructed with great care and ceremony. The builders used brightly colored soils to create surfaces of red, yellow, and white, colors that symbolized concepts such as war, peace, and purity. The other large mounds also had colored surfaces, giving the mound group a spectacular appearance at its zenith. While the people who lived along the river within 30 miles viewed this site as the center of their lives, the leaders here had contact with leaders much farther away. An exquisitely carved pipe found in one of the mounds was made of Missouri flint clay and came from the Caho-kia area near St. Louis. Some of the pottery the Shiloh Indians used came from major Mississippian centers such as Etowah, Moundville, and Cahokia.

When this chiefdom fell, no comparable mound-building society rose to replace it in this area of the Tennessee River Valley. The people moved elsewhere, and their descendants include the Chickasaw, who ceded their lands west of the river to the U.S. government in 1819. The Chickasaw Nation in Oklahoma considers the Shiloh Mounds as part of their homeland.

FURTHER READING: *Archaeology at Shiloh Indian Mounds, 1899–1999*, by Paul D. Welch.

122. Sellars Farm State Archaeological Area, TN

James V. Miller

Off U.S. 70 on Poplar Hill Rd., southeast of Lebanon

This is a place of nature and of the memories of an ancient people. Overhead a red-tailed hawk soars, a deer springs from a cedar grove, and a blue heron skims over the waters of Spring Creek. We are in the natural world of the Mississippian people who lived in this village 1,000 years ago. The village, originally surrounded by a double earthen wall and a dry moat with a wooden stockade on the inner wall's half-mile circumference, is dominated by a truncated pyramidal mound standing at the western edge of an open plaza, around which the people built houses of daub and wattle with thatched roofs. Ruled by an elite hierarchy, they were farmers, as were the other Mississippians who lived in the central Cumberland River basin from A.D. 900 to 1500, and their corn crops thrived in the fertile creek bottoms. They are known as the Stone Box Grave people because of the limestone-lined graves in their burial mounds and under the floors of their houses.

Among the people were master artists who sculpted siltstone statues of their honored ancestors. One of the four statues found at the site is considered the best Native stone statue of a human unearthed in North America. It is in the McClung Museum at the University of Tennessee in Knoxville. The protected village site serves as a monument to these ancient Mississippian people.

FURTHER READING: *Speaking with the Ancestors: Mississippian Stone Statuary of the Tennessee-Cumberland Style,* by Kevin E. Smith and James V. Miller

123. Pocahontas Mound, MS

On U.S. 49, Pocahontas

Between A.D. 1000 and 1300, Mississippians built a 22-foot-high rectangular platform mound with a wooden building on top of it. Their village surrounded the platform mound and the dome-shaped burial mound nearby.

124. Natchez Trace Parkway, MS: Boyd Mounds Site

Natchez Trace Parkway at milepost 106.9, Jackson

This small burial mound was begun after A.D. 800 as two parallel mounds. Sometime before 1100, Mississippian people covered the mounds with more earth, creating a large burial mound that is about 110 feet long, 60 feet wide, and 4 feet high.

125. Tombigbee National Forest, MS: Owl Creek Mounds

Off Natchez Trace Parkway at milepost 243.1 on Davis Lake Rd., Tupelo

Mississippians built these two platform mounds between about A.D. 1100 and 1200. The largest is 17 feet high, and on top of it are the remains of a building. Since there is little evidence of debris, it is likely that this was a ceremonial center where few, if any, people lived.

126. Natchez Trace Parkway, MS: Bear Creek Mound and Village Site

Natchez Trace Parkway at milepost 308.8, Tupelo

The Mississippians who lived in the nearby village built a flat-topped mound with a building on top of it between about A.D. 1100 and 1300. The National Park Service restored the mound to the estimated original size, 8 feet high and 85 feet square.

127. Natchez Trace Parkway, MS: Emerald Mound

Ian W. Brown

Natchez Trace Parkway at milepost 10.3, Natchez

The people of the Mississippian tradition known as the Plaquemine culture built and occupied Emerald Mound between A.D. 1250 and 1600. It is an enormous quadrilateral platform mound about 255 yards long, 145 yards wide, and 30 feet high with two (of the original eight) mounds on top of it, one of which is 30 feet high. Its east-west axis honors the sun, which was critically important to these agricultural people. They had a powerful principal chief, and the succession was matrilineal. They raised corn, beans, and squash and hunted, fished, and gathered wild fruits, nuts, and vegetables. Most of the people lived in hamlets along the banks of St. Catherine Creek and its tributaries and on hilltops. They journeyed to Emerald to participate in annual rituals, ceremonies, and games and to trade. When the eighteenth-century French explorers encountered their descendants, the Natchez Indians, the only chiefdom society in the Mississippi Valley to have survived relatively intact, they named the chief the Great Sun. Power shifted to the Grand Village of the Natchez in the eighteenth century, but the glory of Emerald must have still been strong in their oral tradition. Today people come to learn about and honor the remarkable people who built the mounds, once one of the centers of the Plaquemine culture.

FURTHER READING: "Natchez Indians and the Remains of a Proud Past," by Ian W. Brown, in *Natchez Before 1830,* edited by Noel Polk

128. Natchez Trace Parkway, MS: Mangum Mound

Natchez Trace Parkway at milepost 45.7, Port Gibson

This natural hill was a cemetery for people who lived during the same period as those at Emerald Mound.

129. The Grand Village of the Natchez Indians, MS

Jim Barnett

400 Jefferson Davis Blvd., Natchez

Museum

The Natchez built the three Grand Village mounds between 1200 and 1600. The mounds, which range in height from 8 to 14 feet, are along St. Catherine Creek, 3 miles east of the Mississippi River. Their most sacred temple building was on one of the mounds. On another was the house of the Great Sun, their hereditary chief. The tribe was divided into two moieties, which the Europeans interpreted as social ranks. Kinship and descent were determined by a matrilineal system, with the family name and social

affiliation passing down from mother to daughter. The Natchez people lived on family farms in five settlement districts. They grew corn, beans, and squash, gathered wild plants, hunted, and fished. The abundance of food meant that the people had time for religious and social activities, including mound building. They had a calendar year divided into thirteen months or moons, beginning in March with the Moon of the Deer. They had feasts and ceremonies on each new moon and major celebrations in July (Moon of Little Corn) and September (Moon of Great Corn).

This was the main ceremonial mound center for the Natchez Indians when the French began to settle the area in the early 1700s to counter English control. The French became the primary trading partners of the Natchez, but over time, tension between the two groups increased, culminating in the Natchez Rebellion of 1729. In the brief war, the French defeated the Natchez, took captives, including the last Great Sun, and sold them into slavery in the Caribbean islands. Many Natchez became refugees and joined the Chickasaw and, later, the Creek and the Cherokee in the southern Appalachian Mountains. Today their descendants still recognize their Natchez heritage.

FURTHER READING: *The Natchez Indians: A History to 1735,* by Jim Barnett

130. Winterville Mounds, MS

Jeffrey P. Brain

North of U.S. 82 on Rte. 1, Greenville

Museum

The people who built the first mounds at Winterville, known as the Coles Creek culture, arrived in about A.D. 1000 and lived along the banks of the Mississippi River from Winterville south into Louisiana. These agricultural people had an organized political system and well-developed religious beliefs. The mounds were their religious center and the principal abode of their leaders. Most of the common people lived in small hamlets and farmsteads scattered over the surrounding countryside; they came to the mound center for religious ceremonies and social occasions. In the rich land of the Yazoo Delta they must have led a successful and rewarding life.

In about A.D. 1200, people from an even greater cultural tradition, the Mississippian, arrived. Their mound center at Cahokia influenced a vast area, and their effects upon Winterville were dramatic. The small mound group was transformed into a great center that towered over the flat, alluvial land — the reigning queen of the delta for the next 200 years. During these centuries Winterville was primarily a ceremonial center; probably only the social elite, the priests, and their retainers lived there year-round. Their houses, on and around the lesser mounds, were of wattle and daub with thatched roofs. The largest structure was the tribal temple on the great central Mound A, where they kept their sacred objects. In the center was a fire — the symbol of the sun — maintained by the priests and elders. At death the most important people were interred in the mounds with pottery vessels, tools, and other personal effects.

The people left before Hernando de Soto arrived, and there is no evidence of a great catastrophe. It is probable that they moved away because the fields were worn out or the banks of the river were no longer safe and attractive places to live. The preservation of Winterville honors them today.

FURTHER READING: *Winterville: Late Prehistoric Culture Contact in the Lower Mississippi Valley,* by Jeffrey P. Brain

131. Angel Mounds State Historic Site, IN

Off I-164 at exit 5 to Pollack Ave., Evansville

Native American Museum and Education Center

Between A.D. 1100 and 1450, several thousand Mississippians lived in a village along the Ohio River and raised crops in the rich soil. They built ten platform mounds (the temple mound has been reconstructed) and surrounded the village with a stockade enclosing 105 acres. There is a mound nearby built by earlier people.

132. Moundville Archaeological Park, AL

Vincas P. Steponaitis

East of Rte. 69 and north of County Line Rd., Moundville

Jones Archaeological Museum

Moundville is a remarkable place, not only because of the scale of its earthworks but also because these ancient monuments are so well preserved. The large scale is a testament to the ancient builders; the preservation is a happy consequence of the foresight of local citizens who worked together in the 1920s and 1930s to protect the site as a 185-acre state park. This ancient town was built by Mississippian people who lived here from the eleventh through the sixteenth century. Most of the mound construction took place between A.D. 1200 and 1300, a time when the town reached its largest size. It was the political capital and religious center for a province that included thousands of people, many living in outlying communities.

Today visitors are struck by the majesty of the earthworks that surround the plaza. Twenty of these mounds are still clearly visible. Most, if not all, had wooden buildings on top. Some were temples, and others were the residences of chiefs. The mounds were arranged around a large rectangular plaza used for public ceremonies and other gatherings. The mounds and plaza were at one time surrounded by a bastioned stockade made of pine logs that defended all approaches to the site. The people dug and hauled thousands of cubic yards of earth, basketload by basketload, to build the mounds. Archaeologists estimate that the stockade, which was rebuilt several times, consisted of more than 10,000 logs, 10 to 14 inches in diameter. Without modern machinery or even metal tools, the labor required to build these monuments and fortifications was staggering and is evidence of the ingenuity of the people who once lived here and the power of their chiefs.

FURTHER READING: *Archaeology of the Moundville Chiefdom,* edited by Vernon J. Knight, Jr., and Vincas P. Steponaitis

133. Wickliffe Mounds State Historic Site, KY

Kit W. Wesler

94 Green St., Wickliffe

Welcome center, museum

Mississippian people built a village on the bluffs near the confluence of the Mississippi and Ohio rivers about A.D. 1100. It was a commanding site for the river trade and included rich bottomlands. It was also on a major migratory bird flyway. The people constructed a plaza with a large building on the west side and a smaller one on the north. About 100 years later they built platform mounds over the earlier buildings, successively raising similar buildings higher than the rest of the village. The thatched wattle and daub houses and the gardens were on the high ground of the ridge. Their pottery included flared bowls with incised decoration on the rims, negative-painted pottery, and elaborate effigy vessels. The Mississippians traded widely —

for pottery from Cahokia, for marine-shell gorgets reflecting styles from eastern Tennessee and northern Alabama, for mica from the Appalachians, for copper from the Great Lakes, and for shark's teeth from the Gulf of Mexico or the Atlantic.

After 1250 the people expanded the village along the bluff, but mound building slowed. The villagers molded the final caps over the platform mounds and constructed buildings on top of them. They built a few small mounds, perhaps as burial areas for chiefs. After 1350 they left their village, and within the next hundred years the Mississippians left the region. A shroud of silence hung over the area until Europeans and Americans arrived in the eighteenth century.

Today the historic site works with Native Americans, including Shawnees, Chickasaws, and Choctaws, and is a center for Native American culture and education. In the 1990s researchers from Murray State University uncovered a hard-fired clay floor north of the plaza and a rare red and white painting of a Sun Circle, the cross-in-circle symbol characteristic of the Mississippians.

FURTHER READING: *Excavations at Wickliffe Mounds,* by Kit W. Wesler

134. Santee National Wildlife Refuge, SC: Santee Indian Mound

On Rtes. 301/15 south of Summerton: Bluff Unit

Visitor center

According to the Paleoindian Database of the Americas (http://pidba.tennessee.edu/), the first people came into this area more than 13,000 years ago (11,000 radiocarbon years B.P.) and began to hunt and camp. The river swamps of today began to form about 8,000 years ago. Between about A.D. 1200 and 1450 a major Mississippian chiefdom was centered at the edge of one of the largest hardwood cypress swamp forests in the Southeast, now under the waters of Lake Marion. In their village were two mounds. The one near the shore of Lake Marion had large structures on top that were temples or residences for chiefs. The smaller may have been a burial mound. Santee Indians were living in this area in the early eighteenth century. During the Revolutionary War the British forces built a fort on top of the mound.

135. Chucalissa Archaeological Site, TN

Off I-55 at exit 9 to T. O. Fuller State Park, Memphis

C. H. Nash Museum

Chucalissa is the Choctaw word for abandoned house. Mississippian people were in this area by about A.D. 900 and built the first mound in their village, Mound B, probably before A.D. 1300. They constructed Residential Ridge about 1300, and research suggests that they were no longer using it in 1400, when they began construction of the flat-topped temple mound — Mound A, now 25 feet tall with a base of about 100 by 150 feet — on a central plaza. On top of the mound they built a large residential structure, which burned and was rebuilt at least twice. The final burning or abandonment occurred about 1500. While it is likely that some people lived at Chucalissa after 1500, its significance as a population center lasted from about 1300 to 1500. The people farmed, hunted, fished, and participated in a wide trade network. The ongoing research includes more precise documentation of the dates of construction and abandonment of the mounds, increase and loss of population, and changes in the sociopolitical power structure. During the annual Choctaw Festival in August there are exhibits, music, dance, and stickball games.

136. Towosahgy State Historic Site, MO

Off Rte. 77, east of East Prairie

The Osage word *towosahgy* means old town. The Mississippians who lived here until about 1450 built a large mound (250 by 180 by 16 feet), six other mounds around a central plaza, and hundreds of wood and thatch houses. They grew beans, maize, and squash in fields outside their protective stockade. The Mississippi River was then just a few hundred yards away. Fissures near the large mound show where a strong fourth-century earthquake along the New Madrid fault forced white sand upward into the dark sand above.

137. Washington State Park, MO: Petroglyphs

On Rte. 21, south of DeSoto

Between about A.D. 1000 and 1450, when this area was used as a ceremonial site, people carved several hundred petroglyphs into dolomite boulders and outcrops. The images include a mace, arrows, birds, feet, squares, and meandering serpents. The petroglyphs are under a protective shelter with interpretive signs. Research suggests that the Mississippian culture evident in the petroglyphs is the result of the spread of powerful Mississippian ideas emanating from Cahokia.

138. Shawnee National Forest, IL: Millstone Bluff

Brian M. Butler

On Rte. 147, northeast of Robbs

Interpretive trail

In the late 1200s Mississippian people founded a small village, known today as Millstone Bluff, on an isolated sandstone mesa — a prominent topographic feature with a flat top, visible for miles

— in the rugged uplands of the eastern Shawnee Hills. They had moved into the upper Bay Creek Valley from somewhere along the Ohio River. The 4-acre hilltop has never been plowed, so the plan of their village is clear today. They built a central plaza about 35 yards across, surrounded by their houses, which were semisubterranean. About twenty-five house basins have been identified. There are petroglyphs on the northern edge of the escarpment that surrounds the hilltop. The village was the political and ritual center for the agricultural people who lived in the adjacent creek valleys. They left about 1450, and most of the people in southern Illinois were gone by 1500.

FURTHER READING: "Mississippian Cosmology and Rock Art at the Millstone Bluff Site in Southern Illinois," by Mark J. Wagner, in *The Rock-Art of Eastern North America: Capturing Images and Insight,* edited by Carol Diaz-Granados and James R. Duncan

139. Town Creek Indian Mound, NC

Malinda Maynor Lowery

509 Town Creek Mound Rd., Mt. Gilead

Visitor center

Town Creek Indian Mound is peaceful, ancient, and holy. It is a wellspring of sacred knowledge for Indians in North and South Carolina, one of the places our ancestors lived, worshipped, died, and were buried. The mound is one of the thousands of man-made and divinely inspired earthworks that were built in the centuries before the arrival of Europeans. Today the area is a state historic site, with a visitor center, exhibits, and a reconstruction of the mound and some of the community's main structures.

I am a Lumbee Indian from North Carolina and a descendant of the people who lived at Town Creek. Our ancestors constructed the mound as a platform for a house or place of worship in the twelfth century. Then it would have been surrounded by fields of corn, vegetable gardens, houses made of wood, clay, straw, and cane, trash piles of animal bones, broken tools, and smoke from perpetually burning fires. The town square was used for ceremonies, and at other times it served as a playground for both children and adults. Town Creek was a civilization where teachers, artists, farmers, hunters, and philosophers lived. Their important, knowledge-generating activities were not all that different from ours today. They prayed, sang, studied their natural surroundings, celebrated with family and friends, told stories, buried their dead, and cried over them. The details about the place don't survive in our memories, but one piece of information has been passed down over the generations: our ancestors are buried there, making Town Creek a sacred place.

Town Creek people did not write things down, but there is a reason that our people didn't — and still don't — write a lot of things down. Not writing it down means we pass on only the most important knowledge rather than the incessant stream of "information" that sometimes passes for, but is not always, knowledge. Town Creek is our history book. For us, "history" means living, useful knowledge of ourselves and our world; a "book" is the source of that knowledge, whether written down or on the land. Books that are on the land can be very useful, since they cannot be burned, and their meanings can be reinterpreted to meet the needs of generations to come. Indians in North and South Carolina are people with longstanding residence in and ownership of the blessed land of rivers, swamps, forests, and beaches. We have ministered to the land, and it has given us its gifts for many, many generations. The earth has received our dead and has transformed their bodies into spirits that live with us now, even though we do not live at Town Creek.

29. Serpent Mound, OH

41. Acadia National
Park, ME:
Jordan Pond

43. Cape Cod
National Seashore, MA:
Nauset Marsh

52. Marquette Mission Park and Mackinac State Historic Parks, MI:
Straits of Mackinac

74. Grand Portage National Monument, MN: Pigeon River

116. Cahokia Mounds State Historic Site, IL: Twin Mounds and Monks Mound

132. Moundville Archaeological Park, AL

153. Great Smoky Mountains National Park, NC

LEFT:
175. Cherokee National Capitol
(now the Cherokee Nation Courthouse), OK

ABOVE:
176. Osage Tribal Museum, OK

LEFT:
177. Creek Council House
Museum, OK

178. Chickasaw Nation Capitol, OK

182. Choctaw Nation
Tribal Capitol, OK

198. Seminole
Canyon State Park
and Historic Site, TX

201. Medicine Wheel National Historic Landmark, WY

202. Devils Tower National Monument, WY

212. Mount Rushmore National Memorial, SD

243. Palo Duro Canyon
State Park, TX

246. Little Bighorn Battlefield
National Monument, MT

FURTHER READING: *Town Creek Indian Mound: A Native American Legacy,* by Joffre Lanning Coe

140. Lake Jackson Mounds Archaeological State Park, FL

Off Rte. 27 to Crowder Rd. to Indian Mounds Rd., Tallahassee

For several hundred years before 1500 this was the capital of the Apalachee Indians, the descendants of the people known as the Fort Walton culture, who had built the mounds. The largest of the six flat-topped earthen mounds is about 150 feet by 200 feet and 35 feet high. In Mound 3 there were copper breastplates, copper and stone axes, shell gorgets, pearl beads, ceramic and stone pipes, as well as items of lead, mica, anthracite, graphite, steatite, and greenstone. There are wooden stairs and ramps for visitor access to the summits of some of the mounds.

141. Indian Temple Mound Museum and Park, FL

139 Miracle Strip Parkway, Fort Walton Beach

This large sand and shell temple mound was the base for the ceremonial structures built by the people who lived along this beach and the bay from about A.D. 1200 until the 1600s. The adjacent shell middens were built between about 500 B.C. and A.D. 1500. The museum collection includes ceramic vessels. One of the finest is a polychrome urn with figures and faces of the people of that time.

142. Spiro Mounds Archaeological Center, OK

Dennis Anthony Peterson

Off Rte. 9, northeast of Spiro

Visitor center

Spiro Mounds was a Mississippian religious and political center between A.D. 850 and 1450 with ceremonial areas, a burial mound, two temple mounds, and nine mounds that had houses on them. The Caddoan-speaking elite lived in this center. Some of the people who lived in the large surrounding town created works of art of great distinction. They engraved conch shells, embossed copper, carved stone and wood, and wove cloth and lace that were used in ceremonies and that showed the status of the leaders. The leaders traded widely to acquire the materials for the artisans, from the Gulf of California to the Gulf of Mexico, from Virginia to the Great Lakes. When treasure hunters dug into the burial mound at Spiro in the 1930s, they removed — and sold — great works of art from Cahokia, Etowah, and Winterville as well as those made at Spiro. These remarkable creations point up the interconnections between leaders at Spiro and those in other Mississippian centers, provide insights into their ceremonies, such as the First Fire and the Green Corn and Deer dances, and show how the Mississippian people saw themselves.

Works of art from Spiro are in many museums, including the Sam Noble Oklahoma Museum of Natural History and the National Museum of the American Indian. This spiritually and artistically powerful art enables modern artists from many tribes, such as the Cherokee, Muscogee, Choctaw, Caddo, and Wichita, to journey into their heritage.

FURTHER READING: *From Mounds to Mammoths,* by Claudette Marie Gilbert and Robert L. Brooks.

The Rise and Fall of the Mississippians

T. R. PAUKETAT

Something happened at Cahokia in the Mississippi Valley almost a thousand years ago, something big — really big, as the twenty-seven Mississippian places described above show. The grass-covered, four-sided earthen pyramids are the hallmarks of a civilization: the abrupt, dramatic founding of pre-Columbian North America's only well-populated city, which in turn led to powerful rulers, a religious cult, elaborate artwork, migrations, wars, and the emergence of social classes. An army of Spaniards, Old World diseases, and the ensuing flood of European immigrants ended it all, but the Mississippians left permanent legacies.

Between about A.D. 700 and 1050, farmers in the central and lower Mississippi Valley began a sedentary village lifestyle. Some started to build pyramidal mounds — at Toltec and at Winterville — but these were typically vacant ceremonial centers, not populated towns. There is little in the art, the architecture, or the daily lives of these people to explain what happened next, as civilization came a-knocking. About 1050, and in one fell swoop, Cahokians dismantled their old village, designed and constructed a spacious Grand Plaza, and began work on the huge pyramids, including Monks Mound, which became the third or fourth largest mound in the entire New World. They founded the great city of Cahokia, the most significant single event in pre-Columbian North America.

The population of "new" Cahokia swelled to 10,000 or more by the close of the eleventh century, as migrants and pilgrims came to see what was happening. They witnessed the unimaginable: a city under construction. Human labor poured in. There were public works projects, calendrical devices (the woodhenges), festivals attended by thousands, and human sacrifices at which scores were executed. The monuments and ritual events commemorated the new idea of Cahokia, an idea that mixed religion and politics in a way that underlay all of Mississippian culture. Cahokia's powerful rulers appear to have presented themselves as personifications of sky-world thunderbirds. Their "bird-man" ideology spread out from Cahokia, and would-be rulers elsewhere attempted to duplicate it. By 1100 there were small Cahokia-like centers at Moundville, Etowah, and Angel — which seem to have been based on their own versions of the cult of the bird-man rulers. Some Mississippians migrated to new territories, such as Ocmulgee and Aztalan, displacing indigenous Woodland people. So, by hook or by crook, Mississippian culture spread.

As Cahokia began to fall apart in the thirteenth century, other regional powers emerged to fill the vacuum: Towosahgy and the dramatically enlarged and redesigned capitals of Moundville, Winterville, Etowah, and Lake Jackson. Each of these towns was a historical force, but none recaptured the glory of Cahokia. They dominated portions of the South until they, too, collapsed by about 1400. The last hurrah of the Mississippian world may have been the elite tomb mound at Spiro, where, about 1400, art objects and ornamental finery from Cahokia, Moundville, and Winterville were interred with the bodies of the nobility. By the time Hernando de Soto passed through the South (1539–1543), most Mississippian capital towns were reduced to small chiefdoms fighting over territory. In some places, such as Parkin in Arkansas, fear of violent death prevented many people from living outside the walls of their towns.

Finally, widespread warring and death from European diseases encouraged people to flee their homelands, leaving huge areas of the interior of the continent empty. Some European colonists — such as the French in the Illinois country — moved into the vacant lands. Elsewhere the descendants of the Mississippians regrouped, frustrating colonial administrators. The likely descendants of the Cahokians even prevented, for a time, the expansion of Jefferson's America.

FURTHER READING: *Hero, Hawk and Open Hand: American Indian Art of the Ancient Midwest and South,* edited by R. F. Townsend

143. De Soto National Memorial, FL

Margo Schwadron

End of 75th St. NW, Bradenton

Visitor center/museum

Hernando de Soto's expedition in 1539 was the first Spanish exploration of the interior of today's southern United States. The expedition consisted of as many as 700 people, including 2 women, 220 horses, large attack dogs, food supplies for eighteen months, and a herd of pigs. The fleet carrying the expedition anchored off the Gulf coast of peninsular Florida, west of the present-day De Soto National Memorial, before moving up the Little Manatee River from Tampa Bay. (There is no evidence that de Soto was ever at the memorial site.) The Spaniards built a camp in an Indian village whose chief was Uzita. The small village had several timber and palm leaf houses. The chief's house was on top of a mound near the beach opposite a temple on top of which was a carved wooden bird with gilded eyes.

From Uzita, de Soto's army marched north through peninsular Florida. Along the way they traded with chiefs, but they also used force to take food from the Indians as well as women and bearers. After traveling through the territory of the Timucua Indians, the army arrived among the Apalachee in the Florida panhandle. They made their winter camp in Anhaica, the Apalachee capital (today's Tallahassee). Breaking camp in the spring, de Soto's army traveled through Georgia, the Carolinas, and into Tennessee before turning southwest along the Coosa River into central Alabama. There, at Mabila, Chief Tuscaluza nearly defeated the expedition by luring part of the army into that stockaded town, where he had hidden hundreds of warriors. The Spaniards spent the winter of 1540–41 among the Chicaza (Chickasaw) Indians in Mississippi before traveling in Arkansas for a year, searching for gold. In the spring of 1542 they returned to the Mississippi River, where de Soto died. The survivors of the expedition made it to Mexico in September 1543.

On their trek they had encountered nearly 100 Indian tribes but found no gold. The written accounts of the expedition by Rodrigo Ranjel, the Gentleman of Elvas, Hernández de Biedma, and Garcilaso de la Vega provided important information about the Native peoples and enabled scholars to reconstruct the route. The impact of the expedition upon the peoples was great. Warfare as well as epidemics resulting from exposure to new European diseases resulted in the deaths of many, changing their lifeways forever.

FURTHER READING: *Knights of Spain, Warriors of the Sun: Hernando de Soto and the South's Ancient Chiefdoms,* by Charles Hudson

144. Colonial National Historical Park, VA: Jamestowne and the Powhatan Indians

Helen C. Rountree

At the end of Colonial Parkway, Yorktown

Visitor center

Visitors to Historic Jamestowne on Jamestown Island hear about the English settlement and view the excavations of the English fort. The significance of the place to Native Americans during the last 400 years is harder to discern while touring the park. To American Indians in Virginia and elsewhere, Jamestown represents the first permanent English-speaking foothold, a jumping-off place for foreign domination, first of the Chesapeake region and, later, of the rest of North America. For the Powhatan people in particular, Jamestown Fort was initially a place of *tassantassas* (strangers), then a place of opponents.

In 1607 the island was part of the foraging territory of the Paspaheghs, subjects of the paramount chief, Powhatan, the father of Pocahontas. Captain John Smith's map shows many Powhatan villages upriver from the island, where there are more rich alluvial farmlands, more tuber-producing freshwater marshes, and more freshwater fish-spawning areas. Jamestown Island is at the changeover from brackish to fresh water, something the English colonists learned when they drank the river water and developed salt poisoning. Powhatan's capital, Werowocomoco, was in the brackish-water portion of the York River, but its central location within his eastern Virginia domain probably outweighed its ecological disadvantages.

The English chose Jamestown Island for its lack of villages and its deep-water anchorage, but they soon realized that the Native people still considered it an integral part of their homeland. The Powhatans were offended when the newcomers, calling themselves visitors, stayed on and on. They became angry when the "visitors," with their inadequate supply lines from England, became aggressive about food, especially during drought years. The English colony nearly foundered at first, giving the Powhatans the mistaken impression that waging guerrilla warfare and withholding food would be enough to drive the squatters out. They learned otherwise after 1610, when stronger foreign leaders and better-organized personnel and supplies began arriving at Jamestown. The tide really

turned after 1616, when the settlers seized upon Orinoco tobacco as a cash crop. After that there was no holding back the influx of migrants determined to get rich by farming the supposedly "empty" land throughout Tidewater Virginia. The Powhatans were all but driven out of their homeland, a process merely punctuated by wars. For the Powhatans of the 1620s onward, Jamestown symbolized both the false legitimation of squatters' claims and the growing military muscle to enforce those claims.

Yet the Native people were neither wiped out nor completely pushed out. Descendants of the Powhatans live all over Virginia today, and some of them still live as tribal Indians. There are two surviving reservations, the Pamunkey and the Mattaphoni near West Point, Virginia, and several "citizen Indian" enclaves: Chickahominy, Eastern Chickahominy, Nansemond, Rappahannock, and Upper Mattaponi. Today these Powhatans bring visiting friends and relatives to see Historic Jamestowne — but they know well that there is another side to the main story being told there.

FURTHER READING: *Pocahontas, Powhatan, Opechancanough: Three Indian Lives Changed by Jamestown,* by Helen C. Rountree

Franciscan Designs for the Native People of La Florida

DAVID HURST THOMAS

❖ Unlike their European competitors along the Atlantic seaboard, the Spaniards who colonized La Florida made no pretense of separating Church and State. Institutional religion so thoroughly permeated everyday life in sixteenth-century Spain that all aspects of individual and collective life were touched by it. Spanish-Indian contact in La Florida was ruled by formal policies designed to apply Christian principles of governance and to reap economic benefits. Spanish policy was grounded in a sense of duty to change the Indians from heathen barbarians into good Christians. The southland was not settled by private individuals acting on their own. Throughout Spanish Florida, Native Americans were confronted by the priest, the soldier, and the bureaucrat, each of whom answered to a higher authority.

The Spaniards gathered the scattered Indians into new settlements where they could convert them to Catholicism, teach them European methods of cultivation, and try to raise them from the perceived primitive state to that of civilized and responsible citizens of the Spanish empire. Because colonists were in short supply, the Spanish crown used the missions to occupy, hold, and settle its frontier. Years of experience in the New World enabled the Spanish friars to perfect their techniques for converting Indians to the Catholic faith. Although Pedro Menéndez de Avilés imported the newly founded Jesuit order to Spanish Florida in 1566, that group was soon replaced by energetic Franciscans, who built some of the first churches in the present-day United States, mastered numerous Native languages, and wrote the first dictionaries based on Indian dialects. Their mission chain ultimately extended from St. Augustine to St. Catherine's Island and west to Tallahassee. The friars provided instruction in the catechism, music, reading, and writing. These churchmen influenced religious and social conduct as well as agrarian policy and determined the location of new settlements and defensive installations. As Father Francisco Pareja said, "We are the ones who are conquering and subduing the land."

Spain's intrusion into the New World was a regimented endeavor, more "conservative" than the evolving Anglo-American culture of New England. The Spanish tried to regiment everything from economy to religion, from art to architecture. "The Royal Ordinances Concerning the Laying Out of Towns," issued in 1573 by Philip II, dictated site selection, city planning, and political organization. Each new Hispanic town was to be established on vacant land or with the Indians' consent, located on an elevated site, surrounded by abundant arable land for farming and pasturage, and near fresh water, fuel, timber, and Native people (presumably for labor). Sufficient space was to be left in the original town site to allow for growth. The legacy of these Spanish principles can be seen today in Santa Fe, Los Angeles, St. Louis, and St. Augustine. The Royal Ordinances required a detailed town plan, with the principal plaza (its length 1.5 times the width) near the landing place in coastal towns and in the center of the community for inland settlements, with the church and friary fronting on the main plaza.

Hispanic documents reveal little about the associated Indian pueblos. The most important structure was the council house (or *buhio*), a massive circular building 100 feet in diameter where 300 people could sleep. The missionaries recognized the importance of the *buhios* and encouraged the Indians to build them on the mission grounds, so they would think of the mission as their "home." The Indians at these missions lived a regimented life, and the Hispanic architecture of these settlements reflects the rigid organization of space, an idealized Spanish template upon which New World forms were modeled.

FURTHER READING: "Saints and Soldiers at Santa Catalina: Hispanic Designs for Colonial America," by David Hurst Thomas, in *The Recovery of Meaning in Historical Archaeology*, edited by Mark P. Leone and Parker B. Potter, Jr.

145. Mission San Luis, FL

Bonnie G. McEwan

At the corner of Tennessee St. and Ocala Rd., Tallahassee

Visitor center

Mission San Luis, atop one of Tallahassee's highest hills, was one of the more than 100 Spanish missions founded in north Florida and coastal Georgia between 1565 and 1700. Moved to the present location in 1656, the mission served as the Spaniards' western capital and was the home of one of the most powerful Apalachee leaders. The area's fertile soils and intensive agriculture later attracted Spanish colonists to the region, which served as a breadbasket for St. Augustine. More than 1,500 Apalachees lived under the jurisdiction of the mission. By the end of the seventeenth century, several hundred Spaniards, including settlers, soldiers, and their families, lived here. Although they had converted to Catholicism, the Apalachee maintained their traditional political and social organization. They continued to use stone tools and weapons, make pottery, and play their ball game, despite the call for its abolition by some friars. On July 31, 1704, just two days before a British-instigated Creek strike force reached San Luis, the Spaniards and the Apalachees burned the settlement and left.

The Apalachee council house, the largest known historic-period Indian building in the Southeast, has been reconstructed, as has the Franciscan church, a Spanish residence, and the friary. The only documented descendants of Florida's once numerous Native peoples are the Talimali Band of Apalachee Indians, who live in the Red River area of Louisiana. As practicing Catholics, they visit the mission and have donated animal traps, tools, weapons, baskets, and beadwork for display. They have given a human face to the work of the mission, and they teach us all how to handle life's struggles with determination and dignity. In 2004, on the 300th anniversary of the end of the Mission San Luis, Chief Gilmer Bennett said, "I could stand here and tell you about all the hardships we have endured over the past 300 years. This would do no good. One day, all of us will face our maker. He said he would know us by our work. We, the Apalachee, have always tried to be people of good character, and walk with the Great Spirit to preserve our land, water, air, and nature that God trusted to us."

FURTHER READING: *The Apalachee Indians and Mission San Luis*, by John H. Hann and Bonnie G. McEwan.

146. Arkansas Post National Memorial, AR

Geary Hobson

1741 Old Post Rd., Gillett

Visitor center

The present location of Arkansas Post, on the north bank of the Arkansas River, is not the original site, although it is near the first of several former locations. Established in 1686 by Henri de Tonti, the faithful lieutenant of the French explorer La Salle, the post was built near the Quapaw village of Osotouy. During the next century the post was moved to various sites along the Arkansas River because of floodwater danger or fear of enemy British attack. Historians, anthropologists, and ethnologists often disagree about whether these same Quapaws were at this location when Hernando de Soto came though a century and a half earlier or whether they came later and totally dispossessed the Tunica people who were living there before them. My personal belief, a combination of these views, is that the Quapaws came to Arkansas in the seventeenth century and both dispossessed and assimilated the Tunicas, so that in effect everyone was Quapaw by 1686, but with a great deal of Tunican culture still retained. Like the

Quapaws and the Tunicas before them, the French — and then the Spanish and the Americans — quickly learned an unchanging law of the region: that living spaces must be relocated from time to time because of the vagaries of an ever-changing river.

Every work of Arkansas history I have ever seen, and now every Web page, too, never fails to mention that all the Quapaw were moved out of Arkansas and into Indian Territory after the third and last treaty that the tribe signed with the U.S. government in 1833. (Oklahoma Quapaw Tribal headquarters are in Quapaw, OK.) Well, I beg to differ. Down toward the end of the wordage of that last treaty are the names of eleven mixed-blood Quapaw chiefs who were granted allotments after opting to remain in the country with their families. I am descended from these folks. Whether we have been called white or Indian, French or Quapaw, Métis or Chicot at any given time, we have stayed on the land. All of us, in fairly complex ways, have retained or lost (depending on which families one looks at, and even particular individuals within these families) various degrees of our original Indianness. We are thus successfully disguised from the public as people of Indian heritage — in many cases, even from ourselves.

On occasions when personnel associated with the Arkansas Post National Memorial relate stories about the post's past, and about the Quapaw people and their role in this past, the descendants of removed Oklahoma Quapaws are often invited to take part, to represent those who were dispossessed — that is, us. Never have any of us who stayed been asked to take part. Even today, some of us "stay-behind" descendants retain knowledge of the locations of some of the old burial sites and holy places and, of course, where coons and possums and deer and catfish are to be found, and where yancopin roots can still be gathered to make the old-time national dish, which some of us Arkansas folks still eat. Even though we are left out, we haven't

forgotten that we belong to this land where the Arkansas Post National Memorial now stands.

FURTHER READING: *The Rumble of a Distant Drum,* by Morris S. Arnold

147. Natchez Trace Parkway, MS: A Glimpse of Chickasaw Nation History from the Chickasaw Village Site

Kirk Perry

Natchez Trace Parkway at milepost 261.8, northwest of Tupelo

Visitor center at milepost 266

From the Chickasaw village, where Chickasaws carried out international affairs with other tribes, with Europeans, and with Americans, the once familiar ancient trails in the homelands stretched to the Atlantic seaboard, the Gulf of Mexico, and the Ohio River Valley. Trails led southeast down the Tombigbee River to Mobile Bay, east to Charles Town, and to the Tennessee and Mississippi rivers, where the Chickasaw were perceived as barriers to European expansion by the French, the Spanish, and the English from contact in the late seventeenth century through the eighteenth century. The site includes part of the large village of Falacheco, where Chickasaws once met European traders, held talks with other tribal nations, and harbored Natchez Indian refugees to protect them from French reprisals in the 1730s. The Chickasaw built secure villages and produced food, tools, weapons, adornments, and household goods from the prairies and forests. As warm as Dutch ovens, winter houses were constructed by standing poles in the ground, weaving cane or strips of branches among them, and then covering the house with daub. There were fire pits in the earthen floors and other fires outside. The cone-shaped roofs were covered with thick layers of long grass. Summer houses were usually square or rectangular with gabled roofs and sides that could be removed. By 1740 the Chickasaw had left this village to consolidate their settlements for protection from their enemies.

Many Europeans noted that the Chickasaw were tall, that the women were beautiful, and that the men were intrepid warriors who protected their people and their homes. Early European visitors wrote that the Chickasaw form of government and social system were as logical, workable, and just as their own. The values inherent in their religious and social systems were superior in many ways to those of the ethnocentric intruders. In 1837 the United States government forcibly removed the Chickasaw from their homelands to Indian Territory. Chickasaws who return to the village site continue to retain the sense of home and connection to their forefathers. Traditional strong family ties are enabling the Chickasaw to retain their identity as a proud and unconquered nation that continues to gain strength today.

FURTHER READING: *Splendid Land, Splendid People: The Chickasaw Indians to Removal,* by James R. Atkinson

148. Osage Village State Historic Site, MO

Andrea A. Hunter

North of Rte. 54, off Rte. C, Walker

Outdoor exhibits

The Osage, Wa-zha´-zhe, are a midwestern/southern Plains tribe that at European contact was living in southwestern Missouri. They belong to the Dhegiha branch of Siouan language speakers, along with the Ponca, Kaw, Omaha, and Quapaw tribes. Since their homelands were along waterways, particularly the Missouri and the Osage rivers, the Osage were known to early explorers, including Jacques Marquette and Louis

Jolliet, who recorded them near the Missouri River on their 1673 map.

Named the Brown site by archaeologists, this historic place was the primary village of the Osage from about 1675 until 1775. After 1700 the tribe split into two factions, the Big Osage and the Little Osage. The Little Osage moved north into central Missouri to take advantage of European trading along the Missouri River. The Big Osage remained here until about 1775.

As remarked by the first Europeans who came into contact with the Osage, they were tall, striking-looking people — the men typically more than six feet — well built, handsome, and stoic in character. Because of their physical nature and prowess, the Osage were described as the most feared by the Europeans in the Louisiana Territory. The men shaved their heads except for a "roach" — a ridge on the top of the head — and wove feathers and beads into it. Both men and women had tattoos on their bodies and pierced their ears and decorated them with bones and shells. Men wore arm and wrist bracelets, deerskin breechcloths, leggings, and moccasins. Osage women wore deerskin dresses, skirts, leggings, and moccasins.

At this village, where between 2,000 and 3,000 people lived, there were about 200 longhouses and ceremonial lodges, constructed of wood frames covered with rush mats, bark, or buffalo skins. In the spring, after the women planted corn, beans, squash, and pumpkins in their fields in the floodplain, the tribe left for their summer hunt on the southern plains. They returned in August, harvested and processed their crops, then took off on their fall hunt until December. During the winter, smaller parties hunted to bring in fresh meat.

The Europeans changed life for the Osage in three major ways. After they got horses in about 1700, the Osage were able to hunt more and travel farther. As the fur trade grew, they farmed less, trapped fur-bearing animals, and increased their use of European trade goods, including rifles and metal tools. This dependence upon manufactured rather than traditional Osage utilitarian and ceremonial items was a significant change from their traditional lifeways. The Osage left behind pottery, chert projectile points, catlinite and claystone pipes, and sandstone effigy pipes from their earlier traditional life as well as knives, brass kettles, crucifixes, glass bottles, and kaolin clay pipes from the years after European contact.

At the close of the eighteenth century the Osage were viewed as an obstacle to America's great westward expansion. In 1808 William Clark negotiated a treaty with the Osage that gave the United States government all Osage lands east of a line drawn from Fort Osage on the Missouri River to the Arkansas River in Arkansas. This began the Osage movement westward. In 1825 the Osage relinquished all remaining lands in Missouri to the United States, and the tribe moved into southern Kansas. In 1872 the Osage were finally removed to a federal reservation in Oklahoma. Despite a long history of losing homelands and cultural traditions, the Osage tribe in Oklahoma is today a thriving and prosperous nation.

FURTHER READING: *A History of the Osage People,* by Louis F. Burns

149. Fort Osage National Historic Landmark, MO

On Osage St., north of Sibley

Fort Osage Education Center

After Meriwether Lewis and William Clark returned from their expedition, Clark was appointed commander of the militia and Indian agent of the Louisiana Territory. Fort Osage was built in 1808 on the Missouri River under Clark's direction to protect the U.S. Factory Trade House and to promote trade with the Osage. Although the fort was north of their core village area in southwest Missouri, the Little Osage were encouraged to live near the fort. Some Kanza (Kaw) also lived near the fort in the fall of 1808. In that year the Osage signed a treaty that began their removal from their homelands. All had apparently left the area of the fort after 1811, returning only to trade and to receive their annuities. When Congress abolished the factory system in 1822, it was the end of Fort Osage as a trade house and military garrison. After the 1825 survey of the Santa Fe Trail, distances on the trail were measured from a point about 1.5 miles south of the fort.

150. Kituhwa Mound, NC: Return to Kituhwa

Joyce Conseen Dugan

Off U.S. 19, west of Cherokee

Kituhwa is the most important mother town of the Cherokee. When I was growing up, our family would drive along the Tuckaseegee River, where we would see Kituhwa, the ancient mound and the town site, in the valley setting. The older Cherokees would tell us the meanings of this place in stories passed down from their ancestors. They also told us that the owners did not permit their ancestors — or them — to visit Kituhwa. When I was elected principal chief of the Eastern Band of Cherokee in 1995, I was determined to make a difference in all the challenges that faced our tribe. Health care, education, and housing were my priorities. When the owner of the great mound offered to sell it to the tribe, I knew that buying it was not on my list of priorities, and certainly our tribe was not in a position to spend money on anything considered noncritical. I discussed the opportunity with others in tribal government and with community members and discovered the deep meaning this place held for our people. Tribal members told stories about Kituhwa and told us that one of the names for Cherokee people means "the people of Kituhwa." Many held it in the highest regard for what it means about our past. Academics told us that people began living here about 9,000 years ago.

By the time of removal in 1838, Kituhwa and its associated towns had given up citizenship in the Cherokee Nation, which was far south of their mountains. Our ancestors began to chart their own course, knowing that Kituhwa was the political starting point in our path toward nationhood. It was here at Kituhwa that we asserted our right to exist as a nation with a central government. However, it was also during this time that our land was taken from our ancestors illegally. Kituhwa continued to be our spiritual and civic homeland, so I knew without any doubts that we must purchase it. In October 1996 we stood together at Kituhwa — with representatives of the Cherokee Nation and the United Keetowah Band of Cherokee Indians — and reclaimed it for our people, almost 200 years after our people had been locked out of it. I believe that nothing else I have accomplished in my life is as important as this. Today we remain the People of Kituhwa.

FURTHER READING: *The Cherokees*, by Joyce Dugan and B. Lynne Harlan

151. Nikwasi Mound, NC

Barbara R. Duncan

At Nikwasi Lane and Main St., Franklin

The Nikwasi Mound was the spiritual, political, and physical center of the town of Nikwasi, one of fifteen Cherokee Middle Towns along the Little Tennessee River from its headwaters to the Nantahala Mountains. The original Cherokee homeland extended over more than 140,000

square miles in eight present-day states. The mother town of Kituhwa was associated with the Middle Towns because it was on the Tuckaseegee River, a tributary of the Little Tennessee. For more than a thousand years the mound was the center of a Cherokee village, with houses, a dance ground, and fields for playing stickball and chunkey, surrounded by hundreds of acres of cornfields, gardens, and orchards. People gathered in a townhouse on top of the mound to make decisions, dance, and hold ceremonies.

In 1730 Sir Alexander Cuming, acting without any authority, called a council of more than 2,000 Cherokees at Nikwasi, where he appointed an emperor and then took a delegation of seven Cherokees to London to swear allegiance to the king of England. Nikwasi was destroyed by the English in 1761 and by the Americans in 1776, but Cherokees rebuilt it both times and lived here until the Treaty of 1819 took this area from them. A Cherokee legend tells that Nikwasi was once defended by spirit warriors who came from the mound. A nineteenth-century version added that spirit warriors appeared during the Civil War, causing U.S. forces to spare the town. In 1946 Macon County children led the fundraising drive that saved the mound, now protected by the town of Franklin, 33 miles from the Qualla Boundary, home of the Eastern Band of the Cherokee Nation.

FURTHER READING: *Cherokee Heritage Trails Guidebook*, by Barbara R. Duncan and Brett H. Riggs

152. Oconaluftee Indian Village, NC: The Eastern Band of Cherokee Indians

B. Lynne Harlan and Tom Hatley

U.S. 441 N, in Qualla Boundary

The Oconaluftee Indian Village lies tightly against a deeply forested hillside across the narrow valley of the river from which it takes its name. At the living-history village, a replica of an eighteenth-century town, craftspeople still make the traditional Cherokee river-cane double-weave baskets and coil-built open-fired pottery. Many of the traditions — in politics as well as crafts and foodways (beanbread and wild greens) — are flourishing against the odds, like the Eastern Cherokee themselves.

The Qualla Boundary, as the reservation is named, adjoins the Great Smoky Mountains National Park. Here in the most important temperate forest reserve in the world, the ancestral landscape of the Cherokee remains a hot spot of diversity shaped by millennia of human residence. During the colonial period, a mountain river was known as a "long person" to the Cherokee. These rivers became the key to controlling the western lands. As a result, alliances with the Cherokee were grand prizes in the geopolitical struggle. The rivers brought trade, conflict, and new opportunities to the Cherokee people. The rich alluvial soil was the agricultural and economic engine. Agriculture was a source of power for Cherokee women, whose sway in diplomacy was troublesome to the imperial "fathers." Diplomacy was complicated by the subtle differences in the interests, dialects, and economies among and within the three Cherokee regions: the Lower Towns (today's upstate South Carolina), the Middle and Valley Towns (central Appalachia), and the Overhill Towns (along the Tennessee River). Each claimed its own mother towns, and each of the towns figured into life, politics, and religion in different ways; some, such as Kituhwa, were more important than others.

Intertribal alliances with the Ohio tribes and with the Creek to the south strengthened Indian resistance during the Cherokee War of 1759–1761, the most important episode of the Seven Years' War in the South. The war was a standoff, with Cherokee victories, as at Fort Loudoun,

and defeats, including the burning of Nikwasi in 1761. Three scorched-earth military campaigns in 1776 and the burning again of Nikwasi were preemptive strikes against the tribe, changing the course of the American Revolution in the South and changing the internal politics of the Cherokee Nation. After 1776 a faction of Cherokees moved south from the old Overhill settlements, constituted themselves as the Chickamauga Towns, and began two decades of warfare with settlers and then with the states for control of the southern Great Valley. The American victory altered the balance of power and changed the lives of the Cherokee, forcing them into either armed resistance or principled peacemaking with an unprincipled partner.

The few families who remained behind when the Cherokee Nation was forced west in 1838 asserted a new political strategy aimed at maintaining their land and nationhood. These "Oconaluftee Citizen Indians," the nucleus of the new Eastern Band of Cherokee Indians, had received reserves or land claims under earlier (1817 and 1819) treaties. However, most of these properties were appropriated by white farmers before Cherokees could take possession of them. Nearly all such "reserves" or land claims were arranged to encompass culturally important or sacred places, such as Kituhwa. After removal, community leaders began to buy their land back, working through white agents such as William Holland Thomas or prominent, sometimes bicultural, families. However, no step toward autonomy was taken without resistance. Rights of citizenship were denied by North Carolina officials, and the Cherokee remained disenfranchised and unable to vote in state elections until 1946, when returning World War II veterans demanded recognition. Like other tribes, the Eastern Band faces ongoing challenges to land ownership and self-governance. These have been made more difficult through the years by the isolation they shared with their neighbors in the southern Appalachians. Only recently has the Eastern Band asserted its sovereignty and had it acknowledged.

The chief and council-led government, the Harrah's casino operated by the tribe, and the downtown revitalization demonstrate the Cherokee will to preserve their sovereignty and their cultural heritage. Traditional values, such as working together cooperatively, as in *gadugi*, or free labor groups, continue, as do craft and farming traditions. The people speak Cherokee, and infants are learning it in a language-immersion nursery. The Eastern Band, one of the world's smallest nations, continues to defy the odds.

FURTHER READING: *The Eastern Band of Cherokees, 1819–1900*, by John R. Finger

153. Great Smoky Mountains National Park, NC: Oconaluftee River Trail

Trail from Oconaluftee Visitor Center on U.S. 441 or the Qualla Boundary

Along the 1.5-mile trail between the Oconaluftee Visitor Center and the Qualla Boundary, there are wayside exhibits with artwork by contemporary Cherokee artists and quotations in English and in the Cherokee syllabary about the Cherokees' spiritual relationship with this place. The signs link features of nature — such as buzzards, trees, mountains, and the river — to Cherokee stories and traditions. The spirit of the exhibits is reflected in the words of the Cherokee elder Jerry Wolfe: "The Great Smoky Mountains are a sanctuary for the Cherokee people. We have always believed the mountains and streams provide all that we need for survival. We hold these mountains sacred, believing that the Cherokee were chosen to take care of the mountains as the mountains take care of us."

154. Unicoi Turnpike Trail, GA, NC, and TN: Nunna'hi-tsune'ga

Brett H. Riggs

From Taccoa, GA, through NC, to Vonore, TN

Wayside exhibits in Hanging Dog Recreation Area at Grape Creek, NC, and at Unicoi Gap at the NC/TN line

An ancient trade route, once known as the Tellico or Quanasee Path, spans the southern Appalachian Mountains from southeast to northwest, linking the upper Savannah River basin to the lower Little Tennessee River basin. For thousands of years, Native travelers followed this path between the Cherokee Lower Towns in modern Georgia and South Carolina and the Overhill settlements of the Tennessee Valley, where it connected with the Great Warriors' Path at Tellico. During the eighteenth century, British colonial traders, soldiers, and diplomats plied the trail in their dealings with the Cherokee Nation. In the heyday of the deerskin trade (about 1710–1759), merchants drove long trains of packhorses along the path, hauling tons of trade goods to Cherokee towns, then returning to Charleston with tens of thousands of deer hides. With the outbreak of the American Revolution in 1775, opposing Cherokee war parties and American militia launched raids and counterraids over the trail between South Carolina and Tennessee.

In 1813 a group of American and Cherokee entrepreneurs formed the Unicoi (from the Cherokee word *unega*, or white) Turnpike Company to develop the first commercial road across the southern mountains. They chose the route of the old Tellico Path through the Cherokee Nation, and for the next three years workers wielded axes, shovels, and picks to widen the ancient trail from Taccoa through Clarkesville and Helen in today's Georgia, then into North Carolina through Hayesville and Murphy, and into

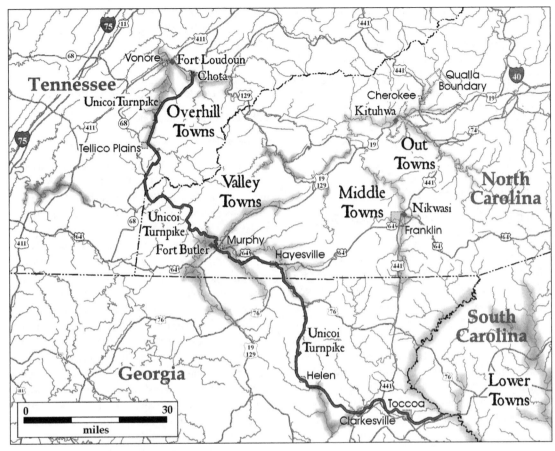

The Unicoi Turnpike, mid-eighteenth-century Cherokee settlement areas (shaded), and several present-day towns

Tennessee through Tellico Plains, ending in Vonore. In 1816 the Unicoi Turnpike opened up a lucrative trade between the burgeoning markets of South Carolina and Georgia and the frontier producers of the Tennessee Valley. The turnpike bustled with heavily loaded freight wagons rolling westward against a tide of livestock driven to eastern markets.

Despite such brisk traffic, the turnpike company neglected the road, and by 1830 the turnpike had fallen into disrepair and disuse. The U.S. Army took over road maintenance in 1836, repairing the turnpike for use in the tragic Cherokee removal of 1838. In June and July 1838, more than 3,000 Cherokee prisoners traveled along the Unicoi Turnpike from Fort Butler, North Carolina, in their westward exodus along the Trail of Tears. Afterward the turnpike funneled Anglo-American settlers into the old Cherokee Nation, and it remained an important route through the southern mountains until the early twentieth century. In 1999 the Millennium Trails Program designated a 68-mile section of the Unicoi Turnpike as a National Millennium Flagship Trail. Much of this segment runs through U.S. Forest Service lands and is accessible to the public.

FURTHER READING: *Cherokee Heritage Trails Guidebook*, by Barbara R. Duncan and Brett H. Riggs

155. Chota Memorial, TN

Off Rte. 360 on County Rd. 455 to Bacon Ferry Rd., south of Vonore

The Overhill Town of Chota was a Cherokee capital and the beloved town of refuge where no blood could be shed. In 1780, during the Revolutionary War, the Virginia militia destroyed the town, and by 1823 settlers had driven out the last of the Cherokee families. Most of the town was flooded over when Tellico Lake was created, except for the area of the townhouse now commemorated by the memorial. The memorial to the Overhill Town of Tenasi, which was covered by the lake, is nearby.

156. Ninety Six National Historic Site, SC

On Rte. 248, south of Ninety Six

Visitor center

The multicultural community that grew up here had a flour mill and a trading post where Cherokees bartered deerskins, horses, and medicinal herbs for bolts of cloth, agricultural tools, guns, and ammunition. The traders gave it the unusual name perhaps because they thought it was ninety-six miles to the Cherokee village of Keowee, in the South Carolina foothills. As more settlers encroached on the Cherokee homeland, violence increased. In 1759 the governor of South Carolina ordered a fort to be built around the trading post to protect the settlers. The Cherokee attacked it twice in 1760 during the Cherokee War.

157. Fort Loudoun State Historic Area, TN

338 Fort Loudoun Rd., Vonore

Visitor center

The expansion of English colonies increased competition between the French and the English, and in 1757 the British built Fort Loudoun to protect their southern colonies from French attacks. In the summer of 1760 Cherokees put the fort under siege. On August 9 Captain Paul Demeré surrendered the garrison in return for safe passage to Fort Prince George in the Lower Towns (in present-day South Carolina) but broke the terms of surrender by destroying guns, ammunition, and cannon when he left. The next day the Cherokee attacked and killed about 20 British soldiers in retaliation for the same number of Cherokees who had been held hostage and killed by the British at Fort Prince George earlier. They killed Demeré and took about 200 captives. The historic area includes reconstructions of the fort and a Cherokee winter house. Across the lake is the Tellico Blockhouse, where troops were stationed between 1794 and 1807 to protect the Cherokee from white encroachment and attacks and to encourage the Cherokee to become more like white farmers. The Cherokee expanded their crops to include cotton, which they sold to the agents at the blockhouse. In the Tellico Treaty of 1798 the Cherokee lost their lands from above the Little Tennessee River to the Clinch River; in the 1805 treaty they lost all of their lands in today's Middle Tennessee. The Sequoyah Birthplace Museum is nearby.

158. Natchez Trace Parkway, MS: Choctaw Agency

Phillip Martin

Natchez Trace Parkway at milepost 100.7, Ridgeland

The second Choctaw Agency, which was active between about 1810 and 1823, was the office and residence of the Choctaw agents Silas Dinsmoor and John McKee, the U.S. government's representatives to the Choctaw Nation. The agency distributed annual treaty payments, negotiated treaties (although no treaties were signed at this site), and conducted "civilization" activities, including educating tribal members in spinning, weaving, "modern" farming, carpentry, and blacksmithing. This was the Western District of the Choctaw Nation (and therefore not within the United States) along the Natchez Trace, the principal land route between Nashville and Natchez and the gateway to the southwestern frontier of the United States.

The years during which the Choctaw Agency operated were very significant for the Choctaw. Before this period they had been able to remain relatively isolated from outside influences, but in the decade after 1810 their traditional life was forced to give way to the American intrusion into the Choctaw Nation. Despite major pressure from the United States in that decade, it was not until 1820 that the Treaty of Doak's Stand forced the Choctaw to cede half of their remaining traditional lands — most of central Mississippi — to the United States. In 1823 the U.S. government moved the agency about 100 miles to the northeast. Then it was just a matter of time before the land-hungry United States forced the Choctaw to cede the remainder of their lands — one-fourth of Mississippi. In the 1830 Dancing Rabbit Creek Treaty, three-fourths of the Choctaw were removed in the first Indian removal to Indian Territory; there they became the Choctaw Nation. The descendants of the Choctaw who remained in Mississippi are now the Mississippi Band of Choctaw Indians, a 9,300-member tribe living on reservation lands in the vicinity of Philadelphia. The Jena Band of Choctaw Indians are the descendants of Choctaws who remained in Mississippi at the time of removal but moved into Louisiana in the late nineteenth century.

FURTHER READING: *The Choctaw Before Removal,* by Carolyn Keller Reeves

159. Horseshoe Bend National Military Park, AL

Robert W. Blythe

On Rte. 49, north of Dadeville

Visitor center

The Battle of Horseshoe Bend was the climax of the Creek War of 1813–1814, which ended Creek military power in the Southeast. Although white Americans decided the outcome, the Creek War is best understood as a civil war within the Creek Confederacy, a loose coalition of tribal towns. The Upper Towns were along the Coosa, Tallapoosa, and Alabama rivers in present-day Alabama. The Lower Towns were along the Chattahoochee in Alabama and Georgia and along the Flint River in Georgia. By the early 1800s many Creeks, especially in the Lower Towns, had established family farms and adopted aspects of Anglo-American culture.

Increasing white settlement, the pressure to assimilate, and debts to traders put great stress on the Creek. In the fall of 1811 the Shawnee leader Tecumseh visited the Upper Creeks and urged them to unite with the Shawnee to revive Indian traditions and resist white inroads. A strong resistance movement, with roots in Creek spiritual beliefs and the desire to retain Creek cultural practices and lands, swept the Upper Towns. Whites called these Creeks Red Sticks. Although far stronger in the Upper Towns, the

Red Sticks had some supporters in the Lower Towns. When a band of Red Sticks killed the civilian and military inhabitants of Fort Mims on the lower Alabama River on August 30, 1813, massive retaliation by the United States was a certainty.

State militia, U.S. Army regulars, Cherokees, Choctaws, and their Creek allies soon invaded the Creek heartland. About 1,000 Red Stick warriors and 400 women and children built a fortified village, Tohopeka, at a horseshoe-shaped bend in the Tallapoosa River. The war chief, Menawa, directed the building of a strong timber breastwork across the neck of land formed by the river bend. The Red Sticks believed that with the river protecting them on three sides and the fortifications on the fourth, they could hold off any assault. Some believed their shamans could call on supernatural protection against bullets. Commanded by General Andrew Jackson, 2,000 whites and Indians attacked Tohopeka on March 27, 1814. Less than one-third of the Red Sticks had firearms, and they were no match for Jackson's larger force. Between 800 and 900 Red Stick warriors died, and 350 women and children were taken captive. Jackson's army suffered 200 casualties. Organized Red Stick resistance collapsed, with devastating effects on Creek society.

FURTHER READING: *Sacred Revolt: The Muskogees' Struggle for a New World*, by Joel W. Martin

160. Fort Toulouse/Fort Jackson Park, AL

2521 W. Fort Toulouse Rd., Wetumpka

Visitor center

The Mississippian people who once lived in the area of the confluence of the Coosa and the Tallapoosa rivers built mounds, one of which remains on a bank of the Coosa. The French built their first fort in 1717 and a second between 1749 and 1751. They abandoned it after the 1763 Treaty of Paris, which ended the Seven Years' War. Parts of this fort and of Fort Jackson, built by the United States after the battle of Horseshoe Bend, are replicated in the park.

On August 9, 1814, General Andrew Jackson forced the Creek to sign the Treaty of Fort Jackson, which required them to cede more than 20 million acres of their homelands, including about two-thirds of the Upper Creek lands and about one-third of the lands of the Lower Creeks, many of whom had fought with Jackson. As Edmunds, Hoxie, and Salisbury wrote in *The People: A History of Native America,* "The treaty provided a portent of things to come. Not even Indian people who befriended the Americans would be immune from their land hunger. Tribes could not rely on the goodwill of the government. The future would be full of empty promises."

161. New Echota Historic Site, GA: Early Cherokee Nationalism in the Nineteenth Century

Julia Coates

1211 Chatsworth Hwy. NE, Calhoun

Visitor center

As Americans continued to encroach on Cherokee lands and as U.S. government demands for additional cessions of Cherokee land persisted into the early 1800s, a generation of leaders emerged among the Cherokee who were convinced that the only way to counter the increasing power arrayed against them was to assert their own nationality as strongly as possible. Although they later had serious differences in their beliefs about how the Cherokee Nation could best be preserved, John Ross and Major Ridge were among the strongest early nationalists on the Cherokee Council. For several decades, the two worked tirelessly to enact their shared vision. New Echota represented the Cherokees' hopes and efforts toward nation building.

After 1800 the Cherokee National Council met annually at Ustenali. By the 1820s they had made it their national capital and named it New Echota, after the old town of Chota, which had for centuries been their religious center and, after the 1750s, their political center until they abandoned it in the late 1780s. New Echota reminded the Cherokee of their long, continuous tradition of self-government. The Council House, the bilingual *Cherokee Phoenix* — the first Indian newspaper — and the Cherokee Supreme Court were in New Echota. By means of these institutions, the Cherokee sought to defend their land and their sovereignty through legislation, public opinion, and the courts. In 1827 they adopted their first constitution, and on the recommendation of Major Ridge, the council selected John Ross to be the principal chief. After Andrew Jackson was elected president in 1828, the Cherokee Nation was under increasing pressure to cede its last lands and remove to the west. Georgia passed legislation to terrorize the Cherokees out of their homes in northern Georgia and to prohibit their government from functioning within the state. In 1829, under threat of violence from the Georgia Guard, a state-supported vigilante organization, the Cherokee National Council was forced to move its meeting place, ultimately settling on Red Clay, Tennessee. Only the newspaper continued to function in New Echota.

In 1832 the U.S. Supreme Court upheld the Cherokees' sovereignty within their own territories, but President Jackson did not enforce the Court's ruling. Major Ridge, his son John Ridge, and Elias Boudinot, the editor of the newspaper, decided that the only way to preserve their nation and the people was to remove to the Indian Territory. John Ross continued to work to keep the Cherokee Nation in its homelands, which was the desire of the majority of the Cherokee people. By the early 1830s, divisions deepened among the Cherokee leaders as the debate about how to save their nation grew more heated. In

December 1835 the Cherokees who believed that removal was their best hope signed the Treaty of New Echota, in which they ceded the remainder of Cherokee lands and agreed to remove to the Indian Territory. Their action was clearly illegal under Cherokee law, as the signers, including Major Ridge and Elias Boudinot, knew. Many Cherokee regarded the Ridges and Boudinot as traitors, and they were killed by Cherokees after they arrived in the Indian Territory.

New Echota symbolizes many things to the Cherokee people. Although it was the site of an illegal treaty, for Cherokees today New Echota represents the culmination of two decades of efforts by the leadership to forge a nation. It represents Cherokee commitment and conviction on all sides of a critical debate and, ultimately, the wisdom of ancestors who ensured — by their actions during one of the most devastating times the Cherokee have ever known — that the Cherokee Nation and the people would continue to flourish into the twenty-first century. Today many of the original buildings at New Echota have been reconstructed, including the Council House and the Supreme Court building, Samuel Worcester's mission station, and James Vann's tavern.

FURTHER READING: *The Cherokee Removal: A Brief History with Documents,* by Theda Perdue and Michael D. Green

162. Chieftains Museum/Major Ridge Home, GA

Carey L. Tilley

501 Riverside Parkway NE, Rome

The Cherokee man known as The Ridge (1770–1839) was one of the leaders of the Cherokee nationalist movement that emerged in the first three decades of the nineteenth century. He received the name and rank of major while fighting as an American ally in the Creek uprising of 1813. As speaker of the National Council during the 1810s and 1820s, Ridge was instrumental in the codification of laws that culminated in the first Cherokee Constitution. Initially, Ridge strongly supported the Cherokee government led by Principal Chief John Ross in resisting the federal Indian Removal Bill and attempts by the state of Georgia to extend its laws over Cherokee land. When both the state and President Andrew Jackson ignored a Supreme Court ruling that Georgia's actions were illegal, Ridge shifted his lifelong opposition to land cession and became the leader of a minority faction of Cherokees who believed that a treaty should be made with the U.S. government in order to preserve the Cherokee Nation. On December 29, 1835, Ridge led his party in signing the Treaty of New Echota, which ceded the land of the Cherokee Nation in exchange for $5 million and a guarantee of land in the Indian Territory. Although the treaty was never supported by Chief Ross or the majority of the Cherokee people, the U.S. government ratified it in May 1836. The Cherokee were given two years to leave their homeland. In 1837 Ridge left his plantation, ferry operation, and trading post, which are collectively known today as the Chieftains Museum/Major Ridge Home. The following year most Cherokees were forced to move to the Indian Territory, where on June 22, 1839, Major Ridge, his son John, and his nephew Elias Boudinot were killed by Cherokee opponents of removal.

FURTHER READING: *Cherokee Tragedy: The Ridge Family and the Decimation of a People,* by Thurman Wilkins

163. Chief Vann House Historic Site, GA

82 State Rte. 225 N, Chatsworth

Visitor center

James Vann was the son of Wahli, a Cherokee woman, and a Scottish trader named Vann. He was a slave owner and became so successful in varied businesses that he was one of the richest men in the South. He supported the establishment of the Springplace Moravian Mission, primarily because of his interest in educating Cherokee children. He built a brick mansion on his plantation in 1804. Toward the end of his life, he drank excessively and became increasingly violent. In 1809 he was shot and killed at a local tavern. His son Joseph, "Rich Joe," who inherited the house, was forced out in 1835 during the removal of the Cherokees to Indian Territory.

164. Sequoyah's Cabin, OK: Monument to the Cherokee Genius

Dan Agent

On Rte. 101, northeast of Sallisaw

Ten miles from where I was born in Sallisaw in the house of Annie Fargo Agent, my Cherokee/Choctaw grandmother, and Henry Clay Agent, my grandfather, is the log cabin of the Cherokee genius, Sequoyah. He built his home in 1829 and lived there until 1842. He was born more than 800 miles away in Tuskegee or Tiskigi, near Vonore, Tennessee, about 1778. The Sequoyah Birthplace Museum there and the cabin in Oklahoma are monuments that celebrate the only person who conceived an alphabet and a written language for a people.

Before the Trail of Tears, the illegal forced march in 1838–1839 of the Cherokees from their homeland, Sequoyah began his trek west. He lived in Willston, Alabama, from 1819 to 1824. He demonstrated the efficacy and simplicity of the eighty-six-character syllabary in 1821 and gave the Cherokee people a written language, which enabled nearly every citizen to read and write within a few months. From 1824 to 1829 he lived on a reservation for the Western Cherokee in western Arkansas. On February 21, 1828, news stories written in both the syllabary and

English were printed at New Echota, Cherokee Nation (now Georgia), in the first Native American newspaper and first bilingual publication in the Western Hemisphere, the *Cherokee Phoenix*.

Sequoyah's home in the Indian Territory was not his final resting place. He traveled south of the Rio Grande into Mexico in search of some of the many Cherokees who had dispersed south and west of the Indian Territory before, during, and after the Trail of Tears. Sequoyah set out to find them and bring them home to the Cherokee Nation. It is said that he died in a cave in Mexico, but his remains have never been recovered. Outside the cabin is a statue by Fred Olds of Sequoyah. It depicts him holding his ever-present calumet and his syllabary as he tilts his head at an angle, perhaps listening to the birds or the insects or the shifting winds of the Oklahoma evening playing with the leaves of the trees. It is easy to imagine that while he is listening, he hears through the cacophony the sounds of Cherokee children speaking, reading, and singing in the language that lives because one Cherokee man had a dream and persevered through all obstacles to fulfill it.

Relocated from his homeland and laboring for years to complete the syllabary, only to have it destroyed, then recreating it again from memory, Sequoyah exemplifies what Chad Smith, the first Cherokee Nation principal chief of the twenty-first century, says is a legacy of the Cherokee people: "The Cherokee people face adversity, survive, adapt, prosper, and excel."

FURTHER READING: *Sequoyah: The Cherokee Genius,* by Stan Hoig

165. Red Clay State Historic Park, TN

1140 Red Clay Park Rd., south of Cleveland

James F. Corn Interpretive Center

After they moved their government from New Echota in 1829, the Cherokees went to Red Clay,

Tennessee, where they held eleven general councils until they were forced along the Trail of Tears. The park includes reproductions of a council building and a Cherokee farmhouse.

166. Audubon Acres, TN

Off Gunbarrel Rd. at 900 N. Sanctuary Rd., Chattanooga

Visitor center

This is the site of a Mississippian village, called Little Owl Village, and the extensively remodeled Spring Frog cabin, which may have been the home of Cherokee settlers.

Trail of Tears National Historic Trail: The Forced Removal of the Cherokee

DUANE KING

The value of the Trail of Tears, is to teach and remind us of the lessons of history . . . that will prevent such travesty of justice, sham of public policy, disdain for human dignity and political integrity as was inflicted upon the Cherokee during the forced removal.

— Chad "Corntassel" Smith, principal chief of the Cherokee Nation, June 29, 2005

❖ In 1838–1839 the United States government removed more than 15,000 Cherokee from their ancestral homeland in the southern Appalachians and forced them to travel in adverse conditions for more than 1,000 miles to the Indian Territory, now Oklahoma. The arduous journey over several different routes is known as the Trail of Tears. The government's case for removal had been debated in Congress and in the public media for decades. On December 29, 1835, representatives of the U.S. government, unable to conclude an agreement with the duly authorized leaders of the Cherokee Nation, signed a treaty with a minority faction willing to cede the last remaining portion of the original Cherokee homeland. Despite the protests of the overwhelming majority of the Cherokee people, the United States Senate ratified the fraudulent Treaty of New Echota on May 23, 1836. By the deadline in 1838 only 2,000 Cherokees had voluntarily emigrated.

To force the Cherokee west, the government ordered Brigadier General Winfield Scott, in command of about 7,000 federal and state troops, to the Cherokee Nation in May 1838. On May 25 two regiments of Georgia militia captured more than 3,600 Cherokees and sent them to Ross's Landing at Chattanooga. On June 6 Lieutenant Edward Deas left with 489 Cherokees, and on June 12 Lieutenant R.H.K. Whiteley followed with 776 people. They traveled the 60 miles between Decatur and Tuscumbia, Alabama, by rail to avoid the treacherous shoals in the Tennessee River. On June 17 Captain Gus Drane left Ross's Landing with 1,072 people, who were forced on an overland trek of more than 200 miles to Waterloo, Alabama. By the end of June a dozen emigrants were dead and 293 had escaped to make their way back to the concentration camps in east Tennessee. These Cherokees began their journey again later in the year with other detachments. When the steamboats carrying the Whiteley and Drane detachments were stranded by low water in the Arkansas River downstream from Lewisburg (today's Morrilton), Arkansas, the people were forced to travel overland through western Arkansas in the dry, dusty heat of summer. By August 2, when they arrived at the head of Lee's Creek in the Flint District, 72 people had died on the 1,554-mile journey. When the Drane detachment disbanded on September 5 at

Mrs. Webber's farm at present-day Stilwell, only 635 Cherokees were still with the detachment; 146 people had died.

While the government was forcing these Cherokees west, soldiers drove thousands of other Cherokee families from their homes into thirty-one stockades and military stations scattered throughout the Cherokee Nation in southeast Tennessee, western North Carolina, northwest Georgia, and northeast Alabama. From the stockades, the prisoners were sent to the principal emigrating depots near Ross's Landing, at Fort Cass near Calhoun, Tennessee, and near Fort Payne, Alabama. After receiving reports of the suffering along the routes, General Scott delayed the removal until the fall and transferred supervision of the removal to the Cherokee principal chief, John Ross. Most citizens of the Cherokee Nation spent the summer of 1838 in concentration camps in Tennessee and Alabama, where they were organized for the journey west into thirteen detachments of about 1,000 people each.

The Bell detachment, with about 660 Treaty Party members, was the fourth and last detachment to travel with a military conductor. The people left the Cherokee Agency near Calhoun on October 11 and traveled through Chattanooga, Memphis, and Little Rock. The group disbanded at Vineyard Post Office (today's Evansville, Arkansas) on January 7, 1839, having traveled the shortest distance of any detachment, 707 miles. The remaining thirteen detachments, supervised by John Ross, had Cherokee conductors. Twelve went overland, and one, which included the aged and the incapacitated, went by boat. Eleven detachments went via Nashville, Golconda, and Springfield. One, led by John Benge, traveled 778 miles. The people crossed the Tennessee River at Gunter's Landing and at Reynoldsburg, Tennessee. They ferried across the Mississippi at the Iron Banks in Kentucky, moved down the military road into Arkansas, up the

White River to Fayetteville, and along the Cane Hill Road to the Indian Territory. All of the detachments suffered from the severe winter. They arrived in the Indian Territory between January and March 1839, and most disbanded at one of the depots established to provide rations during the first year in the territory. The primary depot was at Mrs. Webber's farm. Others were at Woodhall's near Westville, at Beattie's Prairie near New Fort Wayne, and near the Illinois River in Tahlequah.

The removal of the Cherokee is a story of hardship and loss — and also of resiliency and survival. In the Indian Territory, the Cherokee rebuilt their homes and their lives. Today the Cherokee Nation, centered in fourteen counties of northeastern Oklahoma with its capital at Tahlequah, is thriving and looking toward the future but always mindful of the past.

FURTHER READING: *The Cherokee Trail of Tears,* by Duane King

167. Trail of Tears Commemorative Park, KY

U.S. 41 and Skyline Dr., Hopkinsville

Heritage center

The Cherokee camped here on the Trail of Tears in 1838 and 1839. Two Cherokee chiefs who died during their forced removal, Fly Smith and Whitepath, are buried here.

168. Mantle Rock Preserve, KY

On Rte. 133, west of Joy

A segment of the Trail of Tears runs through the preserve toward the Ohio River. The Cherokees forced along this route camped under Mantle Rock, a sandstone arch about 188 feet long and 30 feet high. Nearby, along the river, is the site of

a village where people lived between about A.D. 800 and 900.

169. Trail of Tears State Park, MO

Off Rte. 177 on Moccasin Springs Rd., Jackson

Visitor center

This is the site of Green's Ferry, where Cherokees crossed the Mississippi River in the winter of 1838–39. About two miles of the historic Green's Ferry (now Moccasin Springs) Road in the park was on the Trail of Tears.

170. Riverfront Park, AR

Willow St. entrance south of Riverfront Dr., North Little Rock

Cherokee, Choctaw, Creek, Seminole, and Chickasaw camped here as they moved west during their forced removal. Each tribe has a wayside exhibit in the park.

171. Cadron Settlement Park, AR

On Rte. 319 off Rte. 64, west of Conway

Many Cherokees died of disease in camps along the Arkansas River in 1834 while moving west before the forced removal along the Trail of Tears. This place was on the land and water routes of all five tribes during removal.

172. Lake Dardanelle State Park, AR

Off Rte. 326, west of Russellville

Visitor center

The Arkansas River was a water route on the Trail of Tears.

173. Village Creek State Park, AR

On Rte. 284, southeast of Wynne

The old Memphis–Little Rock road was one route of the Trail of Tears through Arkansas. A deeply worn segment of the road is in the park.

174. Fort Smith National Historic Site, AR: The Fort Smith Council, 1865

Daniel F. Littlefield, Jr.

Off Garland Ave., Fort Smith

Visitor center

From its establishment in 1817 until the end of the Civil War, Fort Smith played important roles in the Indian affairs of the old Southwest: keeping peace between the Osage and the newly arrived Cherokee until 1824 and serving as a rations depot for the Choctaw and the Chickasaw during removal in the 1830s. Without question, however, the most significant single event in Fort Smith's long history related to Indian affairs was the Fort Smith Council of 1865. At the end of the Civil War, the U.S. government used the fact that Indian tribes had made alliances with the Confederacy to obtain major concessions from the tribes of the Indian Territory. The council, held on September 8–21, included government agents and Osages, Quapaws, Senecas, Shawnees, Wyandots, Cherokees, Creeks, Choctaws, Chickasaws, and Seminoles.

Because factions of the tribes had supported the South, they had, according to the government, abrogated existing treaties. To reestablish relations, new treaties had to be drawn up containing certain costly provisions: the abolition of slavery and adoption of their former slaves, now freedmen, as citizens of the tribal nations; land cessions for the settlement of other tribes; and organization of the tribes under a territorial government. The parties reached no agreements at Fort Smith, but the council laid the groundwork for the treaties negotiated in Washington in 1866.

Although the 1866 treaties contained a number of provisions destructive to the tribes, those that the United States had demanded at Fort Smith ensured the destruction of the Indian Territory. With a standing army occupying the region and radical Republicans controlling Congress, the tribes had no recourse. The U.S. government forced the tribes to accept the provision to adopt the freedmen as tribal citizens, which greatly compromised the tribes' claims to sovereignty and gave the United States the authority to determine tribal membership. The tribes ceded approximately the western half of the Indian Territory, allowing the government to continue its disastrous removal policy with other tribes until the 1880s. The U.S. government's failure to locate any removed tribe on a large area in the center of the Indian Territory led to the establishment of the Oklahoma Territory in 1890, followed by a clamor for allotting land to tribes in the western part of the territory and opening unallotted lands to American settlement. The tribes tried but failed to establish a territorial government under the Okmulgee Constitution, and bills to impose U.S. territorial status were floated in every Congress until it established the Dawes Commission in 1893 to dismantle the tribes and prepare them for eventual statehood. The chain of events set in motion by the Fort Smith Council of 1865 laid the groundwork for the Dawes era, perhaps the darkest period in the tribes' histories.

FURTHER READING: *Fort Smith: Little Gibraltar on the Arkansas,* by Edwin C. Bearss and Arrell M. Gibson

175. Cherokee National Capitol, Cherokee National Supreme Court Building, and Cherokee National Prison, OK

Chad Smith

Tahlequah

Within the Cherokee Nation three historic landmarks are testaments to the will and perseverance of the Cherokee people: the Cherokee National Capitol, the Cherokee National Supreme Court Building, and the Cherokee National Prison. All were erected during the years that the Cherokee Nation held title to its lands. All three buildings stand within one block of one another in what has been called the Cherokee Square. The square not only symbolizes the Cherokee constitutional government during the years from 1839 — when the new constitution was adopted — until 1907, it is also the icon of its reemergence, which began in 1970.

While there are older buildings in northeastern Oklahoma (the 1844 Cherokee National Supreme Court Building is the oldest public building in Oklahoma), none holds the same degree of importance, both socially and philosophically, as the Cherokee National Capitol. The 1867 capitol was erected on the site of the first one, a log cabin burned during the Civil War by General Stand Watie's troops. Ironically, a monument to General Watie stands on the capitol grounds, recognizing him as the only full-blooded Indian brigadier general in the Confederate Army and the last general to surrender. The capitol served as the political center of the Cherokee Nation, where the chief delivered the state-of-the-nation address and where the Cherokee Nation, as a government, carried out its renascence by building roads and bridges and establishing an educational system that rivaled and surpassed others in the United States. The capitol housed the executive branch, the National Senate and Council, the Supreme Court, and the superintendent of schools.

In 1898, following federal orders to cease operations, the capitol and the courts of the Cherokee Nation shut down. Allotment was forced upon the Cherokees, and in 1907 the state of Oklahoma came into existence, a state that owed much of its foundation to the Cherokee and other American Indian tribes. With the establishment of the state, the Cherokee Nation's operations were severely restricted by the United States. The Cherokee National Capitol, the Cherokee National Supreme Court Building, and the Cherokee National Prison were sold to Cherokee County in 1914, and the capitol became the Cherokee County Courthouse. This, however, did not mark the tragic end of the capitol as an emblem of what had been the Cherokee Nation.

Following a resurgence of tribal sovereignty, the Cherokees eventually reformed their nation and in 1971 had their first election since William C. Rogers was elected chief in 1903. W. W. Keeler was elected principal chief, and the Cherokee Nation as a government reemerged. In 1979 the capitol, the Supreme Court Building, and the prison were returned to the Cherokee Nation. After renovations, the capitol was rededicated in 1991, signifying the ongoing rebirth of the Cherokee Nation. The capitol, now also known as the Cherokee Nation Courthouse, houses the judicial branch, which hears criminal and civil cases. During the annual Cherokee National Holiday on Labor Day weekend, the principal chief gives the state-of-the-nation address at the capitol to more than 1,000 Cherokee people in a scene reminiscent of the glory days of the Cherokee Nation. In 2003 the Cherokee National Capitol, the Cherokee National Supreme Court Building, and the Cherokee National Prison were placed in trust by the federal government.

FURTHER READING: *The Cherokee Nation: A History,* by Robert J. Conley

176. Osage Tribal Museum, OK

Jim Gray

Grandview Ave., Pawhuska

The Osage Nation's museum, library, and archives, established in 1938, are the repositories for the major collections of Osage artifacts and photographs that tell about the Nation's culture and lifeways. The building, constructed in 1872 in the Indian Territory community that became Pawhuska, was a two-story school, dormitory, and chapel with a distinguishing cupola. In major renovations in 1937–38, 1967, 1987, and 1994, it became a one-story building with space for displays about contemporary life and a gift shop with an extensive inventory of merchandise, resources, and crafts. The museum is a focal point on the Osage Nation campus, which includes tribal government buildings, tribal senior citizen housing, and BIA and IHS facilities.

Our ancestors moved from Kansas to the new reservation in 1871–1872, ending an era of land cessions to the United States that had begun in 1804–1806. They had ceded most of today's Missouri, Arkansas, Oklahoma, and Kansas and received in return one-fifth of a penny per acre for the approximately 80 million acres. In 1803 the Osage population was estimated to be about 10,000. When the Osage reservation was allotted in 1906, there were only about 990 full-blooded members of the Nation and about 1,200 of mixed blood. The tragic loss in population was the result mainly of disease and infant mortality. The decrease in population and the intruding Euro-American culture had significant effects on the cosmology of the Osage Nation — the foundation of life for our people, including government, society, economy, and religion. The priest-leaders of the Osage represented twenty-four fireplaces, or clans, as the Euro-Americans called them, grouped into two divisions to represent the sky and the earth. The population loss meant that there were too few representatives of the fireplaces to hold ceremonies, so the foundation of Osage life began to weaken.

In 1881 the Osage adopted a constitution that established a three-branch government similar to that of the United States. The federal government illegally abolished this government in 1900 and replaced it with a council. The 1906 allotment act established another new council. In 2006 we established a new government and a new standard for citizenship. There are approximately 17,000 persons now eligible for citizenship in the Osage Nation with the right to vote and hold office. Our movement to a new reservation fulfilled an ancient prophecy when oil was discovered in 1896. Since then over 2 billion barrels of oil have been produced, with approximately $1 billion in revenues to the tribal members who own royalties. This great wealth has produced both benefits and hardships to our people. Recently we have entered the gaming industry, and it will produce an almost equal amount of wealth for our people in the next generation. We are preparing plans to use the money wisely.

FURTHER READING: *The Osage and the Invisible World: From the Works of Francis La Flesche*, edited by Garrick A. Bailey

177. Creek Council House Museum, OK

A. D. Ellis and Ted Isham

106 W. 6th St., Okmulgee

During 1837 and 1838 the U.S. government forced the Creek people to move from today's Georgia and Alabama, where our ancestors had lived for centuries in related towns in a collective group called the Creek Confederacy. It was divided into the Upper Creeks, who lived along the Coosa and Tallapoosa rivers, and the Lower Creeks, who lived along the Chattahoochee and Flint rivers. They spoke different but related languages. After their traumatic removal to the Indian Territory, the Creek reconstituted their lives and their government. They reestablished their division councils as well as the national council, in which the division councils met periodically to conduct the business of the Creek Nation and to deal with problems such as those with the United States and with other Indian tribes. This division of Upper and Lower Creek had a long, rich history and was ideal for organizing the nation in the new land. The Civil War disrupted the Creek Nation's stability and order, and the national council stopped meeting. During the war, Creeks fought for both the United States and the Confederacy. Afterward, under pressure from the U.S. government, the Creek Nation adopted a new constitutional government with a bicameral legislature, the House of Kings and the House of Warriors. The new government selected its new capital, named it Okmulgee, and in 1867 built the Muscogee Creek Council House, a 20-by-40-foot, two-story log building at the edge of the thick timber that fringed the Deep Fork River.

The Creek held important intertribal gatherings in the council house to encourage peaceful coexistence among the Indians forced to relocate to the Indian Territory. In 1878, after prosperity came back to the industrious tribe, Chief Ward Coachman led the Nation in building a new council house on the site of the original one. It is a large, two-story sandstone building. After passage of the Dawes Severalty Act, which allotted some tribal lands to individual members and opened the rest for white settlement, and of the Curtis Act of 1898, followed by Oklahoma statehood in 1907, the governments of the Five Tribes were dissolved. The Department of the Interior took possession of the council house, and in 1919 the city of Okmulgee purchased it. In 1923 Judge Orlando B. Swain formed the Creek Indian Memorial Association to be the governing body of the council house to preserve it and educate the public about Native Americans, especially the Muscogee Creeks. In

1961 the Creek Council House was designated a National Historic Landmark, and in 1969 it became a museum. After the historical restoration, which was completed in 1993, the building received the National Trust's National Preservation Honor Award.

Today the Muscogee (Creek) Nation still has its government headquarters in Okmulgee, and although the Nation has not yet regained ownership of its council house, it is making strides in doing so with the newfound prosperity of the Nation's economic base. The Creek Council House is a symbol of the perseverance of the Creek people. The Nation, which has 2,800 employees and an annual operating budget of $152 million, contributes $385 million to the economy. Central to the goal of self-sufficiency for the tribe are the traditional ideals of the Mvskoke Etvlwv, the Muscogee tribal towns, particularly the ideal of *etehvlvtetv* (pronounced e-tee-huh-luh-tee-duh), which means pulling together and taking care of each other. We are achieving these ideals.

FURTHER READING: *The Road to Disappearance: A History of the Creek Indians,* by Angie Debo

178. Chickasaw Council House Museum and Chickasaw Nation Capitol, OK

Richard Green

Fisher and 8th sts., Tishomingo

Following their forced removal to the Indian Territory, the Chickasaw settled on land purchased from the Choctaw, but since it was within the Choctaw domain, the Chickasaw were not independent. In 1855 the tribe purchased full title to the land (now in thirteen counties in south-central Oklahoma) from the Choctaw and declared its sovereignty. In 1856 tribal members assembled at Good Spring near Pennington Creek, where they wrote a constitution and held elections. In so doing they replaced the traditional council of clans with three branches resembling the structure of the U.S. government. They also changed the name of the little town that was springing up around them to Tishomingo, after one of the tribe's last great warriors and orators, who had died on the Trail of Tears. Tribal leaders met in a one-room log council house to draft and pass the first laws of the Nation. This council house was the seat of tribal government until the Nation erected the two-story brick capitol in 1858. (The council house was refurbished in 1965 and eventually became the namesake exhibit inside the Chickasaw Council House Museum.)

During the next forty years non-Indian intruders flooded into the Chickasaw Nation, and the United States signaled its intent to abolish the Indian Territory tribal governments and their land titles. As the U.S. Congress incrementally diluted the Chickasaw government, the capitol deteriorated. In 1898 the Nation demolished the brick structure and replaced it with a striking, durable building constructed of large granite blocks from the quarry of the sitting governor, Robert Harris. But just sixty years after removal, the federal government forced the Chickasaw Nation to agree to relinquish its tribal lands and end its government by 1906. Why did the tribe build such an expensive capitol when the U.S. government was threatening to end tribal government? Because the granite building on the hill — no matter who owned it or what the tribe's future — would stand as a permanent monument to the Chickasaw Nation. Today the Chickasaw Capitol houses a permanent exhibit on tribal government from 1855 to Oklahoma statehood in 1907.

The government of the Chickasaw Nation consists of three branches, executive, legislative, and judicial, just as it did in 1855. In 2006 the tribe had approximately 10,000 employees and capital investments in excess of $350 million. Since he became the Nation's governor in 1987,

Bill Anoatubby has focused his administration on providing better health care, educational assistance, and housing and on increasing economic development and heritage preservation.

FURTHER READING: *The Chickasaws,* by Arrell M. Gibson

179. Chickasaw National Recreation Area, OK

Jeannie Barbour

Rtes. 7 and 177, Sulphur

The Chickasaw National Recreation Area has been a place of rest and renewal for Native people for about 7,000 years. Thirty freshwater and mineral springs bubble up through the surface rock formation here. These springs are in one of Oklahoma's most beautiful natural areas and have been valued for generations for the water's medicinal qualities. The terrain at Chickasaw National Recreation Area is part of an ecotone in which the eastern deciduous forest meets the mixed-grass prairie. Because of this, a rich diversity of wildlife lives among the densely wooded areas, rugged slopes, and rolling prairie lands.

Chickasaw families have come together for generations at the springs, having first settled here in 1839. They continued to share the precious springs with their Choctaw cousins after the Chickasaw separated from the Choctaw Nation in 1856 and established their own sovereign nation. Enterprising businessmen saw the economic benefits of the springs and established the town of Sulphur amid the springs. In 1902, when tribal land was being allotted and tribal governments were being extinguished by the federal government, the Chickasaw and Choctaw agreed to sell to the federal government 640 acres that included the springs, ensuring the protection of the springs and the surrounding area. In 1906 Sulphur Springs Reservation became Platt National Park, and in 1976 the park was renamed the Chickasaw National Recreation Area in honor of the Chickasaw Nation.

Removal and Recovery

LOUIS COLEMAN AND ROBERT POWELL WEST

❖ In 1830 Congress passed the Indian Removal Act, and the Choctaw signed the Treaty of Dancing Rabbit Creek, in which they gave up their homelands and were removed to the Indian Territory. Disease, severe weather, and logistical mismanagement caused great suffering and death. Approximately 2,000 Choctaws died on the trail. The Choctaw were resilient, however, and wasted no time in recrimination. Instead, they set to work clearing land, building homes, and reestablishing their government, including a new constitution in 1834. Christian missionaries came with them from Mississippi and established missions, churches, and schools. In 1832 they founded Wheelock Mission and organized a church. Between 1844 and 1847 the congregation built a stone church that still stands, the oldest church in Oklahoma. The day school, founded in 1833, was expanded into a boarding school. It was incorporated into the Choctaw national school system in 1842 and was active until 1861. In 1884 Wheelock Academy opened and became a model for tribal schools. It closed in 1955. The six surviving structures symbolize the Choctaw commitment to education.

Fort Towson, established in 1830 to defend the Choctaw from the Plains Indians, was abandoned in 1854. The store has been reconstructed, and the small museum tells the history of the fort. In the early 1830s a trading post,

Doaksville, was established. It grew into the largest town in the Indian Territory, a center of official and commercial life, and was the Choctaw capital from 1850 until 1863, when the capital was moved to Chahta Tamaha. On June 23, 1865, Stand Watie, a Cherokee who was a Confederate brigadier general, was the last Confederate general to surrender in the Civil War. He surrendered at Doaksville. When the railroad was built through the Choctaw Nation in the early 1900s, it bypassed Doaksville, ending the life of the town. An interpretive trail through the site tells the town's history.

Traditionally, tribal lands were held in common, with members developing acreage as needed. But in the late nineteenth century, amid growing pressure from new settlers in Oklahoma, the tribe agreed to allot tribal lands in severalty; each member received a homestead with the privilege of claiming surplus land. The Choctaw Nation lost its sovereignty for seventy years but regained it with the new federal policy of Indian self-determination in the 1970s.

180. Wheelock Academy, OK

Off Rte. 7, Millerton

181. Fort Towson Historic Site and the Doaksville Site, OK

Northeast of Fort Towson

Museum; interpretive trail through Doaksville site

FURTHER READING: *Indian Removal: The Emigration of the Five Civilized Tribes of Indians*, by Grant Foreman

182. Choctaw Nation Tribal Capitol, OK: Tushka Homma

Gregory E. Pyle

Council House Rd., Tuskahoma

Oklahoma has been the home of the Choctaw Nation since the 1830s, when the U.S. government removed our ancestors from their Mississippi homelands. They endured many hardships, and those who survived are examples of the determination and stamina of Choctaw people. In 1884 our ancestors built Tushka Homma (Red Warrior), the two-story red brick capitol. Today the building includes a court, a museum, and a gift shop. In front of the building is the monument area, where Choctaws who served in the military are honored. The Veterans Cemetery is nearby. In 1891 the U.S. Post Office changed the spelling of the town to Tushkahomma, and in 1901 shortened it to Tuskahoma. The Choctaw Nation continues to use the original spelling of the name of the capitol.

Tribal leadership has evolved into a three-branch government with headquarters in Durant: the executive (chief and assistant chief), the legislative (twelve tribal council members), and the judicial (three judges), as mandated by the constitution, which was ratified in 1983. There is a tribal office in each of the twelve districts (in Bryan, Choctaw, Pushmataha, McCurtain, LeFlore, Haskell, Pittsburg, Coal, Latimer, Atoka, and Hughes counties), so services are accessible to all people of the Choctaw Nation. The Nation has a history of putting families first, with priorities on education, health, and jobs. Today we place an emphasis on increasing education opportunities, expanding health care, and creating high-quality jobs. Scholarships, language classes, opportunities to receive a general equivalency diploma, child development centers, and school programs assist tribal members with their education. We have built a new hospital, clinics, wellness centers, and a recovery center. We have created employment opportunities in gaming, manufacturing, and other businesses. Profits from these businesses make it possible for the tribe to provide services to the Choctaw people.

FURTHER READING: *The Choctaw of Oklahoma,* by James C. Milligan

183. Fort Gibson Historic Site, OK

907 North Garrison, Fort Gibson

Reconstructed stockade; fort buildings

The fort was established in 1824 on the Grand River near the confluence of the Grand, the Verdigris, and the Arkansas rivers. Renamed Fort Gibson in 1832, it became the Headquarters of the Southwestern Frontier. Before railroads, supplies came by boat up the Mississippi and Arkansas rivers to unload near the fort. It was a supply center for the Cherokees, Seminoles, and Creeks moving into the Indian Territory after being forced from their homelands. During the Civil War it was a U.S. fort. When the Confederates tried to capture it in July 1863, they were stopped and defeated at the battle of Honey Springs. The fort was closed in 1890.

Constitutional Government Among the Five Civilized Tribes

BOB L. BLACKBURN

❖ Many people know about the rich cultural tapestry of Indian art, from dance and literature to painting and music. Less well known is the remarkable evolution of constitutional, representative government by five tribes removed to the Indian Territory, the Cherokee, Choctaw, Chickasaw, Creek, and Seminole. Prior to contact with Euro-Americans, they were regulated internally by complex law-ways and customs that had evolved according to the conditions and dynamics of tribal life. Civil affairs were usually based on consensus, with leaders limited by their ability to persuade others to follow their example. Social control came from clans and elders as well as social and religious norms.

The Choctaw wrote their constitution in 1834; the Cherokee adopted a new constitution soon after their arrival in 1839; the Chickasaw wrote theirs in 1856; and the Creek adopted their written constitution in 1867. The Seminole, the last of the southeastern tribes removed to the Indian Territory, established their government in 1856. Today these tribes continue as sovereign nations. The Cherokee National Capitol in Tahlequah, the Chickasaw National Capitol in Tishomingo, the Choctaw Nation Tribal Capitol, and the Creek Council House in Okmulgee stand as evidence of the tribes' self-determination and adaptation.

FURTHER READING: *Social Order and Political Change: Constitutional Governments Among the Cherokee, the Choctaw, the Chickasaw, and the Creek,* by Duane Champagne

184. Dade Battlefield Historic State Park, FL

Donald L. Fixico

On Battlefield Dr., east of I-75, Bushnell

Museum

On December 28, 1835, the U.S. military entered into a conflict that began the longest war fought between the United States and an Indian tribe. From 1835 to 1842, the diverse Muscogee Seminole and Mikasuki Seminole bands, including towns of Creek allies and escaped African Americans, fought twelve U.S. Army generals in eight important battles. The warfare began in late 1835 when the great Seminole war leader Osceola and a small force killed the Indian agent Wiley Thompson. Major Francis Dade volunteered to lead a rescue expedition to support Fort King, and on December 23 he marched northward from Fort Brooke with a force of 108 soldiers. Every night for five evenings, Dade and his men could hear the Seminoles preparing for war. On the morning of the fated day, 180 Seminole warriors led by Micanopy concealed themselves in the high grass along the road. The battle began when Micanopy shot Major Dade through the heart. The soldiers readied their one cannon and forced the Indians to retreat, but the Seminoles concealed themselves and then attacked again and again. By three o'clock in the afternoon, 105 soldiers were dead and 3 were badly wounded.

Known to white Americans as a massacre and to the Seminoles as a victory, this battle triggered more warfare. Osceola led his warriors to victories at Camp Clinch, Great Cypress Swamp, Camp Monroe, Clear River, Mosquito Inlet, and Lake Okeechobee. In October 1837 he was taken prisoner under a flag of truce near St. Augustine. He died at Fort Moultrie the following January. Other leaders took charge, and after Coacochee surrendered in 1841, the Seminole lost five engagements in 1842. After seven years of fighting, and without a peace treaty, the defeated Seminole accepted removal. Band after band traveled more than 1,200 miles to the Indian Territory west of the Mississippi. Those who remained sought safety in south Florida.

FURTHER READING: *The Seminole Wars: America's Longest Indian Conflict,* by John Missall and Mary Lou Missall

185. Tree Tops Park, FL: Pine Island Ridge

Brent Richards Weisman

3900 SW 100th Ave., Davie

Today's Florida Seminoles have learned to thrive in the modern world just as their ancestors did in earlier times. Now most Seminoles live on reservations in south Florida, but once Seminole towns and villages could be found throughout Florida, from the banks of the St. Johns River in the east to the bluffs of the Apalachicola River in the western panhandle. They grew corn, pumpkins, squash, melons, and potatoes, herded cattle, and raised horses. Some villages had orange and peach trees nearby. Spanish and British traders based in St. Augustine were eager to exchange cloth, beads, and iron tools for Seminole cattle, deerskins, honey, and oranges. This era of good feeling and prosperity changed when the Americans took control of Florida in 1821. The U.S. government immediately made plans to remove the Seminoles to Indian Territory in the West. Three wars fought between 1817 and 1858 did not achieve complete removal of the Seminoles, but the wars did greatly reduce their numbers and territory. By the mid-1800s almost all of the Seminoles remaining in Florida lived around Lake Okeechobee or in the Everglades and in the Big Cypress regions of south Florida. This was a period of isolation from the outside world. The Seminoles were seeking out areas where they could continue their traditional way of life. One place they came to was Pine Island Ridge, a finger of high ground on the eastern edge of the Everglades. A part of Pine Island Ridge is now preserved in Tree Tops Park. The Seminole Tribe's Hollywood Reservation is nearby.

Tree Tops Park is a quiet place and provides a small refuge from the hustle and bustle of the twenty-first century. Hiking trails lead through deep, shady hammocks and beside fields where Seminole voices once rang out. On Pine Island Ridge, Seminoles were once again able to grow corn, potatoes, and pumpkins, adding crops of lima beans and bananas. Photographs taken in 1897 give us a tantalizing glimpse of Seminole activity on Pine Island Ridge before the encroachment of modern life. One picture shows Seminoles playing the ball game at the ceremonial dance ground. A group of people are standing around the tall, slender ball pole watching a man with ball sticks held high over his head. He has probably just used the sticks to hurl the deerskin ball toward the target near the top of the pole. Today the ball game continues to play a very important role in the Green Corn Dance and is a vital part of traditional Seminole culture. Another photograph shows Seminole families standing in a clearing outside a cluster of palmetto-thatched open-air *chickees,* complete with their raised split-log sleeping platforms. By the end of the nineteenth century, at least three major clan camps had their homes on Pine Island, numbering perhaps 200 people in all. Many Seminoles today can trace their lineage back to a Pine Island family.

Outside the park visitor center is a bronze statue of Sam Jones, or Abiaka. The statue was commissioned by Broward County to preserve the memory of this quiet warrior. The statue shows him pointing the way to safety for a Seminole woman and her child. His concern for the safety and well-being of the people makes him one of the greatest leaders in Seminole history. Without the courage, wisdom, and sheer determination of Sam Jones to keep the Seminoles in Florida, the modern Seminole Tribe of Florida would not exist. Other exhibits tell of Sam Jones and early Seminole history at Pine Island Ridge.

FURTHER READING: *Unconquered People: Florida's Seminole and Miccosukee Indians,* by Brent Richards Weisman

186. Ah-Tah-Thi-Ki Museum and Living Village, FL

On Big Cypress Seminole Reservation, off I-75 at exit 49; 17 miles north on Rte. 833 to West Boundary Rd.

In the Seminole language, *ah-tah-thi-ki* means a place to learn. Near the museum is a recreated Seminole village, where tribal members work on traditional arts and crafts.

American Indians and the Civil War

LAURENCE M. HAUPTMAN

❖ At the same time that Americans were fighting the Sioux in Minnesota, incarcerating about 9,000 Apaches and Navajos at a concentration camp at Fort Sumner, New Mexico, and massacring Cheyenne at Sand Creek, Colorado, nearly 20,000 American Indians were serving in the U.S. and Confederate militaries. From April 1861 until well past General Robert E. Lee's surrender, American Indians served as infantrymen, cavalrymen, scouts, sharpshooters, and even as commissioned and noncommissioned officers. Stand Watie, the principal chief of the Cherokee Nation (South), was a brigadier general in the Confederate army. On orders from Lieutenant General Ulysses S. Grant, his military secretary, the Seneca sachem Lieutenant Colonel Ely S. Parker, drew up the surrender papers that General Lee signed at Appomattox Court House, Virginia, on April 9, 1865. Two and a half months later Watie surrendered at Doaksville in Indian Territory.

American Indians believed that participation in the war effort was their last best hope to stem the loss of their land and the tribal destruction that had begun in the East centuries before. There were other reasons for joining the war effort — poverty, the search for adventure, past treaty alliances, divergent views on slavery, validation of tribal leadership — but the primary one was their increasing dependence on the non-Indian world for economic and political survival. They fought on all fronts of the war; however, their largest participation was in the Trans-Mississippi West. In April and May 1861, Delaware scouts led by Black Beaver successfully evacuated U.S. forces from Indian Territory. On December 26, 1861, Confederate Cherokees led by Colonel Stand Watie defeated the U.S. Indian force led by Chief Opothleyahola at the Battle of Chustenahlah. In the U.S. victory in the Battle of Pea Ridge on March 6–8, 1862, two mounted Confederate Cherokee regiments participated, one led by Watie and the other by John Drew, the nephew by marriage of Watie's Cherokee rival, Principal Chief John Ross. Later, many in Drew's 2nd Cherokee Mounted Rifles defected to the U.S. side. On July 17, 1863, Major General James G. Blunt's command, which included the 2nd U.S. Indian Home Guard (Creeks, Delawares, Quapaws, and Seminoles), defeated the Confederates at Honey Springs, the most decisive U.S. victory in Indian Territory. In September 1864, in the Second Battle of Cabin Creek, Watie and his brigade of 800 Cherokees, Creeks, and Seminoles joined with 1,200 Texans to capture a 300-wagon mule train loaded with $1.5 million worth of food, clothing, medicine, guns, and ammunition headed to Fort Gibson. In April 1864 at Poison Spring, Arkansas, the 1st Regiment of Choctaw and Chickasaw Mounted Rifles, commanded by Colonel Tandy Walker, a Choctaw, helped defeat a U.S. foraging party returning to Camden.

American Indians also contributed significantly to both sides of the conflict on battlefields east of the Mississippi River. Company K of the 1st Michigan Sharp Shooters, comprising mostly Ojibwes, Ottawas (Odawas), and Ottawa-Ojibwes, as well as a few Delawares, Oneidas, and Potawatomis, received official praise from the U.S. government for their service in the first assault on Petersburg on June 17, 1864, and in the federal fiasco at the Battle of the Crater on July 30, 1864. U.S. Indians at the crater also included the 1st Michigan Sharp Shooters as well as Senecas in the 14th New York Heavy Artillery, Indians from New England and New York in the 31st U.S. Colored Troops, and Indians from Wisconsin in the 37th Wisconsin Volunteer Infantry. Confederate Indians included the Catawbas in the 12th South Carolina Volunteer Infantry, who served in Lee's Army of Northern Virginia from Antietam onward. The Pamunkey served as river pilots for Major General George B. McClellan in the Peninsula Campaign, the Lumbee aided Major General William T. Sherman in his march through the Carolinas, and the Iroquois of the "Tuscarora Company," Company D of the 132nd New York State Volunteer Infantry, guarded the rails and stopped Confederate forces in North Carolina around New Bern in February 1864 and at Wyse Forks in March 1865. The Eastern Band of Cherokees, led by their adopted spokesman William Holland Thomas, an influential white secessionist, served the Confederates by guarding the Appalachian mountain passes and enforcing conscription in western North Carolina and eastern Tennessee.

The Civil War had a devastating impact on American Indians. Their significant military contributions failed to improve the overall conditions of their peoples, and the massive military firepower developed in four years of warfare was soon employed in "pacification" campaigns against Indians defending their homelands on the Great Plains and in the Southwest.

FURTHER READING: *Between Two Fires: American Indians in the Civil War*, by Laurence M. Hauptman

187. Pea Ridge National Military Park, AR

Rte. 62, west of Garfield

Visitor center/museum

About 800 Cherokees, the 1st and 2nd Cherokee Mounted Rifles, fought for the Confederacy in the Civil War battle of Pea Ridge on March 6–8, 1862. The park includes the Elkhorn Tavern segment of the Trail of Tears, on the Springfield–Fayetteville Road, and areas where the Cherokees camped and received supplies.

188. Battle of Honey Springs Historic Site, OK

Off Rte. 69, north of Checotah

Interpretive center

This battle, on July 17, 1863, was designated by the Civil War Sites Advisory Commission as one of the 384 principal battles because the victory of about 3,000 U.S. troops over about 6,000 Confederates enabled U.S. forces to gain control of the Indian Territory and much of Arkansas. The forces included the 2nd U.S. Indian Home Guard (Creeks, Delawares, Quapaws, and Seminoles), African Americans, and white soldiers.

189. Petersburg National Battlefield, VA

Off Rte. 36/Wythe St., Petersburg

Visitor center

In the Civil War battle at Petersburg on June 15–18, 1864, the Third Division of Major General Ambrose E. Burnside's IX Corps included American Indians in Company K of the 1st Michigan Sharp Shooters: Ottawas (Odawas), Ojibwes, Ottawa-Ojibwas, Delawares, Hurons, Oneidas, and Potawatomis. The Sharp Shooters and the American Indians in the 14th New York Heavy Artillery, the 31st U.S. Colored Troops, and Company K of the 37th Wisconsin Volunteer

Infantry served the United States in the tragic battle of the Crater on July 30, 1864. Catawbas in the 12th South Carolina Volunteer Infantry fought for the Confederacy. Lieutenant General Ulysses S. Grant's headquarters were in City Point at Petersburg. His military secretary was Lieutenant Colonel Ely S. Parker, a Seneca sachem.

190. Castillo de San Marcos National Monument, FL

South Castillo Dr., St. Augustine

The Spanish built the massive masonry fort in the late sixteenth century. When Spain ceded Florida to the United States in 1821, the Americans renamed it Fort Marion. About ninety Seminoles, including Osceola, were imprisoned at the fort for two months in 1837 before most were moved to Fort Moultrie in South Carolina. Between 1875 and 1878 seventy-four Kiowas, Cheyennes, Arapahos, Comanches, and Caddos were sent here from Oklahoma and held at the fort. Captain Richard Henry Pratt was in charge of the prison. When he left in 1878 to found the Carlisle Indian Industrial School, all but twenty-two of the younger men were sent back to Oklahoma. Some of the twenty-two went to Carlisle and some to the Hampton Institute. About 500 members of the families of the Chiricahua Apaches who were imprisoned at Fort Pickens were held here in 1886–1887.

191. Gulf Islands National Seashore, FL: Fort Pickens

Gulf Breeze

Museum/visitor center; fort accessible by boat or bicycle

Beginning in October 1886, Geronimo and sixteen other Chiricahua Apaches were held prisoner at Fort Pickens. Their families were sent to Fort Marion, where they were held until the following April, when they were sent to Fort Pickens. In May 1888 the government sent all of them to Mount Vernon Barracks, 30 miles north of Mobile, except for six children, including one of Geronimo's, who were sent to the Carlisle Indian Industrial School in Pennsylvania. In 1894 the Apaches were transferred to Fort Sill, Oklahoma, where they were held prisoner until they were finally freed in 1914. Geronimo died in 1909 and was buried in the Fort Sill prisoner of war cemetery.

192. University of North Carolina at Pembroke, NC: A Part of Lumbee Indian Heritage

Helen Maynor Scheirbeck

Pembroke

Every July Lumbee Indians come from across the United States for a week of homecoming at their tribal headquarters in Pembroke. Their activities include the customary homecoming events and also the celebration of their educational heritage and its connection with the University of North Carolina/Pembroke. The quest for education began in 1885 when the Lumbee, committed to education for their children, petitioned the state for separate schools for their children, for their own school committees, and for the right to select teachers from among their own people. North Carolina appropriated $500 to pay teachers for the school. Local Lumbees provided personal funds to buy the land for the school, and they built and paid for the schoolhouse. Several years later, the school was moved to Pembroke. It grew into a high school, with a separate normal school to train local Indian teachers, and into the college that today is part of the University of North Carolina system. The student body includes students from all over the world.

While striving to educate their children, the Lumbee have survived the whites' coercive tactics and assassinations of their leaders. During the Civil War, when North Carolina tried to use Lumbees in the munitions factory at Fort Fisher, many decided they would not be conscripted to work for the Confederacy. A young Indian man, Henry Berry Lowrie, organized a band of Indians, along with a few blacks and whites, to fight back and protect the poor people in the county. Between 1864 and 1872, the Lowrie band took money and supplies from the white community and gave it to impoverished people in the county. The tribe became the Lumbee officially in 1952, when the state approved its petition to be named after the river along which they live. Congress passed a law approving the name in 1956. But challenges to the Lumbee continued. On January 18, 1958, the Ku Klux Klan came into our homeland and threatened us with violence. The grand wizard had just begun to speak when shots rang out from the Lumbees, knocking out the one light bulb over the speaker. As the Klansmen disappeared into the woods, they abandoned their fallen flag and cross. The Lumbees had routed the Klan from Lumbee country. Indians from all over the country sent congratulations and pledges of support.

On July 4, 2003, Jimmy Locklear, the volunteer coordinator at the National Museum of the American Indian, and I had the honor of joining fifty other Lumbee family members at the university outside of "Old Main" to receive the Victory Medal, honoring the work of our fathers. Jimmy's father was one of the Lumbees who had defended our homeland in 1958, and my father was the judge who had tried the Klan's grand wizard. We thought how wonderful it was that the Lumbee victory over the Klan could be celebrated forty-five years later at Pembroke — another achievement that became part of the Lumbee heritage at Pembroke.

FURTHER READING: *The Lumbee,* by Adolph L. Dial

SECTION THREE

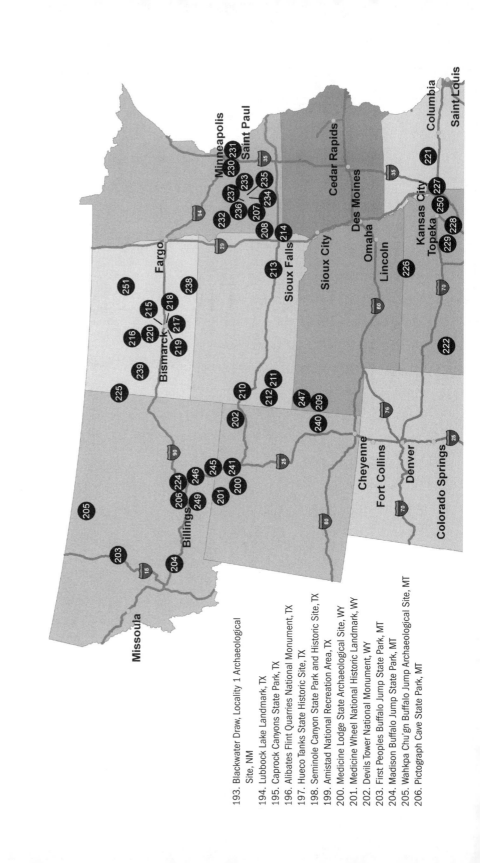

193. Blackwater Draw, Locality 1 Archaeological Site, NM

194. Lubbock Lake Landmark, TX

195. Caprock Canyons State Park, TX

196. Alibates Flint Quarries National Monument, TX

197. Hueco Tanks State Historic Site, TX

198. Seminole Canyon State Park and Historic Site, TX

199. Amistad National Recreation Area, TX

200. Medicine Lodge State Archaeological Site, WY

201. Medicine Wheel National Historic Landmark, WY

202. Devils Tower National Monument, WY

203. First Peoples Buffalo Jump State Park, MT

204. Madison Buffalo Jump State Park, MT

205. Wahkpa Chu'gn Buffalo Jump Archaeological Site, MT

206. Pictograph Cave State Park, MT

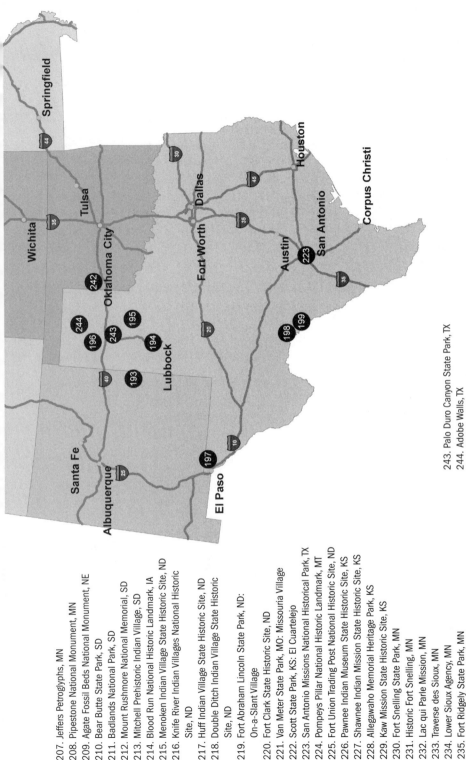

207. Jeffers Petroglyphs, MN
208. Pipestone National Monument, MN
209. Agate Fossil Beds National Monument, NE
210. Bear Butte State Park, SD
211. Badlands National Park, SD
212. Mount Rushmore National Memorial, SD
213. Mitchell Prehistoric Indian Village, SD
214. Blood Run National Historic Landmark, IA
215. Menoken Indian Village State Historic Site, ND
216. Knife River Indian Villages National Historic Site, ND
217. Huff Indian Village State Historic Site, ND
218. Double Ditch Indian Village State Historic Site, ND
219. Fort Abraham Lincoln State Park, ND: On-a-Slant Village
220. Fort Clark State Historic Site, ND
221. Van Meter State Park, MO: Missouria Village
222. Scott State Park, KS: El Cuartelejo
223. San Antonio Missions National Historical Park, TX
224. Pompeys Pillar National Historic Landmark, MT
225. Fort Union Trading Post National Historic Site, ND
226. Pawnee Indian Museum State Historic Site, KS
227. Shawnee Indian Mission State Historic Site, KS
228. Allegawaho Memorial Heritage Park, KS
229. Kaw Mission State Historic Site, KS
230. Fort Snelling State Park, MN
231. Historic Fort Snelling, MN
232. Lac qui Parle Mission, MN
233. Traverse des Sioux, MN
234. Lower Sioux Agency, MN
235. Fort Ridgely State Park, MN
236. Upper Sioux Agency State Park, MN
237. Birch Coulee Battlefield, MN
238. Whitestone Hill Battlefield State Historic Site, ND
239. Killdeer Mountain Battlefield State Historic Site, ND
240. Fort Laramie National Historic Site, WY
241. Fort Phil Kearny State Historic Site, WY
242. Washita Battlefield National Historic Site, OK

243. Palo Duro Canyon State Park, TX
244. Adobe Walls, TX
245. Rosebud Battlefield State Park, MT
246. Little Bighorn Battlefield National Monument, MT
247. Fort Robinson State Park, NE
248. Fort Buford State Historic Site, ND
249. Chief Plenty Coups State Park, MT
250. Haskell Indian Nations University, KS
251. Fort Totten State Historic Site, ND

People and Place

PHILIP J. DELORIA

❖ Human beings everywhere develop attachments to the places they call home. For American Indian people, those ties have a particularly rich character, one that starts with origin stories, which recount beginnings in order to define the group's very nature. Tribal peoples do not simply name their home territories; they point specifically to the places of creation that anchor those territories. Here is the site of emergence; over there lies the route of original migration; this mountain centers the entire world. Origin stories use such specific places to situate Native societies not only in space but also in an ancient time that is continuous with the present. Other stories are concerned less with the people's origins than with those of the place — and every people will have a large number of such places, each evoking layers of sacred and historical narrative, with the stories of the past always helping to explain lessons vital to the present. Sometimes it isn't necessary to tell the stories; the place name itself serves as shorthand. Listeners already know the place, its stories, and the lesson to be learned.

Places are also important sites for individuals. Vision-quest sites, for example, marry spiritual experience, individual subjectivity, and community wisdom. After a person who has gone away and had a vision returns home, the vision is often interpreted by and performed for the community, which recognizes a new identity emerging from an encounter in a specific location. Sites of particular power, such as Bear Butte in South Dakota, are likely to be used repeatedly. Such places are often linked to the possibility not only of knowing the past and present but also of seeking prophecies of the future.

Indian people define place in more prosaic terms as well. Many of the names that continue to define the North American landscape refer to places where Indian people engaged in simple acts of everyday life: water crossings, gaps in the hills where bison emerged, bogs where cranberries grew, buttes where eagles nested. Nor are such names merely relics of earlier centuries. Indian people today continue to name places in ways that reflect everyday life and labor on the land.

When they arrived in North America, Europeans immediately pronounced it a space, an empty wilderness devoid of names or stories. In fact, North America had always been a collection of well-known neighborhoods, places thickly named and storied by Indian people. Where Europeans insisted that they saw meandering hunters following game (even when they were looking at sedentary farmers!), Indian people were in fact moving through sequences of familiar places. The contest for North America, then, was defined not only by military domination and resistance; it was also defined by the claiming, translating, erasing, and renaming of Indian places.

That contest left indelible marks on American Indian peoples and places, including the creation of several new kinds of places. Among the most visible "Indian" places on the continent, for example, are the killing sites of battles, massacres, and removals: Wounded Knee, Sand Creek, Prophetstown, the Trail of Tears, and Bosque Redondo, among many others. Less visible, but just as important, are the archeological sites, in which (primarily) white Americans have assembled a continental past by exploring ancient Indian places and claiming them as a national legacy. Reservations, devised as zones for the containment and reeducation of Indian people, have become critical places in Indian Country. Turned by Native people from spaces of confinement into new homelands of cultural persistence and reimagination, they are places of history and possibility. In this sense, Indian-defined places continue to link Native people with their own pasts, presents, and futures.

193. Blackwater Draw, Locality 1 Archaeological Site, NM: People and Water

John L. Montgomery

On Rte. 467, north of Portales

The discoveries at Blackwater Draw provided the first clear evidence — spear points associated

with Ice Age mammoths — of the presence of Paleoindian people here 11,300 years ago. They became known as the Clovis culture (after the nearby town). Also fascinating is the place. In those cooler and wetter times an ancient spring-fed lake enabled plants to grow and attracted animals and the people who hunted them. Since then the lakebed has slowly filled with sediment, effectively sealing and protecting a detailed record of the past, including Clovis spear points embedded in the bones of mammoths as well as artifacts characteristic of later Paleoindian periods (such as the Folsom culture) and historic times.

The stratified archaeological record also reveals how prehistoric peoples responded when temperatures rose, rainfall declined, and the dependable sources fed by groundwater dried up. They dug deep wells — some of the earliest in North America — to reach the underlying water table. They used available manpower and technology to maintain a source of water, critical to survival, in response to the challenge of coping with climate change.

FURTHER READING: *Blackwater Locality No. 1 — A Stratified Early Man Site in Eastern New Mexico*, by J. J. Hester

194. Lubbock Lake Landmark, TX

Near the intersection of Rte. 84 and North Loop 289, Lubbock

Nash Interpretive Center

Lubbock Lake Landmark, an archaeological and natural history preserve, is one of the few places in North America where there is evidence of a complete sequence of human existence beginning about 10,000 B.C. On the nature trails, visitors can see life-size sculptures of four of the extinct animals that were attracted to the water in a meander in Yellowhouse Draw, now Lubbock Lake: ancient bison, Columbian mammoth, short-faced bear, and giant pampathere.

195. Caprock Canyons State Park, TX

On Rte. 1065, north of Quitaque

Interpretive center

People began hunting among the red rock canyons about 10,000 years ago. Several Folsom points and the remains of an Ice Age bison were found near Lake Theo. People quarried Tecovas jasper from sites now in the park and made stone tools. The Texas State Bison Herd is in the park.

Tools from the Earth

CATHERINE M. CAMERON

❖ Today we are surrounded by manufactured materials: steel, plastic, and glass. For millennia, however, American Indians' most important material was stone, the hardest, sharpest, and most durable medium for spears and arrow points for hunting, knives and scrapers for cutting meat and working hides, axes for cutting wood, hoes for tilling the soil, and grinding stones for processing food. The people stacked stone to make their houses, fashioned it into beads, pendants, and other ornaments, and carved it into bowls or pipes.

For tools that required a sharp edge, such as arrowheads, spear points, knives, and scrapers, they used chert or flint (terms that include geologically distinct varieties of siliceous stone) because it has an even texture but is brittle enough to be chipped, or "knapped," into the required shape. They prized obsidian, a volcanic glass, for its razor-sharp edges. Flakes of obsidian could be used as informal cutting tools, and larger pieces could be fashioned into knives, arrowheads, or spear points. Tools such as manos and metates for grinding corn and hammerstones for pounding tasks had to be abrasive and dura-

ble, so they were made from tough, resistant stone such as quartzite, rhyolite, or sandstone. For ornaments and containers, people chose softer stone, such as steatite or soapstone.

American Indians had a vast knowledge of the properties of stone and often traveled great distances to obtain the best-quality materials. Their quarries were most often simply gravel terraces or rocky streambeds, where they could easily collect pebbles or cobbles, test them for quality, and then fashion them into tools. But they also constructed complex mines with holes, pits, shafts, and tunnels; the debris included tons of broken rock and large stone hammers and hammerstones for rough shaping. Many of the quarries were worked generation after generation. The methods for quarrying varied with the deposit. At quarries in southern Illinois, the miners found flint nodules in a layer of clay almost 25 feet below the surface, dug deep pits through the clay to the nodules, and then, risking cave-ins, tunneled laterally to collect them.

At Flint Ridge in Ohio, a hard grayish flint bed lies 10 to 20 feet below the surface. The miners dug away the earth, kindled fires, and, when the flint was hot, doused it with water to shatter it. They discarded the outer fragments and repeated the process until the flint bed was exposed. At the Big Obsidian Flow in Newberry Volcanic National Monument in Oregon, people could knock off large chunks of the shiny black glass from the ancient volcanic flow. The miners seldom made finished tools at the quarries. They made simple "preforms" or "bifaces," big chunks of material roughly shaped into convenient carrying sizes for their own use or for trade. The extensive trade of high-quality stone demonstrates its importance to American Indians. Enormous quantities of obsidian from the area that is now Yellowstone National Park were found in a burial mound in Ohio. Alibates flint from north Texas has been found at sites on the Great Plains and in the Southwest. Those who quarry pipestone at Pipestone National Monument traditionally leave an offering of food or tobacco, a gift of thanks. Quarries are sacred places for American Indians.

FURTHER READING: *Prehistoric Quarries and Lithic Production,* by Jonathon E. Ericson and Barbara A. Purdy

196. Alibates Flint Quarries National Monument, TX

By tour only from the Lake Meredith National Recreation Area, Fritch

The Alibates flint is in layers just below the surface on a ridge above the Canadian River north of Amarillo. The beautiful multicolored flint — agatized dolomite — holds a sharp edge, so it was a vital source for weapons and tools for the people who lived in this area. The flint was so valuable that it was widely traded across the Southwest and the plains. The monument includes more than 730 large quarry pits surrounded by piles of flakes, chips, and broken tools, the debris of mining begun more than 10,000 years ago.

Pictographs and Petroglyphs in Texas

SOLVEIG A. TURPIN

❖ Hueco Tanks State Historic Site encompasses three towering volcanic outcrops that contain hollows, crevices, and caves formed by erosion. Rainwater trapped in the hollows — *huecos* — has attracted prehistoric and historic travelers for millennia. The cracks, crevices, and caves shelter an impressive array of pictographs and petroglyphs attributable to successive waves of Native artists from at least three distinct cultural periods. The earliest paintings are scenes of game animals and humans generally attributed to Archaic hunting and gathering people. Puebloan influence is evident in the kachina dancers, horned serpents and toads, goggle-eyed figures, masks, and rain altars. The Plains Indian artistic tradition is evident in horsemen, dancers, and other action scenes sometimes credited to the Mescalero Apaches.

Seminole Canyon State Park and Historic Site, just downstream from the confluence of the Pecos River and the Rio Grande, was created to preserve examples of all five of the regionally defined pictograph styles — Pecos River, Red Monochrome, Red Linear, Bold Line Geometric, and Historic Paintings — and their archaeological context. The seventy-two archaeological sites in the park include the largest rock shelter in Texas, Fate Bell, as well as many smaller shelters where people once lived, a vertical-shaft burial cave, cairn burials, tipi rings, open campsites marked by burned rock ovens and stone tools, extensive outcrops of chert for making stone tools, a hunting blind constructed of rock slabs, and remnants of railroad camps from the 1880s.

Amistad Dam was erected in 1969 to impound the waters of the Rio Grande just below its confluence with the Devils and Pecos rivers. The reservoir was built to provide water for irrigation and power, with the added benefit of recreational sports, such as sailing, fishing, and water skiing. A side effect was increased access to hundreds of archaeological sites on both sides of the border with Mexico. A ten-year-long effort to salvage information from sites that would be inundated or otherwise affected by increased access led to numerous excavations and documentation of pictographs. The two most famous sites accessible by boat are Panther and Parida caves as well as many lesser-known pictographs and shelters where people once lived.

197. Hueco Tanks State Historic Site, TX

On Rte. 2775 off Rtes. 62/180, northeast of
El Paso

By tour only from the visitor center

198. Seminole Canyon State Park and Historic Site, TX

Off Rte. 90 west of Comstock

Interpretive center; Fate Bell Shelter by tour only;
some tours include the White Shaman Preserve

199. Amistad National Recreation Area, TX

On Rte. 90, northwest of Del Rio

Visitor information center

FURTHER READING: *The Rock Art of Texas Indians,*
by Forrest Kirkland and W. W. Newcomb, Jr.

200. Medicine Lodge State Archaeological Site, WY

Off Rte. 31 on Cold Springs Rd., north of Hyattville

Visitor center exhibits

Research has documented the presence of people here beginning about 10,000 years ago. There are petroglyphs and pictographs on a 300-foot-long sandstone cliff face.

201. Medicine Wheel National Historic Landmark, WY

Jeanne Oyawin Eder

Rte. 14A, between Burgess Junction and the western edge of the Bighorn National Forest

I first saw this Medicine Wheel fifty years ago, before it was surrounded by a high fence. We could stand near it, marvel at its site, and offer prayers to the Great Spirit. It is an 80-foot circle of boulders with twenty-eight large rocks radiating in spokes from the center. On a treeless plateau at an elevation of 9,642 feet in the Bighorn Mountains of Wyoming, it seems as if it is on top of the world — a good place to offer prayers to the Creator. Some people say it represents a calendar, while others say it is connected to major astronomical events such as the summer and winter solstices. For others it represents a layout for the Sun Dance ceremony because the twenty-eight spokes represent the twenty-eight poles in a Sun Dance circle. The Sun Dance is used for prayers for our relatives and for a renewal of the Earth Mother. For certain, to many American Indians today it is a sacred place to offer prayers or hold a sacred event. Many people have left tobacco ties fastened to the fence; each one carries a prayer.

Since rocks have always been an important part of American Indian religion — a broad statement but one with validity — ponder this. A Dakota (Sioux) creation story points up the importance of rocks. The first rock, Inyan (EE-yah), was a fluid mass of matter and debris floating in the universe. Inyan was very lonely and wanted to have someone to talk with and share his experiences. One day he realized that he had the power and energy to use part of himself to create someone to be with him. Inyan closed his eyes and squeezed all of his energy together. The blue blood that flowed from his veins became the waters of the earth, and the rocks in the universe gathered around him. Inyan eventually became as hard as rock and found that he had created Makah, the Earth Mother, and things were good. One of the important American Indian ceremonies is the sweatlodge ceremony, in which rocks are heated until they are very hot; the steam formed when water is splashed on the rocks cleanses people's minds and bodies.

My adopted father, Herman Bad Bear, told

me that there are other Medicine Wheels in Montana, Wyoming, and Canada and that they are all connected — reminders that American Indian people have a responsibility to protect and care for the Earth Mother.

FURTHER READING: *Medicine Wheels: Ancient Teachings for Modern Times,* by Roy L. Wilson

202. Devils Tower National Monument, WY: Mato Tipila Paha — The Hill of the Bear's Lodge

Karen Lone Hill

Off Rte. 13 on Rte. 24, Devils Tower

Visitor center

Devils Tower National Monument stands 1,267 feet tall and is near the Belle Fourche River in northeastern Wyoming. The summit of this great tower is 400 feet by 200 feet and is supported by columns of phonolite, an igneous rock, that are 10 to 17 feet in diameter. The sedimentary rock between the phonolite columns has worn away over the years. Devils Tower, as it is popularly known, is a rock climber's paradise, but it is also a spiritual sanctuary for some of the Native American tribes in the surrounding area.

The Oceti Sakowin (Seven Council Campfires), which include the Dakota, Nakota, Lakota, and Assisiboine — one of many tribal groups in this region — has known Devils Tower as Mato Tipila Paha (the Hill of the Bear's Lodge). Their origin story, which has been passed down through the generations, tells of a time when one of the bands was camped near where Devils Tower now stands. A brother and his sister strayed from the camp and were chased by bears. A voice directed them to a small butte. The bears surrounded them and began to close in. Fallen Star, a hero in the Oceti Sakowin's *ohunkakan* (long-ago stories), commanded the earth to rise. The bears clawed at the earth as it rose, protect-

ing the children, who were later returned safely to the earth. That clawed hill has become known as Devils Tower.

Mato Tipila Paha represented the last part of the annual ceremonial journey of the Oceti Sakowin. The journey began with the Pipe Ceremony and the welcoming back of the thunders at Hinhan Kaga Paha (Harney Peak) during the spring equinox, then proceeded to Pe Sla (Center of the Black Hills), welcoming back all of life, and ended at Mato Tipila Paha with the Sun Dance at the start of the summer solstice.

During this spiritual journey, Mato Tipila Paha became Pte He Gi (Gray Buffalo Horn); Inyan Kaga (south of Devils Tower) became Pte He Sapa (Black Buffalo Horn), and Bear Butte (Mato Paha) became Pte Pute Ya (the Buffalo's Nose). The triangle formed by these three mountains was called the Buffalo's Head, which faced east toward the rising sun.

In addition to the Oceti Sakowin, other tribes that have a cultural connection to Devils Tower are the Eastern Shoshone and Arapaho of Wyoming; the Blackfeet, Crow, and Northern Cheyenne of Montana; the Three Affiliated Tribes and Turtle Mountain Chippewa of North Dakota; the Blackfeet and Piegan of Canada; and the Kiowa and Southern Cheyenne of Oklahoma.

Conflicts have occurred between the rock climbers and people engaged in ceremonial practices during the summer solstice. Adherence to equal respect and the sharing of this unique place between spiritual practitioners and rock climbers is evolving. The understanding that Devils Tower (Mato Tipila Paha) is a spiritual place must continue to grow.

FURTHER READING: *Lakota Star Knowledge: Studies in Lakota Stellar Theology,* by Ronald Goodman

Buffalo Jumps

ROSALYN R. LAPIER

❖ D. H. Lawrence wrote, in "The Spirit of Place," that "every continent has its own great spirit of place. Every people is polarized in some particular locality, which is home, the homeland." The Blackfeet homeland is in the shadow of Mokakinisi, "the Backbone of the World," as we call the Rocky Mountains. Our intimate knowledge of this landscape, the animals, and the plants made it possible for the Blackfeet and other Great Plains tribes to hunt and gather strategically. In the buffalo jump, people made ingenious use of the landscape for their survival. Buffalo moved throughout the Great Plains, but in the winter they preferred more protected areas. The people, observing these patterns, placed rock cairns to form drive lanes leading to the edge of high bluffs. Young men lured the buffalo into these lanes to "jump" them over the cliff. The women butchered the buffalo and processed the hides. They cut the meat into thin strips, which they dried on racks in the sun or over hot coals. *Káyiis*, the dried meat, was kept for future use or was pounded and mixed with crushed dried berries and fat to make pemmican, *móókaakin.*

The people revered the buffalo. Elaborate religious rituals surrounded buffalo hunting. The Blackfeet used *iinisskimm*, the buffalo calling stone, in a ceremony to "call" the buffalo. Some rituals help humans cope with the moral dilemma of killing another being, one that potentially provides powerful supernatural assistance. After the American Indians on the northern Great Plains acquired horses — which the Spanish had brought to the continent — the use of buffalo jumps died out. The people no longer had to "call" the buffalo; they could chase them.

Today buffalo jumps are places to learn about our past, to learn how the people of the plains developed an intimate knowledge of this landscape and utilized it to live a rich life.

FURTHER READING: *The Buffalo People: Prehistoric Archaeology on the Canadian Plains,* by Liz Bryan

203. First Peoples Buffalo Jump State Park, MT

On the Ulm-Vaughn Rd., northwest of Ulm

Visitor center

From about A.D. 900 until about 1500, many tribes drove buffalo off the steep drop-offs along this mile-long cliff.

204. Madison Buffalo Jump State Park, MT

Off I-90 on Buffalo Jump Rd., south of Logan

The Shoshone used this jump most frequently, and many other tribes came to the area for its abundant resources.

205. Wahkpa Chu'gn Buffalo Jump Archaeological Site, MT

Off Rte. 2, west of Havre

Until about A.D. 1400, Native people used this site along the Milk River to kill and butcher buffalo.

206. Pictograph Cave State Park, MT

George Horse Capture

Off I-90 at the Lockwood exit to Coburn Rd., south of Billings

Southeast of Billings, across the gentle sloping "breaks" of the nearby Yellowstone River, past the hill of transmitting towers, there is an ancient and peaceful place known as Pictograph Cave State Park. Carved eons ago by the springtime streams of water flowing over the sandstone cliffs near Bitter Creek, three caves nestled in the horseshoe-shaped terrain mark the passage of our Indian ancestors: Ghost Cave, Middle Cave, and Pictograph Cave. They are a sight to behold. About 100 pictographs decorate the walls of the caves, featuring weapons, horses, elk, and other animals, tipis, a beautiful turtle, and anthropomorphic and mystical figures. The paint colors are red, black, and white. Some have been carbon-dated to 3,000 years ago, and others are more recent. Thankfully, some of the more interesting pictographs were copied on paper by WPA artists in 1937, when the site was excavated, and the copies are stored at Montana State University — Missoula. Since then vandals and natural elements have taken their toll. Moisture on the walls forms strange stains as it causes the sandstone to disintegrate, leaving only a few of these ancient pictographs to enjoy today.

When one visits this place there is magic in the air if one sees with more than one's eyes. In addition to some surviving pictographs, outlines of spiritlike images crowd together at the back of the caves. Their haunting human shapes evoke memories of the First People when they lived nearby and are reminders of what happened to them and their descendants. It feels as if they are trying to tell us something important, but because of the noise in this world, we can't quite hear them.

207. Jeffers Petroglyphs, MN

Joe Williams

East off Rte. 71 on County Rd. 10 to County Rd. 2, southwest of Comfrey

Visitor center open daily from Memorial Day through Labor Day

Jeffers Petroglyphs is a living, sacred place on Dakota ancestral lands where indigenous peo-

ple have worshipped for thousands of years. Between 5,000 and 250 years ago, they carved more than 2,000 images into the exposed quartzite along a tall ridge 3 miles wide and 25 miles long. The carvings record thousands of years of interactions with the spiritual world. The images represent the prayers of people seeking spiritual guidance and record their parables and historic events. The carvings document the perseverance of the people, including the Cheyenne, Dakota, Arapaho, Oto, and Iowa, who thrived on this prairie for thousands of years because of their deep understanding of and intimate relationship with their physical and spiritual world. Today American Indians visit and pray at this sacred place.

FURTHER READING: *The Jeffers Petroglyphs: Native American Rock Art on the Midwest Plains,* by Kevin Callahan

208. Pipestone National Monument, MN

Glen H. Livermont

Off Rte. 75, Pipestone

Visitor center and Upper Midwest Indian Cultural Center

> At an ancient time, the Great Spirit, in the form of a large bird, stood upon the wall of rock and called all the tribes around him, and, breaking out a piece of the red stone, formed it into a pipe and smoked it, the smoke rolling over the whole multitude. He then told his children that this red stone was their flesh, that they were made from it, that they must all smoke to him through it, that they must use it for nothing but pipes — and as it belonged to all tribes, the ground was sacred, and no weapons must be used or brought upon it.

In 1836 the artist George Catlin recorded this Sioux origin story. Other Plains Indians have stories of pipestone, showing its importance in the traditional beliefs and practices at the red pipestone quarries.

The tree-lined Pipestone Creek flows through the grass-covered valley and creates a rich riparian corridor for animals and plants. From the quartzite formations, American Indians have for generations quarried pipestone to carve their sacred *chamupa* (pipes). The National Park Service manages the fifty-six quarries, allocating permits to Indians enrolled in federally recognized tribes. There is a two-year waiting list, attesting to the demand for this sacred stone, in spite of the hard physical labor required to quarry it. Using hand tools, quarriers laboriously smash through up to 15 feet of quartzite to expose the thin layer of pipestone, a great personal investment of labor and religious commitment and a testament to the reverence in which the sacred red stone is held. The pipes fashioned from the stone are an integral part of American Indian religion and culture and are central to all sacred ceremonies. The use of tobacco, *cansasa*, in the pipes conveys through the smoke the prayers and desires of the users to their Great Spirit. This ritualistic use of pipes and pipestone by American Indians gives the quarries their cultural and religious importance.

FURTHER READING: *Pipestone: A History,* by Robert A. Murray

209. Agate Fossil Beds National Monument, NE: A′bekiya wama′k′ aśk′ an s′e — Animal Bones Brutally Scattered About

Sebastian C. LeBeau II

On Rte. 29, south of Harrison

Visitor center and museum

The old Lakota name for Agate Fossil Beds National Monument is *A 'bekiya wama 'k'aśk'aŋ s'e* — Animal Bones Brutally Scattered About. The name refers to the fossil bed below Carnegie Hill containing the fossilized remains of prehistoric animals, or *Uŋhce 'ġilahu* (bones of the monster) to the Lakota. Far back in their cultural past, during the time period known as *Wico 'icaġe P'e 't'a kiŋ* (the Age of Fire), their ancestors, the *Ikce Oya 't'e* (Real People), hunted and camped in the area. In the old days the people believed that *Wakiŋ 'yaŋ* (Winged One) destroyed the *Uŋhce 'ġila,* turning their skeletons into stone and placing them in the ground, where their presence could not harm people. However, *Gnaśk'iŋ 'yaŋ* (the Spirit of Folly) tricked a young man into using the bones as *Wi 'hmuŋġe* (witch medicine). To counter this, *Wakiŋ 'yaŋ* asked if any animals would sacrifice themselves and become stone so that they would always be on hand to protect people. The beavers volunteered, and *Wakiŋ 'yaŋ* changed them into stone so they will exist for as long the *Uŋhce 'ġilahu* exist. The ancient land beaver, *Paleocastor,* was a creature known to the *Ikce Oya 't'e.* Its fossilized burrows, known as *Daemonelix,* dug into the bank of the Niobrara River, are called *Capa Ti* (beavers' lodge) by the Lakota. The burrows exist to balance the effects of *Gnaśk'iŋ 'yaŋ* and his *Wi 'hmuŋġe.* These Native stories express the cultural significance of the park's landscape to the Lakota.

At the visitor center and museum, visitors can learn about the 19–21-million-year-old Miocene-epoch mammal fossils, the people who camped along the Niobrara River about 2,500 years ago, and the many American Indians who were in the Agate Valley in the eighteenth and nineteenth centuries, including the Apache, Arapaho, Arikara, Cheyenne, Comanche, Crow, Dakota Sioux, Kiowa, Lakota Sioux, Nakota Sioux, Omaha, Pawnee, Ponca, and Shoshoni. The exhibits in the James Cook Gallery include beadwork, catlinite pipes, and quillwork made by American Indians and information about the Cheyenne, Chief Red Cloud, and other Oglala Lakota who gathered here.

FURTHER READING: *Fifty Years on the Old Frontier,* by James H. Cook

210. Bear Butte State Park, SD: Mato Paha — Sacred Sentinel of the Northern Plains

Jace DeCory

On Rte. 79, northeast of Sturgis

Education Center

The bear made his journey from Mato Tipila (Bear Lodge/Devils Tower) to rest on the periphery of He Sapa, the Black Hills of South Dakota. Known by the Lakota as Mato Paha and by the Cheyenne as Noahvose, Bear Butte serves as a sentinel on the plains. An occasional snore or growl reminds us of the bear's powerful presence. Approaching this icon, one is filled with overwhelming joy, anticipation, and hope that prayers will be heard — knowing that one will leave a better person. We offer prayers in the form of tobacco wrapped in colorful cloth, crying that prayers will be answered, reminded by our elders to come with humbleness and a good heart. Bear Butte is a gift from the Creator. For thousands of years, travelers came to fast, pray, seek visions, find direction, and receive sacred laws at this volcanic laccolith, where ceremonies are validated, our spiritual beliefs are rooted, and holy pilgrimages are made.

At Mato Paha, Fools Crow, a Lakota spiritual leader, received visions and guidance to be a healer. Crazy Horse and Sitting Bull prayed here. In 1857 the Lakota held a great reunion to resist further encroachment on treaty lands. The hard work of preserving Mato Paha must continue because there is adult entertainment nearby with unholy behavior and alcohol abuse, which threatens the sanctity and meditative calm. While most come to pray, others come to play. The bear will sleep well as long as we maintain our

spiritual ties to Mato Paha. Because traditional cultural rites provide human beings with healing connectedness to the land, our stewardship of open spaces and sacred sites is a duty to our Creator and to future generations. Mato Paha deserves our respect. We must continue to pray and listen. *Mitakuye oyasin* — We are all related.

FURTHER READING: *Where the Lightning Strikes: The Lives of American Indian Sacred Places,* by Peter Nabokov

211. Badlands National Park, SD: Mako Sica and the Oglala Lakota

Paul M. Robertson

Off I-90, southeast of Rapid City

Cedar Pass Visitor Center and White River Visitor Center

The Lakota call it Mako Sica — Badlands — and in a departure from the common practice of renaming natural features in Lakota country after white settlers, cavalry officers, or frontier agents, the name stuck. Drive north on BIA Highway 27 through the Oglala Lakota Nation, past the Wounded Knee Massacre site, to the White River Visitor Center in the Southern Unit of Badlands National Park, and you get a hunch about why the name stuck. The White River, near the southern boundary of the quarter-million-acre national park, is a light, smoky hue, while dramatic mud buttes and pinnacles carved by rain and wind, tables rising hundreds of feet above the mixed-grass prairie, extensive alkali flats, and the ubiquitous circling turkey vultures lend it a forbidding beauty. Lakota people say that before the long knives (whites) came, they traveled through the area only if they absolutely had to. Good water and game were scarce, and travel was difficult — hence the name. Lakota elders still call the Cheyenne River, just north of the park, Wakpa Waste (Good River), because the abundant wood, game, and pasture for horses made it a good place to travel along. Although the Lakota did not dwell in the badlands, their oral tradition tells of an ancient warlike tribe, the *wa sesa un* (people who wear the red paint), who once lived there. Tipi rings, earthen fireplaces, and stone implements that are about 12,000 years old are said to have been left by the *wa sesa un.*

Richard Two Dogs, an Oglala Lakota spiritual leader who lives in Porcupine, not far from the park, told me that his grandfather said the people tried to avoid being downwind from the badlands when the wind blew hard, believing that something in there could make them sick. In the 1980s Lakotas stopped an initiative to mine the rich zeolite deposits in the badlands, arguing in part that dust from the planned strip mining would be a health hazard. But the Lakota also regard the badlands as a source of healing. The sediment that gives the White River — Maki Zite (smoky earth water) — its color was once used on wounds to draw out infections. Spiritual leaders still go into the park to collect plants for traditional medicines, and Lakota people conduct ceremonies there, including *hambleceya* — crying for a vision. Visitors in the southern area of the park are alerted not to disturb any flags or tobacco offerings.

The park supports *wanbli gleska* (spotted eagles) — golden eagles — and a recently introduced population of highly endangered black-footed ferrets, which thrive on their chief prey, prairie dogs. Herds of Rocky Mountain bighorn sheep, pronghorn antelope, and buffalo roam in the protected area. The Oglala Sioux Tribe's Department of Parks and Recreation, which jointly administers the park's Stronghold Unit, has reported an increase in mountain lion sightings. The joint management agreement provides an opportunity for the Oglala Lakota people to manage their own resources. The tribal employees' perspective is critical to culturally sensitive

development in the park, and they are keen to protect its many historic, prehistoric, and sacred sites. The Stronghold Unit is a particularly important area. It was there that Lakota people danced the Ghost Dance in the late nineteenth century, praying for the return of the buffalo and the end of colonial domination. It is also the site of the natural fortress where Lakota people fled for protection after the 1890 Massacre of Wounded Knee. Wiwang Wacipi — Sun Dance — ceremonies have been held there in recent years.

The Oglala Lakota people have a proud history. Although they have suffered a great deal from unjust and cruel colonial policies before and during the reservation era, they are intent on reclaiming their land, their language, and their culture. They are starting new businesses, asserting their treaty claims, working to rebuild their governance structures, teaching their children Lakol Wicohan (Lakota Ways), and arming them with education.

FURTHER READING: *Insiders' Guide to South Dakota's Black Hills and Badlands,* by Thomas D. Griffith and Dustin D. Floyd

212. Mount Rushmore National Memorial, SD: Paha Sapa — Ancestral Homeland of the Lakota

Rhonda Buell Schier

On Hwy. 244, south of Keystone

Lincoln Borglum Museum

"Why is there a tipi here?" asks a visitor upon arriving at Mount Rushmore National Memorial. "These are two completely different stories." This greeting signals an opportunity for the National Park Service interpretive rangers to engage visitors in an exploration of American history from multiple points of view. As people of ever-changing diversity arrive at Mount Rushmore to discover our nation's history, the rangers help them investigate the story of the human experience from different perspectives and with an appreciation for the contributions of the many cultures of our country. Why, indeed, is there a tipi in the foreground of the giant sculpted portraits of Washington, Jefferson, Lincoln, and Roosevelt?

The answer is in the towering granite cliffs of Rushmore Rock, in the forest of Ponderosa pine, in the streams of Grizzly Gulch, along the rugged path in Starling Basin, and in the vivid blue sky that serves as the canopy to this "island in the plains." This is the Paha Sapa — the hills of black — named by the Lakota, who for centuries have considered the area sacred, "the heart of all that is," a part of Mother Earth and Father Sky, from which all life comes and to whom all life returns. The oral histories of the Native people tell us of a kinship with nature. Nicholas Black Elk, the Oglala Lakota holy man for whom our neighboring wilderness area is named, said, "It is the story of all life that is holy and good to tell of us two-leggeds sharing with the four-leggeds and the wings of the air and all green things, for these are children of one another and their father is one spirit."

This park is small compared to the enormous parks such as Yellowstone and Glacier, but within its boundaries is an ecosystem that comprises what the sculptor of the four presidents, Gutzon Borglum, described as a "veritable garden of the Gods." Long before Borglum had the vision of American history marching along the skyline, that history was already present among the people of the first nations. The indigenous people, the original inhabitants of the Black Hills, turned to the animals, plants, and landscape for food, medicine, and spirituality, enabling them to sustain their cultures, which still thrive today.

When we look at Mount Rushmore, we see more than the portraits of leaders who created our democratic form of government. We also see a granite mountain preserved as a cornerstone of the ancestral homeland for the Arikara, Cheyenne, Kiowa, Pawnee, Crow, and Lakota. Here at Mount Rushmore we honor the stories of our nation's heritage. We strive to create a place of respect for diverse cultures and revitalization for Native people.

Why is there a tipi at Mount Rushmore? Why indeed!

FURTHER READING: *Black Elk Speaks,* by John G. Neihardt

213. Mitchell Prehistoric Indian Village, SD

3200 Indian Village Rd., north of Mitchell

Boehnen Memorial Museum and Thomsen Center Archeodome

About 1,000 years ago, 600 or so people lived in about seventy earth lodges in this fortified earth-lodge village. They grew crops, hunted bison, and fished in Firesteel Creek and the James River. Research suggests that they lived here for about fifty years and then moved to the Missouri River. The Archeodome, a teaching and research facility, covers the remains of three earth lodges.

214. Blood Run National Historic Landmark, IA: Peace on the Prairie

Lance M. Foster

Off Rte. K10, west of Granite

An area near Rte. K10 is open daily; tours are by appointment with the Lyon County Conservation Board

Even commonplace landscapes can have mythic importance, and Blood Run is such a place. It is along a loop of the Big Sioux River in Iowa and

South Dakota. The people of the Oneota culture lived here between about A.D. 1200 and 1700 in a large, complex ceremonial center that included cache pits, earthworks, mounds, stone circles, and boulders with cupules (tiny cup-shaped indentations) pecked into them. A study in 1883 reported 276 mounds; there are about 76 today. The descendants of the Oneota, Omaha, Ioway, and Otoe tribes had their village here as part of a wider tribal landscape that stretched from Nebraska east to today's Pipestone National Monument and Effigy Mounds National Monument. Blood Run also has spiritual significance as the place where intertribal peace was established in about 1680 through the ceremony of the Calumet or Pipe Dance, ending the strife among the Arikara, Cheyenne, Ioway, Omaha, and Otoe. The dance brought about peace through the various tribes' adoption of one another's children.

By 1750 these tribes had left Blood Run as a result of epidemics and the rise to power of the Sioux. The Arikara and Cheyenne moved northwest, up the Missouri; the Omaha, Otoe, and Ioway moved south, down the Missouri. Today these tribes have reservations throughout the region: the Cheyenne in Montana and Oklahoma, the Arikara in North Dakota, the Omaha in Nebraska, the Otoe in Oklahoma, and the Ioway in Kansas, Nebraska, and Oklahoma. Although these tribes left Blood Run, the peace they made still rests here. On a quiet evening, in the rustle of grass, in a small gust of wind, their ceremonial song of the Calumet Dance may be remembered: "This is what I seek: Peace, which has come as a small child."

FURTHER READING: "A Closing Circle: Musings on the Ioway Indians in Iowa," by Lance M. Foster, in *The Worlds Between Two Rivers: Perspectives on American Indians in Iowa*, edited by Gretchen Bataile, David Gradwohl, and Charles Silet

The Myth of Nomadism and Indigenous Lands

DAVID E. WILKINS

❖ Land and its flora and fauna are vital to indigenous nationhood and provide the foundation for Native identity. European settlers and their descendants had very different concepts of the ownership and use of land from those of America's Native peoples. The idea of a legalistic separation of ownership from the use and care of land was foreign to American Indians. Historically, most Native people maintained that no one had the right to own or sell the earth, which was viewed as the fountain of life. Non-Native intruders have persistently sought to disrupt Native relationships to the land in an effort to establish hegemony over it. Therefore it is appropriate to review some of the more notable rhetorical devices employed then and now by non-Native interlopers, which have enabled them to gain effective control over about 98 percent of Native land in the continental United States.

Felix S. Cohen, a great legal scholar, was often said to have been the dean of federal Indian law. In his 1945 article "Indian Claims" (included in *The Legal Conscience: Selected Papers of Felix S. Cohen*) he discussed the three most powerful "myths" then used by whites and white government officials to justify the usurpation of Indian rights and lands: the Myth of Moral Progress, the Myth of the Vanishing Indian, and the Myth of Indian Nomadism.

The Moral Progress myth allowed non-Indians to benefit from past depredations by asserting that the predators were morally superior to their prey. It declared that Native peoples were culturally retarded and therefore had no business resisting the efforts of their allegedly more enlightened and progressive non-Indian neighbors and their governments to "improve" the lands and more effectively "utilize" the resources on, coursing through, or below the land's surface.

The Myth of the Vanishing Indian holds that Indians were slowly but inexorably dying out, opening the continent to the whites' "manifest destiny" to replace them. This destiny was thought to be ordained by God because whites were the hardier race, but as Cohen wrote in the 1940s, Indian people were actually "the most rapidly increasing part of our population."

The Myth of Nomadism, probably the most pernicious of the three, has been used since the early colonial era to justify the diminution and dispossession of Native peoples' land rights. According to the mythmakers, as Cohen put it, "a white man 'travels' or 'commutes' [while] an Indian (like a buffalo) 'roams.'" Accordingly, even some Supreme Court justices argued that Indian "roamers" were not "owners" and thus had no bona fide land titles that could be legally recognized, enforced, or respected by whites. Thus non-Indian "discoverers" and their successors could assert an act of "discovery" that gave them superior claims to territory that had been for millennia the homelands of Native nations. This myth was propagated even though it was not the reality. The first Native Americans the Europeans met along the Atlantic and Pacific coasts lived there year-round. Tribes in the Midwest and the South planted vast fields of corn. Since they did not have domesticated farm animals, many Indians left their farms for part of the year to hunt, returning to harvest their crops and live in their villages during the rest of the year. Very few traveled for the entire year.

However, as recently as 2005 the effects of the Myth of Nomadism were evident in the U.S. Supreme Court decision *City of Sherrill v. Oneida Indian Nation*. Writing for the court, Associate Justice Ruth Bader Ginsburg said: "Under the 'doctrine of discovery' . . . fee title to the lands occupied by Indians when the colonists arrived became vested in the sovereign — first the discovering European nation and later the original States and the United States." As the language of the *Sherrill* decision shows, the Myth of Nomadism continues to permeate the national legal system by implication, causing profound difficulties for Native nations in their efforts to stabilize or expand their minuscule land holdings. Until all such myths are explicitly disavowed and federal, state, and indigenous lawmakers make a clear attempt to identify and codify the actual status of Indian nations and their land holdings, tribal nations will find it difficult to continue their national reconstruction and improve intergovernmental relations with the surrounding polities.

FURTHER READING: *The Legal Conscience: Selected Papers of Felix S. Cohen,* edited by Lucy Kramer Cohen

215. Menoken Indian Village State Historic Site, ND

North of I-94, east of Bismarck

About A.D. 1200, hunters and gatherers lived in this small community east of the Missouri River. They built about thirty earth-covered houses protected by a bastioned fortification ditch. It was apparently destroyed by fire about A.D. 1215.

216. Knife River Indian Villages National Historic Site, ND

Gerard (Yellow Wolf) Baker

On Rte. 37, north of Stanton

Visitor center

The confluence of the Knife and Missouri rivers is the traditional homeland of the Mandan and the Hidatsa. The historic site preserves the remains of some of their villages, one of which was the home of Hidatsa as early as about A.D. 1400 to 1450. The people lived in earth lodges in the winter, some of which were 60 feet in diameter, sheltered by the big cottonwood trees. In the summer they lived on higher ground. They raised crops — the responsibility of the women — in the river bottomlands. They had elaborate ceremonies relating to the crops, believing that all living things have a spirit. They stored the harvests in deep cache pits. In good years they had enough to last the winter and to trade with other tribes. The active northern plains trade network included Knife River flint as well as crops. The people were organized into matrilineal clans and age-determined societies. The seasons dictated their activities. In the spring, when the ice broke in the river and the geese returned, it was time to plant. In the summer the women tended their gardens and the men hunted for game. This was also the time for ceremonies. Fall was harvest time for the women, while the men went out on the prairies to hunt buffalo. The cold winters kept people close to home.

Smallpox arrived in 1837 with the infected people and their blankets on the steamboat *St. Peter,* which visited nearby Fort Clark in June; about 90 percent of the Mandans and 70 percent of the Hidatsas died as a result. The remaining Mandans left their Fort Clark village in 1837, and when they returned the next year the Arikara had arrived, having migrated northward along the Missouri River. In 1845 the Hidatsa and the Mandan left their Knife River villages and their way of life and established Like-a-Fishhook Village about 80 miles up the Missouri River. The Arikara joined them in 1862. Here even more of the "old ways" were taken away, not only by the government but also by organized Christianity. The Dawes Act of 1887 forced the people to leave their village way of life behind and move onto allotments. Like many tribes in America, we continued to suffer from broken treaties and from the loss of our homeland. But today we are still a proud people, and most, though not all, live on the Fort Berthold Indian Reservation. We include ranchers, farmers, teachers, judges, park superintendents, doctors, lawyers, and other professionals. We still have our clans, and we are bringing back the societies. We know that our ancestors still live in the Spirit Villages, so when you visit the Knife River Indian Villages, stop, go off by yourself, and you may hear them sing.

FURTHER READING: *Women of the Earth Lodges: Tribal Life on the Plains,* by Virginia Peters

217. Huff Indian Village State Historic Site, ND

On Hwy. 1806, south of Huff

About A.D. 1450, Mandans built this carefully planned village of earth lodges and protected it with a fortification ditch about 2,000 feet long with ten bastions. The village has been so carefully preserved that the rectangular shapes of the lodges can still be seen in the depressions in the ground.

218. Double Ditch Indian Village State Historic Site, ND

On Hwy. 1804, north of Bismarck

Mandans lived in this large earth-lodge village between about 1490 and 1785. The remains of many circular earth lodges can be seen within the two visible fortification ditches. Two earlier outer ditches found recently show that the village was reduced in size over time, probably because of disease. Large refuse middens surround the village.

219. Fort Abraham Lincoln State Park, ND: On-a-Slant Village

Tracy Potter

On Rte. 1806, south of Mandan

Museum

More than 400 years ago, families from three nearby Mandan villages built a new community on about five sloping acres tucked between the Missouri River and a high bluff. The Mandan chose the site for their village, which became known as On-a-Slant — Miti-o-pa-resh — for two reasons. The first was defense. The site was protected on the south by a steep ravine and on the north by a natural cut bank. On the western edge of the village, these remarkable people completed a huge public works project. They dug a 600-foot-long ditch — a dry moat — with stone, bone, and wooden tools and backed it with a high palisade of cottonwood, elm, and ash poles. It is likely that they built palisades to encircle the entire village, doubling the natural defenses with their man-made ones.

The Mandans' second consideration was access to the rich bottomland along the Missouri. The broad, flat field below Miti-o-pa-resh and to the north beckoned the women, who were the gardeners, to plant their crops. The Mandan were genetic engineers who developed and grew thirteen varieties of corn, matching their thirteen clans. The number thirteen appears repeatedly in Mandan culture. They also grew sunflowers, nine varieties of beans, and five kinds of squash. The men grew tobacco and hunted, bringing meat and hides back to the lodges. The villages used every part of the buffalo, including the droppings left behind on the prairie, which they dried for fuel.

Their success in farming and hunting meant that the Mandan had surplus food, which they stored in cache pits under and near their lodges, enabling them to live in their villages year-round. They also traded their surplus, and their permanent towns became trading centers. About 1,000 people lived in perhaps eighty-five round, earth-covered lodges in Miti-o-pa-resh, built and owned by the women. The lodges were sensibly constructed for the wild swings in the climate of the northern plains. They could be heated to stay warm when winter temperatures dropped to 20 below zero and were cool in the 100-degree summers. Extended families of ten, twelve, or twenty lived within their comforting circle. Life in On-a-Slant ended after the dreadful smallpox epidemic of 1781. The Mandan abandoned Miti-o-pa-resh, but they are honored today with five reconstructed lodges and the lessons in Mandan history and culture given by tour guides.

FURTHER READING: *Mandan Social and Ceremonial Organization*, by Alfred W. Bowers

220. Fort Clark State Historic Site, ND

On Rte. 200, southeast of Stanton

Open mid-May through mid-September

In 1822 Mandans built an earth-lodge village, Mitu' tahakto's (first or east village), on the Missouri River. In the early 1830s the American Fur Company built the Fort Clark trading post near the village. In 1837 most of the Mandans died in a smallpox epidemic, and many of the survivors fled to join the Hidatsa. The next year, Arikaras moved into the village, where they lived in the summer and grew crops. In 1850 a competitor built Primeau's Post between the village and the fort. Part of Fort Clark burned in 1860, and the owners bought Primeau's Post. When the American Fur Company abandoned the post that year and moved their operations to Fort Berthold farther upriver, the Arikara abandoned the village and moved to Star Village, across the river from that fort. Depressions in the ground reveal the site of Mitu' tahakto's and its fortification. While he was there in 1833–34, Karl Bodmer, a Swiss artist, painted watercolors — now in the

Joslyn Art Museum in Omaha, Nebraska — of the village and its people.

221. Van Meter State Park, MO: Missouria Village

Matthew Jones

On Rte. 122, northwest of Marshall

Missouri's American Indian Cultural Center

Along the great river Nyi Shuje — Smoking Water — there once lived a people who were great warriors. They used Nyi Shuje like a modern highway and traveled from its junction with Nyi Tan — Muddy Water (the Mississippi) — all the way into southwestern Iowa. Many tribes told stories about the people's skill and bravery in battle. Known by many names — Neotacha, Massorites, Ouemessourit, and Missouria — they were respected and feared. They had originated in the Great Lakes region of southern Canada and had migrated south with three other nations — the Hotonga, Hochungra, and Aiouez. Over time the nations separated, and the Hotonga and Ouemessourit continued their migration until they found fertile land for agriculture along Nyi Shuje. They built a village and lived in peace until an argument between the two nations split them. The Hotonga left and traveled up Nyi Shuje to southeastern Nebraska, where they settled. The Ouemessourit stayed in their village and made a good life for themselves, raising crops, fishing, and hunting buffalo on the plains. They were such a dynamic force in the region that the French renamed Nyi Shuje after them, calling it the Missouri River. The French explorers Jacques Marquette and Louis Jolliet showed the Ouemessourit on their 1673 map.

As Native nations were forced out of their traditional areas and onto the plains, old enemies began to confront the Ouemessourit, and wars erupted. In 1798, as the Ouemessourit were moving to a new village site down the Missouri River, they were ambushed by the Sauk and Mesquakie and nearly annihilated. After this massacre, a small number of the Ouemessourit sought refuge with the Kansa and the Osage, while a larger group fled farther up the Missouri River and took refuge with the Hotonga, who called themselves Wahtohtana. These two nations were still living together in July 1804 when Meriwether Lewis and William Clark found them along the Platte River in Nebraska. Earlier in June these explorers had written in their journals about seeking an old, decaying Missouri Indian village on the north shore of the Missouri River.

This great nation has been honored by having a river and the state of Missouri named after it. The site of one of the Ouemessourit villages and the earthworks that they built, known as the Old Fort, have been preserved in the state park. The homeland of the Otoe-Missouria Indian Tribe of Oklahoma is in Red Rock. To learn more about the Otoe-Missouria Tribe, visit their Web site at www.omtribe.org.

FURTHER READING: *The Otoes and Missourias: A Study of Indian Removal and the Legal Aftermath,* by Berlin Basil Chapman

222. Scott State Park, KS: El Cuartelejo

520 West Scott Lake Dr., Scott City

Plains Apaches were living in a village here when Taos Indians arrived in 1664, having fled Spanish rule before the 1680 Pueblo Revolt in present-day New Mexico. The Taos built a small seven-room pueblo — the outline of which has been restored — where they lived for several years. It became known as El Cuartelejo. Late in the century, Picuris Indians fled Spanish rule and lived here for several years until the Spaniards returned them to their pueblo. The conflicts during the early eighteenth century between the Apaches and other tribes moving into the area resulted in the Apaches abandoning their village and moving south.

223. San Antonio Missions National Historical Park, TX:
Mission Nuestra Señora de la Purísima Concepción de Acuña, Mission San José y San Miguel de Aguayo, Mission San Juan Capistrano, Mission San Francisco de la Espada

David J. Weber

Visitor center at 6701 San Jose Dr., San Antonio

The park preserves the remains and reconstructions of four missions that Indians built under the guidance of Spanish Franciscans on the upper reaches of the San Antonio River. Drawn to this well-watered area by a seasonal Coahuiltecan village, Spaniards established a town, fort, and mission at San Antonio in 1718 as part of a larger effort to block the French from expanding from Louisiana into Texas. A few miles downstream, Franciscans established the San José mission in 1720 and transferred Nuestra Señora de la Purísima Concepción de Acuña, San Juan Capistrano, and San Francisco de la Espada from eastern Texas in 1731. The park comprises these four missions with their stone chapels and outbuildings; the 1718 mission, San Antonio de Valero, known today as the Alamo, is outside the park.

Like Spanish missions elsewhere, the San Antonio missions attracted Indians who sought security from other tribes, from Spanish laymen and soldiers, or from disease and hunger. While the militarily powerful Comanche and Apache avoided the San Antonio missions, the Coahuiltecan-speaking peoples of the region, squeezed from the south by Spaniards and from the north by Apaches, sought refuge behind mission walls.

Once there, Natives learned that the Spaniards would employ force as well as persuasion to eradicate indigenous religions and indigenous ways and replace them with Christianity and Western ways. Although they might have entered a mission willingly, Indians were not allowed to leave after receiving baptism. Franciscans feared that they would fall into apostasy and lose their chance to reach the Christians' heaven. Under the tutelage of Franciscans, Spanish soldiers, and Christianized Indians, new converts learned European trades and methods of farming and ranching, along with the form and substance of Christianity. In these nearly self-sufficient missions, Indians raised crops, tended livestock, made tools, pottery, cloth, and clothing, and constructed chapels, houses, granaries, stables, corrals, dams, and irrigation ditches. Those who openly resisted this regimen might receive physical punishment; runaways were hunted down.

By the mid-1740s, the Native population of the five San Antonio missions reached a high point at about 1,000, with individual missions seldom housing more than 250. Coahuiltecan speakers from a great variety of small bands, most of which are now extinct, made up the majority of the mission populations. Most of the Indians in the missions either succumbed to disease or stayed only long enough to recover their strength, regroup, and flee. Others remained willingly, making the mission their permanent home and mingling with Spaniards who moved onto mission lands as the Native population declined. Over time the last mission Indians blended into Hispanic society. When the missions were dismantled in the late 1700s, few culturally Indian people remained. Today several groups claim descent from Indians of the San Antonio missions and seek to recover their cultural heritage.

FURTHER READING: Essays by Gilberto M. Hinojosa, Anne A. Fox, and Elizabeth A. H. John, in *Tejano Origins in Eighteenth-Century San Antonio*, edited by Gerald E. Poyo and Gilberto M. Hinojosa

224. Pompeys Pillar National Historic Landmark, MT

Off I-94 at exit 23, east of Billings

Interpretive center

Over the ages people have carved petroglyphs into and painted pictographs on this tall, broad sandstone outcrop near a ford on the Yellowstone River in the homeland of the Crow. They also built two rock cairns on top of the outcrop. William Clark added his name in 1806 and named the butte for Sacagawea's baby, Baptiste Charbonneau, whom he called Pompy, the Shoshone word for little chief.

225. Fort Union Trading Post National Historic Site, ND

Off Hwy. 1804, 25 miles southwest of Williston

Visitor center

John Jacob Astor's American Fur Company built Fort Union in 1828, and it was the most important fur-trading post on the upper Missouri until it closed in 1867. It was a center of peaceful exchange, where Assiniboine, Blackfeet, Cree, Crow, Hidatsa, and Ojibwe traded buffalo robes and other furs for trade goods such as guns, knives, kettles, blankets, cloth, and beads. The rebuilt trade house is part of the partially reconstructed trading post.

226. Pawnee Indian Museum State Historic Site, KS

Robert Fields

North of U.S. 36 on KS Hwy. 266, Republic

In the 1820s this was a thriving and productive village. About 2,000 of the Kitkehahki band of Pawnee lived in forty to fifty earth lodges on a bluff overlooking the Republican River Valley, where the women raised corn, beans, and squash. Their round lodges, 30 to 40 feet in diameter, with a smoke hole in the center, looked like earth mounds. They had a strong framework of timbers with a final cover of sod. The Kitkehahki fortified their village with a wall of sod and timbers for protection from their enemies. In the spring and fall the entire village moved onto the High Plains, where they lived in tipis, to hunt bison. As I stood among the sites of twenty-two of their circular lodges, I imagined hearing a grandmother calling to the children who were at play here not so long ago: *"[Ati ka'] Suks atku! [D]aktiki•Ka ruh' [d]at'sa'us?"* (Listen, grandchildren, are you hungry?).

I walked inside the museum building, which encloses one of the larger earth lodges, 50 feet in diameter. The Kitkehahki had made a hard floor by spreading wet clay and then building fires on it to dry and harden it. I took a tour, which included a recording in both English and Pawnee, explaining what I was seeing. Visitors are privileged to listen to a ninety-eight-year-old Pawnee elder, Maude Chisholm, speaking her ancient language. Visible on the original floor are postholes, the remains of burnt timbers that once supported the lodge's thick walls, and the hearth with ashes from the last fire. The large storage pit was probably lined with bark or grass and used to store food, such as corn and dried meat. When the Kitkehahki abandoned their village, they left a ceremonial bison skull, hoe blades made of bison bones, and metal trade goods, including knife blades and an ax. The museum also preserves the presence of the Kitkehahki in exhibits that include maps, photographs, and prints of seven Pawnee warriors painted by George Catlin in 1832; four of the warriors lived in this village.

After living along the Platte and lower Loup rivers in Nebraska and on the Blue and Republican rivers in southern Nebraska and northern Kansas, the Pawnee were removed to the Indian Territory in 1876. In the nineteenth century the Pawnee population declined as a result of wars with their traditional enemies, disease, and the terrible conditions on the reservations; by the end of the century there were only 600–700 tribal members. Today, there are 3,190 enrolled Pawnee. The Pawnee Nation in Pawnee, Oklahoma, is governed by the Pawnee Business Council; the Nation also has a traditional council of chiefs, the Nasharo Council, made up of two chiefs from each of the four bands: Chaui, Pitahawirata, Kitkehahki, and Skidi.

FURTHER READING: *The Lost Universe,* by Gene Weltfish

227. Shawnee Indian Mission State Historic Site, KS

Bertha Cameron and Greg Pitcher

3403 W. 53rd St., Fairway

Museum

Three of the original sixteen buildings, built between 1839 and 1845 as a mission and a manual labor school, remain today. The school, established by the Methodist missionary Rev. Thomas Johnson, provided classroom instruction and manual arts training for Shawnee children and students from other tribes. The students' day, which began at 4 A.M. and ended at 8 P.M., included six hours of classroom instruction. The boys were trained to abandon hunting and become farmers, so they worked on the farm and in the shops for six hours each day. The girls were trained to stop farming and learn domestic skills, so they cooked for the students and employees and sewed clothing for six hours each day. In the spring and fall the students were permitted to return to their families to help with planting and harvesting. The Shawnee on the Kansas River Reserve were primarily farmers

who lived in comfortable log houses and raised vegetables in their fields.

By 1850 many parents had become dissatisfied with the school and began to keep their children at home. Manual-labor instruction ended in 1854 when Kansas became a territory, and the school population dwindled until the school closed in 1862. The mission housed territorial offices from 1854 to 1856. The 11th Kansas Volunteer Cavalry Regiment was stationed there during the Civil War, when Kansas was known as "Bleeding Kansas" because of the violence between those for and those against slavery. Although the Kansas River Reserve was never formally extinguished, nearly all of the land in it was sold to white settlers or given to Civil War veterans by 1870. Congress forced the Shawnee into an agreement that gave them citizenship in the Cherokee Nation, but the Shawnee maintained separate communities and their own cultural and political identities.

The Shawnee Tribe's headquarters are in Miami, Oklahoma, and the tribal enrollment is just under 2,000. It is one of three federally recognized Shawnee tribes; the other two are the Eastern Shawnee Tribe of West Seneca, Oklahoma, and the Absentee Shawnee Tribe of Shawnee, Oklahoma.

FURTHER READING: *The Shawnees and Their Neighbors, 1795–1870,* by Stephen Warren

228. Allegawaho Memorial Heritage Park, KS

James Pepper Henry

On County Rd. K-525, southeast of Council Grove

Kanza Heritage Trail (map available at the Kaw Mission State Historic Site); interpretive panels

On the crest of a grass-covered hill rising high above the treeline of the Neosho River Valley stands a lone sentinel of limestone, a tribute to the Kanza Indians. Erected by the citizens of Council Grove, the monument entombs the remains of an unknown Kanza warrior discovered on the bank of a nearby creek. U.S. Vice President Charles Curtis, a Kanza descendant, attended the August 1925 dedication along with a delegation of Kaw Indians from Oklahoma. The Kanza, or Kaw, for whom the state is named, are a Siouan-speaking people whose homelands once included nearly half of today's Kansas. Beginning in 1825, treaties were signed that reduced the Kanza territory. The U.S. government established an Indian agency and built 138 rectangular stone huts for the Kanza on a 9-by-14-mile reservation near Council Grove. Accustomed to living in round lodges, the Kanza refused to live in dwellings with corners, fearing that evil spirits would be trapped. They preferred living in tipis and used the stone houses as stalls for their horses. This prompted local white residents to declare that the Kaws "treated their horses better than their women." In 1873, when the state of Kansas and the U.S. government prepared to remove the Kanza to Indian Territory, Allegawaho, the principal chief of the Kanza, resisted and declared to the officials in the Indian agency: "Great Father, you whites treat us Kanza like a flock of turkeys. You chase us to one stream, then you chase us to the other stream. Soon you will chase us over the mountain and into the ocean." Despite his desperate plea, the government forced the Kanza to leave their homelands in Kansas and move to today's north-central Oklahoma. As a result of disease and malnutrition, by 1900 fewer than 200 of the more than 1,600 Kanza who left were still alive.

Today the Kanza have rebounded in strength and numbers and are reclaiming our history and our cultural heritage. Now known as the Kaw Nation of Oklahoma, the tribal administration, including Luther Pepper (great-grandson of Chief Allegawaho), negotiated with an area resident, Willis Houston, for the donation of ten acres encompassing the monument and the agency building in the 1990s. The Nation next purchased 148 adjoining acres. Working in partnership with the Kansas State Historical Society and the Kaw Mission State Historic Site, the Kaw Nation established the Allegawaho Memorial Heritage Park and Kanza Heritage Trail, which they dedicated in 2002. The park includes a two-mile trail loop to the stone monument, the remnants of two stone huts, the partially restored and stabilized agency building, restored prairie, and Little John Creek. As a prominent member of the tribe stated at the dedication: "This is a proud day for the Kaw Nation, the 'People of the South Wind.' The Kanzas are returning to a small part of the land which was once their home. We are designating a park to preserve our heritage and to tell people the story of the tribe that gave its name to the state of Kansas."

FURTHER READING: *The Kansa Indians: A History of the Wind People, 1673–1873,* by William E. Unrau

229. Kaw Mission State Historic Site, KS

500 North Mission, Council Grove

The Methodist Episcopal Church South built a mission and school where Kaw boys lived and studied for three years until it closed in 1854.

230. Fort Snelling State Park, MN

Neil (Cantemaza) McKay

Rte. 5 and Post Rd., St. Paul

Thomas C. Savage Visitor Center

Bdote (Mendota) — where the Mississippi and Minnesota rivers meet — is the traditional home of the Dakota *Oyate* (nation). For many Bdewakantunwan Dakota, this is Eden, the middle of all things and the exact center of the earth. The Dakota lived in summer villages on the Mississippi and Minnesota rivers, and Bdote was a stopping place as they traveled along the rivers. Overlooking the confluence is an ancient Dakota burial ground, Oheyawahe (a hill much visited).

After the War of 1812, the United States took control of the vast Northwest by building forts and licensing traders. Fort Snelling was completed in 1824 on the bluff above the confluence of the Mississippi and the Minnesota. Nearby were Dakota villages, trading posts, and the U.S. Indian Agency. Treaties in 1837 and 1851 opened Dakota homelands to settlement. As a tragic consequence of U.S. Indian policy, the Dakota went to war in August 1862. In November the government forcibly removed approximately 1,700 Dakota elders, women, and children from their reservations and marched them to Fort Snelling. There they were held in an internment camp, where about 130 died. The following spring the survivors were sent away from their homeland to a miserable reservation called Crow Creek on the Missouri River. Soon the Ho-Chunk were also forcibly removed from Minnesota. As Jim Anderson, a member of the Mendota Mdewakanton Dakota Community, has stated, "Mendota is the place of genesis and genocide of the Dakota people."

The Dakota Commemorative March, held on November 7–13 every other year since 2002, honors the Dakota who were forced to march in 1862. By walking the 150 miles from the Lower Sioux Agency to Fort Snelling, Dakota from the United States and Canada share the continuous grieving and healing process caused by the ill treatment of their ancestors. To remember the thirty-eight Dakota men who were hanged in Mankato in 1862, the Memorial Run has been held annually on December 26 since 1987. It begins at midnight at Fort Snelling and ends at Mankato about noon. As a people, the Dakota

are in various stages of grieving and healing. Bdote will always be a part of this process.

FURTHER READING: *Citadel in the Wilderness: The Story of Fort Snelling and the Northwest Frontier,* by Evan Jones

231. Historic Fort Snelling, MN

Off Rtes. 5 and 55 near the airport, Saint Paul

The U.S. government built the fort at the confluence of the Minnesota and Mississippi rivers to secure American control of the Upper Mississippi Valley and to support the nearby U.S. Indian Agency. It was completed in 1824. The reconstructed stone fortress is a Minnesota Historical Society historic site museum.

232. Lac qui Parle Mission, MN

Off Rte. 59 on Rte. 13, northwest of Montevideo

Open from May through Labor Day

Joseph Renville, son of a Dakota mother and a French father, established a fur-trading post on the Minnesota River in 1826. He invited missionaries to establish a mission in 1835, which closed in 1854 because the Dakota were opposed to it.

233. Traverse des Sioux, MN

On Rte. 169, north of St. Peter

Treaty Site History Center

This shallow crossing of the Minnesota River, called Oiyuwege (the place of crossing) by the Dakota and Traverse des Sioux (crossing place of the Sioux) by the French, was a gathering and trading place. In 1851 it was the site of a treaty between the United States and the Sisseton and

Wahpeton bands of the Dakota, opening nearly all of their lands to settlement.

The Dakota in Minnesota 1851–1862

LENOR A. SCHEFFLER

❖ The Dakota agreed, in the 1851 Treaty of Traverse Des Sioux and in the Treaty of Mendota, to give up nearly all of their homelands in today's Minnesota and move to two small reservations along the Minnesota River. The U.S. government established the Lower Sioux and Upper Sioux agencies to administer the treaty responsibilities to the Dakota and to turn them into English-speaking farmers. Problems soon arose. The Dakota and the government negotiated a new treaty in Washington, D.C., on June 19, 1858, in which the Indians sold their reservations on the north side of the Minnesota River. The price was to be determined by the U.S. Senate, with part of the money set aside to pay debts to the traders. But when the Senate set the price at only thirty cents per acre, the Lower Sioux bands received little money, and the Upper bands far less than they had expected. After an 1861 crop failure and a delay in the 1862 annuity payments, the Dakota had little food and no credit at the traders' stores. The warriors' groups among the Dakota disagreed with the farmers' groups about their treatment by the government. Little Crow, who had tried to mediate between the groups, agreed to lead the warriors into battle. The Dakota attacked the Lower Sioux Agency on August 18 and Fort Ridgely on August 20 and 22, 1862. They destroyed the Upper Sioux Agency on August 28 and attacked Minnesota militia volunteers at Birch Coulee on

September 2. Henry Hastings Sibley, the former governor of Minnesota, who was in command of volunteers, defeated the Dakota later in the month, took many prisoners, and ended the warfare. Little Crow escaped, but the following July he was shot and killed by a farmer.

Sibley appointed a military commission to try the prisoners for "murder and other outrages." More than 300 Dakota were convicted and sentenced to death. The Episcopal bishop of Minnesota, Henry Whipple, had written an open letter to President Lincoln in March 1861, deploring the treatment of the Indians. After the war he traveled to Washington and told the president about its causes and about the plight of the Dakota. President Lincoln changed the sentences of all the convicted Dakotas except for 38, who were hanged in Mankato on December 26, 1862. The others were imprisoned until 1866, when President Andrew Johnson ordered that the 177 survivors be released and sent to a reservation.

234. Lower Sioux Agency, MN

Off Rte. 71 to County Rd. 2, Morton

Interpretive center, open on weekends from Memorial Day through September

The Dakota attacked the Lower Sioux Agency, the government's operations center for the Mdewakanton and Wahpekute bands of Dakota, on August 18, 1862. One stone warehouse, which withstood the battle, has been restored. There are markers at the sites of several traders' stores, the military commission where some of the trials of the Dakota were held, Chief Wabasha's village on the prairie above the Minnesota River Valley, and the Myrick Trading Post, where the trader had denied credit to the Indians, saying, "Let them eat grass." After the attack, his body was found with his mouth stuffed with grass. The government once built houses for those Dakota who had begun to assimilate by becoming farmers, cutting their hair, and wearing white men's clothes. As Indian people today we continue to struggle to maintain our culture and our identity. Some of the struggles we face, in maintaining our own way of life or assimilating partially or completely, are similar to those the Dakota faced in 1862. Our struggles today are no less challenging than theirs.

235. Fort Ridgely State Park, MN

Off Rte. 4, south of Fairfax

Restored fort, open from Memorial Day through Labor Day

The government established Fort Ridgley in 1853 to keep peace between the Dakota and the settlers moving into the area. During the warfare, the fort became a refuge for settlers. The Dakota attacked the fort first on August 20, 1862, and again on August 22. After suffering heavy casualties from artillery and rifle fire, the Dakota ended their attacks.

236. Upper Sioux Agency State Park, MN

5908 Hwy. 67, Granite Falls

The park includes the site of the Upper Sioux Agency near the mouth of the Yellow Medicine River, established to serve the Sisseton and Wahpeton bands of the Dakota. The Dakota name for the area is Pejuhutazizi Kapi (the place where they dig for yellow medicine). The Dakota destroyed the evacuated agency on August 28, 1862.

237. Birch Coulee Battlefield, MN

East of Rte. 71 at the intersection of Rtes. 2 and 18, north of Morton

Open from May through October

Markers along the interpretive trail tell about the battle between the Dakota and the settlers from the perspectives of a Minnesota militia captain, Joseph Anderson, and a Mdewakanton, Wamditanka (Big Eagle). The battle began at dawn on September 2, 1862, when the Dakota, led by Big Eagle, surrounded the militia camp and held the soldiers under siege for thirty-six hours, until Henry Hastings Sibley arrived from Fort Ridgley with a 1,500-man command.

FURTHER READING: *Kinsman of Another Kind: Dakota-White Relations in the Upper Mississippi Valley 1650 to 1862,* by Gary Clayton Anderson

238. Whitestone Hill Battlefield State Historic Site, ND

Off Rte. 56, southeast of Kulm

Museum

On September 3, 1863, Brigadier General Alfred Sully, in command of the military mission into Dakota Territory, attacked a tipi camp of Dakota, Hunkpapa Lakota, Blackfeet (Sihasapa Lakota), and Yanktonai, killing about 200 men, women, and children. They burned about 500,000 pounds of dried buffalo meat, increasing the pressure upon the Sioux to move to reservations.

239. Killdeer Mountain Battlefield State Historic Site, ND

Off Rte. 22, northwest of Killdeer

Brigadier General Alfred Sully, in command of 2,200 troops, continued his military campaign against the Sioux. On July 28, 1864, he attacked a camp of Dakota, Nakota, and Lakota; used artillery to shell the camp, killing men, women, and children; and burned their lodges and food supplies.

240. Fort Laramie National Historic Site, WY

Troy D. Smith

On Rte. 160, south of Fort Laramie

Visitor center

Fort William, a cottonwood-walled fur-trading post built in 1834, was replaced by the adobe-walled Fort John in 1841. Both served as major fur-trading posts in the central Rockies, where traders and Plains Indians met to trade buffalo and other furs. The U.S. Army purchased Fort John in 1849 and founded Fort Laramie. The army had planned to build a stockade around it but did not because of the cost, leaving the fort dependent upon its location and its garrison for protection. The fort was the second built along the Oregon Trail. Travelers on the trail were killing or driving away game, which caused conflicts with the Indians, and there were also intertribal conflicts as a result of the expansion of the powerful Lakota and their allies, the Cheyenne and the Arapaho, into Pawnee, Crow, and Arikara areas. U.S. officials' efforts to keep the peace included compensating tribes for the game that was lost and drafting a multilateral peace treaty with boundaries, which would enable them to assign culpability for any subsequent depredations. Ten thousand Indians arrived at the treaty conference in 1851, including Lakota, Cheyenne, Arapaho, Crow, Arikara, Hidatsa, Assiniboine, and Shoshone — so many that the conference had to be moved to the mouth of Horse Creek, 30 miles to the east. The treaty provided that Indians would allow safe passage for settlers and would allow roads and forts to be built on their lands. In return, the United States pledged

that the Great Plains area would remain theirs and promised to provide annuities for fifty years. The treaty was signed with great fanfare, although the peace it brought about — both between tribes and with the United States — was fragile and short-lived. So were the annuities; Congress later limited them to ten years, and some tribes received none at all.

Another council was held at the fort in 1866 in an attempt to gain Lakota approval for a route through their hunting grounds to the Montana gold mines. Red Cloud opposed the proposed route, the Bozeman Trail, and a large faction joined him in withdrawing from the negotiations. The remaining Indian leaders agreed to the treaty, but those who had opposed it did not recognize it. Before the treaty was signed, soldiers arrived at the fort with orders to begin establishing posts on the Bozeman Trail, ensuring the failure of the treaty. After two years of warfare, Red Cloud agreed in 1868 to negotiate another Fort Laramie Treaty, but only after the three forts along the Bozeman Trail — Reno, Phil Kearny, and C. F. Smith — were closed. This treaty reserved most of present-day western South Dakota, including the Black Hills, as a reservation for the "absolute and undisturbed use" of the Sioux. It set aside the area north of the North Platte River, west of the Missouri, and east of the Bighorn Mountains as hunting grounds for the Indians to "roam and hunt while the game shall be found in sufficient quantities to justify the chase." It provided that there would be no revisions of the treaty without the approval of three-fourths of the adult males of the tribes and that the Bozeman Trail was unceded Indian territory where whites could not settle and where no military forts could be built, so the three forts were abandoned. It stipulated that white teachers, blacksmiths, and farmers would come to live on the reservation to teach the Indians "civilization." Red Cloud agreed to the treaty.

After gold was discovered in the Black Hills,

the U.S. government ordered the tribes to report to their agencies. Knowing that they would refuse to leave their lands, the military mounted a campaign led by Brigadier General George Crook out of Fort Laramie. By 1890, when it was closed, Fort Laramie had been the military's center of operations on the High Plains and on the routes of the Oregon Trail, the Pony Express, the transcontinental telegraph, and the Deadwood Stage.

FURTHER READING: *Fort Laramie and the Pageant of the West, 1834–1890,* by Le Roy R. Hafen and Francis M. Young

241. Fort Phil Kearny State Historic Site, WY

Off I-90 at exit 44, Banner

Visitor center/museum

Forts Phil Kearny, Reno, and C. F. Smith were built in 1866 to protect travelers on the Bozeman Trail but were abandoned two years later. The historic site also includes the sites of Forts Reno and Fetterman, and of the Connor (August 1865), Fetterman (December 1866), and Wagon Box (August 1867) battles.

242. Washita Battlefield National Historic Site, OK

Lawrence Hart

Off Hwy. 47, west of Cheyenne

In an outstanding address on September 8, 2000, to mark the 175th anniversary of the Bureau of Indian Affairs, Kevin Gover, then the assistant secretary for Indian Affairs, Department of the Interior, remorsefully mentioned the battles of Sand Creek, Washita, and Wounded Knee as national tragedies. Of the three, two were perpetrated against the Cheyenne. One

cannot discuss the so-called battle of the Washita on November 27, 1868, without reference to the Sand Creek Massacre of November 29, 1864. During those four years, four incidents stand out. One: the great peace chief Black Kettle held a peace council at Camp Weld near Denver in September 1864 with the commander of the 1st and 3rd Colorado Volunteers, who led the Sand Creek Massacre two months later. Two: Medicine Woman Later, the wife of Black Kettle, received nine bullet wounds at Sand Creek. Three: in another remarkable peace effort, Black Kettle signed the 1865 Treaty of Little Arkansas nine months after surviving Sand Creek. Four: the Cheyenne Dog Soldiers, who blamed the council of forty-four Cheyenne peace chiefs for the massacre at Sand Creek, sought revenge against whites continually for four years.

In 1868 Major General Phillip Sheridan launched a winter campaign against Indian warriors who were attacking and raiding throughout eastern Colorado and western Kansas. He assigned Lieutenant Colonel George Armstrong Custer, 7th U.S. Cavalry, to command the expedition. Riding south from Camp Supply, Custer's scouts found Black Kettle's village of fifty-one lodges along a river the Cheyenne people had named the Lodge Pole River. The scouts mistakenly thought it was the main Cheyenne village, where the Dog Soldiers were camping, and attacked the peaceful village. Black Kettle and his wife, Medicine Woman Later, were shot dead as they attempted to escape on horseback. Fifty-three women and children were captured. Twenty soldiers and twenty-nine Indians were killed.

Some Cheyenne escaped and survived. Several are notable. One was White Buffalo Woman, who rescued two youngsters. Two others were Moving Behind and her aunt, Corn Stalk Woman. Another was Magpie, who was at the Little Bighorn in 1876 when Custer's 7th Cavalry was annihilated. Another was my great-grandfather, Afraid of Beavers, a brother to Medicine Woman Later. He searched for his sister and Black Kettle after Custer and his troops returned to Camp Supply. He found their bodies in the Washita River and buried them in an undisclosed location. The survivors of the Washita and their descendants became members of Cheyenne Chief Red Moon's band. Moving Behind, White Buffalo Woman, and Afraid of Beavers are buried at a cemetery near present-day Hammon, Oklahoma, known by the Cheyenne as the Red Moon Community. As a member of the Red Moon Community and a great-grandson of Afraid of Beavers, I testified in Congress to help establish the Washita Battlefield National Historic Site, dedicated on November 12, 1996.

Today more than 12,000 Cheyenne and Arapaho people are on the rolls of the Cheyenne and Arapaho Tribes of Oklahoma. The government consists of a governor, a lieutenant governor, and eight legislators. The tribal offices are in Concho. In 2006 the Tribes established the Cheyenne and Arapaho Tribal College, now being developed on the campus of Southwestern Oklahoma State University in Weatherford. We are planning to have our own campus in the future.

FURTHER READING: *Washita: The U.S. Army and the Southern Cheyennes, 1867–1869,* by Jerome A. Greene

243. Palo Duro Canyon State Park, TX

Dan L. Flores

On Rte. 217, east of Canyon

Interpretive center

Palo Duro Canyon is one of those singular landforms that affects virtually every first-time viewer in the same way. With no advance warning, the flat, oceanlike Texas High Plains quite suddenly reveal a hidden world: a mile-wide, 1,000-foot-deep roar of color and form that is a quite astonishing antithesis to the linear plain and the blank blue bowl of the sky. The effect is pure magic.

Surprising and beautiful, diverse in geology (four major exposed formations reaching back 200 million years) and ecological diversity, this 50-mile-long canyon created over the past million years by the headwaters of the Red River has been astonishing and delighting us humans since we first came to the continent. Within a 200-mile radius of it lie the two type locations of North America's most ancient Paleolithic sites (Clovis and Folsom, both nearby in New Mexico) as well as one of the most important flint quarries of the Americas, now Alibates National Monument, less than 75 miles to the north. The Archaic campsites that litter the rim of Palo Duro and the incised and painted images on its sandstone walls leave no doubt that for thousands of years the canyon drew Native people to its embrace. Below the winds that scour the surface of the Llano Estacado (as European Spaniards named the raised tableland in which the canyon is carved), Palo Duro and the other canyons of the escarpment offered protected camps shaded by cottonwood canopies, with abundant streams and springs, firewood, and medicinal and food plants. The herds of buffalo that sought shelter in the canyon during winters were so immense that the Kiowas and the Southern Cheyennes linked Palo Duro to a widespread Plains tradition that buffalo had their ultimate origins underground in its secret depths.

The Comanche are the Native people most closely associated with Palo Duro during historic times. In the wake of the Pueblo Revolt (1680) against Spanish control in New Mexico, which liberated Spanish horses to the tribes of the interior West, Shoshonean-speaking Comanches astride newly acquired ponies rode through the Rocky Mountain passes to displace the resident Apache bands of the southern High

Plains. For Comanches, the Llano Estacado and its suite of escarpment canyons seemed to be two halves of their world, the "Top-of-the-Badlands" — a place to hunt *cuhtz* (buffalo) but otherwise *nimiwahti* (without people) — and the "Red Badlands" of the canyon world, full of power spots, campsites, and sanctuaries. Their names for the Red River itself were Peopassa Neovit (Big Sand River) and Kecheahque Hono (Prairie Dog Town River).

When the united tribes fought hide hunters and the American military (the so-called Red River War) to defend their buffalo country from invasion, Palo Duro Canyon became their last sanctuary. Within its bold red and yellow walls, speckled with the junipers that give the canyon its Spanish name, the Comanche may have believed they could not be found; red, yellow, and green were their sacred colors. But at daybreak on September 28, 1874, Colonel Ranald Mackenzie's troops plunged their horses down the canyon wall in an attack that surprised the last free village of combined Comanches, Kiowas, and Cheyennes. Their lodges and winter supplies burned, 1,450 of their ponies driven into nearby Tule Canyon and shot in a frenzied execution, the tribes walked to their designated reservations in Oklahoma.

Palo Duro did not save the Plains tribes in 1874, but in the years since the state of Texas created the 16,000-acre Palo Duro Canyon State Park in the 1930s, descendants of the three tribes have returned regularly to this canyon, which is central to their sense of themselves and their place in the world.

FURTHER READING: *The Texas Panhandle Frontier,* by Fred Rathjen

244. Adobe Walls, TX

Thomas W. Kavanagh

Rte. 207 to a right turn on County Rd. F, north of Stinnett

The site of the 1874 battle is owned by the Panhandle-Plains Historical Society.

The Canadian River Valley had been a favorite Comanche campground since the early eighteenth century, and by the early nineteenth century local bands of the Yamparika had villages along the river. They traded buffalo meat, hides, and horses with Spaniards and Pueblo Indians from New Mexico, who visited their villages as Comancheros. Charles and William Bent and Ceran St. Vrain built the first trading post along the river in the early 1840s. While it operated for only a few years (and no longer exists), the post's adobe walls gave the area its name.

The 1865 Treaty of the Little Arkansas River set aside the Texas Panhandle as a reservation for the Comanche and the Kiowa. The 1867 Treaty of Medicine Lodge Creek reduced their reservation to a portion of southwestern Oklahoma, but it gave them the right to hunt buffalo in the panhandle as long as there were enough buffalo to justify the chase. The treaty also restricted white settlement in the panhandle for three years. After the invention in the early 1870s of an industrial process to tan buffalo hides, commercial hunters began killing herds just for the hides, and by 1874 they had decimated the herds north of the Arkansas River. Since the treaty no longer prevented them from settling in the panhandle, hunters, merchants, and storekeepers moved in. The community that grew up about a mile from the old adobe trading post included a store, a blacksmith shop, and corrals. It was of particular concern to the Yamparika Comanches because it was competing with them in the trade in buffalo products. As a result of this competition, the killing of the buffalo herds, and the murder of warriors in Texas, the Comanches made plans to attack the buffalo hunters, then seek revenge for the warriors' deaths. They felt protected by *puha* (bullet-proof power). A young Kwahada man, Quenatosavit (White Eagle), announced that he had *puha* and could share it, not just with a few, as had been claimed traditionally, but with all. In late June 1874, a combined force of several hundred Comanches, Kiowas, and Cheyennes attacked the Adobe Walls compound. When *puha* failed, the Indians withdrew. Quenatosavit was soon renamed Isatai (Female Wolf).

Adobe Walls continues to be an important symbol in Comanche culture. A family-owned "honoring song," composed by a participant in the battle, is still known as the "Adobe Walls Song."

The Comanche Nation's headquarters are in Lawton, Oklahoma, and about half of the more than 13,000 tribal members live in that state. The Nation administers social programs under contracts with the federal government. Revenues from casinos and a water park fund additional programs and per capita payments to tribal members.

FURTHER READING: *The Comanches: A History,* by Thomas W. Kavanagh

245. Rosebud Battlefield State Park, MT

Jeffrey Ostler

Off U.S. 212 on Rte. 314, southeast of Crow Agency

On June 17, 1876, Lakota and Cheyenne military forces defeated U.S. Army troops led by Brigadier General George Crook. The ground the Lakotas and Cheyennes defended that day was part of the territory they had secured during the 1850s when they fought the Crows for control of the rich buffalo ranges in present-day southeastern Montana. The United States recognized Lakota ownership of this area in a treaty negotiated in 1868, which established a "permanent reservation" for the Lakota in what is now western South Dakota, an area that included their sacred Black Hills. It also defined much of eastern Wyoming and southeastern Montana as "unceded Indian territory."

Following rumors of gold, in 1874 the United States sent an exploring expedition into the Black Hills, led by Lieutenant Colonel George Armstrong Custer, which found a few flecks of the precious metal. After the Black Hills were publicized as the next El Dorado, prospectors swarmed into them. At first the army upheld the Lakota treaty rights and ordered the miners to leave, but in late 1875 President Ulysses Grant and other officials decided to withdraw the troops from the Black Hills. They ordered the Lakotas and the Cheyennes in the unceded territory to move to the permanent reservation by January 31, 1876, and threatened them with war if they did not. The government also made plans to pressure the Lakotas already living on the reservation to sell the Black Hills and the unceded territory.

Knowing that the Lakotas and the Cheyennes in the unceded territory would reject the government's demand that they vacate their country, the army began preparing for a winter campaign. On March 17, 1876, Crook led 700 troops in an attack on a small camp of Cheyennes and Lakotas on the Powder River, burning their lodges but inflicting few casualties. Crook returned to Fort Fetterman; in May he resumed his offensive with two other columns, one led by Brigadier General Alfred Terry and Colonel John Gibbon and the other by Custer.

In early June, Sitting Bull held a Sun Dance on Rosebud Creek a few miles north of present-day Lame Deer. After offering 100 pieces of his own flesh as a sacrifice to Wakan Tanka (the Great Spirit), Sitting Bull had a vision in which he saw U.S. soldiers and their horses falling into the Indians' camp. This prediction of victory gave the 3,000 Lakotas and Cheyennes in attendance immense confidence and courage. Among these was the Lakotas' major war leader, Crazy Horse, who had earlier vowed to defend the Black Hills and the unceded territory. Now he promised to strike a devastating blow against the invaders of his country.

During the next few days, the Lakotas and Cheyennes moved up Rosebud Creek. Before dawn on June 17, Crook, his troops, and 250 Shoshone and Crow auxiliaries marched down the Rosebud. When they halted for breakfast, Lakotas and Cheyennes, led by Crazy Horse, attacked. Crook fended off this assault, but Crazy Horse regrouped and continued attacking into the afternoon, eventually causing Crook to withdraw his forces to a base camp in northern Wyoming. Casualties were light, with both sides losing about ten men. Although Crook claimed victory, the battle of the Rosebud was a resounding triumph for the Lakotas and the Cheyennes. Despite being significantly outnumbered, they had met Crook and repulsed him. Although the Lakotas and the Cheyennes rejoiced in Crook's retreat, they realized that Sitting Bull's prophecy had not yet been fulfilled. That happened eight days later on the Little Bighorn.

FURTHER READING: *Crazy Horse: A Lakota Life,* by Kingsley M. Bray

246. Little Bighorn Battlefield National Monument, MT

Herman J. Viola

Off I-90 at exit 510, Crow Agency

The Little Bighorn Battlefield National Monument memorializes the battle fought on June 25–26, 1876, which pitted the charismatic Lakota leader Sitting Bull against the colorful and controversial Lieutenant Colonel George Armstrong Custer of Civil War fame. In 1876 Sitting Bull was at the peak of his spiritual and political power. About forty-five years old, he was still strong and nimble. He had probably never seen Custer, but the battle of the Little Bighorn forever united them.

After Brigadier General George Crook attacked a small camp of Cheyennes and Lakotas on the Powder River, the Lakota and Cheyenne bands began camping together for mutual protection. By June 24, Sitting Bull's camp stretched for about two miles along the Little Bighorn River, which the Indians called the Greasy Grass. More than 1,000 tipis and brush wickiups stood in large tribal circles: Northern Cheyenne, Lakota-Hunkpapa, Oglala, Miniconjou, Brule, Two Kettle, Sans Arc, and Blackfeet Sioux. There were about 7,000 people, including between 1,500 and 2,000 fighting men and an estimated 25,000 horses. "It was a very big village and you could hardly count the tipis," recalled Black Elk, the Oglala holy man, who was thirteen years old at the time.

Custer located the village and attacked with twelve companies of the 7th U.S. Cavalry and thirty-five Indian scouts, including Dakota Sioux, Arikara, and Crow. Key to his strategy was the expectation that the Indians would run away, but instead they counterattacked. After pinning down five companies, the majority of the warriors, led by Crazy Horse, Gall, Lame White Man, Low Dog, Two Moons, and other leaders, surrounded Custer's troops, killing them to the last man. The fighting lasted a short time. "It was like hunting buffalo," one of the Indians said. The Indians killed 263 men, including 3 Arikara scouts: 212 with Custer and 51 with Major Marcus A. Reno's command in a separate battle 4 miles upriver. Five more of Reno's men died later of their wounds. In 2001, during the ceremony on the 125th anniversary of the battle, the names of the 54 Indians known to have died in the battle were read. On June 25, 2003, an Indian Memorial was dedicated to honor and recognize all the tribes that fought and died in the battle.

The Northern Cheyenne insist that Custer's defeat was the result of his failure to keep a solemn vow he made to their tribe in March 1869 in a sacred pipe ceremony. The keeper of the Cheyenne sacred arrows, speaking in Cheyenne, warned Custer of disaster if he ever betrayed the pact of friendship he had just made with the tribe. By attacking them at the Little Bighorn, the Cheyenne believe, Custer broke the pact and angered the spirits that protected the tribe. The inevitable outcome — Custer's personal annihilation and all the consequences of that — was proof of the working of great spiritual power.

Sitting Bull had indeed won a great victory, but it hastened the end of Plains Indian life. The U.S. Army proved so vengeful that by the end of 1877 the only Indian survivors of Little Bighorn were either on reservations or in Canada, where about 3,000 of them had fled. But life was lonely and hard there. As the buffalo disappeared and hunger became a constant companion, the refugees slowly and quietly began returning to friends and families south of the border. In July 1881 Sitting Bull and fewer than 200 men, women, and children — starving and wearing threadbare clothes — and their fourteen gaunt ponies arrived at Fort Buford. "I wish it to be remembered," he said, "that I was the last man of my tribe to surrender my rifle."

The Battle of the Little Bighorn

GERARD BAKER — MANDAN, HIDATSA, AND ARIKARA NATION

❖ When Indians visit the battlefield today, some cry. Many get angry. They are upset for the loss of the way of life, the freedom they once enjoyed. It's something we Indian people will never retrieve. That is what the battlefield means to us. That's why as its superintendent I tried to make it a welcoming place for Indians as well as non-Indians. No one should demean Custer's soldiers, who made the ultimate sacrifice here for their government and their way of life. But visitors should also be aware that the battlefield is on an Indian reservation and that the 7th Cavalry was here to force the last independent Indians to give up their freedom and become wards of the government, a decision in which they had no voice or choice.

JEANNE OYAWIN EDER — DAKOTA SIOUX

Tremendous changes have taken place in the lives of the Sioux and all Plains Indian peoples from 1800 to the present. After the War of 1812, U.S. officials began signing treaties whose ultimate purpose was to acquire and exploit lands that belonged to the Native peoples of the Far West. The 1868 Fort Laramie Treaty stipulated that no future treaties would be ratified unless three-fourths of all adult Sioux males signed the agreement. From the Sioux perspective, the Great Sioux War was a war to remain independent and to guarantee the rights of the Sioux people to their homeland. It was a war to guarantee their treaty rights. It was a war to guarantee their hunting rights. Theirs was a sacred fight for freedom. It was born of the Sioux people and fought for the Sioux people. This was a people's war.

WILLIAM WALKS ALONG — NORTHERN CHEYENNE

I believe it is important to know the pain our ancestors experienced during the period of history in which the U.S. government's Indian policy was genocidal in nature. Also, it is important to know our own pain, because I believe it destroys our self-pride, our arrogance, and our indifference toward others. The treatment of our people has sometimes been cruel and inhumane and filled with an intense moral attitude. We Indian people have a determination to make the United States live up to its highest ideals. We all have received abundantly from our ancestors, who made a difference on this ground. The eternal values — faith, trust, hope, life, justice, mercy, honesty, service, sacrifice, humility, and charity — will assist us in giving back to our communities and allow us to focus on issues and problems that have been ignored for too long.

JOSEPH MEDICINE CROW — CROW

At age ninety, I am perhaps the one living person who has had the longest association with the battle of the Little Bighorn. My interest in the battle began as a youngster listening to the stories of White Man Runs Him, the brother of my grandmother. I often interpreted for my grandfather when various white people would come to interview him about the battle. Thanks to him, I met and befriended all but one of the six Crow scouts who were at the battle. As a boy I greatly enjoyed listening to all their stories about their scouting for Son-of-the-Morning-Star, the Crow name for George Armstrong Custer. They often expressed admiration for him, especially for his courage. In their minds only a person of great personal courage would have attacked that huge camp filled with the dreaded enemies of the Crow and Arikara people.

FURTHER READING: *Little Bighorn Remembered: The Untold Indian Story of Custer's Last Stand*, by Herman J. Viola, from which this essay is excerpted.

247. Fort Robinson State Park, NE

On U.S. 20, west of Crawford

Fort Robinson Museum; original and reconstructed buildings

The post named Camp Robinson was established to assert U.S. military authority at the Red Cloud Agency, which was located here from 1873 to 1877. Thousands of Northern Cheyenne, Arapaho, and Oglala lived in the area. In 1877 the agency was moved to Pine Ridge, and in December 1878 Camp Robinson was redesignated Fort Robinson.

On September 5, 1877, Crazy Horse was killed in front of the post guardhouse. He had surrendered the previous May and had brought his people to the Red Cloud Agency. After hearing rumors that Crazy Horse was organizing a plot, Brigadier General George Crook ordered him taken into custody. When Crazy Horse resisted, he was stabbed and mortally wounded in the struggle.

In 1877 the Northern Cheyenne, forced by the U.S. government to leave their homelands and live on a reservation with the Southern Cheyenne in Indian Territory, were suffering from disease, primarily malaria, and lack of food. The following year about 350 of them escaped and headed back north toward their homeland. Those led by Little Wolf evaded capture and by early 1879 were in Montana Territory. Dull Knife and his people had planned to join Red Cloud but were captured on October 24 and taken to Camp Robinson, where they were held. After several months, the army was ordered to force them to return to the reservation. To escape from imprisonment in the cavalry barracks and avoid removal to Indian Territory, they broke out on a freezing night in January 1880. Many were killed or captured, but Dull Knife and some of his family escaped and made it to the Pine Ridge Agency. Eventually a reservation was established for the Northern Cheyenne in southeastern Montana, where Dull Knife and the other survivors settled.

248. Fort Buford State Historic Site, ND

Off Rtes. 1804 and 58, southwest of Williston

Missouri-Yellowstone Confluence Interpretive Center; restored buildings

The fort was built in 1866 near the confluence of the Missouri and Yellowstone rivers to protect immigrants heading west. After the battle of the Little Bighorn, Sitting Bull led his band into Canada to escape the military. By 1881 game had become so scarce that the group was forced to return to the United States. In July of that year Sitting Bull surrendered at Fort Buford. The army abandoned the fort in 1895.

249. Chief Plenty Coups State Park, MT

Timothy Bernardis

On the Crow Reservation, west of Pryor

Visitor center and museum

This was the home of Plenty Coups (Many Achievements), the last traditional chief of the Apsaalooke, the Crow people. He was born about 1848 and became a chief in his twenties because of his battlefield accomplishments in raids against the Lakota, the Blackfeet, and other tribes. He chose to settle on Pryor Creek near present-day Billings in 1883 because as a young man he had had a vision in which the buffalo disappeared and were replaced by cattle. He also saw himself as an old man sitting on his future homestead with its sacred spring. This vision encouraged the Crow to continue to be allies of the whites in their wars with other Indian tribes to retain Crow country. Plenty Coups' greatness was as a leader by example for the Crow when

they were forced to change to reservation life and adapt to the new ways and yet remain Crow.

Plenty Coups lived in a tipi in the summer and in his log house in the winter. He was both a Catholic and a member of the Crow Tobacco Society. His famous words to his people were: "Education is your most powerful weapon. With education you are the white man's equal; without education you are his victim." His new battles to preserve Crow land were fought not against other tribes but against the railroads, trespassers, and congressional attempts to open the reservation to general homesteading. Beginning in 1880 he traveled to Washington, D.C., at least ten times, especially between 1908 and 1918, along with other old chiefs and young, educated Crows. After they succeeded at the congressional hearings in turning back the attempts to open the reservation, he returned home and enlarged his house to two stories. Upstairs was the Honors Room, where he kept his medicine bundles and other sacred items. He had visited Mount Vernon during a trip to Washington and saw that it was a place of honor, so he gave his homestead to be a park for both Crows and whites. In the dedication ceremony in 1928, he stated that the park was to be a memorial not to him but to the Crow people and that it should remind Indians and whites to live and work together in harmony. Near his house are his sacred spring, general store, apple orchard, and grave. Since 1928 the Crow people have made continuous use of the homestead park for feasts and arrow-throwing tournaments.

Today there are about 12,000 enrolled members of the Crow Nation, about 9,000 of whom live on the 2.3-million-acre reservation in south-central Montana. Social and ceremonial expressions of culture take place year-round, including sweats, Tobacco Society dances, dance society activities, giveaways, peyote meetings, naming ceremonies, and medicine bundle ceremonies. During the annual Crow Fair, tribal members and visitors camp in tents and in 1,000 tipis in what is known as the Tipi Capital of the World. The Crow people have maintained, perpetuated, and created their culture while taking advantage of educational opportunities both on and off the reservation. Little Big Horn College, chartered in 1980, has as its mission to provide education "in areas that reflect the developing economic opportunities of the Crow Indian reservation community" and a commitment to the "preservation, perpetuation, and protection of Crow culture and language."

FURTHER READING: *Plenty-Coups, Chief of the Crows,* by Frank B. Linderman

250. Haskell Indian Nations University, KS: From Assimilation to Self-Determination

Karen Gayton Swisher

155 Indian Ave., Lawrence

The Carlisle Indian School, established in 1879 in Pennsylvania, was the model Congress used in 1882 to authorize setting aside vacant army posts or barracks and purchasing land to establish off-reservation boarding schools for Indian youths. Congress appropriated $150,000 to found three boarding schools in Nebraska, Oklahoma, and Kansas. The United States Indian Industrial Training School opened in Lawrence, Kansas, on September 17, 1884. In his 1936 introduction to *Highlights of Haskell Institute,* Rev. William P. Ames wrote that the school was established "to provide an opportunity for the American Indians, lacking such a privilege elsewhere, to acquire an education which would fit them for useful citizenship in the mature years of life and in the community or region of their future residence." Twenty-two American Indian children began an educational experience designed to prepare them for assimilation into the American mainstream. The training school evolved into Haskell Institute, then Haskell Indian Junior

College, and is now Haskell Indian Nations University. The history of Indian policy is reflected in the twelve-decade history of Haskell.

No longer an institution that promotes assimilation, Haskell takes pride in promoting the philosophy of self-determination for American Indian and Alaska Native people and nations while continuing to serve their educational needs, though very differently from 1884. Our 320-acre campus, with its historical and contemporary structures, is a National Historic Landmark. Haskell combines the intellectual, physical, social, emotional, and spiritual components of American Indian life into a unique university experience. Supported by the Bureau of Indian Affairs, Haskell provides a tuition-free education and a culturally based curriculum for a culturally rich student body of 900 students representing approximately 130 tribes and nations. Haskell has several associate degree programs and four bachelor's degree programs: elementary education, American Indian studies, business administration, and environmental science. The degree programs offer students broad options from which to choose as they prepare themselves to be future leaders in tribal management, science, education, and other professional fields. Culturally based courses include Native and Western Views of Nature, Philosophy of Indigenous Thought, Biography of American Indian Leaders Past and Present, and American Indian Theatre History.

Dedicated to "building our future . . . preserving our traditions . . . through educational excellence," Haskell holds a unique place in the history — and future — of Indian education and of Indian Country.

FURTHER READING: *Boarding School Seasons: American Indian Families, 1900–1940,* by Brenda J. Child

251. Fort Totten State Historic Site, ND

Off Rte. 57, Fort Totten

Interpretive center

The U.S. Army built Fort Totten between 1867 and 1873 and left it in 1890. Between 1891 and 1959, it was an industrial boarding school for Indian children from the Dakota and Turtle Mountain reservations and others, then a tuberculosis preventorium — where Indian children who were at high risk for the disease were sent for special care as well as education — and then a school until 1959. Sixteen of the original buildings are in the historic site.

SECTION FOUR

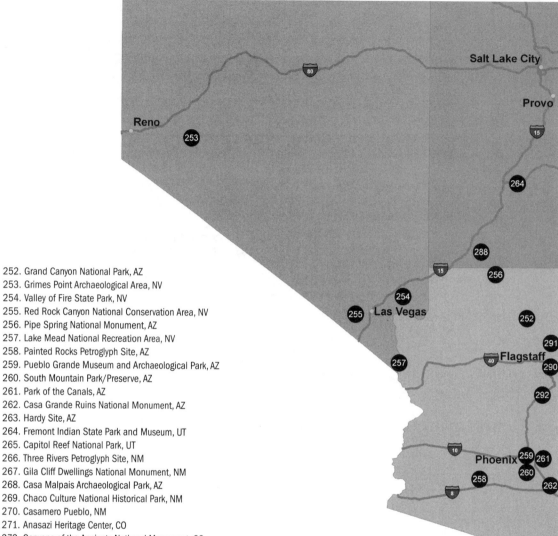

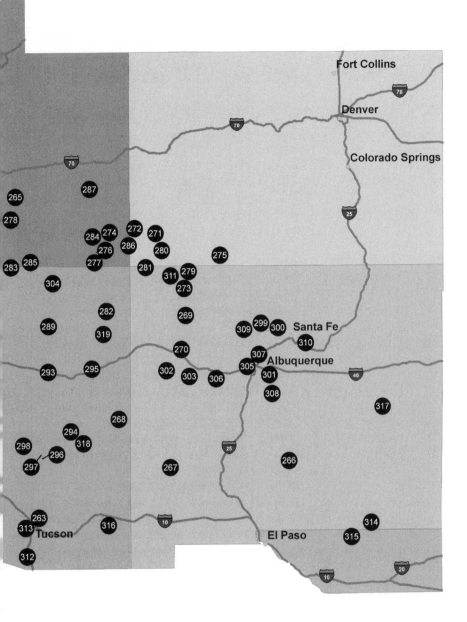

301. Tijeras Pueblo, NM
302. El Morro National Monument, NM
303. El Malpais National Monument, NM
304. Navajo National Monument, AZ
305. Petroglyph National Monument, NM
306. Pueblo of Acoma, NM
307. Coronado State Monument, NM
308. Salinas Pueblo Missions National Monument, NM
309. Jemez State Monument, NM
310. Pecos National Historical Park, NM
311. Navajo Pueblitos of the Dinétah, NM
312. Tumacácori National Historical Park, AZ
313. Mission San Xavier del Bac, AZ
314. Carlsbad Caverns National Park, NM
315. Guadalupe Mountains National Park, TX
316. Fort Bowie National Historic Site, AZ
317. Fort Sumner State Monument, NM
318. Fort Apache and Theodore Roosevelt School Historic District, AZ
319. Hubbell Trading Post National Historic Site, AZ

Places and Spaces

DAVE WARREN

❖ "Historic sites" appear on maps as interesting side trips or destinations of curiosity. For most people who come to these places, the experience is filtered through terms devoid of the meaning they had for the people who used the place — what they felt, thought, and sought. Instead, science organizes reality and human meaning into compartments and segments, which we can stand and view only from the outside. Consider, for a moment, these places as eddies in the currents of large events, places where meaning resides in human memories, the spiritual hearths, even places of personal sacredness.

Your space is part of a place. Others have stood where you are, not just yesterday but long ago. In some places, you see the handprints of human beings who plastered earthen walls generations ago or laid their hands against a cave ceiling and silhouetted the outline with paint or created intricate etchings on a rock face. All are signatures of simple yet profound human experience and happening.

For some observers, these archaeological or historical artifacts are "ruins." Others know them as evidence of civilizations that entered from an origin place lost in memory, now remembered in prayer and ceremony. Those who need time markers will bracket the beginnings and endings of eras, epochs, ages. These places are monuments, impressive evidence of achievement, sometimes of difficulty and tragedy — eloquent imprints of long-absent but not forgotten people. Their precincts may be quiet now, but they are swept by occasional winds that flow across flat lands or down from sacred peaks that those who came before also knew. These places are crucibles of human stories and daily events that we may come to understand if we are attentive. They are the living memory of ancestral life and are testaments to human continuity. Long ago our ancestors lived a daily routine that we can understand as our own.

In some parts of our land these meanings are dramatic testimony to what we say. Ancient homelands of Native peoples in the Southwest literally bear the imprints of ancestral lifeways. One finds among cliff dwellings deep impressions in the stone. At first they appear to be wind-worn cavities in the soft strata. Upon closer view, these features become clear: they are human footprints, worn deep in the stone, marking countless comings and goings of the men and women who scaled the cliffs along these paths. You see, it is indeed possible to walk in the path of forebears, to hold hands with them when steadying yourself by grasping handholds worn by countless generations in the soft volcanic-ash stone.

Entering these places is more than visiting. It is taking part in the continuum of human experience. Here events of the past become elements of the present, and how we observe that connection determines in great part how others who follow us will share and understand its meaning. Yet if we pause for a moment, it is obvious that these places, and the space we occupy in them, are our past and our present. Do we not look out over the same mountains as others did? Are we not still embraced by the same cosmos, encircling the people and the land in sacred space, marked by sacred places? All — the people, the sounds, and the silence — create places of remembrance and renewal. As we traverse these places, we move in the paths of those who have gone before and move a little closer to the ones who gave us life.

252. Grand Canyon National Park, AZ

Canyon View Visitor Center; Tusayán Museum, 23 miles east of Grand Canyon Village

On the South Rim of the Grand Canyon, in about A.D. 1185, ancestors of Pueblo people known as the Kayenta built a small U-shaped Pueblo, today called Tusayán Ruin, where about twenty people lived and farmed on nearby land. They left about 1225. On the North Rim between A.D. 1050 and 1150 about twenty Kayenta lived in a small linear room block called Walhalla Glades Ruin during the summer months and farmed on the slopes nearby.

The following statements relate the significance of the Grand Canyon to these tribes.

HAVASUPAI: To this day, the Havasupai still reside within a segment of the Grand Canyon, their traditional and ancestral home since around A.D. 1100. The Colorado River is a key element of their traditional life. They consider the Colorado River the spine of their lifeline and as such sacred in itself.

HOPI: The Hisatsinom, ancestors of present-day Hopi people, were among the earliest to make use of the Grand Canyon, or Ongtupka, and it remains a special place of great importance to every Hopi. The Hopi continue to make pilgrimages to Ongtupka to collect resources, make offerings, and reinforce their present-day relationship.

HUALAPAI: The Grand Canyon and the Colorado River have intrinsic spiritual values for the Hualapai people. The river is revered as a life-giving source known as Ha'yidtadta, the backbone or spine. In Hualapai belief, the people cannot survive without the spine, the river. The river through the canyon makes a lifeway connection that flows through the hearts of the Hualapai people. Through emergence, survival, subsistence, and struggle, the Hualapai have had the canyon and the river for hunting, gardening, and collecting plants and minerals. The Hualapai have sought to maintain and protect their ancestral homelands since time immemorial.

NAVAJO: For centuries the Navajo have used resources in and around the Grand Canyon for farming, grazing, plant gathering, hunting, and religious purposes. Several times through history the canyon has been used as a refuge from non-Navajo peoples. The Tooh, or Colorado River, is a sacred male being and forms a protective boundary on the western border of Navajo land.

SAN JUAN SOUTHERN PAIUTES (Southern Paiute Consortium/Kaibab Band of Paiute Indians, Paiute Indian Tribe of Utah, including the Shivwits): The Grand Canyon is the origin for songs, stories, and dances about the water, animal brothers in the Paipaxa' uipi Canyon, and minerals that the Kaibab Paiute gather. Where the Colorado River passes through their traditional lands, they have hunted, collected plants, and farmed for centuries and continue their practices in modern times.

ZUNI: From the moment that the Zunis arrived on the surface of the earth, the Grand Canyon (Chimik ana ya) and the Colorado River have been sacred. In order to successfully carry out the prayers, offerings, and ceremonies necessary to ensure rainfall for crops and a balanced universe, Zunis collect samples of water, plants, soils, rocks, and other materials from the Grand Canyon.

Great Basin Indigenous Places

CATHERINE S. FOWLER

❖ The Great Basin lies between the sharp uplift of the Sierra Nevada–Cascade Range on the west and the equally impressive chain of the Rocky Mountains on the east, the drainage of the Snake River and its flat, level plain on the north and the Colorado River with its many steep canyons on the south. Because the mountain masses on the east and west block the rain, this vast region is semiarid. Rather than being one large basin, as its name implies, it is an area of many basins separated by mountain ranges. Because many of the ranges are isolated from one another, some have developed endemic floral and faunal species over time. This area is the homeland of the Washoe, Northern Paiute,

Owens Valley Paiute, Southern Paiute (including the Chemehuevi), Shoshone, and Ute. Each major group had various subgroups with contiguous territories, often defined from mountain crest to mountain crest, in keeping with the biogeography. Today combined subgroups live on reservations that are but a small fraction of their former territories.

These Native peoples were once hunters of large and small game, gatherers of a wide variety of food and medicinal plants, and fishermen in the Great Basin's widely scattered lakes, rivers, and streams. This vast area contains many places that are particularly meaningful to Great Basin peoples: water sources, hot springs, isolated rock formations, mountain peaks, pictograph and petroglyph sites, and caves. Water sources, particularly the springs, seeps, and *tenajas* (rock tanks), have descriptive names such as Coyote's-Water-Comes-Out, Navel Water, Water on the End, and Eagle's Water. All are respected and approached with care and with requests to the spirits that dwell therein for permission to visit and for special favors. People may leave offerings as an additional show of respect. Such offerings should never be disturbed. Hot springs dot this tectonically active region and are sources of healing water and mud used to relieve pain. It is particularly important to leave offerings at these healing waters and not to desecrate them by using them merely for recreation or without showing respect.

Mountain peaks and other rock formations, which are often places of origin, are sacred. They are named and become the focus of prayers as people move across the landscape. Many peaks have two names, one that a person can use in reference and the other to be spoken only in prayer or another sacred context. Some common names of reference are Nībagantī (Has Snow), for Charleston Peak in the Charleston Range; Wangikudakwa (Fox Peak), for Jobs Peak in the Stillwater Range; and Aga (Tall), for Spirit

Mountain. Native people look upon the sites of pictographs and petroglyphs with respect and as places to be protected from vandalism. Caves and rock shelters are often places of supernatural power, where a person might seek the power to doctor the sick or perform certain other tasks or to request special favors or contact spiritual helpers. Caves used long ago to inter the dead are to be avoided by the living.

The people look after the land and the habits and habitats of its plants and animals through prayer and careful tending, including cleaning and clearing the camps and collecting areas, tending water sources, and offering prayers to this living landscape. They believe that the land and its resources need the hand and the respect of people to produce and be at their best. Outsiders often see this region as a vast desert, but Native people see the Great Basin's life and soul and feel a sense of custodianship for the entire region.

FURTHER READING: *Great Basin*, edited by Warren L. d'Azevedo, vol. 11 of the *Handbook of North American Indians*

Petroglyphs and Pictographs in the Great Basin

ALANAH WOODY
AND ANGUS R. QUINLAN

❖ The petroglyphs and pictographs in the western Great Basin are often in the settled landscape or near water. They are tangible signs for Native Americans of the continuing presence of their ancestors.

253. Grimes Point Archaeological Area, NV

On Rte. 50, east of Fallon

Along the shoreline of the ancient Lake Lahontan are more than 150 basalt boulders where early people, perhaps 10,000 years ago, engraved petroglyphs, most of which are nonrepresentational, including cupules. These very small, rounded depressions are among the oldest petroglyphs in the area. The petroglyphs are difficult to see because the dark coating that forms on basalt has covered them again.

254. Valley of Fire State Park, NV

Off I-15, Overton

Visitor center

The petroglyphs on the wind-carved red sandstone formations — which appear to be ablaze at sunset — in a valley near Lake Mead are both representational and nonrepresentational. Some of the images resemble an atlatl, a spear-throwing stick used before the introduction of the bow and arrow about 1,500 years ago.

255. Red Rock Canyon National Conservation Area, NV

On Rte. 159, west of Las Vegas

Visitor center

Among the pictographs and petroglyphs is a series of painted handprints made by mixing red ochre as a pigment with a wetting medium and then pressing a hand into the paint and onto the rock.

FURTHER READING: "Rock Art," by Polly Schaafsma, in *Great Basin*, edited by Warren L. d'Azevedo, vol. 11 of the *Handbook of North American Indians*

256. Pipe Spring National Monument, AZ

Angelita S. Bulletts

406 North Pipe Spring Rd., Fredonia

Kaibab Band of Paiute Indians Visitor Center and Museum

This land, south of Zion National Park and north of the Grand Canyon, which many consider inhospitable, isolated, and barren, is the place of creation of the Kaibab Paiute people, the Kaivavits, or Mountain Lying Down People. It is here that the Creator placed us to care for the land and those that live on it. We are taught that all things on this land have life, just as humans do, and we must consider this as we make decisions that affect the land, rocks, plants, water, animals, mountains, and all other things.

Paiute people believe that water has life and is powerful. The red cliffs that surround us have yielded pure, filtered water. Our knowledge of water sources and the power they hold has carried our people into this century. Our small reservation, which encompasses Pipe Spring National Monument, is a mere portion of the traditional lands of our people. Euro-American encroachment caused Paiute people to congregate in the Pipe Spring area in the 1800s, when we were pushed out of southern Utah and northern Arizona. Today our homeland includes national parks, monuments, and forests. We share it with all our brothers and sisters of the world.

These red cliffs, deep canyons, staircases of rock, and rushing rivers are part of our birth land, our Holy Land, which has sustained us in our traditions of being stewards of the land. We care for this land not as owners but as we would care for our mother or father. Our ancestors traveled from Pipe Spring to the Grand Canyon, then up to the Kaibab Plateau, following the seasons to hunt and gather for the winter months. Through the generations, mythical and historical stories have been told about the water,

the mountain ranges, and the keepers of the animals. Here on our homeland life began, and we believe that here all life will die and come back once again to this Holy Land.

FURTHER READING: "Southern Paiute," by Isabel T. Kelly and Catherine S. Fowler, in *Great Basin*, edited by Warren L. d'Azevedo, vol. 11 of the *Handbook of North American Indians*

257. Lake Mead National Recreation Area, NV: Wikame – Spirit Mountain: The Hualapai Perspective on Creation

Loretta Jackson

Off Rte. 163 off Christmas Tree Pass Rd., northwest of Laughlin

Wikame (Spirit Mountain) is the place of origin for the Hualapai people. Rising to an elevation of 5,600 feet, it is a striking granite mass on the landscape. A sacred spring called Ha' thi-el (Salty Spring) flows from a side canyon, which supports native plants including giant reed, desert tobacco, bear grass, various cacti, and edible grass seeds, once harvested by the Pai people. Petroglyphs tell an awesome story of the world covered with water and depict the creation of the Hualapai people and other Yuman-speaking tribes. Hualapai traditional belief assigns sacred significance to the Colorado River; the people believe they were created and formed from the sediment, clay, and giant reeds found along its banks. The river's midsection is called Ha'yipapa, which means the backbone or spine of the river. The Creator instructed the Hualapai people to live on their ancestral homelands, more than 7 million acres in northwestern Arizona. This is where they roamed and resided from time immemorial. Today the Hualapai Tribe lives on 1 million acres of those ancestral lands, known as the Hualapai Indian Reservation, in Peach Springs on the Colorado Plateau and the Grand Wash Cliffs escarpment. The northern boundary of the reservation follows the Colorado River for 108 miles in the Grand Canyon.

FURTHER READING: *Spirit Mountain: An Anthology of Yuman Story and Song,* edited by Leanne Hinton and Lucille J. Watahomigie

Expanding the Dialogue Between American Indians and Non-Indian Archaeologists

JOE E. WATKINS

❖ The Antiquities Act of 1906 cemented American archaeology's role as the steward of the past, and archaeologists have developed and presented an "objective" scientific body of knowledge about American Indians within a social and scientific isolation that has too often precluded the opinions of nonscientists. The Society for American Archaeology holds stewardship as the first principle in its Principles of Archaeological Ethics. The failure of scientists to share that stewardship with American Indians generated an "us-versus-them" atmosphere. Occasionally, some non-Indian archaeologists called attention to this atmosphere, but it was not until the massive social unrest of the 1960s and 1970s that a dialogue was truly initiated. While American Indians made it known that their perspectives on heritage management did not always agree with the scientific views, they have gradually chosen to participate in managing their heritage.

Laws such as the National Historic Preservation Act (1966), the American Indian Religious Freedom Act (1978), the Archaeological Resources Protection Act (1979), and the Native American Graves Protection and Repatriation Act (1990) created some processes for protecting the national heritage of the United States from impacts resulting from federal actions. The 1992 amendments to the National Historic Preservation Act gave American Indians more control over research on their heritage, but tribal perspectives were still held to be secondary to scientific views. Additionally, these laws do not protect heritage sites on private land, in direct conflict with the idea of a truly "national" heritage program.

Dialogues between American Indians and non-Indian archaeologists have expanded steadily. In 1935 the Society for American Archaeology elected Arthur C. Parker, an archaeologist of Seneca descent, its first president. Until the last decade there were few American Indian archaeologists, but since then their number has increased, as have the areas of archaeology within which they work. The Hopi, Navajo, and Zuni have strong historic preservation programs that protect tribal heritage, and the archaeologists in these programs work with tribal advisory groups in a constant dialogue on these issues. There are currently sixty-six tribal historic preservation offices nationwide, and the Indian and non-Indian archaeologists in these programs offer additional voices to the ongoing dialogue.

In addition to the tribal heritage programs, American Indian archaeologists are becoming more numerous in the academy. Their varied heritages and social backgrounds influence their research and teaching, allowing them to offer new insights into the interpretation of the past. Their perspectives complement archaeology and help expand its utility beyond the scientific realm. Their voices offer fresh concepts in the ongoing dialogue among archaeologists — American Indian and non-Indian alike — who are working to integrate American Indian sensitivities with archaeological concerns so that the artificial boundaries between "us" and "them" are being torn down. Such integration requires not only recognizing different facets and definitions of "heritage" but also overtly accepting various interpretations of what an "archaeologist" can and should do to be considered ethical.

FURTHER READING: *Working Together: Native Americans and Archaeology,* edited by Kurt Dongoske, Mark Aldenderfer, and Karen Doehner

The Hohokam: People of the Desert

PATRICIA L. CROWN

❖ The southern Arizona desert was, for the Hohokam, a place of broad, gently flowing rivers lined with trees. Elaborate canal networks crisscrossed their fields of corn, beans, squash, and cotton, which stretched for miles away from the river. They built more than 500 miles of main canals in the Salt River Valley. Crops on the ancient river terraces beyond the canals were watered by rainfall and runoff. The surrounding desert provided abundant edible fruits and greens.

About A.D. 1 the people in southern Arizona settled in permanent villages, produced their first pottery containers, and increased their dependence on cultivated crops. Until about A.D. 1150 the Hohokam (a Pima word meaning "all used up") built shallow pithouses with a single entry. The walls were of wood and woven reeds and twigs, covered with a thick layer of dirt. Seen from afar, their villages appeared to be a series of low mounds along the canals. The construction and maintenance of the canals and the allocation of water required great cooperation. After A.D. 900 they constructed flat platform mounds, probably for rituals that drew people from distant villages. They also united for ball games in the villages that had ball courts. The largest of the more than 200 Hohokam ball courts was more than 16 feet high and nearly 200 feet long. After A.D. 1150, many Hohokam lived in aboveground, Pueblo-like adobe structures with adjacent walled courtyards.

The Hohokam traded widely in pottery, shells, and textiles as well as food and animal skins. (Their pottery has been found on a beach near Los Angeles.) They were skilled weavers and potters, created elegant stone palettes, and are best known for their shell ornaments. Over the centuries the Hohokam culture expanded to encompass a larger area of the Southwest — from the Mexican border to Flagstaff and from western Arizona to the New Mexico border — defined by the presence of their distinctive red-on-buff pottery and their ball courts.

Our knowledge of the Hohokam has lagged behind that of other cultures, such as Chaco, because of problems in dating and site visibility. The desert woods they used cannot be tree-ring dated, and development has obliterated many large villages along the rivers in the Phoenix and Tucson areas. There are reconstructions of early Hohokam houses at the Gila River Arts and Crafts Center, the Desert Botanical Gardens in Phoenix, and the Arizona–Sonora Desert Museum in Tucson.

No one knows why nearly all of the Hohokam left the Phoenix Basin after A.D. 1350.

FURTHER READING: "The Hohokam of Southwest North America," by James M. Bayman, in *Journal of World Prehistory*

258. Painted Rocks Petroglyph Site, AZ

Off I-8 on Painted Rock Dam Rd., northwest of Gila Bend

There are more than 750 Hohokam petroglyphs on basalt boulders in the site.

259. Pueblo Grande Museum and Archaeological Park, AZ

Washington and 44th sts., Phoenix

About 1,000 Hohokam lived in a village here at the head gates of several of their major irrigation canals. They irrigated thousands of acres of farmland on the north side of the Salt River. They built two ball courts and, after A.D. 1150, a large platform mound about the size of a football field and at least 20 feet tall.

260. South Mountain Park/Preserve, AZ: Petroglyphs

Off Central Ave. and south of Baseline Rd., Phoenix

South Mountain Environmental Education Center

The Hohokam who lived and hunted in this mountain range left petroglyphs throughout what is now the largest municipal park in the world, more than 16,000 acres.

261. Park of the Canals, AZ

1710 North Horne, Mesa

The park includes Hohokam canals and a botanical garden.

262. Casa Grande Ruins National Monument, AZ

Off Rte. 287, Coolidge

Visitor center/museum

During the 1300s Hohokam people built a large, multistory structure in a village near the Gila River. They used caliche mud, which becomes very hard after it dries, and beams cut from forests as far away as 60 miles. They built the walls layer by layer, 4 feet thick at the base and as

high as 35 feet. The first floor was a platform mound measuring about 60 feet long and 40 feet wide. The next two floors each had five rooms, large ones at the north and south ends and three smaller rooms in between. The top floor had one room. Although the actual uses of the building are not known, there are openings in the walls that line up with the seasonal movements of the sun and moon, which may have guided the farmers in planting their crops. Near the building is an elliptical depression about 81 feet long and 46 feet wide, which was a ball court.

263. Hardy Site, AZ

2900 N. Craycroft Rd. in Fort Lowell Park, Tucson

The Hohokam lived in a large village here from about A.D. 300 to 1250. There are displays about Hohokam life, but the village itself was backfilled after excavation to preserve it.

The Fremont

DAVID B. MADSEN

❖ The Fremont people were loosely affiliated farmers and foragers who lived on the northern margin of the Greater Southwest from about 1,500 to 500 years ago. Their farming hamlets and larger villages were centered along the many drainages of the upper Green River on the Colorado Plateau in Utah and on the numerous small streams draining the mountain ranges of the eastern Great Basin. Fremont hunter-gatherers ranged as far west as central Nevada, north to southern Idaho, and east to northeastern Colorado and southwestern Wyoming.

The Fremont were the descendants of local hunter-gatherers. Beginning about A.D. 500, they began to adopt some of the characteristics of their southwestern neighbors. While their pottery, pithouse architecture, coursed adobe and masonry granaries, and corn, bean, and squash horticulture were modeled on those of the Ancestral Pueblo peoples and the people of the Mogollon region south of the Colorado River, their distinctive moccasins, one-rod-and-bundle coiled basketry, clay figurines, and, among the eastern Fremont, elaborate pictographs and petroglyphs of large trapezoidal horned figures were unique. No single trait was shared universally, and no single characteristic distinguishes the Fremont as a whole from the surrounding peoples. Some Fremont lived in large, socially stratified, year-round farming villages, while others lived in small, isolated hamlets of one or two families that farmed for part of the year and often went out on extended foraging expeditions. Other Fremont lived year-round in small, mobile foraging groups. An individual might have lived in all of these various ways over a lifetime.

Beginning about A.D. 1250 the Fremont groups began to disappear, and by about 500 years ago they had left their last places in northwestern Colorado. The cause continues to be debated, but it seems to have been a combination of drastic episodes of climate change and an influx of competing foraging societies related to the Ute and Southern Paiute.

FURTHER READING: *Exploring the Fremont*, by David B. Madsen

264. Fremont Indian State Park and Museum, UT

3820 W. Clear Creek Canyon Rd., Sevier

Fremont people painted pictographs and carved petroglyphs in Clear Creek Canyon.

265. Capitol Reef National Park, UT: Petroglyphs

On Rte. 24, east of Torrey

Visitor center

Fremont people carved petroglyphs on the Wingate sandstone cliff east of the visitor center.

Ancestral Pueblo Peoples

LINDA S. CORDELL

❖ The Spanish word *pueblo,* meaning village or town, was applied by the conquistadors to the settled Native American farmers they encountered in what is now the U.S. Southwest. Today Pueblo peoples, speaking six different languages and differing among themselves in details of social organization and belief while manifesting great similarities in settlement pattern, economy, religion, and overall sociopolitical organization, live in nineteen indigenous villages in New Mexico and twelve Hopi villages in Arizona — a small portion of their former territory. Pueblo peoples have successfully farmed native American crops (especially maize, beans, and squash) for thousands of years in an environment that is only marginal for agriculture. The southwestern landscapes where Pueblo peoples lived are visually magnificent settings, but because they are so dry, they remain relatively sparsely inhabited today.

Places such as Blackwater Draw date back about 11,300 years, when the most temporally remote Pueblo ancestors lived as highly mobile hunters and gatherers. By about 3,500 years ago, groups of hunters and gatherers began planting corn — which had first been domesticated in Mesoamerica — and subsequently established fairly permanent settlements. Archaeologists recognize and name traditions of house form, settlement layout, and pottery style, which they use as shorthand referents for the groups who made and used them. Today's Pueblo peoples derive from two principal archaeologically defined traditions, although no one-to-one correlation exists between a specific Pueblo village or one of the Pueblo language groups and a particular archaeologically defined tradition. Archaeologists called one of the major Ancestral Pueblo traditions Anasazi, a name derived from a Navajo word meaning "enemy ancestors." Because this name is offensive to many people, most archaeologists today use the name Ancestral Pueblo. Sites of the Ancestral Pueblo tradition are found throughout the Colorado Plateau region of southern Colorado and Utah, northern Arizona and New Mexico, and the Rio Grande Valley. A second tradition, also ancestral to modern Pueblos, is the Mogollon, a name taken from the central mountains of New Mexico, where their remains are most abundant. The Mogollon tradition extends south into modern Mexico. As one would expect with cultural traditions extending over such large geographic areas, there is considerable regional variation. Hence archaeologists may use geographic terms as qualifiers and refer to Chacoans or Mimbres Mogollon. A southwestern tradition outside the main lines of Pueblo ancestry is that of the Hohokam of the low Arizona deserts.

The earliest dwellings constructed by Ancestral Pueblo people were thermally efficient, semisubterranean structures called pithouses. Before about A.D. 500, these people made magnificent tightly woven baskets, elaborate woven-fiber sandals, and blankets. They grew corn and squash, gathered wild plant food, and hunted game with snares, traps, and darts thrown with the atlatl (spear-thrower). Their settlements, generally consisting of small clusters of pithouses, were not usually occupied continuously for more than fifteen or twenty years. Bows and arrows replaced

atlatls and darts, and they used pottery containers for cooking, serving, and storage. Ancestral Pueblo pottery is a gray ware with black painted designs on a white background slip. Mogollon pottery is generally brown with red painted designs. Although not simultaneously, both Ancestral Pueblo and Mogollon villages came to be composed of clusters of contiguous aboveground rooms with open plaza areas and, in most regions, special semisubterranean rooms that archaeologists call kivas because of their similarities to ceremonial rooms of that name used by modern Pueblos. By the ninth century, Ancestral Pueblo farming communities were so successful that they had spread throughout the northern and eastern portions of the Southwest.

Between the tenth and eleventh centuries, Ancestral Pueblo communities in Chaco Canyon and the San Juan Basin were distinguished by huge, planned, elaborate multistory masonry structures, with open plazas and great kivas with distinctive features (for example, benches, raised hearths, and wall niches). Many of these Chaco great houses were connected to Chaco Canyon by ancient roadways, and their inhabitants imported wood, pottery, and stone. The communities depended on corn planted in fields designed to be watered by channeled rainwater runoff. After A.D. 1150 the Ancestral Pueblo demographic center shifted to the Mesa Verde region, Zuni, and Canyon de Chelly. Multistory dwellings were built, but most no longer followed the "Chacoan plan." Examples of post-Chaco sites include Yucca House, Cliff Palace, Keet Seel, and Betatakin. By about A.D. 1250, Ancestral Pueblo people and the Mogollon began leaving the northern and southern edges of their former territory. Although the Mesa Verde region and most of the Mogollon Mountains were apparently uninhabited, some of the largest Ancestral Pueblo communities came together around Zuni Pueblo, the Hopi Mesas, and the Galisteo Basin in New Mexico. Most of these fourteenth- and fifteenth-century sites, such as those at Bandelier, feature in Pueblo traditional history as ancestral community sites.

FURTHER READING: *Ancestral Pueblo Peoples*, by Linda S. Cordell

The People of the Mimbres Mogollon Region

MARGARET C. NELSON AND
MICHAEL W. DIEHL

❖ The people living in the Mimbres Mogollon region of southwestern New Mexico during the eleventh and twelfth centuries were master potters. They painted outstanding naturalistic and geometric designs in black on white-slipped bowls and jars and used them in their daily life, included them in funerary offerings in burials, and traded them throughout southwestern New Mexico, southeastern Arizona, western Texas, and parts of northern Mexico.

The early subsistence farmers grew maize, beans, and squash, and also hunted and gathered the diverse wild resources of their basin-and-range landscape. By A.D. 300 they were living in well-insulated wood and mud houses set deep into the ground and clustered in small settlements on high knolls. These locations may have provided protection, offered views of the landscape and key resources, and attracted travelers for trade. By A.D. 850 they had shifted their primary settlements to the banks of rivers and streams and were living in small rectangular pithouses in larger clusters. Although some of these clusters have as many as 100 houses, their size may be attributed to centuries of abandonment and rebuilding. Archaeologists debate whether these pithouse settlements were villages or just important locations where people set-

tled repeatedly. Some of the largest have large, semisubterranean ceremonial structures. During the pithouse periods, before A.D. 1000, people traded extensively with others to the west in the Hohokam region of southern Arizona and possibly south into Mexico. Quartz crystals, large upland game, and woodland products may have been traded for shell bracelets and pendants, parrots, and copper bells.

By the beginning of the eleventh century, pithouse settlements were reorganized into Pueblos — the first in southwestern New Mexico — along the banks of major rivers above the fertile floodplains. The people had mastered floodplain cultivation, constructing channels and check dams to irrigate their extensive fields. Houses were built in blocks clustered to form villages. House sizes and configurations varied considerably. Some room blocks contained large rooms, which are thought to be ceremonial. These Pueblo-dwelling farmers made spectacular black-on-white pottery with both geometric and naturalistic designs.

Life changed dramatically in the mid-twelfth century. As a result of social stresses and lack of food, most people left the large Pueblos. They either resettled in the local area or moved away, some heading south and others north. By the end of the century they had stopped making their classic pottery.

FURTHER READING: *Mimbres During the Twelfth Century: Abandonment, Continuity and Reorganization,* by Margaret C. Nelson

266. Three Rivers Petroglyph Site, NM

Off Rte. 54 on B-30, Three Rivers

People of the Jornada Mogollon area carved petroglyphs here sometime between about A.D. 900 and 1400.

267. Gila Cliff Dwellings National Monument, NM

At the end of Rte. 15, north of Silver City, NM

Visitor center

By about A.D. 550 people in this Mogollon area were living in the area of the TJ Site in the national monument, taking advantage of the Gila River to grow beans, squash, and maize just as others did through the fifteenth century. Before they left, about A.D. 1150, they had built a 200-room pueblo. Adjoining the pueblo is a small block of rooms where Salado people lived from about A.D. 1400 to 1450. After A.D. 1270, Tularosa Mogollon people built cliff dwellings in five natural caves; they left about 1300. Later this area was part of the homelands of the Chiricahua Apache, who were taken prisoner by the U.S. government and sent to Florida in 1886, where they were imprisoned at Fort Pickens and Fort Marion.

268. Casa Malpais Archaeological Park, AZ

Main St., Springerville

Visitor center and museum; daily tours from the visitor center

The people of the Mogollon area built the masonry pueblo, where they lived between about A.D. 1250 and 1325. It is along the upper Little Colorado River on terraced land created by the basalt flow from a volcanic eruption. It had about sixty ground-floor rooms and a great square kiva made of dry-laid masonry. They built a solar calendar: a circular, thick stone wall with gates that are in alignment with the sun on the winter and summer solstices.

269. Chaco Culture National Historical Park, NM: The Place and Its People

W. James Judge

Off Rte. 550, south of Nageezi

Visitor center

Visitors to Chaco Canyon are struck by the stark natural beauty of the wind-sculpted sandstone cliffs and the magnificent ruins of massive stone buildings constructed by people who came here in the tenth century, created a complex, sophisticated society, and left in the twelfth century. They built nine major structures, known as the great houses, beginning with Peñasco Blanco, Pueblo Bonito, and Una Vida — each at the confluence of a major drainage with the Chaco Wash. They next built sites elsewhere in the canyon: Chetro Ketl, Pueblo Alto, and Hungo Pavi. These are massive and formal, resembling public rather than residential buildings. These major buildings, along with Kin Kletso, Tsin Kletsin, and Wijiji, suggest the increasing role of Chaco Canyon as a significant regional center. The Chacoans invested amazing energy in their canyon, an area seemingly devoid of essential resources. They designed and built the structures to be massive in every sense. They hauled roof beams on foot from 50 or more miles away, pecked formal staircases into the rock cliffs, and built catchments to trap and deliver water though irrigation canals for their fields of corn, beans, and squash. They built a system of engineered and maintained roads within the canyon that were links to other Chacoan communities miles away.

They traded with people in Mexico for copper bells and military macaws, imported turquoise, and crafted hundreds of thousands of beads and ornaments in canyon workshops. Their dominance in finished turquoise suggests that Chaco was a major production, trade, and ritual center. The thousands of broken pottery vessels and animal remains found at Pueblo Alto suggest that Chacoans held great ritual feasts in which the ceramic vessels were smashed as a final offering. By A.D. 1050 Chaco was well established in trade as well as in the social and ritual life of the San Juan Basin. Along with its outlying settlements, which had great kivas and great houses that imitated the architecture of the canyon, Chaco comprised a regional economic and ritual system that continued through about eighty years of generally favorable climate.

In the middle of the twelfth century, the people left Chaco and many of the outlying areas. There was a severe drought then, and we assume that whatever the Chaco system was to become — a city-state, perhaps — the plans were effectively curtailed as environmental degradation outstripped the site's technological capabilities.

There is debate about whether Chacoans lived in an egalitarian or a socially stratified society. Did "elite" Chacoans wield power and control over everyone else, or was power held temporarily, as the occasion demanded? Some researchers favor the view that the accomplishments of the Chacoans could not have been met without the concentration of power in the hands of a limited number of people. In this view, Chacoan elites administered the system largely for their own benefit rather than for the welfare of the people as a whole, resulting in an unequal distribution of power and wealth. Some carry this further, adding an aggressive, militaristic dimension to the Chacoan system, with the great houses viewed more as defensive units than as residences or ritual structures.

Others hold that Chaco functioned as a ritual center, perhaps administered by spiritual leaders who lived there but operated communally by a largely egalitarian society dispersed throughout the San Juan Basin. In this view the canyon was not primarily a residential area but was visited periodically and voluntarily by people on pilgrimage to confirm their allegiance to the ritual system. A latent function of such a system might have been the effective redistribution of resources, allowing a larger, more durable population to live in the San Juan Basin than would be expected otherwise. In this sense the Chaco system stands as a true achievement of human enterprise, extracting the most possible from incredibly sparse surroundings.

In either case, Chaco's achievements stand up well with those of vanished societies elsewhere in the world where human ingenuity is tested against the vagaries of nature. Through time the one specific configuration that would best serve a growing population was selected from a diverse array of social and ritual possibilities. All who have worked in or visited Chaco Canyon would agree that it provides an enduring legacy for its Pueblo descendants, not only in its material remnants but in its lessons, which are applicable today, about how a society responds to environmental demands that cannot be met solely by technological change.

FURTHER READING: *Chaco and Hohokam: Prehistoric Regional Systems in the American Southwest*, edited by Patricia L. Crown and W. James Judge

Chacoans Away from Home: Chacoan Outlying Communities

FLORENCE C. LISTER

❖ Not all Chaco Ancestral Pueblo people lived in Chaco Canyon. From the early 1000s to the middle 1100s, as their cultural expression came into full flower, people under pervasive Chacoan influence spread out from the core area over an expanse of more than 67,000 square miles of the Colorado Plateau. They carried with them a distinctive architectural style and probable worldview that they melded into preexisting communities in unknown ways. From 75 to more than 100 Chaco structures representative of a developmental stage archaeologists know as the Bonito Phase have been identified from the Little Colorado River drainage on the south to the borderlands of Colorado and Utah on the north, from west of Chinle Wash to the Puerco River on the east.

In their locations on prominences or other strategic spots and their preplanned tight formats, these Chacoan buildings portray an orderly sense of purpose: no casual random sprawl here. They are Chaco great houses transferred to environmental settings that often differ dramatically from the home canyon. Although not identical, the structures share the attributes of formalized, symmetrical floor plans, relatively large rooms with high ceilings, and kivas incorporated within the room blocks. Some building units are small; others have several hundred rooms. Some are one-story and others have two or three. Although not as finely executed as the buildings in the canyon, most exhibit the hallmark Chacoan core-and-veneer masonry. Frequently a great kiva is within the compound enclosure or nearby, and segments of prepared roadways run off to uncertain termini. Relics of what must have been a grand social scheme or, to use the researchers' term, "system," these outlying Chaco houses now stand as solitary decaying sentinels over seemingly empty landscapes.

The great houses and the roads that appear to radiate like spokes from the canyon hub suggest an elaborate, far-flung linkage with economic, social, political, or religious bases. The satellite settlements, or outliers, may have been administrative posts for overseeing the storage and transport of necessary commodities or tribute into the resource-deficient canyon proper; structures whose placement or size were meant primarily to convey incontestable authority; quarters for participants in periodic rituals held in the great kiva; or simply the homes of colonists displaced from the canyon by depleted acreage or water sources. Some now believe that the outliers may represent provincial attempts to imitate a vogue favored by the movers and shakers at Chaco Canyon. While definitive interpretations await future research, the outliers probably do reflect some sort of either implicit or explicit control, perhaps through hierarchical sociopolitical or theocratic structure, that underpinned the unique development now termed the Chaco Phenomenon.

Whatever the motivating forces behind the expansion of the Chaco outliers, within about eighty years (1070–1150) they had dissipated. Some of the dispersed great houses were vacated at the same time as those in Chaco Canyon, and others were taken over by Ancestral Pueblo people who followed a variant lifestyle. But within several generations those structures, too, were abandoned.

FURTHER READING: *The Chacoan Prehistory of the San Juan Basin,* by Gwinn R. Vivian

Seven Great House Communities of the Chacoan Era

JOHN KANTNER

❖ More than 200 villages in the Four Corners region of the Southwest are associated with Chaco Canyon, and like Chaco, these outliers or great-house communities include monumental great houses, huge subterranean great kivas, long ceremonial roadways, and substantial soil platforms and berms.

For decades, authorities have debated whether these outlying great houses and their communities were ruled or simply influenced by Chaco. Did these villages provide Chaco Canyon with food, labor, and wealth? Was a Chacoan "system" designed to redistribute food from those with surpluses to those without? Or did the builders of the great houses, impressed by the canyon's monuments, emulate them? Or did they believe in a Chacoan religion? While current knowledge suggests that emulation is the most likely answer, research and the controversy continue.

270. Casamero Pueblo, NM

Off Rte. 66 on County Rd. 19, north of Prewitt

Casamero Pueblo (A.D. 1016–1100) was built using the distinctive core-and-veneer masonry style that defines Chacoan architecture, with twenty-one ground-floor and six second-story rooms, a plaza, and a blocked-in kiva — a circular ceremonial room hidden inside the room block. Aerial photographs show an ancient road approaching from the southeast.

271. Anasazi Heritage Center, CO: Escalante Pueblo and Dominguez Pueblo

27501 Hwy. 184, Dolores

Visitor center/museum

Escalante Pueblo is a small, twenty-five-room great house, begun about A.D. 1100. The masonry is not Chacoan, but its symmetry is typical of the planned great houses, and it has T-shaped doorways and a kiva style like those in Chaco Canyon. People reoccupied it twice, in the late twelfth and the early thirteenth centuries. The nearby Dominguez Pueblo, built by Northern San Juan people, is not a great house.

272. Canyons of the Ancients National Monument, CO: Lowry Pueblo

For directions: Anasazi Heritage Center, 27501 Hwy. 184, Dolores

The people who built Lowry began it as a roughly rectangular structure with about thirty-four rooms, three kivas, and a great kiva nearby. They added to it until it had more than forty rooms and eight kivas, and they built a road approaching the great kiva. Pottery and tree-ring samples suggest that the people built it in the 1080s and lived there until at least 1150. Today there is a reconstructed blocked-in kiva, complete with the original wall paintings.

273. Salmon Ruins, NM

Rte. 64, west of Bloomfield

San Juan County Archaeological Research Center

Salmon, on the San Juan River, is a multistory great house of 175 rooms built quickly between 1088 and 1094. The people moved away in the early 1100s, although a second occupation occurred in the late 1100s and early 1200s.

274. Edge of the Cedars State Park, UT: Pueblo

660 West 400 North, Blanding

Visitor center and museum

The Edge of the Cedars great house rises two stories above the surrounding eleventh-century village and has twelve rooms, two blocked-in kivas, and a large, attached great kiva. It was built in several stages, beginning about 1100, by people who had a detailed knowledge of Chacoan architecture.

275. Chimney Rock Archaeological Area, CO

Off Rte. 160 onto Rte. 151, southwest of Pagosa Springs

Chimney Rock great house, on a precipitous mesa just below two towering stone spires, has seventy rooms and two kivas elevated above an extensive eleventh-century community. Scholars suggest that it was established to harvest nearby pines for use in building Chaco Canyon. It may also have been positioned to observe lunar standstills, which occur every 18.6 years. At those times the moon rises between the two enormous stone pillars. Tree-ring dates suggest that the great house was constructed between 1076 and 1093.

276. Bluff Great House, UT

Rte. 191, Bluff

The Bluff great house once rose three or possibly four stories and contained as many as forty rooms and at least four kivas. A great kiva is southwest of the great house. In front of the great house is a series of earthen berms broken by entrances for at least two roads. A wide, flat terrace behind the structure extends to the back wall. Research at Bluff has documented two occupations, one during the late eleventh and early twelfth centuries and a second one extending from the late twelfth through the thirteenth century.

FURTHER READING: *Great House Communities across the Chacoan Landscape,* Anthropological Papers No. 64, edited by John Kantner and N. M. Mahoney

277. Sand Island Campground, UT: Petroglyphs

Off Rte. 191, southwest of Bluff

Below the rugged cliffs along the San Juan River is a 300-foot-long sandstone face where prehistoric and historic peoples carved hundreds of petroglyphs.

278. Anasazi State Park Museum, UT: Coombs Site

Rte. 12, Boulder

People were living in this area beginning about 11,000 years ago. The Ancestral Pueblo people who lived here between A.D. 1150 and 1250 built their masonry structure aboveground. While little of the pueblo is visible today, it and the artifacts at the site suggest a wide trade network with other Ancestral Pueblo peoples as well as with Fremont people, who once lived in pithouses nearby.

279. Aztec Ruins National Monument, NM

Peter J. McKenna

North of Rte. 516, Aztec

Visitor center

In the late eleventh century, at the height of the cultural efflorescence, Ancestral Pueblo people in the San Juan Valley of northwestern New Mexico began to construct a large community modeled after those in Chaco Canyon. They built their first pueblos around an adobe great house atop a terrace above the Animas River. During the second decade of the 1100s, they erected an enormous masonry great house with more than 500 rooms. It rose to four stories, with an enclosed plaza containing a great kiva. Today this excavated West Ruin forms less than half of the large public ceremonial complex named Aztec Ruins by nineteenth-century Euro-Americans laboring under mistaken assumptions about the community's origins. The great kiva was rebuilt in 1934 by the archaeologist Earl Morris, who followed the architectural evidence he had recovered during his excavation.

Northeast of the West Ruin are the unexcavated portions of this grand ceremonial center. These include the East Ruin: a masonry great house, three tri-wall structures (circular structures with concentric rings of rooms around a central kiva), great kivas, roads, earthen mounds, formal middens, and long, low walls that appear to have defined the various sectors of public space. The West and East ruins are on either side of a road that leads into a large central tri-wall structure between the two ruins. The builders designed and planned the entire complex as a unit, although its present, final form is the result of two centuries of effort. The Aztec community is the largest concentration of Pueblo Bonito–style public buildings outside of Chaco Canyon, rivaling those in central Chaco in size and scale.

The social evolution of the community is shown by changes in construction style and by subtle differences in the layout of the East Ruin, begun in the late 1100s. Tree-ring dates show intermittent additions and remodeling in the Chaco style through the 1280s. While both the West Ruin and the East are formal structures, the West is more rigid in design and in its orientation toward the large plaza. The East is composed of several buildings bounded by massive walls. The internal open space is divided into smaller, linked plazas that suggest increasing segmentation of the community's social units. While the East Ruin was occupied through the 1200s, as evidenced by the lack of household trash and the absence of burials, the West Ruin appears to have been partially abandoned. Although some of the rooms and the great kiva continued to be used, much of the rest of the structure became a repository for trash and human burials.

Today a continuous thread of material culture, architectural features, and oral traditions links Aztec Ruins with the modern Pueblos. The Hopi Tribe and the Keresan Pueblos, notably Acoma and Zia, have ancestral affiliations with Aztec Ruins.

FURTHER READING: *Aztec Ruins on the Animas: Excavated, Preserved, and Interpreted,* by Robert H. Lister and Florence C. Lister

The Chaco Meridian

STEPHEN H. LEKSON

❖ Chaco began about A.D. 900, and by 1020 it had developed into a small but important central place, with far-ranging regional ties. Canyon leaders administered the distribution of food and other goods, and real political power based on garnered surpluses developed within the canyon. Elite power became institutional and probably hereditary. Buildings and built environments were the principal expressions of power: great houses, ritual landscapes, regional sight lines, earth monuments (now called roads), and astronomical alignments that were rapidly evolving toward regional geomancy. The ceremonial city grew around a north-south axis — the Chaco meridian — manifest in the alignment of two remarkable buildings, Pueblo Alto and Tsin Kletsin. The meridian was a north-south alignment at approximately 108 degrees longitude. Aztec Ruins was 50 miles north of Chaco; Paquimé was 375 miles to the south. Both of these later centers — the most important sites of their respectives places and times — were built within a few miles east or west of the Chaco meridian. Intriguingly, the largest and most complex sites of earlier periods, before Chaco, were also on or very close to this north-south alignment. The people who determined the locations of Chaco and later sites valued symbolic continuity with the locations of earlier centers, fixed by shared alignment with celestial north. The astronomy was simple, but the underlying cosmology was probably controlling and authoritative. The meridian shaped much of the region's political history.

By the early twelfth century, power had moved from Chaco to today's Aztec Ruins, a huge, Chaco-style ceremonial city. The old Chacoan world split into northern and southern spheres. To the south, kachina ceremonialism and other newly developed ritual patterns unified the burgeoning Pueblos of Hopi and Zuni and those along the Rio Grande without hierarchies or oppressive governments. In the north the San Juan and Mesa Verde regions perpetuated at Aztec the older Chacoan patterns — stately, formal, rigid, even grim. The political elite marked the historical connection of the new center at Aztec to the old center at Chaco with a major landscape monument, the Great North Road. Aztec was about half the size of Chaco, and its architecture continued the use of Chacoan sandstone masonry — except for one very intriguing building, a massive puddled adobe structure (perhaps anticipating things to come at Paquimé) that faced nearly due south and was just 2.48 miles off the Chaco meridian.

The Great Drought (about 1275–1300) was disastrous for the rainfall farmers. Aztec — like Chaco before it — fell because rain did not. Aztec's end was probably one reason for the dramatically complete abandonment of the Four Corners. The totality of outmigration can only be understood as politically directed — proof in the breach of regional integration. Conditions would have supported a sizable portion of the 1275 population, but everyone left. Tens of thousands joined the Pueblos, from Hopi to the Rio Grande. Many continued beyond, founding new villages in southern Arizona and New Mexico.

The several hundred elite residents of Aztec, heirs of Chaco, appear to have reversed cosmological directions. They headed south — seeking (among other things) a region whose economy could support their Chaco-Aztec lifestyle — down the Chaco meridian, presumably with much pomp and ceremony. After a march of more than 375 miles, they built their new city, Paquimé, on the Rio Casas Grandes, an area ripe for major canal irrigation. Or at least Paquimé rose due south of Chaco at almost the same time that Aztec fell, and evidence suggests that Paquimé's timing and placement were not coincidental.

Paquimé was the most wonderful city ever built in the Pueblo Southwest: Mexican ball courts, effigy mounds, and "pyramids" surrounded a huge, poured-adobe great-house pueblo. The local populations that built the city and supported its elite were not, in the main, plateau peoples. They were, instead, desert-dwelling descendants of the Mimbres, and they carried Mimbres memories and traditions. Chaco, to them, was not a vague fable about a mythical city but the principal political center of their great-great-grandparents' world. Aztec was a more distant place, where Chaco lived on in their own lifetimes. However they presented themselves, the Chaco-Aztec elite would not be strangers — historical or cosmological — in the desert. The Chaco meridian alignment validated the new city and its governors.

The Paquimé people were heirs of the master canal builders, the Mimbres. The great Pueblo city was supported by canal irrigation in the fertile river valley and was filled with exotic goods. The political-prestige economy of Chaco and Aztec exploded into a mercantile economy at Paquimé. Much of that commerce fed the evolving popular religions of the north with colorful feathers from exotic birds. At Paquimé a more authoritarian cosmology was commemorated by structures adopted from distant, more hierarchical regions: ball courts and pyramid mounds. Something like the grim old Chaco cosmology was perpetuated through new versions of old Chacoan forms and the manipulation of new symbols and materials from the south.

After 1275 the stories of the Pueblo people of

252. Grand Canyon National Park, AZ: Marble Canyon

269. Chaco Culture National Historical Park, NM: Pueblo Bonito

280. Mesa Verde
National Park, CO:
Square Tower

282. Canyon de
Chelly National
Monument, AZ

304. Navajo National
Monument, AZ

305. Petroglyph National
Monument, NM:
Morning Star as warrior
with eagle tail-feather
headdress and projectiles

306. Pueblo of Acoma, NM

315. Guadalupe Mountains National Park, TX: El Capitan

317. Fort Sumner State Monument, NM

321. Channel Islands National Park, CA: San Miguel Island

322. Carrizo Plain National Monument, CA: Painted Rock

334. Point Reyes
National Seashore, CA:
Drakes Estero

345. Olympic National Park, WA

346. The Makah Reservation, WA: Makah Bay

356. Lolo Trail, ID and MT: View from the trail

today's Arizona and New Mexico diverged from the political history of the three great cities. The Pueblos developed strong internal controls to prevent the rise of any new elites like those of Chaco, Aztec, and Paquimé.

This essay includes excerpts from *The Chaco Meridian,* by Stephen H. Lekson, with permission from AltaMira Press, www.altamirapress.com.

280. Mesa Verde National Park, CO

William D. Lipe

Off Rte. 160, east of Cortez

Visitor center and Chapin Mesa Archeological Museum

The Mesa Verde (Spanish for green table) is an immense canyon-dissected upland in southwestern Colorado. Mesa Verde National Park was established in 1906 and is a World Heritage Site. Although people have been in the American Southwest for at least 12,000 years, Mesa Verde was visited only sporadically until maize farmers settled there about A.D. 600. For the next 700 years, it supported a densely settled population with cultural and social ties to the many other Ancestral Pueblo communities spread across the Four Corners. Mesa Verde was one of the best places to farm in a region where drought and a short growing season posed great challenges. High enough in elevation to catch rain and snow from passing storms, the mesa slopes to the southwest, allowing the sun to warm its deep, fertile soils. By the 800s, the Mesa Verde people were building reservoirs to catch runoff from storms to supplement the water available from the small springs and seeps in the canyons. Two centuries later, these diligent farmers were expanding their cropland by building terraces on slopes and check dams across small drainages.

The earliest communities were clusters of pithouses located close to farmland on the mesa top. Each house was built and lived in by a nuclear or small extended family. As the centuries passed, people began to build groups of adjoining surface rooms (pueblo architecture), initially of poles and mud and then of masonry. The pithouses became more elaborate and more like the kivas used for religious ceremonies in today's Pueblo Indian communities. The Mesa Verde kivas, however, were family living spaces as well as places for ritual. Most of the time, people lived in small hamlets close to their fields, but in the 800s and again in the late 1100s and 1200s, they moved into compact villages of fifty to several hundred people. One such village has been preserved in Yucca House National Monument, just west of Mesa Verde and administered by the park staff.

In the 1200s the Four Corners area suffered frequent droughts as well as increased warfare, evidently among the Pueblo communities. Many of the people living on the mesa moved into more defensible locations on canyon rims and in natural shelters just below the rim. There they could also protect and easily access the springs that were their most reliable water sources. They built hundreds of masonry cliff dwellings in the natural shelters, including those now named Cliff Palace, Spruce Tree House, Balcony House, and Long House. The largest is Cliff Palace, once home to perhaps 150 people. A multistory apartment house, it has 141 rooms, 21 kivas, and numerous small courtyards that remain marvelously preserved, protected from the elements by the overhanging rock. The walls are of large, well-fitted stone blocks, many laboriously shaped with stone hammers to present a uniform facade. On the opposite canyon rim is Sun Temple, a massive thick-walled building with internal courtyards and storerooms, which must have played a central role in the symbolic and ceremonial life of

Cliff Palace as well as the other cliff villages in the vicinity.

In the late 1200s the population declined in the Four Corners area, including Mesa Verde. By 1300 everyone was gone. The reasons include droughts and shorter growing seasons, disruptions from continuing hostilities, and the attractions of the growing Pueblo communities to the south. The people who left Mesa Verde and the adjacent areas did not disappear; they moved south, often to areas where related Pueblo people lived. Today's Pueblo Indians of the Rio Grande, Acoma, Zuni, and Hopi tribal regions of New Mexico and Arizona have diverse cultural histories. Their oral traditions often speak of migrations from the Four Corners area and, in some traditions, from other parts of the Southwest. The many cliff dwellings and other places where people lived on Mesa Verde stand as a tangible record of the Pueblo peoples' deep history in the Southwest.

FURTHER READING: *Troweling Through Time: The First Century of Mesa Verdean Archaeology,* by Florence C. Lister

281. Ute Mountain Tribal Park, CO

Ute Mountain Ute Reservation

By tour only from the visitor center/museum on Rte. 160, south of Cortez

In 1972 the Ute Mountain Ute Tribe established the tribal park, which includes cliff dwellings — Eagle's Nest, Lion House, Tree House, and Morris 5 — built by the people who built those in Mesa Verde National Park. There are also large pictographs painted by Utes.

282. Canyon de Chelly National Monument, AZ

Off Rte. 191, on Rte. 7, Chinle

Visitor center

THE PLACE AND THE PEOPLE
AILEMA BENALLY

Canyon de Chelly National Monument lies within the Navajo Reservation and is called Tseyi (In the Rock) by the Diné (Navajo). Stream cutting and the uplift of the Defiance Plateau created the steep-walled canyons: Canyon de Chelly, Canyon del Muerto, and seventeen tributary canyons. Its physical grandeur, while inspirational, does not reveal the cultural significance held within the canyon walls. People began coming to the canyons about 5,000 years ago, attracted by flowing water, abundant plants and animals, and cliff-face shelters. The early people are the ancestors of the Hopi, Zuni, and other Ancestral Pueblo peoples. Between about A.D. 1000 and 1300 the canyons were alive with villages. The people built stone houses protected by the deep overhangs in the canyon walls, including those known today as White House Ruin in Canyon de Chelly and Mummy Cave and Antelope House in Canyon del Muerto. They carved images in the rock walls and grew corn, squash, and beans. Then they began moving away. Hopi traditional history documents centuries of life in the canyons, both seasonally and longer when conditions allowed. The Hopi continue to be connected to Canyon de Chelly.

After the Athabaskan-speaking Navajo migrated into the canyons, they raised crops and herded sheep. The Diné have stories that connect them with the land, and the communities, families, and clans identify themselves according to where they are from. Spider Rock is the home of the Navajo deity Spider Woman, the teacher of Navajo weaving, whose web assisted those emerging from the last world to the present world.

The peace of the canyon was broken in 1805 when 100 Navajos were massacred by Spaniards. Life changed tragically in 1864, when the U.S. government forced about 8,500 Navajos to leave their homes and make the Long Walk to Bosque

Redondo, where they were held captive. The Treaty of 1868 created the original Navajo Reservation and allowed them to return home, to the beginning of a new way of thinking and living.

The Navajo of today are a bicultural people: they observe their traditional values, beliefs, and practices while maintaining modern-day lifestyles. They continue their traditional chores of herding sheep, raising livestock, hauling wood and water, and caring for the farmlands, but they also go to work and attend school. Participating in traditional ceremonies is part of family life; this is balanced with participation in community and school activities. The Navajo language threads all of these events and activities together to perpetuate Navajo culture as it evolves through time to keep the hearts and minds of the People together.

TELLING ITS STORY
WILSON HUNTER, JR.

The Navajo guides who take all visitors into the canyons help them understand the sacred balance and harmony among all life systems. People are a part of nature, not separate from it. Nature has its own rhythms and its own cycles. People can work with nature, but people cannot dominate it without upsetting that delicate balance. At Canyon de Chelly we talk about the people because they are part of the system: people and land, taking care of each other. The canyon provides shelter, food, water, wood for warmth, and refuge in times of strife. People take care of the canyon, primarily by showing it respect. In training new park interpreters, we help to broaden their viewpoints, to include ideas and values from other cultures, and to integrate them with National Park Service ideas. By integrating different perspectives, they can become aware of their own perspectives and prejudices.

I recall that when my grandmother told sto-ries of the land, she would ask us to close our mouths and listen. In the canyon we can listen to the land. We can walk in it quietly and "do nothing." By being peaceful, being still, emptying our minds, we can begin to be aware of the land and of our responsibility for it. We cannot underestimate the power of the land. The history of the human spirit and its relationship with the environment is both rich and complex. By developing a sense of place and being part of nature, we can establish an order, a balance, that will enrich our lives on earth and help us find our place in the universe and our oneness with all life and with God.

FURTHER READING: *Navajo of Canyon de Chelly,* by Rose Houk

283. Glen Canyon National Recreation Area, AZ: A Pueblo and Pictographs

Page

Carl Hayden Visitor Center

People have hunted and gathered food in this area for thousands of years. From about A.D. 1250 until 1300, Ancestral Pueblo people lived in a small pueblo high on a sandstone cliff three miles up the middle fork of Forgotten Canyon. It is called Defiance House because of its sheltered location and because of the large pictographs on the rock of three figures with shields and clubs. The canyon continues to be significant to American Indians, including the Hopi, Kaibab Paiute, Kanosh Band of Paiute Indian Tribe of Utah, Koosharem Band of Paiute Indian Tribe of Utah, Navajo, San Juan Southern Paiute, and Ute Mountain Ute (White Mesa Ute Band).

284. Mule Canyon Ruin, UT

Off Rte. 95, southwest of Blanding

Interpretive ramada

Ancestral Pueblo people built the small pueblo, which includes a tower and rooms connected by a tunnel to a kiva.

285. Rainbow Bridge National Monument, UT

Access by boat on Lake Powell

This towering natural bridge has been and continues to be revered by many peoples. In 1995 the Navajo, Hopi, Kaibab Paiute, San Juan Southern Paiute, and White Mesa Ute, along with the National Park Service, developed ways that visitors could show their respect for this sacred place. Visitors are asked to consider not walking up to the bridge or under it. This is the world's largest known natural bridge, with a span of 275 feet. Water flowing from the nearby Navajo Mountain cut through the soft sandstone in the canyon and enlarged the cut, forming the bridge.

286. Hovenweep National Monument, UT

Ian Thompson

Off Rte. 191 on Rte. 262, southeast of Blanding

Visitor center

The thirteenth-century towers of Hovenweep are on bare rim rock surrounding the heads of small canyons and on huge boulders in the canyon heads. The canyons are cut into a vast expanse of sage and juniper known as the Great Sage Plain, which is encircled by distant mountains. Springs enclosed in the heads of the canyons are shaded by stands of ancient hackberry trees. At dawn and dusk the trees fill with bird song, at noon swallows feed their young in nests above the springs, and at night the calls of owls float along the canyon rims beneath countless stars. It is the stone towers, known for their beauty and excellent state of preservation, that first catch the eye at Hovenweep. The first question that comes to mind is "What purpose did the towers serve?"

In the centuries before A.D. 1200, the Puebloan farm families of the Great Sage Plain lived on mesa tops away from the canyon rims. At times their communities were made up of small, dispersed hamlets scattered across a large area. At other times their communities were tight clusters of multiple-family residences or even a single large pueblo containing several hundred rooms. Just as the settlement patterns changed over time, so did the architectural styles.

By 1250 the people had moved from the long-occupied mesa tops into the canyon area. They built their new, tightly clustered pueblos around canyon-rim springs. The towers of Hovenweep appeared at that time. A close look will reveal that many more structures — small kivas and rectangular room blocks — once stair-stepped down the talus slopes immediately below the canyon rims. The population of the pueblos was too large to have been housed in the towers alone. An even closer look reveals low stone walls encircling the canyon pueblos and linking the structures within them. The enclosed plazas may have accommodated community events.

Archaeologists have long hypothesized about the towers' function. Explanations range from defense to communication; many towers are along a line of sight across the Great Sage Plain. However, artifacts from the few towers that have been excavated are similar to those found in the houses and kivas of the time. One possible explanation for the towers, then, is that they were not built to serve a particular function. Instead, they may represent an innovative architectural style as opposed to a functional structural style.

The placement of the towers in the enclosing canyon heads may architecturally symbolize significant elements of Puebloan cosmology in the thirteenth century.

The canyon-rim pueblos were the final Puebloan communities to occupy the Great Sage Plain. By the end of the thirteenth century the people had moved a few days' walk away to join other Puebloans already living in the Rio Grande and Little Colorado River drainages in New Mexico and Arizona. Today the silent towers of Hovenweep are testimony to the architectural beauty and balance achieved by the Puebloan communities of the Great Sage Plain.

FURTHER READING: *The Towers of Hovenweep,* by Ian M. Thompson

287. Canyonlands National Park, UT

Headquarters: 2282 SW Resource Blvd., Moab

Wind and water cutting into the Colorado Plateau created the dramatic but hostile landscape of canyons and sandstone spires, where people began hunting and gathering about 12,000 years ago. About 2,000 years ago, they painted pictographs on rock walls in Horseshoe Canyon and in the remote area known as the Maze. Between about A.D. 650 and 1300, Ancestral Pueblo farmers grew corn, beans, and squash and built small cliff dwellings, kivas, and granaries for food storage. After they left about 1300, the area was uninhabited until the Ute, Paiute, and Navajo peoples came seasonally to hunt and gather.

288. Zion National Park, UT

Off Rte. 9, Springdale

Visitor center, Zion Human History Museum

Between about A.D. 700 and 1300, the Ancestral Pueblo people of the Virgin River area built storage structures for food on a knoll above the North Fork of the Virgin River. It is known as the Watchman Site.

The Pueblo Diaspora

JAMES E. SNEAD

❖ The collapse of the Ancestral Pueblo world on the Colorado Plateau in the 1200s rippled through southwestern society for a century. This was an era of migration, conflict, and reorganization — the severing of old bonds and the making of new ones — as people left places where they had lived for generations and established new communities. No part of the region remained unchanged, and in this turbulent time the foundations of today's Pueblo society were laid. According to tradition, the Tewa people of such northern New Mexico pueblos as San Juan and Nambe came from farther north, and they have been linked to Mesa Verde; farther south, people who speak the Keres language, such as those of Zia or Acoma Pueblo, derive their history in part from Chaco Canyon. Although it may have been new to them, the Rio Grande country had its own indigenous Pueblo peoples, with whom the newcomers intermingled in complex ways.

The details of this encounter, indeed, remain frustratingly vague. In some parts of the Southwest, such as at Betatakin and Keet Seel in Navajo National Monument, it is possible to identify whole communities built by the newcomers in the late thirteenth century. Elsewhere their presence is indicated either by more abstract evidence — rapid population growth, as seen at Bandelier National Monument — or by tiny details, such as the black-and-white ceramic ladle, a fairly common implement in the Four Corners region, found broken in a pottery kiln near Santa Fe, hundreds of miles away.

We have to assume that this complex pattern of evidence mirrors an equally complex process in which people moved as individuals, families, or entire villages, depending on circumstances, most intensely over a period of perhaps fifty years. Near Nambe Pueblo in northern New Mexico, it is possible to trace the progressive founding and abandoning of villages, one after another. We can visualize the historical trajectory by which newcomers gradually made themselves familiar with the land, remaining — as told by Tewa tradition — on the periphery until it was possible to establish a more enduring foothold.

Several places in the Southwest are particularly associated with the migrations of the thirteenth century. One of these is Homolovi State Park in eastern Arizona, where an entire cluster of villages was founded and abandoned by Hopi people in the decades around 1300. Another is the Galisteo Basin, a windswept and generally marginal district near Santa Fe. In 1200 the Galisteo was sparsely inhabited, home to a few small villages and perhaps used as a hunting territory by people living in the more amenable valleys of the nearby Santa Fe River and Rio Grande. By 1350, however, the Galisteo landscape was booming, with nearly a dozen new communities dotting the landscape, largely inhabited by Tewa-speaking Tano people. This thriving population persisted for centuries, until it was torn apart by the forces unleashed in the Pueblo Revolt of 1680. The earliest of the Galisteo villages dates to the late 1200s and reflects not this prosperous era but its more uncertain beginnings. The founders of Burnt Corn Pueblo (not open to the public) built carefully, ensuring their descendants a defensible position high on a ridgetop and a ritually appropriate placement. The prominent hill on the eastern horizon is heavily inscribed with petroglyphs. Their precautions were ultimately inadequate, however, because sometime after the turn of the fourteenth century the pueblo was completely destroyed by fire, along with many of the small farmsteads in the surrounding countryside. This suggests that while accommodation between different social groups was possible in some cases, violence was also a way by which new traditions were established.

Ultimately this period of shifting settlements, mobility, and warfare came to an end, and a new order arose. In the reborn Pueblo world, the old great houses, ritual roads, and family-scale kivas were replaced by community houses arranged around multiple plazas and kivas built to hold larger social groups. It was the pueblos built in the fourteenth century, with caciques, curing societies, and kachina dances, that the Spanish encountered centuries later. Standing in a plaza of the great community houses of Pecos National Historical Park or Tyuonyi in Bandelier National Monument or Kuaua in Coronado State Monument, we see the link between past and present, and from this landscape we gain a greater understanding of how this new order came to be.

FURTHER READING: *In Search of the Old Ones: Exploring the Anasazi World of the Southwest,* by David Roberts

The Sinagua

CHRISTIAN E. DOWNUM

❖ In about the fifth century, small groups of pithouse-dwelling agriculturalists lived in the pine forests of northern Arizona. By about 700 these people, known today as the Northern Sinagua, were living in the high country near modern Flagstaff. Their origins are not well known, but they seem to have been shaped by the Mogollon and Ancestral Pueblo cultures. The Southern Sinagua lived in the Verde Valley and drew upon the Hohokam culture to the south. In these early times, the Sinagua lived in small groups of pithouses, loosely clustered in areas where they could farm. They grew corn and squash, gathered and hunted, and made a distinctive thin brown pottery, Alameda Brown Ware.

Life changed for the Northern Sinagua about A.D. 1065, when Sunset Crater Volcano erupted and covered about 800 square miles with black volcanic ash. Though initially destructive, the ash formed a moisture-conserving mulch that improved farming. This event caused local populations to move to lower elevations. People of adjacent cultures moved in, bringing changes to the Northern Sinagua. Between 1130 and 1220 they built large, multistory pueblos such as Wupatki and Elden. They built communal gathering places, such as the Hohokam-style ball courts, the Chaco-like great kivas at Wupatki, and the large, rectangular structures that suggest "community rooms" at Elden. Trade expanded, and there is evidence of new, more complex forms of social organization and religious expression, particularly in the Wupatki area. During this time they built the relatively inaccessible cliff dwellings and alcove structures in Walnut Canyon. By about 1250 the Northern Sinagua had left the Flagstaff and Wupatki areas. There is no one satisfying explanation, but population growth, worsening climate, degraded agricultural conditions, and ethnic conflict may have played related roles. Since populations at Homol'ovi, Anderson Mesa, and the Hopi Mesas increased, it may be that the Northern Sinagua moved east.

The Southern Sinagua were skilled farmers whose crops included cotton, which they irrigated with water from the Verde River and its tributaries. They wove cotton into garments that sometimes were painted with elaborate designs. They built the dramatic cliff dwellings in the Verde Valley, including Montezuma Castle, and large pueblo communities, such as Tuzigoot, between about 1125 and 1400. By about 1450 they had moved and joined other Pueblo communities, principally the Hopi but also perhaps the Zuni and others farther east.

289. Taawa Park, AZ: Stories of the Ancient Hopi

Leigh Kuwanwisiwma

By guided tour only from the Hopi Cultural Preservation Office, Rte 2, Kykotsmovi

Taawa Park, in the heartland of the Hopi people, contains approximately 5,000 petroglyphs, concentrated in a large alcove. They capture a time period about 1,500 to 2,000 years ago. There are pithouses above the rim of the alcove, where people lived about A.D. 600. There is also a fifty-room ruin where Hopi clans lived from about 1000 to 1300. Hopi traditions speak of many clans traveling through this area and visiting these ancestral villages as they returned home to the Hopi mesas. This area has strong traditional connections to the Rattlesnake, Sand, Lizard, Flute, Bearstrap, Eagle, and Badger clans. Recognizing its importance in Hopi history, the Hopi Tribal Council protected the area as a park in 1985.

The Hopi name for the area is Paaqapa, which means Bamboo Spring. This spring, east of the petroglyphs, is an important religious shrine of the Hopi Snake Society. Taawa means sun, a revered deity in Hopi religious beliefs. Several of the petroglyphs may have been used as seasonal calendars, sometimes referred to as sun daggers. The petroglyphs show great diversity, from the popular *kokopelli* symbol to the anthropomorphs of southern Utah, which found their way to Hopi land. The Hopi word for petroglyphs is *tutuveni*, meaning "the mark of others." In traditional knowledge, Hopi refer to petroglyphs as a mark of their "footprint," evidence of their long presence in the Southwest from the time of emergence to this present way of life.

Today the Hopi reside in twelve villages, as they have for at least 1,000 years. Retaining much of their culture, including their religious ceremonies, the Hopi people have made the transition into the modern world, albeit with some hesitation, but with a positive outlook. Indeed, many Hopi youths have gone on to higher education, earned degrees, and become leaders of the tribe. The Hopi Cultural Preservation Office is an example of a department where Hopi professionals in archaeology and history work diligently on the tribe's many programs and initiatives.

FURTHER READING: *Pages from Hopi History,* by Harry C. James

290. Coconino National Forest, AZ: Elden Pueblo

Rte. 89, northeast of Flagstaff

The Sinagua built the large, sixty- to seventy-room masonry pueblo from about A.D. 1070 to 1250, and it became an important gathering place. Exotic items in the pueblo included shells from the Pacific Ocean, decorated pottery, and turquoise. These ancestors of the Hopi left about 1275, migrating north and east, and settled on the Hopi Mesas.

291. Walnut Canyon, Wupatki, and Sunset Crater National Monuments, AZ

Lyle Balenquah

Wupatki and Sunset Crater: off Rte. 89, northeast of Flagstaff; Walnut Canyon: off I-40, east of Flagstaff

Visitor centers

These three monuments hold special meaning for many Native American tribes in the South-west. The Hopi remember them as the ancient homes and landscapes where our ancestors once lived. They are sacred landmarks that continue as tangible reminders of the cultural history of the Hopi people.

For modern Hopi clans, such as the Rattlesnake, Bear, Greasewood, Parrot, and others, Wupatki is the home of their ancestors, who in the twelfth century built their pueblo of mud, stone, and wood beams. The National Park Service offers one translation of the Hopi word Wupatki: Long House; it also means It Was Cut Long, referring to a prehistoric event here. Although hunters and gatherers roamed the land at least 11,500 years ago, evidence for occupation of the Wupatki area before A.D. 1100 is sparse. Between 1100 and 1250, different cultures, which archaeologists have named the Sinagua, the Cohonia, and the Kayenta, migrated here and settled the land. Many of the homes built by these peoples were small, one- to two-room structures and pithouses; however, a few large villages dotted the landscape. Wupatki was once four stories high, with more than 150 rooms, and served as a large trade center, where local items such as cotton textiles, turquoise, and obsidian were traded for goods from far away, such as shell jewelry and macaws. The largest concentration of macaws in the prehistoric Southwest was found at Wupatki. There is a Hohokam-style ball court north of the pueblo. Most of the Hopi ancestors had left the Wupatki area by the mid-thirteenth century and had migrated elsewhere. Other Native groups continued to use the Wupatki area, including the Havasupai, who hunted and gathered here seasonally, and Navajo herders, who made nomadic forays into the area. For Hopi people, Wupatki is where much of our culture and religion and many of our ceremonies were formalized.

There is evidence that people were in Walnut Canyon beginning about 4,500 years ago. Between about A.D. 1100 and 1250, ancestors of several Hopi clans, including the Bear, Bearstrap, Greasy Eye Socket, and Bluebird, established farming communities and raised cotton, corn, beans, and squash. Using the materials at hand, they built hundreds of small structures, none larger than a few dozen rooms, in and around the cliff faces of Walnut Canyon. They lived well here for about 150 years before migrating to other areas. Other peoples — the Yavapai, Havasupai, Apache, and Navajo — have since used the area seasonally for herding, gathering, and hunting. Hopi people know Walnut Canyon as Wupa'tupqa, meaning Long Canyon, and we continue to view this area respectfully, honoring our ancestors who once lived here.

Sunset Crater Volcano, known as Pala'tsmo (Red Hill), is a sacred landmark for the Hopi. Current estimates are that it erupted briefly sometime between 1064 and 1100. Before this eruption, the Sinagua farmed the area and lived in small pithouse villages. When the eruption occurred, those living near and far witnessed the spectacular lava flows and clouds of cinders in the sky. The sheer power of the eruption left an indelible mark that has carried through the generations, such that modern Hopi people still recount the birth of this 1,000-foot cinder cone. Afterward, many of the farmers were forced to move. Although it was destructive, the eruption did create fertile farming areas, for the ash increased the soil's water retention and added minerals to it. For Hopi people, Pala'tsmo is proof that great forces inhabit our world, and to this day we visit this place to make humble offerings.

FURTHER READING: *Wupatki and Walnut Canyon, New Perspectives on History, Prehistory, and Rock Art,* edited by David Grant Noble

292. Montezuma Castle National Monument, Montezuma Well, and Tuzigoot National Monument, AZ

Matthew Sakiestewa Gilbert

Off I-17, north of Camp Verde

Visitor center and museum

The discovery of eight Paleoindian-style projectile points in the Verde Valley suggest that people lived here as early as 7000 B.C. By about A.D. 700, people known as the Southern Sinagua were living in shallow pithouses in the valley. They were irrigation farmers and grew cotton, squash, corn, and beans. After about 1000, the population increased, and they began building cliff dwellings. About 1130 they began to build Montezuma Castle, a twenty-room, five-story dwelling in a limestone cliff 100 feet above Beaver Creek. Adjacent to it are the remains of a forty-five-room pueblo and rock shelters. These structures demonstrate the remarkable engineering capabilities of the Southern Sinagua. By about 1300 there may have been 6,000 to 8,000 people living in small villages a few miles apart in this well-watered valley.

About 11 miles away is an immense sinkhole that formed when an underground cavern collapsed long ago. Known as Montezuma Well, it is 55 feet deep and 368 feet in diameter. About 1.4 million gallons of water flow continuously each day through the well, creating an oasis in the desert. The farmers channeled the water to irrigate their crops, and many of the ancient irrigation ditches are still visible today.

The Southern Sinagua also built Tuzigoot — the Apache word for crooked water — a massive stone structure on a ridge 120 feet above the Verde Valley. Parts of the pueblo were two and three stories high, and by about A.D. 1300, it had 110 rooms. Most of the entrances were openings in the roofs. The Verde River provided the farmers with a dependable water supply.

By the mid-thirteenth century Yavapai Indians were living in the valley. Hopi oral tradition recounts that by 1450 the Southern Sinagua had left the Verde Valley, migrated north, and become part of Hopi society. Western Apache came into the valley after about 1500.

293. Homolovi Ruins State Park, AZ

E. Charles Adams

Off I-40 at exit 257 on Rte. 87, Winslow

Visitor center

Homol'ovi, a Hopi word meaning place of the mounds or rolling hills, describes the area near modern Winslow. Seven pueblos were built between A.D. 1250 and 1400 along a 20-mile stretch of the Little Colorado River, 60 miles south of the Hopi villages in northeastern Arizona: Homolovi I, II, III, and IV; Cottonwood Creek Ruin; Chevelon Ruin; and Jackrabbit Ruin. They are ancestral to the Hopi people, and four of them are in Homolovi Ruins State Park.

Beginning in the mid-1200s, the builders of the Homol'ovi pueblos moved south from villages near the Hopi Mesas and northwest from villages ancestral to the Zuni. Taking advantage of excellent environmental conditions and a large labor pool, they farmed the broad, fertile floodplain of the Little Colorado River. They grew several varieties of corn, beans, and squash as well as cotton. On their looms in the kivas, they wove the cotton into textiles, which probably enabled them to trade for exotic goods: shells from the Sea of Cortez, copper bells and macaws from western and northern Mexico, obsidian from the nearby San Francisco Mountains, and pottery from numerous sources. During the mid-1300s a 1,200-room pueblo, Homol'ovi II, was established and came to dominate the area politically. The Homol'ovi villages became even more specialized in growing and weaving cotton.

For reasons that may have included floods, droughts, and crop losses, the people left the area about 1400. Most of them apparently moved to villages on the Hopi Mesas, and some may have moved east to the Zuni area. The legacy of the Homol'ovi pueblos and their people has been preserved by their descendants, the Hopi people.

FURTHER READING: *Homol'ovi: An Ancient Hopi Settlement Cluster,* by E. Charles Adams

294. Kinishba Ruins National Historic Landmark, AZ: Decolonizing Kinishba

White Mountain Apache Tribe Heritage Program: Mark Altaha, Nick Laluk, and John R. Welch

White Mountain Apache Reservation, Fort Apache Historic Park, off Rte. 73, Fort Apache

Nohwike' Bagowa (House of Our Footprints), White Mountain Apache Tribe Cultural Center and Museum

Above a now-dry spring in a pine-fringed alluvial valley near the center of the White Mountain Apache Tribe's lands is the 600-room Ancestral Pueblo village known since 1931 as Kinishba. Hopi and Zuni ancestors built it beginning about A.D. 1160 and lived here for about 200 years. Like the Zuni and the Hopi today, the people were maize farmers, and their villages and domestic arts reflect their unwavering focus on the land, the water, and the community, which was required to sustain their lifeway in a challenging environment. Oral traditions, along with pottery fragments, petroglyphs, and masonry styles, establish eternal linkages between Pueblo people and Kinishba.

In 1931 Byron Cummings, the director of the Arizona State Museum, chose an Anglicized version of the Apache name for the ruin — Kii Dah Ba (Brown House). He hired Apaches and used archaeological field schools, Depression-era works programs, and funding from the Bureau of Indian Affairs to excavate about 220 rooms, rebuild about 140, and create a "living museum." The partnerships necessary to incorporate Kinishba into the Fort Apache Historic Park and address the site's escalating stewardship needs began in the 1990s through consultations with Apache, Zuni, and Hopi elders. These discussions revealed cultural mandates to protect Kinishba's most sensitive elements and maximize peaceful and respectful visitation to and interpretation of Kinishba as a resting place, sacred site, and community important in various Native cultural and oral traditions. Hopi consultants confirmed that Kinishba is probably the site known in their oral traditions as Mäi'povi (Place of Abundant Snakeweed).

With support from the White Mountain Apache Tribe's Council, ongoing intertribal consultations, and financial and technical assistance from the Save America's Treasures and the Arizona Heritage Fund, the Tribe's Heritage Program has worked to restore an indigenous sense of place. By training tribal members in ruins preservation and by installing interpretive signs and trails, we have made Kinishba a place to experience the Ancestral Pueblo legacy on Apache lands as well as the authentic Apache, Hopi, and Zuni perspectives. Explaining these perspectives to visitors through interpretive media has helped decrease vandalism and has deepened visitors' understanding of all the people who lived here.

FURTHER READING: "A Monument to Native Civilization: Byron Cummings' Still-Unfolding Vision for Kinishba Ruins," by J. R. Welch, in *Journal of the Southwest*

295. Petrified Forest National Park, AZ

Anne Trinkle Jones

Off Rte. 40, east of Holbrook

Visitor centers and museums

About 10,000 years ago, wild game hunters began coming to the high desert that today is Petrified Forest National Park. It is still mostly wilderness and has the largest collection of petrified trees in the world. By A.D. 300 Ancestral Pueblo and Mogollon farmers had settled in villages near their small gardens. They built pithouses, lining the floors with thin stone slabs and covering the structures with domes of poles, brush, and mud. Later they built pueblos — rectangular stone-and-mud houses with courses of sandstone blocks and petrified wood chunks. They managed the precious rainfall — less than 9 inches annually — by channeling the runoff along stone alignments into their fields.

Through the centuries people pecked petroglyphs into rock surfaces blackened by desert varnish: geometrics; lizards and other desert animals and their footprints; human beings with elegant hairdos, jewelry, and solemn masks; and figures dancing. There are nearly 3,000 petroglyphs on the boulders below the overlook at Newspaper Rock, and more than 850, including a solar calendar marker, below the trail at Puerco Pueblo.

The petrified logs along the Rainbow Forest trail to Agate House were fossilized more than 250 million years ago. Between A.D. 1100 and 1300, the people flaked pieces off the stone logs to make tools and set jasper-colored chunks of petrified wood in mud mortar to construct a small farmstead of eight rooms. The reconstruction of Agate House in 1934 reflects the excavators' vision more than historical accuracy. However, the setting is breathtaking, and the stroll through the "forest" is exhilarating.

About 1250, people from the surrounding areas built a pueblo, known today as Puerco Pueblo, south of the confluence of the Puerco River, Dead Wash, and Nine Mile Wash. It had more than 100 rooms, with living quarters and storerooms, three deep, opening onto an unroofed central plaza. The only entry to the pueblo was over the roof by ladder. The people descended ladders into three rectangular subterranean rooms (kivas), where they held their sacred rituals. About 200 people lived in the pueblo and farmed the broad river bottoms below. After their pueblo burned in 1380, the last inhabitants departed, leaving only the whistle of wind and the scurry of lizards. These places are ancestral to the Hopi Tribe and to the Pueblo of Zuni.

FURTHER READING: *Stalking the Past: Prehistory at Petrified Forest,* by Anne Trinkle Jones

So Far and Yet So Near

CLARA SUE KIDWELL

❖ There is a certain irony in the fact that the University of Arizona and several research institutions are planning to construct an array of telescopes on top of Mount Graham in Arizona, a site held sacred by members of the Apache tribe living near the mountain. The heavens, perceived by astronomers to be of vast extent and enormous distance from Earth, play a very immediate role in many American Indian cosmologies. The boundaries of the Navajo world in the Southwest are defined by four sacred mountains — Sis Naajiní (Blanca Peak), Tsoodzi» (Mount Taylor), Dook'o'oos»ííd (the San Francisco Peaks), and Dibé Nitsaa (Hesperus Peak) — with four layers of sky above, the highest of which is occupied by the sun, moon, and stars. The hogan, the typical Navajo dwelling, a round structure with a domed roof and four support poles, is a microcosm of the universe. The fire in the center of the structure is the earthly representation of the sun above. The constellations, the main markers of the yearly passage of time, were originally placed on the ceiling of the first hogan by Black God, one of the Navajo Holy People, the deities who are manifest in the forces in the environment. Hogans may still be constructed as sites for curing ceremonies in con-

temporary Navajo communities, and they are still the characteristic dwellings in remote sheep camps, where Navajo families graze their flocks in the summer. In towns, however, hogans have generally been replaced by cinderblock houses funded by the U.S. Department of Housing and Urban Development (HUD).

The Pueblo of Zuni also has a spatial orientation in the concept of the Center. Zuni traditions explain the powerful significance of the Center, which is associated with the emergence of the Zuni ancestors from worlds below this one. The Middle Place, the Center of the Zuni world, is equated with fertility, the power of the sun, and the Zuni system of ceremonies. The Center is a metaphor for completeness and harmony in Zuni life. It collapses time and space into a single unified understanding of the relationship between the human and spiritual worlds. As M. Jane Young observes in her book *Signs from the Ancestors,* "Significantly, the Zunis' name for their village, their 'center,' *itiwana,* is also their word for the winter solstice; one is a center in space, the other a center in time, yet both are 'the same thing.'"

The monolith known by most Americans as Devils Tower in Wyoming is actually a site sacred to several Plains tribes. Its distinctive appearance marks it as a powerful site. A Kiowa story relates how a young boy and his seven sisters were playing one day, when the boy was seized by spirit power and turned into a bear. He began to chase his sisters, who climbed up a tree trunk to escape. The trunk grew upward as the boy/bear clawed at the trunk, scratching deep grooves into its sides in a vain attempt to reach his sisters. They were borne up into the sky, where they now live as the seven stars of the Big Dipper. This relationship between the permanent physical place and the Big Dipper, with its constant progression through the sky, reminds the Kiowa of the spiritual powers that reside in the world around them.

As markers in the sky, certain stars also define

the seasonal patterns of events on earth. The Pleiades, the closely bunched seven stars in the constellation Taurus, are a winter group. In the Seneca villages in upstate New York, the first appearance of the Pleiades in the night sky marks the approximate date of the first killing frost, and their disappearance the date of the last frost. They thus determine approximately the length of the planting season. The timing of the Seneca Midwinter Ceremony is determined by the Pleiades. It begins five days after the new moon that follows the appearance of the Pleiades directly overhead at dusk.

The cycles of the stars, sun, and moon are intimately intertwined with the cycles of human life. Certain Hopi men watch the horizon from places near their villages to observe the exact points of the summer and winter solstices, the resting places of the sun in his journey across the sky. In the Soyal ceremony, prayers and dances are necessary to give the sun the energy to get up from his resting place and continue his journey. When celebrants in the semisubterranean kivas see the three stars of Orion's belt pass over the opening in the roof, they know that the seasonal cycle will continue. Celestial events determine human events, but human events also determine celestial events. The Hopi sense of place is defined by markers both in the landscape and in the sky.

Historical places are earthbound. They are a function of human activity at a particular time. In American Indian cultures, places are important because of particular actions in time, for example, places where the Zuni, Hopi, and Navajo people emerged from worlds below, and because they are sites where people experience their ongoing relationships with the spiritual beings of earth and sky.

FURTHER READING: *Earth and Sky: Visions of the Cosmos in Native American Folklore*, edited by Ray A. Williamson and Claire R. Farrer

The Elusive Salado

JEFFERY J. CLARK AND
PATRICK D. LYONS

❖ The people known as the Salado, who lived in southern Arizona and southwestern New Mexico from about A.D. 1250 until 1450, have been a vexing puzzle for archaeologists. Who were these people, who left such diverse and rich assemblages of artifacts, such as different types of marine shells, turquoise jewelry, obsidian arrowheads, remains of macaws, copper bells, baskets, and cotton textiles? Even their domestic and ceremonial architecture varied from village to village. The only artifact found throughout the area is their finely crafted, decorated pottery, which is stylistically and technologically related to that of the Ancestral Pueblo peoples in northeastern Arizona.

New research has yielded a vast body of evidence and new insights into the lives of the Salado, indicating that between 1250 and 1350, many small groups of Ancestral Pueblo peoples, because of chaotic weather conditions in their homelands, migrated south into river valleys occupied by the Hohokam. In some valleys, the migrants fought with local groups until one or both moved away. In other areas they formed stable communities that included both Hohokam and Ancestral Pueblo traditions. Migration and the uneven mixing of Ancestral Pueblo peoples with the Hohokam help explain who the Salado were and at least partially solve the puzzle.

By 1450, nearly a century before the arrival of the Spanish, the Salado had left their villages, including Besh-Ba-Gowah, Gila Pueblo, and the Tonto Cliff Dwellings. Their departure was preceded by a century of steady population decline. This decline may have been related to climate change, overexploitation of local resources, and social tensions. The final inhabitants may have moved to Zuni, the Hopi Mesas, or northern Mexico. Some may have remained behind but adopted a mobile lifestyle that left few traces. They may be ancestors of the Tohono O'odham (Papago) and Akimel O'odham (Pima).

FURTHER READING: *Salado*, edited by Jeffrey S. Dean

296. Besh-Ba-Gowah Archaeological Park, AZ

Off Rte. 60, Globe

Museum

Salado people built this pueblo along Pinal Creek between A.D. 1250 and 1275. It had about 250 ground-floor rooms and may have had as many as 200 upper-story rooms. The people moved away between 1375 and 1400 and left Roosevelt Red Ware (Salado polychromes) as well as ceramic plates with perforated rims and Maverick Mountain Series painted pottery, both of which are characteristic of Ancestral Pueblo people who had moved into the area from northern Arizona.

297. Gila Pueblo, AZ

Gila Pueblo campus of Eastern Arizona College, Globe

Between A.D. 1275 and 1450, Salado people lived in this large (more than 200-room) pueblo. According to tree-ring dating, they built portions of the pueblo during the 1340s and 1380s. They left their characteristic perforated plates and Maverick Mountain Series pottery.

298. Tonto National Monument, AZ

Owen Lindauer

Rte. 188, east of Roosevelt Dam, Roosevelt

Visitor center and museum

About A.D. 1300, Salado people living in the Tonto Basin built pueblos of unshaped masonry

blocks and adobe mortar in the large recesses that erosion had carved in a layer of siltstone on the hillside above the Salt River Valley. The one called Lower Cliff Dwelling had twenty rooms and the nearby Upper Cliff Dwelling had forty. They cleared terraces, which, along with the rooftops, provided space for work and play. At the time that some Salado moved into these hillside pueblos, those in the valley moved from small to larger villages, such as Besh-Ba-Gowah.

They ate corn grown in the Tonto Basin — and left behind more than 1,500 corncobs in one room — as well as wild fruits and seeds that they had gathered in the highlands. They wove cotton, also grown in the basin, into cloth and participated in a trade network in the Southwest and as far west as the Gulf of California. The polychrome pottery and cotton fabrics left behind by the Salado show their remarkable talents as potters and weavers. Some of these are in the museum in the visitor center. In the first part of the fifteenth century, when the Salado began to move elsewhere, these people were among the last to leave.

FURTHER READING: *Salado*, edited by Jeffrey S. Dean

American Indians' Spirituality and Land Use

CHARLES WILKINSON

❖ American Indians today continue to revere their ancestors' homelands, including those they no longer own, lands now managed by public agencies. Because of their reverence for Rainbow Bridge, the National Park Service asks visitors not to walk under it. At Devils Tower, which the northern Great Plains Indians call Bear's Lodge, the NPS asks rock climbers not to climb on the sheer walls in June when tribes conduct ceremonies. The Tenth Circuit Court of Appeals ruled that climbing companies lack standing to challenge the NPS's voluntary ban and suggested in a dictum that Congress has recognized the agency's right to close the area to climbing as well as to ask visitors not to climb. In 1999 Blackfeet elders urged the protection of about 500,000 acres along the Rocky Mountain Front. The chief of the U.S. Forest Service and the Lewis and Clark National Forest supervisor, Gloria Flora, led the effort to withdraw the area from mining. American Indians are helping all Americans to have a greater reverence for our public lands.

Excerpted from "Land Use, Science, and Spirituality: The Search for a True and Lasting Relationship with the Land," by Charles Wilkinson, in *Public Land and Resources Law Review*

FURTHER READING: *God Is Red: A Native View of Religion,* by Vine Deloria, Jr.

299. Valles Caldera National Preserve, NM

William deBuys

On State Hwy. 4, west of Los Alamos

After miles of rugged canyons and high-altitude forests, travelers along Highway 4 experience an explosion of space when they enter the Valles Caldera's vast, tawny grasslands — a seemingly misplaced prairie that stretches away to the foot of darkly forested mountains. The caldera is a bowl 14 miles in diameter, formed in the aftermath of a stupendous volcanic eruption 1.22 million years ago. Having emptied itself, the volcanic field collapsed inward, creating the bowl. Subsequent volcanism pushed up arcs of mountains that divide the bowl into grassy basins called valles. These include Valle Grande, which is visible from the highway, Valle Toledo, Valle San Antonio, Valle de los Posos, Valle Seco, and

more. All of this landscape, and its peaks and springs, flora and fauna, carry significance for American Indians, especially for the people of four Pueblos — Jemez, Zia, Santa Clara, and San Ildefonso — ancient and still vibrant communities close to the southern and eastern edges of the caldera.

The act that established the preserve in 2000 recognized the "historical and religious significance" of the caldera to American Indians and directed the Valles Caldera Trust, which administers the preserve, to consult closely with neighboring pueblos on matters affecting them. In deference to Pueblo concerns, the act restricted the use of the upper elevations of the preserve's tallest mountain, Redondo Peak, which at 11,254 feet is also the tallest of the surrounding Jemez Mountains. It also specifically authorized the trust to "set aside places and times of exclusive use" of the preserve lands in order to accommodate religious and cultural needs. The Trust and its Pueblo neighbors have worked hard to honor these directives, with the result that permission for such use is rarely an issue; only coordination is, the goal being to eliminate conflict between the Pueblos' needs for privacy and the activities of the general public, which include hiking, horseback riding, hunting, fishing, cross-country skiing, general touring, and wildlife viewing. The silent, sun-swept beauty of the valles and the abundance of elk, eagles, and other wildlife suggest only a few of the reasons that the caldera stands so emphatically as symbol and manifestation of both the soulfulness of untrammeled nature and of the heritage of Native America.

FURTHER READING: *Valles Caldera,* by William deBuys and Don J. Usner

300. Bandelier National Monument, NM

Robert P. Powers

Off Rte. 4, south of Los Alamos

> The grandest thing I ever saw. A magnificent growth of pines, encina, alamos, and towering cliffs, of pumice or volcanic tuff . . . The cliffs are vertical . . . and their bases are for a length as yet unknown to me, used as dwellings.
>
> — Adolph Bandelier, October 23, 1880

The grandest thing Adolph Bandelier had ever seen was Frijoles Canyon on the Pajarito Plateau and the cliff pueblos hand-hewn into the north wall of the canyon by Ancestral Pueblo people, who left the Colorado Plateau between A.D. 1150 and 1300.

Initially, these immigrants settled on the plateau's mesa tops in rough masonry pueblos of a few dozen rooms; they hunted, gathered, and raised crops of corn, beans, and squash. About 1270 they built larger, carefully constructed pueblos of ninety or more rooms, one to two stories in height, in tight blocks surrounding a plaza containing one or more kivas. Within fifty years they had aggregated into a few larger pueblos and had become more dependent on agriculture. Research suggests that the families with the best agricultural land banded together in the large pueblos to establish permanent land-use rights and to share food in ritual ceremonies. The increasingly frequent and severe droughts in the 1400s may have made agriculture too risky, particularly for residents of large pueblos farming on the dry mesa tops. By 1450 they had abandoned two of the largest mesa pueblos, San Miguel and Yapashi.

After forsaking the mesas, Puebloans regrouped in a few well-watered canyon locations. Over the next century Frijoles Canyon, with its perennial stream and rich, loamy soils, became one of the most important communities. At the center of the Frijoles community are the large canyon-bottom pueblo called Tyuonyi and a great kiva built about 1520. Perhaps to preserve the canyon floor for agriculture, the Puebloans built thirteen cliff pueblos with more than 1,000 cave rooms along the canyon's north face. These "cavates," which so intrigued Bandelier, preserve a wealth of architectural detail: fire hearths, smoke-blackened ceilings, storage pits, sleeping areas, painted plaster murals — and a glimpse into the lives of these long-vanished people. Together, Tyuonyi and the cave dwellings created one of the largest prehistoric communities in the Southwest. Despite its size, or perhaps because of it, the people left Frijoles Canyon by 1550. Approached with reverence, this special place can convey to people today an understanding of these remarkable people.

FURTHER READING: *The Peopling of Bandelier: New Insights from the Archaeology of the Pajarito Plateau*, edited by Robert P. Powers

301. Tijeras Pueblo, NM

Off I-40 on Rte. 337, Tijeras

Interpretive center

Ancestral Pueblo people lived in Tijeras Pueblo from about A.D. 1300 to about 1425 and were among the first in the Rio Grande region to make beautiful red pottery, decorated with black lead-glaze paint, which they exchanged with neighboring settlements. They raised corn, beans, and squash, which, with wild game, supported about 300 people. Since the pueblo is at the crossroads of the east-west route from the Great Plains to the Rio Grande Valley and the north-south route from northern Mexico to northern New Mexico, the people had ties to all four of these areas.

302. El Morro National Monument, NM

Jonathan E. Damp

On Rte. 53, west of El Morro

Visitor center/museum

El Morro is a massive bluff of Zuni-formation sandstone that towers 250 feet above the surrounding landscape. The pool at its base, the only source of water in the area, marks a stopping place along the trail from Zuni to Acoma. It is also known as Inscription Rock because of the ancient petroglyphs and the messages and names etched into the rock by the Spanish and other Europeans, beginning in the sixteenth century. Non-Zuni visitors to the monument usually focus on these signatures and dates and learn little about the ancestral Zuni presence.

Although it is known for the Europeans' inscriptions, the story of El Morro began long before their arrival. For thousands of years it has been in the homeland of the Zuni, the ancestors of the tribe now living at the Pueblo of Zuni, just west of El Morro. It is important in the Zuni migration story and to Zuni religion and culture. Groups of Zuni traveled from their origin in the Grand Canyon in different directions throughout the Southwest. One group journeyed along the Little Colorado River to the round valley near Shohk'onan, Escudilla Peak, in Arizona, then southeast into New Mexico, and then north to El Morro. Between the late thirteenth and the late fourteenth centuries, they built a pueblo called Heshoda Ya do'a — Zuni for village on top — with more than 875 rooms on top of El Morro, nearly 7,400 feet above sea level, overlooking the valley below. The archaeologist Richard Woodbury called it Atsinna, but the Zuni know the entire sandstone monolith as A'ts'ina:wa — place of writing on rock. After they left Heshoda Ya do'a, they settled in Zuni Pueblo. When El Morro was designated a national monument, it became difficult for the Zuni medicine men and priests from the Pueblo to visit the sacred areas near El Morro to collect medicines and to make offerings.

Today approximately 10,000 Zunis live at Zuni Pueblo, a blend of traditional Puebloan architecture and modern housing. The traditional architecture lies at the heart of the village and represents the spiritual center place of the Zuni people.

FURTHER READING: *A Zuni Atlas*, by T. J. Ferguson and E. Richard Hart

303. El Malpais National Monument, NM: The Zuni-Acoma Trail

Jeffery Kevin Waseta

Between Rtes. 117 and 53, south of Grants

Visitor centers

More than fifteen different lava flows occurred in El Malpais from about 700,000 to about 3,000 years ago, during the Pleistocene and Holocene epochs of the Quaternary Period. The Zuni-Acoma Trail lies in the rugged landscape formed by these lava flows. Before automobiles, the trail was part of the route from the Pueblo of Zuni to the Pueblo of Acoma and was the only means of communication and trade between the two pueblos. Zuni runners used the trail during the Pueblo Revolt in 1680 to relay the message of the insurgency against Spanish rule. Fearing Spanish retaliation, the Zuni and Acoma poisoned all the springs and watering holes along the trail. Spanish friars used the trail from Acoma to Zuni to resupply the mission. The Zuni-Acoma trail, like many prehistoric trails, is considered sacred to the Zuni and Acoma people. Visitors to this primitive trail see the rough and raw volcanic scenery as they make the nearly 7.5-mile crossing of the lava flow from Rte. 53 to Rte. 117. This experience in the badlands of northwestern New Mexico is not to be treated lightly. The spirit of the past continues to reside on the trail, as do the perils of the present in this remote and rugged volcanic terrain.

304. Navajo National Monument, AZ

Off Rte. 160 between Tuba City and Kayenta

Visitor center

PEOPLE OF THE RED ROCK CANYONS
BRIAN CULPEPPER AND
CURLINDA HOLIDAY

In the northeastern corner of Arizona, wind and water carved majestic canyons through the petrified sand dunes of the Shonto Plateau. Over the eons many shallow alcoves formed in the walls of the brilliantly red sandstone cliffs. In the thirteenth century, Ancestral Pueblo peoples constructed villages, called cliff pueblos, in many of these alcoves. Nestled in their protective shelters, three of the largest — Betatakin, Inscription House, and Keet Seel — are in the Navajo National Monument, which was created in 1909 to preserve them. These were the largest cliff pueblos in a diverse and complex canyon community. The residents built their villages directly on the bedrock of the alcove, using wood and stone held together by mud mortar. A dozen or more households, each consisting of a large extended family, made their homes in these places. Every family maintained one or two open courtyards surrounded by their living and storage rooms. Shortly before 1300, all the people living here, as well as in the other villages on the plateau, left to continue their lives in the southern deserts, perhaps traveling as far as northern Mexico. Most of the homes they left behind in the canyons remain intact and look almost as they did 700 years ago.

The Diné (Navajo) came to the plateau about 1800 and moved seasonally, maintaining both summer and winter homes called hogans. Herding their flocks of sheep, they used the canyons for protection from severe weather, predators, and young raiders from other tribes. In 1864, when the U.S. government forced Navajos from their homes and imprisoned them at Bosque Redondo, most of the local Diné escaped the forced internment by hiding in the canyons that protect these cliff pueblos. Soon after the horror of Bosque Redondo, the canyons became part of the newly created Navajo Indian Reservation, and the Diné resumed their way of life. Traditional oral history continues to provide lessons to new generations, which help to keep these cliff pueblos undisturbed for future generations.

HISAT'KATSI (HOPI LIFE IN THE PAST) AT BETATAKIN (TALASTIMA), KEET SEEL (KAWESTIMA), AND INSCRIPTION HOUSE (TSU'OVI)
LLOYD MASAYUMPTEWA

Alik sa'ii — Listen. The Hisatsinom, the people who lived in the villages, mastered farming in canyons several hundred feet deep, enabling them to flourish in this high desert environment. They hunted wild game and grew crops such as corn, beans, squash, and cotton. With nourishment secured, they were able to build the architectural wonders Betatakin (Talastima), Keet Seel (Kawestima), and Inscription House (Tsu'ovi). Each was the village of a distinct clan. They are the ancestral homes of Hopi clans today: at Talastima, the Lenwungwa (Flute) and Aalwungwa (Deer Antler) clans; at Kawestima, the Kookopwungwa (Fire) and Iswungwa (Coyote) clans; and at Tsu'ovi, the Tsu'wungwa (Rattlesnake), Tuwawungwa (Sand), and Kuukutswungwa (Lizard) clans. One can envision men, women, and children working together to build their homes in the large alcoves, high above the canyon floor. They shaped the soft sandstone, made adobe bricks, and collected water in pottery vessels to make mortar for bonding the adobe bricks and sandstone. Using narrow trails and hand/toe holes carved into the cliff face, they brought building materials up to the alcoves. At the same time, they had to tend their fields, hunt, and produce their daily-use wares, including pottery, arrow points, and clothing.

Along with all of these activities, these resilient people also made time for ceremonies, as evidenced by their kivas and other ceremonial areas. Here the various clans developed ceremonies that they took with them when they left eventually for the Hopi Mesas. Prayers and offerings continue to be important to Pueblo peoples today. Communal prayers and ceremonies for rain, so that crops can mature for harvest, are central to Pueblo lives. Hopi elders continue today to make pilgrimages to these ancestral villages.

FURTHER READING: *Navajo National Monument: A Place and Its People,* by Hal K. Rothman

305. Petroglyph National Monument, NM

Polly Schaafsma

Off Unser Blvd. north of I-40, Albuquerque

Las Imágenes Visitor Center

The West Mesa borders the Rio Grande Valley in a great 17-mile-long basalt escarpment just west of Albuquerque, and a line of small volcanic cones punctuates the skyline beyond. Within this volcanic landscape are more than 17,000 petroglyphs, some perhaps 2,000 years old — images revealing the worldviews, cosmologies, and values of the peoples who made them. These petroglyphs are on about 7,300 acres in the monument, which was established to protect and honor them.

A few of the carvings, abstract in nature, appear to have been made by early hunter-gatherers in the valley. In contrast, among the most recent carvings are Hispanic Christian crosses, which are scattered over the escarpment in association with older Pueblo petroglyphs. Although some stand alone, many crosses appear to have been placed next to Pueblo figures of mountain lions, snakes, or other elements thought to embody fearsome power. The majority of the petroglyphs, however, were made by Rio Grande Pueblo people, who farmed the valley and lived first in pithouses and later in pueblo-style villages. Between the fourteenth and seventeenth centuries the Pueblo people built towns and villages of several hundred or a thousand rooms arranged around large plazas. This was a time of prolific image-making and innovations in Pueblo religion. The petroglyphs communicated, affirmed, and commemorated their beliefs.

Among the most compelling petroglyphs are the kachina masks. The main function of the kachina supernaturals, as intermediaries between the Pueblo people and their deities, was to bring rain. Their complex and varied headdresses, facial patterning, and features are remarkable in their diversity. Other subjects are star beings with feathered headdresses and eagle claws, the ubiquitous flute player, shields, and shield bearers. Images that combine human and animal attributes reveal the perceived interchangeability of relationships between the human and animal worlds. Other life forms include birds, animals, and insects, all symbolically complex and invested with various powers. Rattlesnakes wearing masks or horns symbolize the powerful Water Serpent, patron of underground water and responsible for floods and earthquakes. Snakes, coyotes, mountain lions, eagles, parrots, toads and/or frogs, and dragonflies are represented for their symbolic roles in the realms of water, rain, warfare, hunting, and fertility. Animal tracks are also plentiful, perhaps as a shortcut to representing the animal itself.

The symbolism of the petroglyphs is a significant part of Pueblo belief today and a continued affirmation of the presence of Pueblo people in the landscape. The petroglyphs hold special meaning for the neighboring Southern Tiwa– and Keresan-speaking Rio Grande Pueblo people. For them the escarpment and the volcanoes remain sacred, and the petroglyphs represent a lasting repository of tribal knowledge inscribed in the arid terrain. As one tribal elder said, "The petroglyphs keep the traditions."

Not only are they important in keeping the traditions, but they are an active force in the landscape. While the boundaries of the monument create an arbitrary separation between the petroglyphs and the surrounding area, visitors to the monument should keep in mind that the Pueblo people regard this remarkable place within the context of the whole landscape. They perceive a vital connection on both the physical and the spiritual level between the volcanoes, the escarpment, the petroglyphs, and Sandia Mountain, across the Rio Grande to the east. At the time the petroglyphs were made, the homes of the Pueblo people were included in this landscape as well. Today only the Pueblo of Sandia remains in the immediate vicinity in the valley.

FURTHER READING: *Rock Art in New Mexico,* by Polly Schaafsma

The History of the Pueblo Indians

JOE S. SANDO

Pueblos: Acoma, Cochiti, Isleta, Jemez, Laguna, Nambe, Picuris, Pojoaque, Sandia, San Felipe, San Ildefonso, San Juan, Santa Ana, Santa Clara, Santo Domingo, Taos, Tesuque, Zia, Zuni

❖ The people of New Mexico's nineteen Pueblo Nations are the descendants of the Natives of the Southwest and pass down their traditional history in reverent narration. Their history since the European invasion has many bitter memories for them. But time has resulted in changes. Today many Pueblo Indians are descendants of Spaniards, Indians, and Anglos, but they remain predominately Indian in culture, spirit, and tradition.

Among the Pueblos, three languages are spoken, Keresan, Tanoan, and Zunian. Tanoan developed into three dialects, Tewa, Tiwa, and Towa. The Hopi in Arizona are also Pueblo people, but they speak Shoshonean. There has been some borrowing of Spanish words in the everyday Pueblo languages. However, in the religious or classic languages, the vocabulary and terminology remain unchanged. When the Spaniards came, their language quickly became the trade language for all groups in New Mexico.

The Pueblo tribes have the oldest form of government in the United States. The ancient Pueblo traditional system consists of a grand council made up of the religious society heads, who govern the interior sovereignty through the war chief and his two lieutenants, who serve for a lifetime; a war captain and his lieutenant, who are selected annually. Each has five assistants to supervise the two moieties, or kivas, and their year-round activities, such as social dances, hunting, running games, and religious activities. In 1620 the Spaniards introduced the secular system of government in the Pueblos and gave each Pueblo a cane, now known as the Spanish Canes. The positions are the governor, two lieutenants, a fiscale with a lieutenant and five aides, and a sheriff with five aides. Thus the Pueblo government system today is both Native and European. The Pueblos have a third system of government, the All Indian Pueblo Council, which is a coalition of the nineteen Pueblos. It may have started when the Pueblos united to fight the Navajo raiders, who arrived about 1500. The U.S. government first learned of the Pueblo Council in 1922; the Bureau of Indian Affairs rejected it at first, but the Pueblos fought for it to exist. Today it is the political arm of the Pueblos.

The first Pueblo contact with Spaniards was with Francisco Vásquez de Coronado in 1540. Juan de Oñate came with the first colonists in 1598. The Spaniards instituted their system of *encomienda* and *repartimiento* on the Pueblo farmers, who no doubt found it heartbreaking to try to cultivate and work their own land and then have to work on the Spanish farms in this dry, semidesert climate. It is likely that the Pueblos had to give some of their own crops to the Spaniards. But this was not all that was tearing at the Pueblo souls. An even worse demand was beginning to bring disorder to the Pueblo communities. This was the Spaniards' attempt to discourage the practice of their age-old spirituality. The Pueblo leaders could not accept this third insult. In 1675 forty-seven Pueblo leaders were brought to Santa Fe for trial. They were charged with sorcery, but the real issue was maintaining and professing their Native religious practices. Four men were condemned to be hanged, and the rest were to be publicly whipped. And so the hanging and whipping took place.

Among those who were whipped was a man from San Juan Pueblo whom the Spaniards called Popé. Upon returning home, Popé began to think about the indignity that he and the other men had suffered. He felt that the Spaniards were getting out of hand after they had received so much help from the Pueblos, and something must be done to stop them. The Pueblo world as they knew it appeared to be falling apart. Popé called a series of local private meetings of war chiefs and war captains from neighboring Pueblos to discuss the Spaniards' actions and demeanor. Soon the meetings included most of the Pueblos except for those they

felt were pro-Spanish. When the revolt began, the Pueblo leaders asked the padres and the Spaniards to leave the province and assured them that serious consequences were the alternative. Out of thirty-two padres, twenty-one refused to leave, so they were killed. At least 375 of approximately 7,350 Spaniards also met their death. On August 21, 1680, the Spaniards left. Meanwhile, Luis Tupatu of Picuris Pueblo replaced Popé as leader, at least of the northern Pueblos. In July 1683 Tupatu sent an emissary, Juan Punsilli, of Picuris to El Paso del Norte (present-day El Paso) to invite the Spanish to return to help the Pueblos defend against the raiding tribes.

When the ousted Spaniards returned, in 1692, their attitude toward the Pueblos had changed. Also the Pueblos had gone underground with their spirituality. That is why today the Pueblos still enjoy many of their Native practices. They have their language and their Native religion along with the Catholic religion, which they accepted. Alfonso Ortiz described this as "compartmentalization." Today the Pueblo people are still on their own lands, with their own governments, religion, and traditions.

FURTHER READING: *Pueblo Nations: Eight Centuries of Pueblo Indian History,* by Joe S. Sando

306. Pueblo of Acoma, NM: Sky City

Brian D. Vallo

Off I-40, Acoma

Sky City Cultural Center and Haaku Museum

Traditional oral history reflects a time far beyond our imagination, a time of creation and emergence into this world. The Acoma people have always known of a special place called Haaku (the place prepared), the spiritual homeland prepared for their eternal settlement. The first clan mothers and fathers migrated from their place of emergence and settled at three locations before arriving at Haaku. At places such as Mesa Verde and Chaco Canyon their ceremonial and social systems evolved; those systems guided their migration and have sustained their eternal livelihood here, at "the place prepared."

Today Acoma is the oldest continuously inhabited settlement in North America. The 370-foot-high sandstone mesa in the New Mexico desert is home to more than 5,000 Acoma people. The first European explorers to describe them were Captain Hernando de Alvarado and his companion Fray Juan Padilla, who were sent with an army by Francisco Vásquez de Coronado in 1540. A member of Alvarado's party described Acoma as "the greatest stronghold ever seen in the world." Alvarado wrote, "The city was built on a high rock. The ascent was so difficult that we repented climbing to the top. The houses are three and four stories high. The people . . . of the same type as those in the province of Cibola [Zuni Pueblo] . . . have abundant supplies of maize, beans and turkeys like those of New Spain." Despite the impacts that resulted from contact with the Spaniards, the Acoma people have endured and have sustained the way of life that was intended for them by the Creator at the time of emergence. While contact and subsequent foreign influences have caused tremendous changes in the way Acoma people live today, the tenacity of this great tribal nation has shaped an appreciation passed down over the generations by the clan elders, ensuring the survival and maintenance of indigenous religious practices, language preservation, and economic prosperity for future generations of Acomas. There is a communal effort to maintain traditional opportunities for learning and sharing between the generations.

In 1904 the Pueblo established a system of controls for the hundreds of visitors who were coming to Acoma. The Acoma leaders — the war chiefs, the governor, the lieutenant governors, tribal sheriffs (or fiscales), and a twelve-member tribal council — established its first economic development project: a tour program that enforced controls over access while providing the Pueblo with a source of revenue. Today the Pueblo of Acoma operates and manages seven tribal enterprises, including a new cultural museum at the base of Haaku that is visited by tens of thousands of people each year. Guided walking tours are modeled after the first ones given by Acoma women. The 40,000-square-foot facility includes the tribe's archives and research library, which enhance the tribe's comprehensive historic and cultural preservation initiative.

Haaku is "the place prepared"; truly, the concept of "preparedness" is exemplified by the survival of the Acoma people and their determination to ensure economic prosperity and self-sufficiency for future generations.

FURTHER READING: *Acoma: Pueblo in the Sky,* by Ward Allen Minge

307. Coronado State Monument, NM: Kuaua Pueblo

West of I-25 on Rte. 44, Bernalillo

Museum

Kuaua Pueblo is one of dozens of very large villages established by people who moved into the Rio Grande region from the Colorado Plateau, the San Juan Basin, and the Mogollon Mountains. The people of Kuaua (the name means evergreen in Tiwa) began building their village about 1300 and left by 1700. It had more than 1,200 adobe-walled rooms around three large plazas and six kivas. The kiva in the south plaza had layers of fine murals. This kiva and one of the mural layers have been reconstructed. Fifteen panels of the original murals are in the museum. Kuaua is considered an ancestral village

by the southern Tiwa-speaking Pueblos of Sandia and Isleta. The Spanish explorer Francisco
Vásquez de Coronado was in this area in 1540.

308. Salinas Pueblo Missions National Monument, NM

James E. Ivey

Visitor center on Rte. 60 in Mountainair

The springs and catch basins around ancient
Lake Estancia, now reduced to large salt ponds,
have attracted visitors since people first moved
through the Salinas Basin about 6000 B.C. About
A.D. 700 they built pithouses and settled permanently in the area. In the fourteenth century,
people built six pueblos, three of which, Quarai,
Abó, and Gran Quivira (known as Las Humanas
until the 1830s), are in the national monument.
These people hunted and gathered wild foods,
but they also farmed extensive fields, some of
which appear to have been irrigated. Since they
were separated from the Rio Grande by mountains, they developed relationships with the
Plains Indians, who by the late sixteenth century
formed part of their daily social life.

The Franciscans established a mission in Abó
in 1622, in Quarai in 1626, and in Las Humanas
in 1629. The missionaries were the hands of the
church, part of a hierarchy of authority that extended to the pope in Rome. At the same time
they were agents of the Spanish crown and its
pacification of new frontiers. They taught Catholicism, farming, ranching, and the ways of
European culture. They demanded labor and
obedience in return, including construction labor on large churches. At Abó about 1645, Fray
Francisco Acevedo began to remodel the convento and double the size of the church. With its
massive sandstone walls and sophisticated but-
tresses, it was spectacular, exceeded in grandeur
only by the church at Pecos. At Quarai, Fray

Juan Gutiérrez de la Chica completed Nuestra
Señora de la Purísima Concepción in 1632. Both
missions have kiva-like structures in the center
of each convento patio, which resemble the
kivas of the pueblos and appear to have been
built with the approval of the missionaries. They
may have been used for the first Christian training of Pueblo leaders. At Las Humanas, San
Buenaventura was completed in 1634, but the
large church begun in 1659 was never completed, and the convento was occupied only
briefly.

Devastating droughts in the 1650s and in
1667 caused famine, resulting in the deaths of
450 people at Las Humanas in 1668. After an increase in raids by Apaches and Navajos, who
were also suffering, the people abandoned their
pueblos. By 1676 the missionaries and pro-
Spanish Indians had left. The efforts of the governor and the Franciscans to reoccupy the Salinas pueblos were stopped by the Pueblo Revolt
in 1680. Spanish settlers moved to Abó and
Quarai in the early 1800s but left about thirty
years later. They did not try to live at Las
Humanas because it was too far from the Rio
Grande and was exposed to Apache and Comanche raids. By the early 1830s Las Humanas
had become so associated with the legends of
the rich "Gran Quivira" sought by Coronado
and several early provincial governors that it became known by that name.

FURTHER READING: *In the Midst of a Loneliness,* by
James E. Ivey

309. Jemez State Monument, NM

Joshua Madalena

On State Rte. 4, north of Jemez Springs

The ancestors of the people of the Pueblo of
Jemez, who began to leave the Four Corners area
between about 1275 and 1300, migrated into this

region. One of the villages they built in the mid-fourteenth century was Giusewa, which means a village by sacred medicinal springs of sulfur. The location in the narrow San Diego Canyon was chosen not only for the hot springs but also for control of the water in the Jemez River. Giusewa Pueblo was four to five stories tall and had seven giant kivas and about 500 rooms. More than 2,000 Jemez lived here. For about 250 years, the Jemez of Giusewa lived in harmony with nature and with the other villages in the Jemez Mountains, growing corn, beans, and squash, performing their ceremonies in kivas, dancing to the music of their songs, and hunting game.

In 1598 the Spanish came to stay in our territory, led by Juan de Oñate. When he left, a Franciscan friar stayed on at Giusewa to force the Jemez to convert to Catholicism. He did not stay long, and many years passed before another Franciscan friar was detailed to convert the Jemez people. Conversion meant they would no longer worship the Great Spirits but instead pray to God and Jesus; no longer practice our sacred religious activities but pray in a foreign language; no longer dance to songs sung in our tongue to the beat of the drum but learn to speak Spanish; no longer pass down traditional values to our children but learn the Spanish folklore and the ways of the Bible. The Jemez secretly continued to live the "old ways," to endure, and to survive through continuing encroachments and suppressions.

Between 1621 and 1625 Friar Gerónimo de Zárate Salmerón coerced the Jemez into building San José de los Jemez, a massive stone-and-earth church with an octagonal bell tower, one of the most beautiful in the Southwest. The mission was active for some years, then abandoned by 1640. In 1680 the Pueblo people revolted against the Spanish, and the Jemez moved from Giusewa to the mesa tops. For the next twelve years the Pueblo people followed the old ways. In 1692 the Spanish returned and began to pun-ish those defying Spanish rule. On July 24, 1694, Governor Diego de Vargas attacked the Jemez in their mesa-top village of Astialakwa, burned it to the ground, and took their corn and sheep. More than 80 people died. They were so petrified of Spanish rule that some chose to jump off the mesa top.

Today the Jemez are still a proud people living in the village of Walatowa. We have endured the unimaginable and survived. Our culture lives on, and as we sing in our language and dance to our songs to the beat of our drum, we are thankful every day, with every breath, to the Great Ones, our ancestors, who sacrificed to keep the old ways alive.

310. Pecos National Historical Park, NM

John L. Kessell

Off I-25, Pecos

Visitor center and museum

By 1450 the Pecos Indians were living in their new, defensible, multistory pueblo, large enough for 2,000 people, on a rocky ridge in a mountain valley of brick-red soil. With the Pecos River a mile to the east and the Rio Grande a day's walk to the west, location determined Pecos Pueblo's prominence and, in the end, its decline. Its people balanced the deep tensions between traders and farmers, guarding the route of trade and of war between the agricultural Pueblo Indians of the Rio Grande Valley and the buffalo-hunting peoples of the Great Plains. As gatekeepers, the Pecos profited from the export of crop surpluses, cloth, and luxury items and the import of buffalo hides, tanned skins, dried meat, and human captives. But in times of famine and war, they were subjected to fierce attacks from the plains.

In 1540 the first Spaniards arrived in Pecos, seeking quick wealth and the lost Seven Cities of Antillia. They found, instead, the people — wearing shell beads, turquoise, eagle claws, grizzly-bear teeth, animal skins, turkey-feather cloaks, and cotton cloth. Deeply disappointed, the Spaniards vacated the Pueblo world after two winters, but in 1598, led by Juan de Oñate, they returned to stay. Oñate had contracted with the king's viceroy in Mexico City to recruit 200 colonist families and manage the "pacification" of New Mexico in return for temporary proprietorship. To make the venture profitable, Oñate sought exploitable resources or subject peoples rich enough to pay tribute in salable goods. He was also on a crusade. "Open the door of heaven to these heathens," he prayed as he took possession in the name of his king and the Spanish church militant.

The Franciscan friar Fray Andrés Juárez, who came in 1621, smashed no Pecos idols. Rather, he caught the people up in a new building project, using adobes, neat sun-dried building blocks of earth weighing about 40 pounds each. Course after course the women laid, while the men dragged in massive pine logs, learned how to adz and carve them, then labored to hoist them aloft. Finally, in 1625, the cavernous structure stood complete, 40 feet high, a fortress-church to match the pueblo.

In 1680, after nearly a century of religious and economic repression, the Pueblo Indians united and drove the Spaniards south to the El Paso area. In a supreme show of defiance, they set fire to the roof of the Pecos church and tore the building down. Twelve years later Diego de Vargas began a hard-fought Spanish restoration, which bitterly divided the Pecos. Juan de Ye and Felipe de Chistoe spoke for those who favored the Spaniards' return; iron knives, horses, and firearms were good for trade and protection. Diego Umbiro hated the Spaniards; they were, he said, "of a different flesh." The two factions clashed violently in the summer of 1696, when most of the northern Pueblos rose for the last

time against Spanish rule. Chistoe, with the concurrence of Governor Vargas, invited opposition leaders to talks in a kiva, where his men murdered them. The brutality of this purge brought the Pecos Pueblo to the verge of disintegration. Chistoe, honored by the Spaniards with fancy dress and titles, won out, and those who opposed him left the community. The population of the pueblo continued to decline. Some of the remnant died at the hands of Comanches, others of smallpox. As they shifted to survive in eighteenth-century New Mexico, Pueblo Indians and Spaniards learned to live together. They built the final church at Pecos sometime between 1705 and 1717. The Franciscans came to accept the Pueblo people's outward show of Christianity, looking the other way as they resumed their ancient ceremonial life. United in poverty, most Spaniards and Pueblo people lived as neighbors, shared cultural traits, and bartered beans and sheep.

Peace with the Comanches in 1786 did not favor the Pecos. By the 1820s Spanish settlers were taking up old fields that they swore were vacant, and protests from the Pecos went unheeded. In 1838 the surviving few moved to Jemez, the only other Towa-speaking Pueblo, taking with them their ceremonial gear and the life-size Pecos bull costume. They prospered at Jemez, but they never forgot. The Pecos bull still dances at Jemez.

FURTHER READING: *Kiva, Cross, and Crown: The Pecos Indians and New Mexico,* by John L. Kessell

311. Navajo Pueblitos of the Dinétah, NM

Harry Walters

Directions available at the Bureau of Land Management, 1235 La Plata Hwy., Farmington

Our people, the Navajo, built hogans here at least as early as the 1540s. No one knows when they arrived here from Canada, where other Athabaskan-speaking people lived. According to anthropologists, they may have arrived sometime during the fifteenth century. However, our people say that this is the place where our ancestors emerged from beneath the earth to this Fourth World. Many of the Navajo creation stories and traditional ceremonies seem to have evolved here. Sacred places and landmarks mentioned in many ceremonies and stories are here. There are many petroglyphs and pictographs, some of which depict images of the Holy People who created the Navajo world. There are few differences between those images and the sand paintings of today, demonstrating that few changes have been made in the ceremonial system. Medicine people and elders make pilgrimages to these sacred places to make medicine and leave offerings.

Pueblitos are defensive structures built on top of boulders or mesas. More than 150 such structures are scattered throughout Dinétah. Some are quite large, with high stone walls around them for defense against enemies such as the Utes, Comanches, and Spaniards; others consist of one or two rooms. All were built between 1680 and 1760. The pueblitos are Puebloan in nature and attest to the close relationship between our people and the Pueblos in the past. When warfare increased in the 1760s, our people moved to be with their relatives in the Chuska Mountains. Today Dinétah lies outside our reservation, but we hold the land sacred, and our ceremonies remind us of that.

FURTHER READING: *Defending the Dinétah,* by Ronald H. Towner

312. Tumacácori National Historical Park, AZ: The O'odham and the Missions

Donald T. Garate

Mission San José de Tumacácori, Mission Los Santos Ángeles de Guevavi, Mission San Cayetano de Calabazas, off I-19 at exit 29, Tumacácori

Visitor center

The O'odham, who had always lived at a village on the Santa Cruz River called Tumacácori, petitioned the Jesuit missionary Eusebio Kino to establish a mission. He came in January 1691 and found that they had built three ramadas for him: one to sleep in, one to eat in, and another for saying Mass. He left them gifts of cattle and wheat and traveled upriver to Guevavi, where he established the headquarters for a mission system that included Los Santos Ángeles de Guevavi, San José de Tumacácori, San Ignacio de Sonoitac, and San Cayetano de Calabazas. The Jesuits introduced new ideas to the O'odham that changed their way of life. In addition to a new religion and culture, the Jesuits brought new farming techniques, wheat — a grain they could grow year-round — and livestock. While many O'odham accepted Catholicism and the Spanish lifestyle, and generally found an easier living by so doing, the missions brought lethal scourges down upon them, including European diseases and incessant raids by Apaches.

The changing cultural, economic, and political winds during the 150 years of mission life sometimes brought growth to these communities but more often deterioration. For a number of reasons — the uprising of a faction of O'odham in the Altar Valley in 1751, the worldwide expulsion of the Jesuits and their replacement by the Franciscans, Mexican independence, the ouster of Spanish-born priests, and the United States/Mexican War — all four missions were eventually abandoned. The O'odham left Tumacácori after the hard winter of 1848 and moved to Mission San Xavier del Bac, south of Tucson. The mission sites became part of the United States in the Gadsden Purchase of 1854, but no one represented the absentee O'odham in the struggles for ownership, and they lost all claims to the land in 1914. Today much of the mission land is protected within the historical park.

FURTHER READING: *Tumacácori National Historical Park,* by Susan Lamb

313. Mission San Xavier del Bac, AZ: O'odham *Himdag*

Marlon B. Evans

1950 W. San Xavier Rd., Tucson

The Jesuit missionary Eusebio Francisco Kino first visited the O'odham community of Wa:k (San Xavier del Bac) in August 1692 and gave the mission its name. After the king of Spain expelled the Jesuits from Mexico in 1767, the first Franciscan missionary came to the mission the following year. In 1783 Father Juan Bautista Velderrain hired Ignacio Gaona from Mexico to design Mission San Xavier del Bac, and the O'odham built it. The mission opened its doors in 1797. With its white stucco exterior, it is often called the "White Dove of the Desert." Spanish missionaries introduced the Catholic religion to the O'odham, and the O'odham included some of their ancient religious practices with Catholicism, creating the vitality and spirituality of their religion as practiced today. The mission continues to be important to the O'odham for daily services, Sunday Mass, holy days, weddings, baptisms, Holy Communion, and funerals.

There are three groups of O'odham. The Tohono O'odham, known as the Desert People; the Akimel O'odham, the River People; and the Hia-Ced O'odham, the Sand People, who live to the west of the Desert and River people. All three tribes share the O'dham language. The 1854 Gadsden Purchase split the O'odham homeland between the United States and the Mexican state of Sonora. Because of Spanish colonization and the proximity to Mexico, the O'odham have adapted and incorporated many Spanish influences into our language, agriculture, and daily lives, including the Catholic religion. Today, about three-fourths of the Tohono O'odham live on three reservations, San Xavier, Gila Bend, and Tohono O'odham.

Father Kino and other missionaries introduced Spanish vegetables such as chickpeas, onions, and melons to our ancestors. These vegetables blended well with the O'odham diet of saguaro fruit, jams and syrups, tepary beans, pinto beans, prickly pear pads, and cholla buds. The high-protein tepary bean, which is native to the Southwest, is still cultivated by the Tohono O'odham and Akimel O'odham.

Mission San Xavier del Bac withstood an earthquake in 1887. The restoration of the exterior and of the paintings and sculptures inside the church was made possible by the nonprofit organization Patronato San Xavier. Today the mission community is a blend of Old World Catholicism, traditional O'odham *himdag* (culture/life), and the contemporary revitalization of language, culture, and religion.

FURTHER READING: *Sharing the Desert: The Tohono O'odham in History,* by Winston P. Erickson

314. Carlsbad Caverns National Park, NM

Off U.S. 62/180, southwest of Carlsbad

Visitor center

For thousands of years American Indians hunted, gathered, and lived in this area. They left pictographs on the south wall of the entrance to the caverns and piles of fire-cracked rocks at the entrance to Desert Loop Road, where they roasted plants, including mescal, agave, and yucca parts. A rock shelter that they used is in Walnut Canyon. Along the trail to the shelter, the park has provided information about the plants that the people gathered and used. The area that is now the national park continues to be important to American Indians, and the park consults with a number of tribes: the Apache Tribe of Oklahoma, Comanche Nation, Fort Sill Apache Tribe, Hopi Tribe, Jicarilla Apache Nation, Kiowa Indian Tribe of Oklahoma, Mescalero Apache Tribe, Pawnee Nation, Pueblo of Isleta, Pueblo of Zia, Pueblo of Zuni, San Carlos Apache Tribe, White Mountain Apache Tribe, and Ysleta Del Sur Pueblo.

315. Guadalupe Mountains National Park, TX: The Mescalero Apaches and the Guadalupe Mountains

Donna R. Stern and Nicole G. Stern

On U.S. 62/180, Pine Springs

Visitor center

For the nomadic Mescalero Apaches, the Guadalupe Mountains, with their precious seeps, springs, and rugged surroundings, were a safe refuge. These agile mountain dwellers lived in the mountains during the summer and camped in the desert in the winter. They also traveled and lived in the Sacramento, Capitan, and Oscura mountains. Their ability to adapt to almost any climate demonstrated their resilience as a people. Guadalupe Peak, which is sacred to the Mescalero Apaches, is the highest point in Texas (8,749 feet). A geological fault associated with regional uplift exposed (as seen from the west) 2 miles of the Capitan Reef, a 400-mile-long ancient marine fossil reef formed during the Permian Period. Subsequent erosion exposed the reef for 50 miles along the southeastern flanks of the Guadalupe Mountains from Guadalupe Peak to the vicinity of Carlsbad.

According to Mescalero Apache legend, the famous Mountain Gods, *ga-he,* were presented to the people in a cave in the mountains. Many Mescalero families continue to travel into these revered mountains for traditional events, including religious puberty rites for young girls and initiation rites and vision quests for young boys as part of their training for Mountain-God dance groups. Traditionally, the Mescalero Apaches gathered mescal, a staple food plant, from the Chihuahua Desert below the peak. The name Mescalero means "the people who eat mescal." They still harvest and prepare the plant by roasting it in deep pits, removing the pulpy white meat, and drying it into a hearty and nutrient-rich food, which will keep for a year. The texture of mescal is stringy, and the taste is sweet, like caramel. There is an annual mescal roast at the Living Desert Museum in Carlsbad, New Mexico.

In 1855, after outsiders encroached on their land, the Mescalero Apaches reluctantly agreed to exchange their land and live on a reservation. The government built Fort Stanton on ancestral tribal lands but never ratified the treaty, resulting in ongoing clashes between miners and Mescalero Apaches. In 1862 General James Carleton ordered all Mescalero Apaches to Fort Sumner, in eastern New Mexico. Breaking his promise that only the Mescalero would occupy Bosque Redondo, Carleton brought more than 8,500 Navajos to live there too. The overcrowded conditions and insufficient resources resulted in conflicts between Mescaleros and Navajos. The Mescaleros escaped in 1865 and lived in the nearby mountains until 1873, when President Ulysses S. Grant established the first Mescalero Apache Reservation near Fort Stanton. Hundreds of thousands of acres smaller than their original lands, the Mescalero Apache Reservation today is bordered on the south by the Sacramento Mountains and to the north by the Sierra Blanca. It is the home of more than 4,000 tribal members today.

FURTHER READING: *The People Called Apache,* by Thomas Mails

316. Fort Bowie National Historic Site, AZ

Leland Michael Darrow

On Apache Pass Rd., 13 miles south of Bowie

Trail to ruins and visitor center

All of our land is sacred, our old people said to us. It takes care of us and must be respected and cared for. The low, rough area called Tsetagułka (white-topped rock), between Naakibitsi (Dos Cabezas, the mountains of the two heads) on the northwest and Tsehadisaa (Chiricahua, the mountains that have standing rocks) to the southeast, is a favorite place of our people. Agave, yucca, mesquite, sumac, and many other plants used for food, medicine, and other supplies grow abundantly. Our people once made their homes in this area, took care of the spring that always flowed, and held their ceremonies before circulating on, leaving little trace of their presence.

The Spanish came to us and to the other Native people, demanding supplies and work. Those who refused were killed or taken away to be slaves. Our people constantly moved to evade them. In the 1700s and early 1800s our people learned to make raids on the Spanish and their allies to capture supplies or avenge attacks. When the Americans came to our land in 1846, we offered to help them fight the Mexicans. The United States laid claim to half of our land. Their people wanted to pass through our land, so we made a treaty in 1852 to allow that. The spring between the mountains became a regular stopping place for any people passing through. One of our leaders, Cochise, arranged for his people to supply firewood for the stage station that had been built in Apache Pass. Friendly relations halted when Cochise and his family were invited to a meeting in the pass, where he was falsely accused of kidnapping. He escaped from the soldiers' tent and later learned that his captured relatives had been hanged. Mangas Coloradas, Cochise's father-in-law, joined him to op-

pose the U.S. soldiers moving toward Apache Pass in July 1862 and was seriously wounded. The soldiers built Fort Bowie to control access to the spring and as a base to support the invasion and occupation of our lands. To promote peace, Cochise agreed to a reservation on Apache homelands in 1872. Cochise died in 1874, and two years later the United States closed the Chiricahua Reservation.

Fort Bowie served as a base for pursuing Chiricahua people who tried to escape from the hot, dry, rocky San Carlos Reservation and return to their homes. San Carlos was a reservation of a different Native nation, used as a dumping ground to remove some Arizona Natives from land desired by the American invaders. In 1886 lies and promises accomplished what soldiers could not, and the Chiricahua Apaches who came in were shipped off into exile in Florida. All Chiricahua men, women, and children, their leaders, and the scouts were sent to Florida. With no Apaches left, Fort Bowie was not needed and was eventually abandoned. Trash and sewage had polluted the spring.

More than 500 Chiricahua Apaches were kept as prisoners in Florida, then Alabama, and later were moved to Fort Sill, Oklahoma. The 261 survivors were finally released in 1913 and 1914, but they were not allowed to return to their ancestral homeland. Their descendants are now either the Fort Sill Apache Tribe or part of the Mescalero Apache Tribe. Today the Fort Sill Apache Tribe, with offices in Apache, Oklahoma, is a federally recognized tribe with 626 tribal members who live all across the United States. The tribe owns about 300 acres in Oklahoma and offers health and educational services to tribal members.

FURTHER READING: *Arizona: Combat Post of the Southwest, 1858–1894,* by Douglas C. McChristian

317. Fort Sumner State Monument, NM

Davina Two Bears

Off U.S. 60/84, southeast of Fort Sumner

Bosque Redondo Memorial

Life for the Diné was good but hard in the nineteenth century in Diné Bikéyah, the Navajo homeland. The Diné prayed to the Holy People and lived in respectful harmony with Nahasdzaan, Mother Earth, her creatures, and nature. They interacted with other tribal nations through trade and intermarriage but also though warfare. The Diné were known for their great herds of sheep, horses, and cattle as well as for their orchards and large fields of corn, melons, and squash. Their riches — their women and children — were the envy of their traditional adversaries, such as the Utes and Comanches who raided Navajo families. When Spaniards and Mexicans took Diné to be slaves on their ranches and in the silver mines of Mexico, they often retaliated in self-defense. The American military tried to put down the violence, but in reality they sought to lay claim to our sacred lands. Diné leaders did not agree to sign treaties while their children were being stolen and enslaved, despite promises of protection by the American military. In the early 1800s the Diné headman and peacemaker Narbona traveled far and wide in his quest to negotiate peace, only to be murdered during a treaty negotiation.

In 1864 the United States government began to remove the Diné from their homelands. Through oral history, the Diné recount the scorched-earth policy practiced by the American military, as they witnessed in horror the death of family members and the destruction of their hogans, livestock, and crops. More than 8,500 Diné were captured and suffered the 400-mile Long Walk to Bosque Redondo, an oxbow in the Pecos River, where the military had built Fort Sumner, a fort and reservation where the government incarcerated the Diné and about 450 Mescalero Apaches. Diné oral history also recounts great acts of heroism by the leaders, who continued to advocate their people's release, and also by the men, women, and children, who evaded troops or survived the internment. Despite the ordeal of the Long Walk, both the Diné and the Mescalero Apache made it back to their homelands. The Mescalero Apache escaped en masse on the night of November 3, 1865, and were never recaptured. The Diné had to endure until 1868, when their powerful prayers and ceremonies came to fruition with their release, negotiated by Diné leaders, including Manuelito and Barboncito. They miraculously persuaded the U.S. government that their homelands were not in the Indian Territory but rather within Diné Bikéyah. Although our people left Fort Sumner with few belongings, we continue to carry within our hearts the resilience of the survivors, confident in the strength of our culture, our prayers, and our Diné society to prosper from this tragic ordeal.

FURTHER READING: *Bighorse the Warrior*, by Tiana Bighorse

Wisdom Sits in Places

KEITH H. BASSO

❖ Long before the advent of literacy, to say nothing of "history" as an academic discipline, places served humankind as durable symbols of distant events and as indispensable aids for remembering and imagining them — and this convenient arrangement, ancient but not outmoded, is with us still today. In modern landscapes everywhere, people persist in asking, "What happened here?" The answers they supply, though perhaps distinctly foreign, should not be taken lightly, for what people make of their places is closely connected to what they make of themselves as members of society and inhabitants of the earth, and while the two activities may be separable in principle, they are deeply joined in practice. If placemaking is a way of constructing the past, a venerable means of *doing* human history, it is also a way of constructing social traditions and, in the process, personal and social identities. We *are*, in a sense, the place-worlds we imagine. As roundly ubiquitous as it is seemingly unremarkable, placemaking is a universal tool of the historical imagination. And in some societies, at least, if not in the great majority, it is surely among the most basic tools of all.

As conceived by Apaches from Cibecue, the past is a well-worn path or trail (*'intin*), which was traveled first by the people's founding ancestors and which subsequent generations of Apache have traveled ever since. Beyond the memories of living persons, this path is no longer visible — the past has disappeared — and thus it is unavailable for direct consultation and study. For this reason, the past must be constructed — that is to say, imagined — with the aid of historical materials, sometimes called footprints or tracks (*biké' goz'áá*), that have survived into the present. These materials come in various forms, including Apache place names, Apache stories and songs, and different kinds of relics found at locations throughout Apache country. Because no one knows when these phenomena came into being, locating past events in time can be accomplished only in a vague and general way. This is of little consequence, however, for what matters most to Apaches is *where* events occurred, not when, and what they serve to reveal about the development and character of Apache social life. Descriptive place names came first: 'Ihi'na' Ha'itin (Trail to Life Goes Up, a butte) and Chaghashé Biké'é (Children's Footprints, a rock in an evanescent stream). The names of clans, which are based upon descriptive place names, came later. Commemorative names were awarded last, after the Apache had made the land their own and were experiencing the rewards — and also the painful problems — that come with community living.

Western Apache history deals in the main with single events, and because these are tied to places within Apache territory, it is pointedly local and unfailingly episodic. It is also extremely personal, consistently subjective, and therefore highly variable among those who work to produce it. For these and other reasons, it is history without authorities — all narrated place-worlds, provided they seem plausible, are considered equally valid — and the idea of compiling "definitive accounts" is rejected out of hand as unfeasible and undesirable. Weakly empirical, thinly chronological, and rarely written down, Western Apache history as practiced by Apaches advances no theories, tests no hypotheses, and offers no general models. What it does instead, and likely has done for centuries, is fashion possible worlds, give them expressive shape, and present them for contemplation as images of the past that can deepen and enlarge awareness of the present. In the country of the past, as Apaches like to explore it, the placemaker is an indispensable guide.

And this in a powerful sense. For the placemaker's main objective is to speak the past into being, to summon it with words and give it dramatic form, to *produce* experience by forging ancestral worlds in which others can participate and readily lose themselves.

FURTHER READING: *Wisdom Sits in Places: Landscape and Language Among the Western Apache,* by Keith H. Basso, from which this was excerpted with permission from the University of New Mexico Press

318. Fort Apache and Theodore Roosevelt School Historic District, AZ: Past Is Present

White Mountain Apache Tribe Heritage Program: Mark Altaha, Doreen Gatewood, Karl Hoerig, Ramon Riley, and John R. Welch

White Mountain Apache Reservation, Fort Apache Historic Park, Fort Apache

Nohwike' Bágowa (House of Our Footprints), White Mountain Apache Tribe Cultural Center and Museum

A premier icon of the West, Fort Apache symbolizes powerful and transformative contacts between cultures. From time immemorial the area was farmland for American Indians, until 1870, when the high ground at the confluence of the East and North forks of White River became a cavalry outpost and an instrument of subjugation. For more than fifty years, army personnel, civilian contractors, and Apache people came together here in occasional conflict but more often in tentative cooperation. It changed the Apache world forever.

In 1922, when the government admitted that the Apache wars were over, the focus turned from military subjugation to educational assimilation. The Bureau of Indian Affairs saw the abandoned fort as an ideal facility for the Theodore Roosevelt School. The Apaches blinked, and bureaucrats replaced officers. Little boys and girls replaced former barracks dwellers. Heavy-handed efforts to force students to adopt non-Indian ways focused on military-style discipline and living conditions, English-only curriculum, and vocational training. Johnny Endfield, the White Mountain Apache Tribal Council vice chairman, remembers sneaking around to speak Apache: "The teachers were always watching," he said. "I learned to like the taste of that soap, and it never washed my language away."

As school enrollments and maintenance budgets declined in the 1960s, the BIA began demolishing some of the site's beautiful historic buildings with little regard for their significance.

The losses obliged the White Mountain Apache Tribe to rescue the place known for generations as Tł'óghagai (White Reeds Growing) and to seek to fulfill Fort Apache's initial promise as a guardian of land, heritage, and prosperity. By envisioning a tourism industry focused on Apache land and cultural heritage, the tribe has attracted support from the Arizona Heritage Fund, the World Monuments Fund, the National Park Service, and the National Endowment for the Humanities. Our partnerships have resulted in the preservation of ten of the district's twenty-seven historic buildings, the completion of our Nohwike' Bágowa (House of Our Footprints) cultural center and museum, and recognition as a Save America's Treasures project, a Preserve America community, and a State of Arizona Culture Keeper. The "Footprints of the Apache" and "Fort Apache Legacy" exhibits are the first presentation of White Mountain Apache perspectives on our culture, our history, and Fort Apache's important roles therein.

The history that has endowed Fort Apache with its immense popularity was not always kind to our ancestors, but by harnessing this popularity in the name of cultural perpetuation and using Fort Apache to tell our side of the story, we have been able to make peace with the past and write a new history of education, jobs, revenue, and intercultural communication and understanding.

FURTHER READING: "Fort Apache, Arizona Territory: 1870–1922," by Lori Davisson, in *The Smoke Signal*

319. Hubbell Trading Post National Historic Site, AZ: Lok'aahnteel

Kathleen Tabaha

Off Rte. 264, west of Ganado

Hubbell Trading Post, Lok'aahnteel, founded in 1876 by John Lorenzo Hubbell in the heart of Diné Bikéyah, is the oldest continuously operating trading post in the Navajo Nation. Mr. Hubbell, who came to trade with the Navajo people after their tragic Long Walk to Bosque Redondo, learned their customs and language and became their good friend whom they trusted. Mr. Hubbell, called Naakaii Sání (Old Mexican) by the Navajos, had a phenomenal influence on the Navajo people, not only by providing a market for their beautiful baskets, jewelry, and rugs but also by bringing them new ideas for rug designs and new sources of dyes and yarns. As a bridge between cultures, he encouraged weavers and silversmiths to take their work to the 1915 Panama Pacific International Exposition. To this day his influence continues.

Ever since the post was established, Navajos have been trading their arts and crafts for money and merchandise. Today the trader operates his business as John Hubbell did. As you walk across the squeaky wooden floors, you immediately think about how people traded here years ago. You mingle with other visitors and hear them speaking various languages. Beautiful antique baskets adorn the ceiling, handmade Indian jewelry lies elegantly in the showcases, and intricately designed rugs, hand-woven by skilled Navajo women, are for sale in the rug room. Since 1967 the National Park Service has protected the original 1883 trading post, the 160-acre homestead with its landscape and structures, and the Hubbell home, with its expansive personal collection. Most important, it preserves the authentic trading tradition established by John Hubbell.

FURTHER READING: *Indian Trader: The Life and Times of J. L. Hubbell,* by Martha Blue

Tree-Ring and Radiocarbon Dating

JEFFREY S. DEAN

❖ "How old is it?" is usually the first question asked by visitors to prehistoric and historic places. Two of the many independent chronological techniques for answering this question are tree-ring and radiocarbon dating.

Tree-ring dating (dendrochronology) was developed in the Southwest early in the twentieth century by the astronomer Andrew Ellicott Douglass. As the first independent dating technique, dendrochronology forced archaeologists to deal with absolute dates, revolutionizing the way they considered time. As a result, a ring sequence that now extends back to 662 B.C. and more than 50,000 tree-ring dates from more than 5,000 sites provide the Southwest with the best prehistoric chronological controls in the world. The use of tree-ring dating has expanded and currently sustains archaeological research in western North America, Europe, Siberia, and the Near East.

Dendrochronology is based on variability in the annual growth layers of trees, the familiar "rings" visible in cross sections of tree trunks. Where tree growth is controlled by external environmental factors, usually climate, trees that live through the same span of years produce identical sequences of wide and narrow rings. Matching the patterns of ring-width variability between trees, called crossdating, identifies contemporaneous rings and specifies the years in which the rings were grown. Combining the cross-dated ring records of living trees, dead trees, archaeological samples, and geological specimens produces long, absolutely dated composite (master) ring chronologies that represent the general pattern of tree growth in a region. Composite chronologies range in length from a few decades to more than 9,000 years and serve as standards for dating samples of unknown age. The unique place at which the pattern of an unknown ring series matches the pattern of a master sequence specifies the year in which each ring in the unknown series was grown.

Unlike dates derived by other methods, a tree-ring date applies to a single calendar year and has no associated statistical error. Under ideal circumstances, the dated outermost ring on a sample specifies the exact year in which the tree was felled. With due caution, this date can be applied to the archaeological feature in which the sample was found. Dendrochronology, however, is restricted to regions where suitable tree species and crossdating exist and where usable wood or charcoal is preserved in archaeological sites. Thus it has not yet been widely applied in the tropics, the Southern Hemisphere, southeastern Asia, or Oceania. Furthermore, the method's time span is restricted to the lengths of the relevant master chronologies.

Because climate controls tree-ring growth, ring widths accurately record aspects of past climate variability. Recent tree-ring research indicates that the normal southwestern precipitation pattern was disrupted between A.D. 1250 and 1450 by chaotic climate conditions that would have adversely affected traditional farming practices in the northwestern half of the region. This climatic breakdown, coupled with other environmental stresses, undoubtedly was an important cause of the abandonment of the Four Corners area and population movements to the south and east in the late thirteenth century.

Just after World War II the physical chemist Willard F. Libby introduced radiocarbon dating, which caused a second global revolution in archaeological time reckoning. This technique measures the passage of time by the transformation (decay) of radioactive carbon-14 atoms into nitrogen-14 atoms through the loss of beta particles. This process occurs at a rate that is expressed as the half-life, the time required for half

the original carbon-14 to decay (5,730 years ± 40 years). Thus in 5,730 years half the original amount of carbon-14 will have decayed, in another 5,730 years half of the remaining amount will have disappeared, and so on. The amount of carbon-14 in any living organism is equal to that in the atmosphere, because the uptake of carbon from the environment offsets loss caused by decay. When the organism dies, replenishment of carbon ceases, and the amount of radioactive carbon begins to diminish through decay. The quantity remaining thereafter indicates how much time has elapsed since the organism died.

Plant and animal remains from archaeological sites are dated by comparing the remaining amount of carbon-14 to the original amount. This procedure produces a radiocarbon age in years with an associated statistical error. Past fluctuations in the amount of atmospheric carbon-14 and other factors cause radiocarbon ages to deviate from true ages. These deviations are measured by comparing the radiocarbon ages to the actual ages of samples of known date. Here dendrochronology comes back into the picture. The radiocarbon time scale is calibrated against absolutely dated wood samples drawn from long tree-ring chronologies. Calibration transforms a carbon-14 age into a calendar date range likely to include the actual year of the organism's death. For example, a radiocarbon age of 2,000 years ± 50 years becomes a calibrated date of 92 B.C. to A.D. 53 with a 67 percent probability of bracketing the true date.

The fact that a radiocarbon date specifies a range rather than a point in time often introduces uncertainty into archaeological dating. This problem is aggravated for periods in which peculiarities of the calibration curve cause abnormally long date ranges. In addition, some materials, such as bone and shell, are difficult to analyze, while other materials, such as perennial plants, produce samples that represent long periods. Careful sample selection and date evaluation are necessary to maximize the archaeological potential of radiocarbon determinations. Because radiocarbon dating can be used anywhere and spans 60,000 years, it is applicable to many contexts that cannot be tree-ring dated. Thus it has become the primary archaeological dating technique in regions and time periods not covered by dendrochronology.

Since each dating system has unique capabilities, archaeologists continue to seek out new techniques whose strengths offset the weaknesses of others. Among the other methods used are archaeomagnetism, obsidian hydration, thermo-luminescence, amino acid racemization, lichenometry, electron spin resonance, and a large family of radioisotopic measures, including argon-40/argon-39, potassium-argon, and uranium series. It is safe to predict, however, that dendrochronology and radiocarbon dating will remain crucial to archaeological chronology building throughout the world.

FURTHER READING: "Dendrochronology," by Jeffrey S. Dean, in *Chronometric Dating in Archaeology*, edited by R. E. Taylor and M. J. Aitken

SECTION FIVE

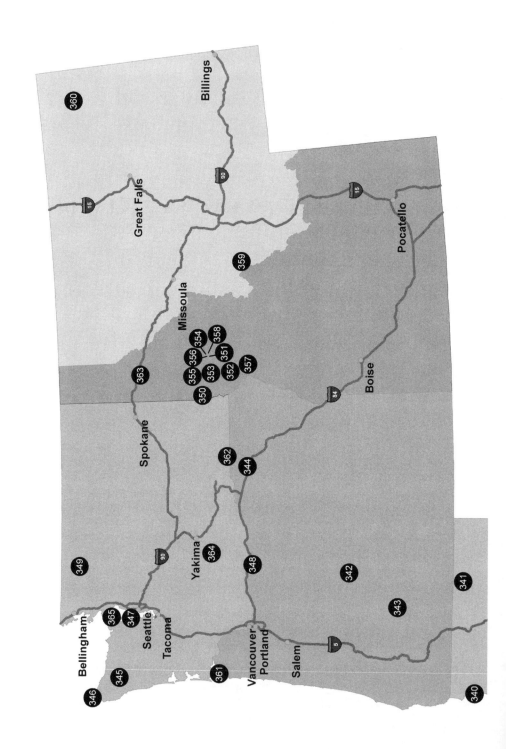

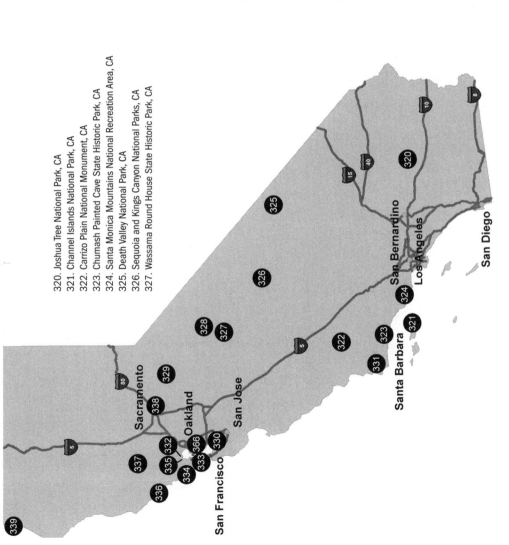

Native Californians

MALCOLM MARGOLIN

❖ People first started appearing in the land that is now California more than 12,000 years ago. They gradually dispersed along the ocean beaches, settled in mountain valleys, moved out into the open desert, and established villages in the oak savannas of the Sierra foothills. They built wooden houses in the redwood and pine forests, underground earthen houses in the grasslands of the Central Valley, and rush and willow houses along the fringes of marshlands. Their languages were — and are — many and varied. Some speak languages of the Algonquian family of eastern North America. Others speak an Athabascan language related to those of Canada, some speak languages from the Uto-Aztecan or Shoshonean language family, some from the Hokan of the Southwest, and some from the Penutian. At least two groups of Yukians speak languages that have not been linked to any other surviving language.

There was great variety as well in the technologies, physical characteristics, customs, and beliefs of Native Californians. For example, they practiced many modes of boat building. The Yurok at the mouth of the Klamath River made blunt and sturdy dugout canoes of redwood logs. The Modoc hollowed their dugouts until the shell was thin, well suited to lake waters. The Chumash built boats of planks, sewn together with deer sinew and caulked with asphaltum, so strong that these maritime people could paddle them to the Channel Islands. The Choinumni of the San Joaquin Valley bound tule (bulrush) together with willow withes to make barges 50 feet long, outfitted so that families could live on them while on fishing expeditions. The people were physically varied: the Mohave of the Colorado River area were the tallest Indians in North America; the Yuki of Mendocino County the shortest. They belonged to more than 500 independent tribal groups. Such diversity has so overtaxed non-Indian systems of categorization and nomenclature that we have tended toward generalization. Today people who, several hundred years ago, were in several dozen independent tribal groups — small nations — are all known as Pomo, and others have been lumped together as Miwok, Maidu, Yokuts, and so on.

It is estimated that in 1769, when the first Spanish colonists arrived, there were about 310,000 Native Californians; by 1900 there were about 20,000. In the 2000 census, 330,000 people identified themselves as American Indians living in California. There are now 107 federally recognized tribes in California. As living cultures, they are changing and adapting. The man who uses a chain saw to carve out a traditional dugout canoe and the woman who uses a blender to process acorns are continuing their cultural traditions, using, as they always have, the best available tools for the job at hand. Their stories, poems, paintings, sculpture, weavings, jewelry, and baskets evidence the continuing vibrancy of their cultural life.

Excerpted from *The Way We Lived: California Indian Reminiscences, Stories, and Songs.* Copyright © 1981. Revised edition copyright © 1993.

320. Joshua Tree National Park, CA: The People and Their Homeland

Clifford E. Trafzer

Off Rte. 62, Twentynine Palms

Oasis Visitor Center

In May 2004 Matthew Leivas, a Chemehuevi, led singers gathered in present-day Joshua Tree National Park in a series of Salt Songs. They sang long into the night, taking a magical journey through the songs from a cave along the Bill Williams River of western Arizona, northwest to Las Vegas, south into the dry deserts and rocky mountains of eastern California, and to the Oasis of Marah in the park. A Southern Paiute elder, Vivian Jake, spoke from the heart, explaining that the place is sacred, the home of many diverse plants and animals and the former village site of Serrano and Chemehuevi people who lived in peace in an isolated part of the Mojave Desert.

Long ago, during the Pleistocene Epoch, the Pinto culture thrived in the desert and mountains of the park. In more recent times, Serrano and Cahuilla Indians used the area for centuries, and the Chemehuevis settled there in the 1860s. Indians gathered mesquite beans, seeds, cactus fruit, and flowers, and hunted antelope, rabbit, squirrels, quail, ducks, and geese. They hunted bighorn sheep, which they revered, singing songs honoring them. They traveled to the San Bernardino Mountains to hunt and to gather piñons and acorns, storing them in huge granary baskets on log stilts. They used songs — in which they described springs, villages, gathering areas, and vast hunting areas — as oral deeds to claim areas of the land. A person, family, or clan then owned that area, which other Indians could use if granted permission.

Women used large stone pestles and deep stone mortars — some of which are still in the park — to pound the nuts into fine, delicious flour for cakes and porridge. While the women gathered, prepared, and stored foods and cared for their families, the men hunted, trapped, and traded. Serranos, and later the Shivawach group of Chemehuevis, grew corn, squash, melons, pumpkins, and beans at the oasis, irrigating the crops with water that rose to the surface from a great underground crevice. They lived in log, brush, and adobe homes with large arbors made of boughs from palm trees. The people did not live in isolation, because travelers to the Pacific Ocean and the Colorado River stopped at the oasis. The ocean, the river, the oasis, and the springs are still significant in their oral traditions.

Beginning in the 1870s, non-Indians started grazing their cattle, prospecting, and claiming land in Joshua Tree. By 1913 some had homesteaded, and most Serranos and Chemehuevis had abandoned their village at the Oasis of Marah. After a death during a tragic Chemehuevi family quarrel, the Indians left Joshua Tree in 1910. The Serranos moved to Mission Creek and then to the Morongo Reservation. Chemehuevis moved first to the Morongo Reservation, then east to Indio, resettling on the Cabazon Reservation. Chemehuevi elders returned to the oasis to burn their village and turn the soil of their homes so that the spirits of the dead would not know the place. They also prayed for their ancestors buried in the cemetery. The government, which never recognized the Serrano and Chemehuevi lands at the oasis, established a reservation on the northern edge of the park where there was no water, so the people never lived there. Some families visited the park occasionally, prayed, and remembered Joshua Tree as a sacred place.

Then in 2000 Dean Mike, chair of the Twenty-Nine Palms Band of Mission Indians, and his cousin, Joe Benitez, returned to Joshua Tree and visited the cemetery, the reservation lands, and the oasis. They formed lasting friendships with Paul and Jane Smith, who own the site of the village, and the National Park staff. In May 2004 they returned to Joshua Tree and heard the Salt Songs sung there for the first time since 1910. Like everyone present, they felt the spirit of Joshua Tree in the cool breeze blowing through the swaying palm fronds and over the rippling waters of the Oasis of Marah, "the little spring with much grass."

FURTHER READING: *Chemehuevi People of the Coachella Valley,* by Clifford E. Trafzer, Luke Madrigal, and Anthony Madrigal

321. Channel Islands National Park, CA

John R. Johnson

Robert J. Largomarsino Visitor Center, Spinnaker Dr., west of Rte. 101, Ventura; Outdoors Santa Barbara Visitor Center, Harbor Way, Santa Barbara

Longtime residents of the Santa Barbara–Ventura coastal region know a bit of Chumash lore: that when atmospheric conditions change and the offshore islands appear close and magnified,

rain is in the offing. Indeed, the Chumash word *anyapax* (ever-changing, or mirage) continues today as Anacapa, the name of one of the five islands in the park. As the Pleistocene Epoch (the Ice Age) drew to an end 13,000 years ago, the appearance of closeness was a reality, for the offshore islands were separated from the mainland by only a narrow strait of water. The first American Indians traveled across the strait by watercraft at this time, when the lower sea level had united the islands as one large landmass. Some of the earliest evidence of human occupation along the Pacific coast, discovered on what are now Santa Rosa and San Miguel Islands, dates to this period.

The Northern Channel Islands have always held a special place in Chumash culture and history, for they were considered to be the original homeland of all peoples speaking Chumashan languages. The very name Chumash was what the island Indians were originally called by their linguistic relatives on the mainland. It was derived from the word *alchum,* bead money, because the islanders manufactured tiny shell disk beads that circulated throughout southern California as currency.

By the time the missions were founded in Alta California in the late eighteenth and early nineteenth centuries, Chumash people occupied at least twenty-one towns on the three largest islands. Today these settlement locations and other residential sites from the prehistoric past exist as shell middens, where sedentary fishing communities built up mounds of discarded shells and bones of fish, marine mammals, and sea birds. House pits are visible at some of these sites, giving visitors the opportunity to envision the layout of the entire village. The *tomol,* a sturdy canoe built of sewn planks split from driftwood and waterproofed with asphaltum, was a major technological innovation that made possible the islanders' maritime economy and trade with mainland Chumash peoples. Fine exhibits of the material culture and social life of Island Chumash Indians are in the Channel Islands National Park Visitors Center at Ventura Harbor and in the Santa Barbara Museum of Natural History in Santa Barbara.

FURTHER READING: "Ethnohistoric Reflections of Cruzeño Chumash Society," by John R. Johnson, in *The Origins of a Pacific Coast Chiefdom: The Chumash of the Channel Islands*, edited by J. E. Arnold

322. Carrizo Plain National Monument, CA: Painted Rock

Georgia Lee and William D. Hyder

On Soda Lake Rd. off Rte. 58, west of McKittrick

Goodwin Education Center

The Carrizo Plain lies along the western edge of its dominant geophysical feature, an open scar called the San Andreas Fault. Dense stands of Carrizo grass, herds of antelope, deer, and elk, and seasonal visits of migratory birds probably drew at least three California tribes to converge here for social gatherings and joint hunts. We find evidence of their ceremonies on massive sandstone outcrops that line the southern edge of the plain.

Painted Rock is the most distinctive outcrop in the Carrizo: its horseshoe shape rises about 120 feet and can be seen for miles. Inside the sheltered curve of the rock are ancient rock paintings. Ethnographies tell of valley tribes traveling here to hunt with the Chumash and the Salinan from the coastal areas. Because of the placement of the paintings and the openness of the site, it appears that Painted Rock accommodated large gatherings; its space would allow for dynamic ritual activities, including chanting, oratory, music, and dance. Multiple art styles can likely be traced to the cultures believed to have gathered here.

Some paintings appear to represent mythological concepts or characters. Coyotes and bears, lizards, turtles, snakes, and hummingbirds, as well as horned figures (shamans?) and many insectlike creatures, are painted on the rocks. Perhaps they were used to reinforce and illustrate traditional legends and the mythological past. Mandalas are prominent, and some figures have zigzag lines emanating from them, suggesting "power lines," which are associated with shamans.

The Carrizo continues to inspire awe today despite the impact of modern society and the uplifting caused by earthquake activity. These events radically altered the environment so familiar to the ancient ones who created the paintings.

FURTHER READING: *The Chumash Cosmos: Effigies, Ornaments, Incised Stones, and Rock Paintings of the Chumash Indians*, by Georgia Lee

323. Chumash Painted Cave State Historic Park, CA

Ernestine Ygnacio-De Soto

Off Rte. 154 on Painted Caves Rd., northeast of Santa Barbara

When my great-grandmother Luisa Ygnacio (1835–1922) worked with the anthropologist John P. Harrington, she told him that the "Painted Cave place" was also known as Alaxuluxen in Barbareño Chumash. My great-grandparents' ranch was at the bottom of the old San Marcos Pass trail at the place called the Indian Orchard. The land had been given to my great-great-grandmother María Ygnacia (1798–1865), the daughter of the last *wot* (chief) of Syuxtun, the principal Chumash town, which was on the Santa Barbara waterfront. Maria Ygnacia Creek, which flows next to Painted Cave, is named for her.

My great-grandfather José Ygnacio (1832–1882) and his sons, who kept cattle in the Painted Cave area, regarded the paintings on the rocks with great respect. The paintings are black (from charcoal), red (from iron oxide), and white (from gypsum) and were probably painted within the last several centuries. Several basic designs seem to have told about events that the artists had experienced and some that were of spiritual significance. My great-uncle Pedro Ygnacio (1863–1942) told the Ogram family, who homesteaded in the area surrounding Painted Cave, that his elders had said that certain paintings in the cave represented funerary *tomols* (plank canoes) taking souls of the dead to Shimilaqsha, the other world.

My mother, María Joaquina Rowe-Yee (1897–1965), told me of the tradition of an old medicine man known as Saximumaseti, who would go into the mountains and paint symbols for magical purposes. He may be the historical figure Andrés Sagimomase (1768–1828), who was the leader of the Barbareño Mission Indians during the Chumash Revolt of 1824.

FURTHER READING: *A Study of a California Indian Culture*, by Campbell Grant

324. Santa Monica Mountains National Recreation Area, CA: Satwiwa Native American Indian Culture Center and Natural Area

Charlie Cooke (Tiq Slow), Dennis Garcia, Ted Garcia, Jr., and Mati Waiya

Visitor center at 401 W. Hillcrest Dr., Thousand Oaks

This area of the Santa Monica Mountains National Recreation Area has been home for thousands of years to American Indians who lived in settled villages and harvested the bounty of the land and ocean without need for agriculture. Steelhead trout streams and chaparral-covered slopes, interspersed with woodland and oak savanna in interior valleys, provided a diversity of food and medicine for our ancestors. The Santa Monica Mountains descend to rugged shores

and secluded coves. The mild Mediterranean climate supports abundant life. Then and now we excel at stone and wood carving and basket making.

Today at the Satwiwa Native American Indian Cultural Center and Natural Area we share with visitors to the recreation area our heritage: stewardship of the land, respect for nature, our cultural values, and their interrelationships. Satwiwa, operated by the National Park Service in cooperation with the Friends of Satwiwa, is a learning center for all people. Satwiwa emphasizes the present and the dynamic cultural life of contemporary American Indian people. Many ceremonies and community dances are organized by contemporary Native American groups. Satwiwa provides a place for children to experience nature. It is a place where Native Americans of all tribes and all ages can gather to share the richness and diversity of their cultures today, as well as learn about the past as a key to understanding the present and the future.

Founding a Tribal Museum: The Malki Museum

KATHERINE SIVA SAUBEL AND
PAUL APODACA

❖ The Malki Museum, founded by Jane Penn (Wanakik Cahuilla), Mariano Saubel (Wanakik and Mountain Cahuilla), Katherine Siva Saubel (Mountain Cahuilla), and Lowell Bean, opened in 1965. We consider it the first Indian museum owned and run by Indian people on a reservation. The Morongo Indian Reservation is known as the home of the Wanakik clan and lineage families of the Cahuilla people, who have lived here since time immemorial. It is our area. The Cahuilla people originated with our creator,

Mukat, and his brother Tamaoit. The people settled here after our creation and still live in this same place. Others, members of different tribes and lineages, now live here with the Wanakik families.

The Morongo Indian Reservation was first known as the Malki Reservation; the name was changed by the Bureau of Indian Affairs. *Malki* is the Wanakik word for hiding or dodging. When the invaders came to this land, Indian people hid in the canyons and ravines here, and so the name came to be. Families were displaced from White Water, the original home village of the Wanakik people, and spread through the Coachella Valley. Some families ended up west of Beaumont.

People are very curious about our concept of the sacred, especially the sacredness of the land. Everything is sacred. This land was given to us, and we were told never to destroy it or the trees or the living things in our world, the way people are doing today with contamination. That is not what we were told to do as Indian people. We are to take care of all things.

The museum hosts an annual traditional gathering of local reservation communities on Memorial Day weekend and offers classes in Cahuilla language, ethnobotany, and other aspects of indigenous Southern California culture. The museum is most famed for the Malki Press, which produces publications concerning all aspects of Southern California indigenous life, including the prestigious *Journal of California and Great Basin Anthropology.* The museum's collection includes Cahuilla basketry, photographs, and documents. It is off I-10 on Fields Road, west of Palm Springs, and is open to the public each day. Please come and visit.

FURTHER READING: *Mukat's People: The Cahuilla Indians of Southern California,* by Lowell John Bean

325. Death Valley National Park, CA: Tüpipüh, Our Timbisha Shoshone Homeland

Pauline Esteves

Rte. 190, Death Valley

Furnace Creek Visitor Center and Museum

This valley and the surrounding places frequented by our ancestors, the Old Ones, is Tüpipüh, our Timbisha Shoshone Homeland. Our people have always lived here. The Creator, Appü, placed us here at the beginning of time. The homeland includes the valley and the nearby mountains, valleys, flats, meadows, and springs. The word *timbisha* refers to a red material found in the Black Mountains, not far from our tribal village at Furnace Creek. The Old Ones used this material, called ochre in English, as paint on their faces, to protect them and heal them. They believed that it strengthened their spirituality. Our people, the Timbisha Shoshone, are named after this material, and so is our valley. The term Death Valley is unfortunate. We refrain from talking about death. Instead, we refer to "one whom it has happened to." Even more important, this is a place of life. It is a powerful and spiritual valley that has healing powers, and the spirituality of the valley is passed on to our people.

The water from Potoin or Poto'inna (Travertine Spring) used to flow into our mesquite groves and into what is now Furnace Creek Ranch. People gathered berries, pine nuts, and seeds near Suunapatun (now the Wildrose campground and spring) and went to Wisi, the spring in Hanaupah Canyon, to gather prickly pears and *wisi* for making cord.

Others came and occupied our land. They gave us diseases, and some of our people died. They took away many of our most important places — the springs, the places we used for food, and those we used for our spiritual practices. They did not want us to carry on our religion or our ceremonies or our songs or our language.

The names of our places became unknown to some of our people. We never gave up. Before 2000 we had no land at all. We now have some of our land back. We have lived in our homeland forever, and we will live here forever. We were taught that we do not end. We are part of our homeland, and it is part of us. We are people of the land. We do not break away from what is part of us. This is our homeland.

FURTHER READING: "Timbisha Shoshone," by Catherine S. Fowler, in *The Cambridge Encyclopedia of Hunters and Gatherers*, edited by Richard B. Lee and Richard Daly

326. Sequoia and Kings Canyon National Parks, CA: The Western Mono and the Foothill Yokuts

Thomas L. Burge

Foothills Visitor Center, State Rte. 198; Kings Canyon Visitor Center, State Rte. 180, east of Three Rivers

More than 400 years ago, Mono Indians moved west across the Sierra Nevada and settled in areas now within the national parks. Known today as the Western Mono (or Monache) Indians, they brought many traits from their Paiute relatives, including a Paiute-based language. Six separate groups or tribes make up the historical Western Mono: the Entimbich, Michahay, Northfork Mono, Patwisha, Wobonuch, and Wuksachi. They were related by culture and language but were politically distinct. Each tribe had its own leaders, villages, and homelands, where they lived well into the 1800s. The Patwisha lived in villages along the Kaweah River, from today's Three Rivers east to the Potwisha Campground and the Hospital Rock area, where there are pictographs. Hundreds of people lived in the larger villages in tall, cone-shaped houses with thatched roofs. Azalea Campground in Kings Canyon National Park is within the homelands of the Wobonuch and was likely visited by Entimbich and Wuksachi peoples, too. There are Indian campsites where women shelled acorns, ground them into flour in the bedrock mortars (grinding holes), leached the flour with water to make it palatable, and cooked it into flat cakes and mushes. A likely Wuksachi campsite is along the Generals Highway near Quail Flat. Descendants of the Western Mono live in Badger, Dunlap, North Fork, Squaw Valley, Three Rivers, and Woodlake.

The Foothill Yokuts include about fifteen named tribes who lived in the foothills of the western Sierra Nevada; three of them lived west of the parks. The Chuckaymina lived in and around Squaw Valley in the Kings River watershed. The Gawia and the Wukchumni lived farther south within the Kaweah River drainage, near Woodlake, Lemoncove, and Three Rivers. They spoke a distinct dialect of Yokuts, which is a Penutian language. The Penutian languages are very different from Paiute and from the dialects spoken by the neighboring Western Mono. As a result, Yokuts and Mono groups were multilingual. Over time, they came to share words and ways of living, such as having independent villages, grinding acorns in bedrock mortars, sharing some hunting/fishing/gathering areas, and making baskets. A fine example of a Yokuts basket is on display at the visitor center in Sequoia Park. Redbud, bracken fern, sourberry, and various sedges are among the raw materials used by Yokuts women in their baskets. Trade across the mountains was very important. Today Yokuts and Mono people live in the nearby communities as well as on reservations at Cold Springs, Santa Rosa, and Tule River. They do not usually define important areas within the parks as belonging specifically to either the Yokuts or the Mono. Many places, such as Potwisha Campground, Hospital Rock, Quail Flat, and Azalea Campground, are considered by all to be traditional or sacred places.

FURTHER READING: "Monache" and "Foothill Yokuts," by Robert F. G. Spier, in *California*, edited by R. F. Heizer, vol. 8 in the *Handbook of North American Indians*

327. Wassama Round House State Historic Park, CA

Linda E. Dick Bissonnette with Les James, Suzanne Ramirez, Karen Sargosa, and Bernice Williamson

Off Rte. 49 on Rd. 628, Ahwahnee

Wassama Round House State Historic Park is on an oak-studded hill in Madera County above Peterson Creek, in a rural residential area south of Yosemite National Park. A semisubterranean assembly-dance house built here in the 1860s was burned by the people in 1893 when an important leader died. An aboveground building, known as the Ahwahnee Round House, was built in 1903 to replace it. It has pine board walls a sugar-pine shake roof, and a smoke hole in the roof. The Ahwahnee Round House leader, Peter Westfall, wanted the roundhouse to remain standing when he passed. After the state acquired its ruins and the surrounding property in 1978, a team that included Miwok descendants restored the 40-foot-diameter octagonal building. The Wassama Round House was dedicated with an intertribal ceremony and celebration on September 28, 1985. Its name is thought to come from the word *wassa*, which means pine in the Southern Sierra Miwok dialect.

In 2005 the community reconstructed a traditional sweathouse downhill from the roundhouse for private healing and renewal ceremonies. Wassama continues to be the spiritual and cultural center for the local Miwok people. Some still speak the language and remember the traditional ways. They established the Wassama Association and are the caretakers of the park, continuing their tradition of teaching the younger generation about their heritage and these sacred grounds. Four association members shared what Wassama means to them:

LES JAMES: It's a gathering place for Native people to share their experiences and traditions. My grandfather explained a lot of things to me, but now I'm learning more. We're putting it into words, especially for younger people. Everything is natural here. It's how we survived.

SUZANNE RAMIREZ: My family, my people, my culture, and my history are here. It's very strong and emotional.

KAREN SARGOSA: To me [it] is unexplainable. It's peaceful. Our people have been here, and you can just imagine what they went through (from the things my grandmother told me) and how they survived. There's a deeper meaning that makes you strive for more. I wish it would stay just like this.

BERNICE WILLIAMSON: I was raised not far from here. Any ceremony here, I was always here with my mom and dad. They put pine needles in the roundhouse so we could sleep in there. They used to bring water up from the creek in buckets, and we (children) would help. All my ancestors are buried here: mom, dad, brother, aunts, sisters, cousins.

FURTHER READING: *Five Views: An Ethnic Historic Site Survey for California*, by the California Department of Parks and Recreation

328. Yosemite National Park, CA: Ahwahnee Village

Off Rte. 140, east of El Portal

Yosemite Museum and Valley Visitor Center

People moved into the Yosemite area about 8,000 years ago. The first to settle in Yosemite Valley were the Ahwahneechee — those who live in Ahwahnee, which means gaping, mouthlike place. In the summer the people lived in *umachas*, shelters made of incense cedar bark. While the men hunted, the women gathered berries, seeds, and materials to weave their baskets. In the fall they gathered acorns and stored them in *chuckahs;* they pounded the acorns into meal flour, which they leached to remove the bitter tannins. They also dried meat to eat during the winter. They traded with coastal people for clamshells and dried fish and traveled the high Sierras to trade acorns for pine nuts, salt, and obsidian, which they used to make tools and weapons. The Sierra Nevada was a conduit of cultural exchange for the Paiute, Miwok, Chukchansi, and Mono.

During the gold rush between 1849 and 1851, thousands of miners invaded the Sierra Nevada foothills, disrupting American Indians' lifeways. To force the Indians out of the valley, the government used treaties and, in 1851, military action by the militia, the Mariposa Battalion. Over the years, American Indians returned to Yosemite Valley to live. Today Native Americans gather in the park for ceremonies in a replica of a late-nineteenth-century Sierra Nevada Miwok village. Ahwahnee Village includes a ceremonial roundhouse, a chief's house, *umachas*, and a sweathouse, as well as *chuckahs* and pounding rocks. The National Park Service consults with the American Indian Council of Mariposa County (Southern Sierra Miwuk Nation), Tuolumne Band of Me-Wuk Indians, North Fork Rancheria of Mono Indians, Picayune Rancheria of Chukchansi Indians, Mono Lake Kutzadikaa Tribe, Bridgeport Paiute Indian Colony, and Bishop Paiute Tribe.

329. Indian Grinding Rock State Historic Park, CA

Dwight Dutschke

14881 Pine Grove–Volcano Rd., Pine Grove

Chaw'se Regional Indian Museum

Chaw'se, a Miwok word meaning grinding or pounding rock, describes the large, marbleized limestone rock where Native Americans processed seeds and nuts by pounding them into meal. The rock has 1,185 mortar holes, the largest collection of bedrock mortars in North America. Elders tell the story that a great creature clawed and pounded the earth until the rock was formed for the Miwok to use; they point to claw marks left on the rock by the creature. There are also more than 300 petroglyphs on the rock; according to elders, they tell the story of the Miwok here at Chaw'se.

After the park was established, Miwok elders gathered together to reconstruct a Miwok village like those of their ancestors before the coming of Europeans. There are *u macha'* (bark houses), *cha'ka* (acorn granaries), and a *hun gé* (ceremonial roundhouse). The roundhouse has become the center of Native American heritage activities. It is semisubterranean, with only its cedar-bark roof above the ground. The State Historic Landmark plaque describes the house well:

> In a village, the roundhouse served as the center of ceremonial and social life. Constructed in 1974, the *Chaw'se* roundhouse continues this tradition. With its door facing the east, towards the rising sun, four large oaks are the focal point of this sixty-foot-diameter structure. Today, ceremonial roundhouses are the most significant architectural manifestation of the continuing Miwok spiritual heritage.

Throughout the year, the Miwok and other tribes gather at Chaw'se for various activities. The most important ceremonial occasion, Chaw'se Big Time, is the weekend following the fourth Friday in September, when Miwok, Maidu, Pomo, Wintu, and other Native American dancers, storytellers, and singers gather to celebrate the coming acorn harvest. Chaw'se continues to serve the Miwok well for ceremonies and for a place to gather together to tell stories.

FURTHER READING: *Indian Life of the Yosemite Region: Miwok Material Culture,* by Samuel A. Barrett and Edward W. Gifford

330. Coyote Hills Regional Park, CA

Beverly R. Ortiz with Carol Bachmann, T. Michael Bonillas, Theodore W. Bonillas, Lisa Carrier, Mary Carrier, Roberta Chew, Ramona Garibay, Sabrina Garibay, Judy Hall, and Ruth Orta

8000 Patterson Ranch Rd., Fremont

Ohlone Visitor Center

Coyote Hills Regional Park is within the traditional homeland of the Tuibun, one of about fifty-seven tribal groups who spoke a variant of a language now designated as Ohlone. During the late 1700s about 400 Tuibun lived in about five villages in the areas now called Alameda Creek and Coyote Hills. They shaped the landscape by burning the grasslands to stimulate the growth of small seed-bearing plants for themselves and tender shoots for the deer. They burned and pruned basketry plants to promote the growth of the long, straight, flexible shoots they needed to make a shapely basket. When they dug bulbs for food, they loosened the soil to promote the growth of more bulbs.

In 1770 the Spanish diarist Pedro Fages described the Tuibun or neighboring Alson people as "friendly" and "good-humored." In 1776 Captain Juan Bautista de Anza's expedition mapped the Coyote Hills. These events foreshadowed a time of severe disruption, dislocation, and suffering for the Tuibun and other Ohlone peoples. Between 1797 and 1804 Spanish priests baptized 141 Tuibun at Mission San José. Many died of European diseases. After the mission system was disbanded in the 1830s, the Ohlone became the labor force upon which Mexican rancho owners relied. In 1850, when California became a state, the Ohlone were subject to state laws that sanctioned the kidnapping and enslaving of Indian people.

Despite two centuries of prejudice and almost overwhelming political and cultural conquest, Ohlone people continue to speak their language and practice their traditional arts, dances, and beliefs. They maintain cultural communities, protect ancient burial sites, and find pride in preserving their heritage. Coyote Hills Regional Park, which includes a Tuibun village site more than 2,000 years old, has become a place to honor ancestors by participating in the annual Gathering of Ohlone Peoples and by teaching the public about Ohlone cultures and history. The following quotations convey the ideas and feelings of ten Ohlone who have made public presentations at the park as part of a year-round cultural interpretive program.

CAROL BACHMANN (Mutsun Ohlone): I am proud to be Ohlone. I feel honored to learn about the foods, baskets, and games the Ohlone people used and played and to teach my children and my grandchildren about them.

T. MICHAEL BONILLAS (Rumsien/Mutsun Ohlone): I am proud to be able to proclaim my Rumsien and Mutsun heritage as an important part of who I am today.

THEODORE W. BONILLAS (Rumsien Ohlone): In the 1930s and 1940s we were raised as Mexican because of the discrimination of the time against Native Americans. Now we're being asked by alternative medical professionals about our plants. It's good to get the recognition.

LISA CARRIER (Mutsun Ohlone): It brings me great joy to teach the children about how the Ohlones were "giving people" who were and are respectful and peaceful. The best part of participating in the Gathering is being with my family and sharing our heritage together with the public.

MARY CARRIER (Mutsun Ohlone): Being part of the Gathering offers me the opportunity to be with my relatives and grow in our culture.

ROBERTA CHEW (Mutsun Ohlone): My father, Marion Moniz, always spoke proudly of his Indian heritage. I know today my spiritual strength comes from the teaching.

RAMONA GARIBAY (Ohlone): I love learning that my ancestors' culture revolved around the word "respect." For me this word sums up what it means to be an Ohlone.

SABRINA GARIBAY (Jalquin/Saclan Ohlone/ Bay Miwok): I'm so grateful that my grandmother, Ruth Orta, told me stories she heard from my great-grandmother, Trina Marine Ruano. In return, I will tell my children those stories too, so our Ohlone heritage will live on.

JUDY HALL (Mutsun Ohlone): I'm excited to learn the ways of my ancestors. I've always known I was Indian, but finding out I'm Mutsun and all the history is fantastic.

RUTH ORTA (Jalquin/Saclan Ohlone/Bay Miwok): In the 1950s my siblings and I used to travel with my mother, Trina Marine Ruano, throughout the state to attend Indian meetings, and she enrolled at least 80 of my relatives and other Indians with the state.

FURTHER READING: *The Ohlone Past and Present: Native Americans of the San Francisco Bay Region*, edited by Lowell John Bean

California Missions

ROSE MARIE BEEBE AND
ROBERT M. SENKEWICZ

❖ In the 1760s Spain became alarmed that the territory it claimed along the Pacific coast of North America could become controlled by Russia or England, so it decided to occupy the territory we now call California. Since 1521, when it conquered the Aztec capital of Tenochtitlán (Mexico City), Spain had expanded its territory in North America by establishing three institutions among the Native peoples: the town (pueblo), the fort (presidio), and the church (mission). The purpose of all three was to assimilate the Indians and turn them into productive citizens of the Spanish empire.

The mission and the presidio were instrumental in the Spanish conquest of California. The Spanish government organized a combined military-religious expedition from Baja (Lower) California to Alta (Upper) California in 1769 and established two presidios and two missions, one each at San Diego and Monterey. Because it was difficult to get soldiers to serve in the remote province of Alta California, Spain established only two more presidios over the next seventy years. However, priests from the Franciscan order were willing to continue to come to California, and they founded nineteen more missions. The mission became the defining institution of colonial California.

Missions had long been part of Spain's expansion in America when it began colonizing California. Over the centuries, Spanish authorities had found that missions were often a cheaper and more effective way of expanding colonial rule than massive military incursions. By 1769 the mission was a well-defined part of the Spanish colonial order, organized to teach the Indians religion and European-style agriculture and turn them into Spanish Catholic farmers. But as the missions became more closely associated with colonial expansion, coercion became important, and the missionaries used soldiers to hunt down the Indians who tried to escape the regimented mission life. This life included required and frequent religious services and instruction sessions. The families lived near the mission compound, at first in their traditional thatched dwellings and later in adobe apartments. Unmarried girls and young women often had to live inside the compound in poorly ventilated dormitories. During the days, the men worked in the fields while the women were assigned domestic tasks, such as cooking and sewing. The Native Californians' lack of immunity to introduced European diseases and the unhealthy living conditions at a number of the missions resulted in the tragic loss of thousands of lives.

In California the term "mission" referred not only to the church but also to the thousands of acres of land around the mission, on which the Indians were forced to grow crops and raise horses, cattle, and sheep. These practices so dramatically altered the California landscape that the Indians' traditional way of life became impossible. More and more joined the missions simply to survive. Those who chose to escape had to head farther inland, beyond the reach of the missionaries and the soldiers. The priests always maintained that they were holding the land in trust for the Indians and that after they were assimilated, the land would be divided among them. But, tragically for the Indians, when the government of newly independent Mexico ended the mission system in the 1830s, nearly all of the land went to the settlers.

The twenty-one missions established between 1769 and 1823 were Mission San Diego de Alcalá in San Diego, Mission San Carlos Borromeo de Río Carmelo in Carmel, Mission San Antonio de Padua on the Fort Hunter Liggett Military Reservation, Mission San Gabriel Arcángel in San Gabriel, Mission San Luis Obispo de Tolosa in San Luis Obispo, Mission San Francisco de Asís (Mission Dolores) in San Francisco, Mission San Juan Capistrano in San Juan Capistrano, Mission Santa Clara de Asís in Santa Clara, Mission San Buenaventura in Ventura, Mission Santa Bárbara Virgen y Mártir in Santa Barbara, Mission La Purísima Concepción near Lompoc, Santa Cruz Mission in Santa Cruz, Mission Nuestra Señora de la Soledad in Soledad, Mission San José in Fremont, Mission San Juan Bautista in San Juan Bautista, Mission San Miguel Arcángel in San Miguel, Mission San Fernando Rey de España in Mission Hills, Mission San Luis Rey de Francia in San Luis Rey, Mission Santa Inés Virgen y Mártir in Solvang, Mission San Rafael Arcángel in San Rafael, and Mission San Francisco de Solano in Sonoma.

FURTHER READING: *Lands of Promise and Despair: Chronicles of Early California, 1535–1846,* edited by Rose Marie Beebe and Robert M. Senkewicz

331. La Purísima Mission State Historic Park, CA

Nicolasa I. Sandoval

On Purísima Rd., northeast of Lompoc

My family now calls the Lompoc Valley home. Although many of our relatives received sacraments, from baptisms to funeral masses, at Mission Santa Inés, my connections to Mission La Purísima are deep. I know the names of ancestors who lived throughout the region, from here to Mission San Buenaventura and Santa Cruz Island. In this place I remember them. They whisper to me in the rustle of the oaks. I see their persistence in the mountains that protect this valley.

I come here often with friends. Starting at the interpretive center, we consider the perspectives of people who walked before us in this place — first known as Amúu. Through the thirteen reconstructed buildings, we learn about how Chumash people lived, labored, and died here in the years between 1813 and 1834. In the infirmary, we imagine those who succumbed to unknown diseases. The infirmary chapel reminds us of the lives that symbolically began and abruptly ended here. Exploring the gardens, we think about the hearts and hands of people who spent countless hours turning the earth. Their work to plant and reap food sustained life in this community. We visit the spare *monjerio* (dormitory) where Native girls and unmarried women were required to live, sleeping on pallets far from the warmth of their families. In the padres' residence, we witness the strength and artistry of the carpenters who built the chairs, benches, and beds that offered comfort and rest to the priests.

In this place we remember people who made irrevocable choices of great consequence. We honor the genius of our first people and their continuing legacy. As I walk here, I feel the gravity of a catastrophic past. I fill my lungs with the fresh air of hope — glad to be alive, triumphant that we are still here.

FURTHER READING: *Prominent Indian Families at Mission La Purísima Concepcíon as Identified in Baptismal, Marriage, and Burial Records,* by G. Farris and J. Johnson

332. Sonoma State Historic Park, CA: Mission San Francisco de Solano

East Spain St., Sonoma

This was the last of the twenty-one missions in California to be completed. Two mission buildings have been reconstructed. The Sonoma Mission Indian Memorial, dedicated in 1999, honors the more than 800 Pomo, Coast Miwok, Patwin, and Wappo — including more than 200 children — who died while living and working at the mission between 1824 and 1839. Their

burial grounds are now under city streets and parking areas near the mission. Their names, recorded by the priests in the mission's death registry, are inscribed on a granite memorial. At the dedication ceremony, one of the speakers was the late Lanny Pinola, a Kashaya Pomo/Coast Miwok, who was a park ranger at Point Reyes National Seashore. Beverly R. Ortiz, in her 1999 article "Honoring the Dead and the Living: Dedication of the Sonoma Mission Indian Memorial," in *News from Native California,* included an excerpt from his speech:

To me and to my people who are here, this is a very emotional time for us. To stand here in memory of our ancestors who toiled [in] these fields, who labored with their hands in the construction of these historic buildings that you see. And to be able to honor them today is something that we waited a generation or so for. We know that we've labored hard and reached out far to make this come to pass. We're grateful that we could be able to unveil this today and have it as a model for the other missions to follow.

333. Golden Gate National Recreation Area, CA: The Ohlone Village Site and the Restored Tidal Marsh at Crissy Field

Paul Scolari and Linda Yamane

Off Rte. 101, east of Golden Gate Bridge, San Francisco

Crissy Field Center

The homeland of the Yelamu people included the San Francisco area at the time of Spanish contact. They were one of approximately fifty independent tribes speaking variations of a language now known as Ohlone. Although we know of no Yelamu descendants living today, the broader Ohlone community has collaborated with the Golden Gate National Recreation Area to preserve Ohlone heritage, shape Ohlone cultural interpretation, and honor the memory of the Yelamu people.

Until 1994 the Presidio of San Francisco was a military post held by Spain (1776–1821), Mexico (1821–1846), and the United States (1846–1994). In 1994 it was transferred to the National Park Service. When an archaeological investigation of the tidal marsh at Crissy Field revealed a seasonal Yelamu village, the park and several Ohlone individuals and groups agreed that the 30-acre marsh could be restored with minimal impact upon the village site and would be planted with native plants recommended by Ohlone basket weavers. The plants include those important for basketry, food, medicines, boats, musical instruments, games, and other traditional uses. Today, visitors can learn about Ohlone/Yelamu history and culture from three outdoor wayside exhibits. Ohlone educators at the Crissy Field Center, an environmental education center run jointly by the NPS and the Golden Gate National Parks Conservancy, offer programs on Ohlone/Yelamu history and culture.

Through the efforts of many, Crissy Field is now a place of natural splendor where land meets sea, past meets present, and Ohlone people can proclaim, "We are still here."

FURTHER READING: *A Time of Little Choice: The Disintegration of Tribal Culture in the San Francisco Bay Area 1769–1810,* by Randall Milliken

334. Point Reyes National Seashore, CA: The Coast Miwok

Gene Buvelot, Sylvia Thalman, and Nick Tipon

Off Bear Valley Rd., west of Olema

Drakes Bay Visitor Center; Bear Valley Visitor Center: Kule Loklo, a recreated Coast Miwok village

For thousands of years, the Coast Miwok Indians of California lived in today's Marin and southern Sonoma counties. Linguists called all the speakers of this language family Coast Miwok, but the people identified themselves by the names of smaller groups or bands. Relationships between bands were usually amiable, with interchanges for ceremonies and trading. They were hunters and gatherers who tended the wild while living in a temperate climate with plenty of food. Oak trees provided acorns, which they made into acorn mush, a staple. Fruit, berries, nuts, and root vegetables were abundant. Tomales, Bodega, and San Francisco bays and the Pacific Ocean were rich sources of fish, shellfish, and edible seaweed. They lived in small villages overseen by a headman and a headwoman. A recreation of a Coast Miwok village, Kule Loklo, in Point Reyes National Seashore, contains a model of a roundhouse or dance house (a ceremonial building), a men's sweathouse, redwood-bark and tule *kotcas* (houses), acorn granaries, and an outdoor dance circle. Adjacent to the village is a garden of native plants with a few labeled examples of many of the plants used by the Coast Miwok. There are more than 140 village sites in the national seashore.

Many places in their homeland are still known by Coast Miwok names. Marin County is named for an Indian leader of the early 1800s. Olema comes from Ole, the name of the coyote creator. Bolinas is named for Bauli'n, a band south of Point Reyes National Seashore. The name of the Sonoma County town Cotati means hit or strike, and Mount Tamalpais means coast mountain. Tomales Bay and the town are named for the Tamal band of Coast Miwok Indians.

The Coast Miwok, like many other California Indians, were severely impacted by the mission system. Thousands died from European diseases, and by 1923 only 75 were living in Graton Rancheria near Sebastopol, established by the Bureau of Indian Affairs. The rancheria was closed in 1962; the excuse given was that the Indians should become "acculturated." Although the land was given to the Indians, they were required to pay taxes on it, and most could not afford to do so. Only one Coast Miwok family still lives at the original Graton Rancheria site. In 1992, in response to potential real estate development on tribal lands, the Coast Miwok people organized to work for federal recognition. In December 2000 they were granted federal recognition as the Federated Indians of Graton Rancheria. The tribe has more than 1,100 members, the fourth largest recognized tribe in California. It is working to restore the Coast Miwok culture and language and to protect their cultural resources from development. The tribe is involved in many projects to enhance the quality of life for its members.

FURTHER READING: *Interviews with Tom Smith and Maria Copa: Isabel Kelly's Ethnographic Notes of the Coast Miwok Indians of Marin and Southern Sonoma Counties,* edited by Mary Collier and Sylvia B. Thalman

335. Olompali State Historic Park, CA

E. Breck Parkman

West of Rte. 101, north of Novato

Olompali State Historic Park is named after the village where several hundred Coast Miwok lived for at least 2,000 years. The park overlooks the Petaluma River and San Pablo Bay and is on the eastern slopes of Mount Burwell. The people named its peak Olompais. The 760-acre park protects reconstructed Coast Miwok houses, nationally significant ancient places such as the village site, bedrock mortars, and petroglyphs, as well as historic structures, including the remains of Camillo Ynitia's adobe. In 1816–1818 more than 200 of the villagers were taken to Mission San Jose, where they were baptized. After the local missions were secularized in 1834, the Coast Miwok returned to Olompali. Their last chief, Camillo Ynitia, was a friend and ally of General Mariano Vallejo, Mexico's powerful commander

of present-day northern California. Through this connection, Camillo was granted title to the Rancho Olompali land grant, the only Mexican land grant to a California Indian that was upheld in a U.S. court. In 1851 Camillo sold his property but continued to live on it until his death in 1856.

FURTHER READING: "Camillo Ynitia: The Last Headman of the Olompalis," by Pamela McGuire Carlson and E. Breck Parkman, in *California History*

336. Fort Ross State Historic Park, CA: The First People

Otis Parrish

On Rte. 1, north of Jenner

The Kashaya, the first people known to have lived in the area that is now Fort Ross, still live in this region. The large villages, such as Metini, were the main residences of the headmen and women. People came together for ceremonial and social events in the assembly house. Family life involved strong, warm, and close emotional relationships. The Kashaya took great pains to make a weary traveler or relative comfortable on an overnight visit. They enjoyed a good time at the drop of a leaf.

During the summer they moved to communities along the coast, where they gathered food from the sea. In the late fall they moved back inland to their main village sites atop the ridges, where shelter was available in the cold winter months. Ceremonies marked the arrival of new fruits and the salmon, the ripening of acorns, the migration of deer, and significant social events. The Kashaya were superbly matched to their environment. They developed successful strategies for hunting, fishing, and collecting and used special processing and storage techniques for the food resources in their territory. The Kashaya have always excelled in creating a wide variety of tools, utensils, basketry, and objects of personal adornment, reflecting a high degree of technical knowledge, design, and artistic ingenuity. Their basketry, a ritual art, has achieved extraordinary respect.

The Kashaya's first encounter with the outside world was with the Russians, who were more interested in hunting sea otters and establishing a food base in California than in dominating the Kashaya or altering their way of life. In 1812 they built Fort Ross. The colony included Russian administrators and workers; Aleut hunters; the Kashaya, who were employed as laborers; and Coast Miwok from Bodega Bay. In 1841 the Russians left, and Mexican and American settlers entered the coastal lands in growing numbers. Land became private property, and this caused great changes in the Kashaya way of life. They moved into villages in the Stewart's Point area, and later some resettled on a small reservation 4 miles inland from the point, high on an exposed ridge with poor soils and little water. It was hardly an adequate compensation for the loss of their homeland. The Kashaya, through all these changes, have continued to preserve the vitality and integrity of their culture. Today many Kashaya reside on the reservation and in areas surrounding Fort Ross, while others continue their careers in Sonoma County and the Bay Area. A growing number of Kashaya occupy positions of political and educational leadership in the area's Indian and non-Indian communities.

This essay includes excerpts from "The First People," by Otis Parrish, in *Fort Ross,* edited by Lyn Kalani, Rudy Lynn, and John Sperry with permission from the Fort Ross Interpretive Association.

337. Anderson Marsh State Historic Park, CA

Jim Brown-Eagle III

On Rte. 53, south of Clearlake

The park preserves 1,065 acres of the pristine aboriginal homelands of the Southeastern Pomo, the stewards of the Clear Lake watershed. Clear Lake, California's largest natural body of water, is set among grass-covered hills, tule marshes, and oak and riparian woodlands. The three Pomo tribes, Elem, Komdot, and Koi, have a 10,000-year history in these homelands. Our ancestors were united under a traditional matriarchal system and blessed with abundant natural and wildlife resources, healing mineral waters, and exceptionally rich soils. They developed the world-renowned Pomo baskets and made arrowheads of obsidian and beads of magnesite and clamshells, which were valuable in their trade with other tribes. Their civilization thrived until the invasion of Europeans and the gold rush brought disease, war, and destruction.

By learning about Pomo history, hiking the trails, and fishing in the lake, visitors can get a glimpse of the peaceful and prosperous lifestyle of the original people of Anderson Marsh State Historic Park. Today only two of the three Southeastern Pomo tribes have survived, the Elem and Koi nations. The Elem Nation has 50 acres of aboriginal homeland near Clearlake Oaks; the Koi Nation, whose traditional territory included Anderson Marsh, has no tribal land base in Lake County.

FURTHER READING: "Southeastern and Eastern Pomo," by Sally McLendon and Michael J. Lowy, in *California,* edited by R. F. Heizer, vol. 8 of the *Handbook of North American Indians*

338. Ancil Hoffman County Park, CA: Effie Yeaw Nature Center — The Nisenan Maidu Lived Here

Vince LaPena

2850 San Lorenzo Way, Carmichael

The Nisenan Maidu have lived in the Sacramento region for a very long time and believe that they were created here. Archaeological evidence found near Arcade Creek, a tributary of the Sacramento River, documents the presence of people in this area for at least 5,000 years. One major Nisenan village was Pusune, at the confluence of the American and Sacramento rivers. Yamankudu, established on a bluff near the nature center, was protected from the seasonal flooding of the American River. Semisubterranean earth houses kept the Nisenan warm during the rainy season and cool in the dry season. Some villages were small, with probably a single, extended family, while others may have had more than 500 people. During the summer some lived in the floodplain and gathered foods from the bountiful river valley while the water was low. Near the nature center is a replica of a Maidu summer village with tule storage houses, an acorn granary, and a grinding rock.

A headman was responsible for each village; certain families provided leadership and had the right to gather acorns or other useful plants from specific places. Villages that spoke a common dialect often banded together to share resources within their district. Marriages were common between families of neighboring districts, and alliances were created for better trading opportunities. Large-scale warfare was uncommon, but there were occasional battles if diplomacy failed. The Maidu held festivals and ceremonies throughout the year, and the people followed strict rules of conduct. Many ceremonies were in the roundhouses of the larger villages. Special runners carried invitations from the host village to the leaders in nearby areas. The Maidu enjoyed eating together, exchanging gifts, singing, dancing, celebrating life, and giving thanks to Worldmaker and to the spirits of the land.

Despite many tragic events during the fur-trapping and gold rush era, some Maidu survived. Today they strive to maintain their languages and cultures within modern society and continue to hold traditional ceremonies. Some groups of Maidu work to educate government agencies about traditional land management practices, while others have businesses that help the community and the state economy.

FURTHER READING: "Nisenan," by Norman L. Wilson and Arlene H. Towne, in *California,* edited by Robert F. Heizer, vol. 8 of the *Handbook of North American Indians*

339. Patrick's Point State Park, CA: The Yurok Village of Sumeg

Joy Sundberg

4150 Patrick's Point Dr., north of Trinidad

The idea for a traditional Yurok village open for public interpretation became a reality when the superintendent of state parks, Bill Beat (whose ancestors include the Wailaki), actively supported the partnership with the Yurok people. They, with the California Department of Parks and Recreation, built the Yurok Village of Sumeg, using old-growth redwood salvaged from winter storms. Sumeg includes three living houses, two sweathouses, a Brush Dance pit with amphitheater-style benches, and three camps for dancers affiliated with the Yurok, Hupa, and Karuk people. A living house is semisubterranean, made of split-redwood planks with a three-pitch roof, and entered through a low circular doorway. In old times the people entered through a maze to keep grizzly bears out. Inside is a rectangular pit with a central fire, where people cooked, worked, and slept during the winter months. Above the pit at ground level is a flat ledge used for sleeping and for storing baskets of acorns, dried fish, dried berries, herbs, teas, basket materials, hides, and chests for regalia.

The Yurok had no dances during World War II. After the war an old man, Albert Grey, said he wanted to dance and sing one more time, and my friend Walt Lara said, "Let's dance again." The dances were revived and were held at Sumeg when it opened in 1992. Each year in June, the nonprofit Sumeg Patrick's Point Lagoons Interpretative Association sponsors the ceremonial Brush Dance for healing a young child. The regalia for the men and young girls includes many necklace strands of shells. Men's headdresses are made of rolled tule covered with the white underbelly of deer hides, eagle feathers, and scalps of red-headed woodpeckers and ducks. Hand-held regalia includes arrows and otter quivers decorated with the scalps of red-headed woodpeckers and red abalone shells, whole woodpeckers mounted on handles, and short-hafted obsidian spears. Young girls wear intricately woven basket caps and white buckskin skirts heavily laden with shells and pine nuts, which make rhythmic tinkling sounds when they dance.

Sumeg Village has inspired a renaissance in the Yurok language, dance, song, and regalia making, with younger generations learning from knowledgeable elders and even old people who never danced before coming out to learn and participate. With great pride we and other Native peoples of the northern California coast watch our grandchildren dancing and living our own culture.

FURTHER READING: *The Four Ages of Tsurai, A Documentary History of the Indian Village on Trinidad Bay,* by R. F. Heizer and J. E. Mills

340. Redwood National and State Parks, CA: Rek-woi, Where the Klamath River Meets the Pacific Ocean, Klamath River Overlook

Elders of the Yurok Tribe Culture Committee

West of Rte. 101 and south of Crescent City

Visitor centers

Below the overlook is the Klamath River, He'lth-kik wa-wroi, central to our world, which extended upriver from here for 40 miles and along the coast in both directions. Rek-woi, the largest village in Yurok country, was on the north side of the river. The village of Welth kwew was on the south side. At Rek-woi a world renewal ceremony, the Jump Dance, Wo-nek-uley-go Puwai, was held. Welth kwew was the site of the Spring Salmon Ceremony each year before the taking of salmon could begin. Below us at the water's edge, the rock of Oregos is a place of purification. And all the places had names — the houses in the villages, the sea stacks, hills, rocks, gathering and fishing places, the creeks and springs. Today the Brush Dance, a curing ceremony, is held annually at the dance grounds on the south side of the Klamath.

This was and is a fine place to live, with salmon (*na poey*), candlefish (*quar rar*), sturgeon (*ka kaa*), and eels (*kay win*) in the river; there is a wealth of foods in the sea and on the land, especially the oak trees and acorns just inland. The salmon and the acorns provide the mainstays of our diet. From here people could travel by trail up and down the coast and by redwood dugout canoe (*aulth way*) upriver to the many villages and towns along the Klamath. Looking down, we see the estuary with its changing sand spit responding to the movement of the mouth of the river from north to south to north. For thousands of years we have lived here, fishing for salmon, eels, and sturgeon, hunting for deer (*po ok*) and elk (*may welth*), and gathering berries, shellfish, and seaweed. Our ancestral lands are vast. Now only the lands on either side of the Klamath River for one mile, from here to Weitchpec, are within the Yurok Reservation. Since 1892 the lands have been divided among many others — the parks, other agencies, and private landowners.

Today the Yurok Tribe is the largest in California, with thousands of members. Most do not live here, but all come at some time to visit, fish, and take part in the ceremonies. We who live here are truly *poh lik la,* downriver Indians.

Copyright © 2008 by Susan Masten.

FURTHER READING: "Yurok," by Arnold Pilling, in *California,* edited by R. F. Heizer, vol. 8 of the *Handbook of North American Indians*

341. Lava Beds National Monument, CA: Modoc Homelands

Douglas E. Deur

Off Rte. 39, south of Tulelake

Visitor center

To outsiders' eyes, the lava beds look forbidding: black rocks protrude from the ground in ancient lava flows, while cinder cones rise abruptly from the beige sagebrush plain. Snow blankets the earth in the winter, and summer winds blow hot and dry. To Modoc eyes, the lava beds look like home. In the beginning of time, Gmukamps, the Creator, walked through this place, leaving his indelible mark. Emerging from Schonchin Butte, he fashioned the Modoc world from Tule Lake mud, blessing this land with fish, plants, and animals for the people who would live here. He then traveled south, leaving footprints in the form of cinder buttes and craters, all the way to Medicine Lake. The Modoc lived well here. For countless generations, they gathered tule reeds, cattails, pond lily seeds, and birds' eggs on the marsh edges, caught mullet in Tule Lake, and flushed deer from the lava flows toward hunting blinds. When storms chased

clouds of waterfowl off the lake, they flew low to the west over Sheepy Ridge, and Modoc were there to capture them with nets. Generations lived, prayed and sought power, died, and were buried here. Everything the people needed was in their homeland.

Not long ago, all of this changed. In the late nineteenth century, immigrants clamored for the removal of the Modoc from their homeland. In 1864 all Modoc were sent to the Klamath Indian Reservation. After Captain Jack (Kintpuash), the young Modoc leader, and about seventy families returned to the lava beds in 1872, soldiers flooded into Modoc country. When negotiations with the U.S. Army failed, Captain Jack made one final request, recorded by A. B. Meacham: "Give me this lava bed for a home, take away your soldiers, and we can settle everything. Nobody will ever want these rocks, give me a home here." The army attacked in November. The Modoc fought well, holding out for five months in their complex volcanic homeland. After their defeat, Modoc leaders were hanged; others were shipped off to Oklahoma or restricted on the Klamath Reservation. Tule Lake was partially drained for agricultural uses. Since then, generations of Modocs have quietly returned to the lava beds, maintaining ties to their homeland. Today Modocs return to Lava Beds National Monument each year to celebrate the endurance of that connection and the endurance of the Modoc people. To Modoc eyes, the lava beds still look like home.

FURTHER READING: *The Indian History of the Modoc War,* by Jefferson C. Davis Riddle

Our Final Place

LARRY MYERS

❖ How do you explain to non-Indians the feelings and meanings of the spirit of our final place?

How do you help them understand that Indian people do not need to know someone to care for that person and to respect that person's spirit?

The link that keeps us bound to our culture and to our ancestors is the ground. It is Mother Earth: the final place where we will all travel to one day.

Caring for our ancestors is more than "treatment and disposition."

It is honor, respect, love, gratitude, and understanding.

It is more than education.

It is more than scientific study.

It is life.

The place where our ancestors are found has life in and around it.

Because it has life, it has a spirit — and that spirit is sacred.

Home is not where the heart is but where our ancestors lie — for that is where we will go on our final journey.

342. Newberry National Volcanic Monument, OR

Off Rte. 97, south of Bend

Lava Lands Visitor Center

The Big Obsidian Flow, which extruded from the Newberry Volcano only 1,300 years ago, covers 700 acres; it was an excellent source of obsidian for people in the Pacific Northwest.

343. Crater Lake National Park, OR: Song of the Lake

Gerald D. Skelton, Jr.

Rte. 138 or Rte. 62, Crater Lake

Visitor centers

Crater Lake is known to my people, the Klamath, as Giiwas. Overlooking the sacred lake from high above on the caldera rim, you feel its power exuding from below to where you stand. You feel the power begin to absorb its way through your skin and into your blood. Your skin tingles as a refrain from an ancient power song comes to your tribal mind filled with the ancient memories and ways of your people. You begin to sing, softly at first:

> *Ktsa'lui ge'-u e'-ush*
> *Ktsa'lui ge'-u e'-ush*

and then with all your heart:

> *Ktsa'lui ge'-u e'-ush,*
> *Ktsa'lui ge'-u e'-ush,*
> *Ktsa'lui ge'-u e'-ush*

The power of the lake pulsates throughout your body, heart pounding, and the power grows stronger inside you as you continue to sing. The power wells up inside your fragile shell of skin, your chest is ready to burst. You continue to sing. Warm tears form in the corners of your eyes, you are overcome by the beauty and power of the lake. The lake has given you its greatest gift, its song and hence its power. Tears trickle down your face. You are one with all creation, the universe. Your power is strong.

The Song of the Lake is *Ktsa'lui ge'-u e'-ush* (my lake is glittering in azure colors).

The Klamath Tribes are spearheading efforts to restore our fisheries and improve water quality in the Klamath Basin. In the 1950s the federal government, faced with the prospect of gaining approximately 1 million acres of forested reservation land, passed the Termination Act, which meant that the Klamath Tribes were no longer officially recognized, a devastating blow. Tribal leaders opposed termination to the end. The federal government then sold the reservation land without tribal consent, paying tribal members a small fraction of what it was worth. Today the Klamath Tribes, which have been a federally recognized tribe since 1986, are working to have more than 600,000 acres of our former reservation land returned to the tribes.

FURTHER READING: *Indian Legends of the Pacific Northwest*, by Ella E. Clark

344. Tamástslikt Cultural Institute, OR: Naamí Níshaycht — Our Village

Susan Sheoships

Rte. 331, east of Pendleton

Naamí Níshaycht, our village in the Tamástslikt Cultural Institute, brings alive the culture of the people now known as Cayuse, Walla Walla, and Umatilla. Naamí Níshaycht embodies the values that inform contemporary tribal life. The village interpreters carry out the seasonal cultural activities much as our ancestors did, speaking in the tribal languages and guided by the teachings of our ancestors. These lifeways sustain us, connecting each of us with our culture. The dwellings express the changing world of our ancestors, who have always lived on this land. The two *wilchí*, the pithouses of the early people, contrast with the more recent tule lodge and tipis. Visitors walk along the path through the village counterclockwise, enacting the individual's lifetime journey toward the dawn.

The earth-covered pithouses evoke the people's link with the earth, *tiichám. Tiichám* encompasses the world, the territory, the country, and relates to the cave, the cache, the earthen oven, the healing mud bath. The sweathouse — *χwiyáytsh* in Umatilla and *ítamash* in Walla Walla — is a small earthen dome for steam baths, but its meaning extends beyond physical cleansing. *Kwáalisimnam naknúwita imíin wáwnakʷshash*, say the elders: always take care of your body. The pool in Naamí Níshaycht stands for the importance of water. Water, *chúush*, is *tawtnúk*, the elemental medicine, always precious and never taken for granted. The centerpiece in the village is the tule-mat lodge, *kʷ'áalk níit*, the longhouse. Until the early twentieth century, such a lodge was the optimal house for a society on the move. It stood for *náymu*, kinship, which bound people together, and its symmetry reflected the orderliness of the natural world. *Tk'ú*, the tule reed, was said to accompany a person throughout life. A person would be born in a tule lodge on a tule mattress, eat meals off tule, and sleep on tule. When departing this life, a person was wrapped in a tule mat, *q'iχlí*. The loss of wetlands means that this versatile cultural resource is less plentiful. The canvas tepees are the most recent addition to Naamí Níshaycht. In the eighteenth century, when the tribes went on buffalo hunts to the east, they lived in tepees. Always open to innovation, they admired this streamlined traveling house. Their adoption of it was characteristic of a people who strive, adapt, and move forward. *Cháwna mún na'ámta* — we will never fade.

The vistas across the wide, open spaces surrounding the village are protected by the tribes' land-use planning, which controls development. Although it took several generations for the tribes to assert sovereignty over our reservation homeland, today our tribal planning helps assure a balance between protection of the land and economic development. The teaching — to live in balance with the land — is central to our people and is perpetuated in the Tamástslikt Cultural Institute.

FURTHER READING: *The First Oregonians: An Illustrated Collection of Essays on Traditional Lifeways, Federal-Indian Relations, and the State's Native People Today,* edited by Carolyn M. Buan and Richard Lewis

345. Olympic National Park, WA

Jacilee Wray

Port Angeles

Visitor center and ranger stations

About 14,500 years ago, the ice began to retreat from the Olympic Peninsula, and people appeared on the landscape, as evidenced at the 12,000-year-old archaeological site of a butchered mastodon. In the mountains and foothills, archaeologists have found fire hearths where people camped between 4,000 and 8,000 years ago, and anthropologists have recorded the oral history of their travels across the mountains; many of their routes are enjoyed by hikers today. As populations grew, commerce increased among the tribes. They built canoes out of large cedar trees and fished and hunted whales and seals along the Strait of Juan de Fuca and along the Pacific coast. Canoes were also important for travel among neighboring villages. One of their villages along the coast, the Makah village of Ozette, was partially buried in a mudslide in 1700 at the time of a tsunami. The site of the village is north of the Cape Alava trail where it enters the beach. There are petroglyphs to the south. Items from the villagers' daily life that were recovered from the village site in the 1970s are in the Makah Cultural and Research Center at Neah Bay. After the establishment of Washington Territory in 1853, the tribes lost their traditional land base and were placed on small reservations. Today the reservation land covers more than 250,000 acres of the Olympic Peninsula, but the entire peninsular landscape continues to have immense importance to the tribes.

The park has many education programs that convey information about the Olympic Peninsula tribes: the Elwha Klallam, Jamestown S'Klallam, Port Gamble S'Klallam, Skokomish, Quinault, Hoh, Quileute, and Makah. The main visitor center features a sealing canoe, with text panels on sea mammal hunting, and a Children's Discovery Room, with interactive exhibits to teach children about tribal lifeways. At the Staircase Ranger Station above Hood Canal, baskets, historical photographs, and text panels represent the Skokomish Tribe; the Quinault Ranger Station on the north shore of Lake Quinault focuses on the Quinault Tribe. Wayside and trail exhibits throughout the park, including the Moments in Time nature trail at Lake Crescent, provide information about the peninsula tribes. Recently the park and the tribes wrote a book, *Native Peoples of the Olympic Peninsula: Who We Are,* which is a comprehensive resource for park visitors.

FURTHER READING: *Native Peoples of the Olympic Peninsula: Who We Are,* by the Olympic Peninsula Intertribal Cultural Advisory Committee, Jacilee Wray, editor

346. The Makah Reservation, WA

Janine Bowechop

Rte. 112, Neah Bay

Makah Cultural and Resource Center; boardwalk trail to Cape Flattery

The drive to Neah Bay on Highway 112 is beautiful, and many people stop to see the scenery along the way, but "keep going, it gets much better." Neah Bay is the hub of the 47-square-mile Makah Indian Reservation at the isolated tip of the Olympic Peninsula, where the Strait of Juan de Fuca meets the Pacific Ocean. This is the homeland of the Makah people. The museum in the cultural center exhibits many of the 55,000 artifacts — including whaling, sealing, and fishing gear — preserved by a mudslide that partially covered the Makah village of Ozette in the early 1700s. Many of the artifacts are decorated with whales and thunderbirds. While contemporary Makah people tend to be private regarding ceremonies in preparation for hunting, the museum exhibits do teach the visitors that ceremonial preparations are critical components of successful whale and seal hunting. There are replicas of canoes and of a cedar-plank longhouse like those in Makah villages several generations ago. The people of Ozette primarily relied on the plenitude of the ocean. They paddled great distances to hunt whales and seals, catch halibut and other fish, and harvest the bounties of the intertidal waters.

There is a boardwalk trail to Cape Flattery, the northwesternmost point of the continental United States, with panels that tell about whale migration, the geology of the region, and the Makah's uses of the forest. Along the trail are cedar trees that have been peeled of part of their bark for use in traditional basketry. At the end of the trail is a view of Tatoosh Island and the entrance to the Strait of Juan de Fuca. Tatoosh Island, which has one of the oldest lighthouses in Washington, was a Makah fishing and whaling station. During the summer months the Makah Cultural and Research Center and the Olympic Coast National Marine Sanctuary provide guided walks along the trail. Those who come to our homeland agree that it does get even better, just down the road.

FURTHER READING: *Coming to Shore: Northwest Coast Ethnology, Traditions, and Visions,* edited by Marie Mauzé, Michael E. Harkin, and Sergie Kan.

347. Old Man House Park at D'Suq'Wub, WA: Ancient Suquamish Winter Village Site

Leonard Forsman

Port Madison Indian Reservation, north of Agate Pass Bridge off Rte. 305, Suquamish

The Port Madison Indian Reservation is the home of the Suquamish Tribe. The tribe's name is derived from this place, D'Suq'Wub, meaning place of clear saltwater. The one-acre park on the shoreline of Agate Passage is the site of Old Man House, a 600-foot-long cedar-plank house, one of the largest cedar-plank houses built in Puget Sound and the home for centuries of hundreds of Suquamish people, including Chief Seattle. Federal officials burned Old Man House in 1870 to discourage communal living. Suquamish families continued to live at D'Suq'Wub until 1904, when the federal government moved them and their houses off their ancient homeland.

The Suquamish conducted winter ceremonials in Old Man House to honor the guardian spirits of individuals, acknowledge the ancestral spirits, and thank the Creator for the gifts that sustained the people. Today Suquamish people visit Old Man House Park to reconnect with their ancestral ways and to honor the sacred ground and the waters that have sustained them for thousands of years. The state of Washington returned Old Man House State Park to the Suquamish Tribe in 2004 after years of negotiations, finally acknowledging the Tribe's cultural and spiritual connection to this place, nearly 100 years after removal. The Suquamish Tribe now manages the land as a tribal park, a symbol of Suquamish cultural resurgence, that is open to all people.

The Suquamish Tribe currently has 900 members, who live primarily in the communities of Suquamish and Indianola on the Port Madison Indian Reservation. The Suquamish are historically a fishing people, and many still rely on clams, crab, and salmon for their livelihood. The Tribe also operates a casino, seafood enterprise, resort hotel, catering/wedding facility, and retail businesses to support community health, education, and the buyback of tribal lands.

Copyright © 2008 by Suquamish Tribe.

FURTHER READING: *The Eyes of Chief Seattle,* by the Suquamish Museum

348. Columbia Hills State Park, WA

Louis Pitt, Jr.

At milepost 85 on Rte. 14, along the Columbia River

The Pictograph Trail is open only on park tours

The Columbia Hills State Park area has been home for the Wishxam people since the beginning of time. Once-great villages, such as Niixcluidix, Waquemap, Collawash, Skin, Squanana, and Wishxam, held firm, exclusive authority over this area's lands and waters. The area was part of the great trade network of the Pacific Northwest; the tribes traded local salmon, roots, and other items for food, clothing, tools, and weapons. All passage through the area, whether upriver, downriver, north, or south, had to be paid in some bartered toll. Explorers such as Meriwether Lewis and William Clark complained about the high price of passage, while at the same time documenting the continued presence of the tribal people in their homelands. The language of these lands is Kiksht, an upper Chinookan language that is also spoken by the Wascos and other relatives downriver to the Pacific Ocean.

The Columbia River provided opportunities to catch *nusux* (salmon) and other fish at Three-mile Rapids, Big Eddy, Five-mile Rapids, and many other sites. Many fishing sites, villages, petroglyphs, and pictographs were covered by the flooding caused by The Dalles Dam, completed in 1956. In Petroglyph Canyon, on a basalt rock wall just east of the park, there were petroglyphs and pictographs. The four treaty tribes (Yakama Nation, Confederated Tribes of Warm Springs, Confederated Tribes of the Umatilla, and Nez Perce Nation), the Army Corps of Engineers, the state of Washington, and the Wishxam people worked together to protect some of the petroglyphs and pictographs by moving them into the park. At the Temani Pesh-wa site, near the parking area at the park, the rock panels are arranged in the same order as in Petroglyph Canyon. The petroglyph Tsa-glalal, she who watches, is also in the area and can be visited on tours. She forever watches over her people as a guardian spirit.

Today the Wishxam — through two treaties — still carry out their way of life by exercising the rights to "take fish . . . at all other usual and accustomed stations; also the privilege of hunting, gathering roots and berries, and pasturing their stock on unclaimed lands, in common with citizens, is secured to them."

FURTHER READING: *The Si'lailo Way: Indians, Salmon, and Law on the Columbia River,* by Joseph C. Dupris, Kathleen S. Hill, and William H. Rodgers

349. North Cascades National Park, WA: Newhalem Rock Shelter

Off Rte. 20, Newhalem

Visitor center

The rock shelter is in the old-growth forest along Newhalem Creek. In about 1500 and again in about 1750, American Indians of the Northwest Coast butchered and preserved the meat of mountain goats and other animals in the rock shelter. Some of the arrow points they left were made of high-quality obsidian from sources in Oregon and Idaho.

350. Nez Perce National Historical Park, ID

39063 Hwy. 95, Spalding

Visitor center/museum

Information on the thirty-eight sites in the park can be found at the visitor center and on the Web site http://www.nps.gov/nepe/.

THE NEZ PERCE BEFORE 1876
JOSIAH PINKHAM

Tribal memory recalls the genesis of the Ni-miipuu, now known as the Nez Perce. Iceyeeye, or Coyote, heard that a monster called Ilcwelcix was devouring all the animal people. Iciyeeye made his way from Celilo to the Kamiah Valley. Ilcwelcix was tricked into inhaling Iceyeeye, who killed Ilcwelcix by severing his heart from the inside and freed all the animal people the monster had devoured. Iceyeeye dismembered the body, and as he threw the body parts, he stated that people would later come from those areas where they landed. Iceyeeye then created the Nez Perce there in the Kamiah Valley. This place is now known as the Heart of the Monster and is highly revered by the Nez Perce.

351. Heart of the Monster, ID

Off Rte. 12, East Kamiah

The rock formation honored by the Nez Perce is near a major Nez Perce crossing of the Clearwater River.

352. Weis Rockshelter, ID

Off Rte. 95 on Graves Creek Rd., south of Cottonwood

The Nimiipuu first began using the shelter about 5,000 to 6,000 years ago. The shelter and the creation story support the idea of indigenous evolution in the Nez Perce homelands rather than migration into them.

353. Musselshell Meadow, ID

On Forest Rd. 100, east of Weippe

Musselshell Meadow was one of the places where families gathered food. The women gathered camas roots, and the men hunted and fished. Chief Joseph and his family traveled all the way from Wallowa to gather camas roots.

354. Weippe Prairie, ID

On Rte. 11, Weippe

Weippe Prairie was a traditional gathering place where the Nez Perce harvested camas roots. On September 20, 1805, the Nez Perce first met men from the Lewis and Clark expedition near here, fulfilling the prediction of an early Nez Perce prophet, who warned of the arrival of a different being that would bring great change to the people and land.

355. Canoe Camp, ID

Rte. 12, west of Orofino

The leader of the Nez Perce village on the Clearwater River was Red Bear. The village became known as Canoe Camp when Twisted Hair, acting during Red Bear's absence, assisted the Lewis and Clark expedition in late September. The Nez Perce gave the men food and showed them how to burn out logs to make canoes, enabling them to again travel by river toward the Pacific Ocean.

356. Lolo Trail, ID and MT

From Weippe, ID, to Lolo, MT

Visitor center at Lolo Pass

For thousands of generations the Nimiipuu, first on foot and then on horseback, traveled the Lolo Trail — part of their vast trail network — to fish on the Yellowstone and Missouri rivers and the Great Lakes and to hunt buffalo on the plains. The Lewis and Clark expedition followed this trail into the Nez Perce country and, on its return, from the Pacific coast. In 1877 the Nez Perce used this trail network when they were evading the U.S. military, which was attempting to confine them to the reservation in Idaho. We, their descendants, continue to travel the trail today.

All of these places, among countless others, were part of an interconnected network of life and culture that had been honed for thousands of generations to ensure the survival of the Nez Perce. This way of life changed immensely as a result of the arrival of Lewis and Clark, followed by traders and settlers and the diseases they brought with them. Some Nez Perce accepted the 1855 treaty, which created a 7.5-million-acre reservation closed to non-Indians, and the Treaty of 1863, in which the Nez Perce lost all but 750,000 acres. Others, led by Chief Joseph and White Bird, refused to live on the reservation, dividing the Nimiipuu.

THE NEZ PERCE SINCE 1876
Diana Mallickan and
Allen Pinkham

Broken treaties, an unjust war, exile, diminished population and land, and disease filled the lives of the Nimiipuu both on and off the reservation for decades after the 1877 war. To commemorate the 100th anniversary of the war, the Nimiipuu began reviving the ancestral ways. The ceremonies conducted at the battle sites by Nez Perce veterans and the Nez Perce Colville, known as the Chief Joseph Band, have helped to restore pride and dignity to all Nimiipuu. The Nez Perce are still seeking healing and reconciliation among the divided tribal groups on the Umatilla, Colville, and Nez Perce reservations. All Americans can identify with the battle sites as places where we seek reconciliation and unity.

357. White Bird Battlefield, ID

Off Hwy. 95, White Bird

After young Nimiipuu men killed settlers in revenge for the tragic wrongs against their people, those opposed to the treaty gathered here at Lamatana. Captain David Perry, leading a force of ninety-nine soldiers, eleven volunteers, and unarmed treaty Nez Perce, arrived on June 17, 1877. They were met by a peace party flying a white flag. A volunteer fired on the Nez Perce, and the battle began. Thirty-four of Perry's force died in the brief battle, the first on the 1,170-mile war trail.

358. Looking Glass Camp, ID

Off U.S. 12, southeast of Kamiah

Interpretive trail

On July 1, 1877, Looking Glass and his band were living in their village on reservation land when Captain Stephen G. Whipple and his force arrived. Looking Glass, who had signed the treaty, was trying to remain neutral in the conflict. Whipple attacked, killed several men, women, and children, destroyed the village and the gardens, and captured hundreds of horses. Knowing they were not safe, they fled to join those opposed to the treaty and headed along the Lolo Trail into buffalo country.

359. Big Hole National Battlefield, MT

On Rte. 43, west of Wisdom

Visitor center

After weeks of fleeing the military, about 800 Nez Perce men, women, and children halted to set up camp, as they had many times before in this beautiful place. At dawn on August 9, Colonel John Gibbon, in command of 163 men of the 7th Infantry and 34 Bitterroot volunteers, attacked, killing 89 Nimiipuu men, women, and children. Under almost impossible odds, the warriors retook the camp, disabled Gibbon's howitzer, and surrounded the soldiers while the women and children escaped. The Nimiipuu continued east through Yellowstone National Park and north toward Canada.

360. Bear Paw Battlefield, MT

On Rte. 240, south of Chinook

Visitor center in Blaine County Museum

After four months on the war trail and the loss of many lives, horses, and possessions, the surviving Nimiipuu camped near the Bear Paw Mountains, 40 miles south of the Canadian border. They had no tipis and few blankets to keep them warm — and the snow fell. General Nelson A. Miles, reinforced by General Oliver O. Howard, attacked the Nimiipuu, killing Looking Glass. After several days of siege under terrible conditions, the battle ended. Some, including the White Bird Band, escaped into Canada with about 150 Nimiipuu, mainly warriors. Chief Joseph and 325 Nimiipuu remained and surrendered. Joseph declared, "I am tired. My heart is sick and sad. From where the sun now stands, I

will fight no more forever." With these words, the war ended. Joseph's people were sent to Kansas and then to Indian Territory, where many died. The survivors were sent to live on the Colville Reservation in Washington, where their descendants live today. Those who escaped to Canada eventually returned to the Nez Perce Reservation. Other descendants live on the Umatilla Reservation.

Today the Nez Perce Tribe on the Nez Perce Reservation in Idaho is actively managing, protecting, and enhancing all of the resources reserved in the treaty of 1855. The Nez Perce Tribal Executive Committee (NPTEC) is the elected governing body, which administers, manages, and coordinates both human and natural resources for the welfare and benefit of the people. They use existing law and agreements to manage resources along with local, state, and federal agencies. The Nimiipuu always strive for social and economic development for the betterment of the people in the Nez Perce community. NPTEC has management authority over two casinos, a gas station, timber, fisheries, land, and natural resources as defined by the 1855 treaty and subsequent treaties and agreements with the United States. In the early twenty-first century, the Nez Perce Tribe became the largest employer in north-central Idaho.

FURTHER READING: *The Nez Perce Indians and the Opening of the Northwest,* by Alvin M. Josephy, Jr.

361. Lewis and Clark National and State Historical Parks, OR and WA

Roberta Conner

Visitor centers: Fort Clatsop and Astoria, OR; Cape Disappointment State Park, Ilwaco, WA

In 1804 the Missouri River tribes and those along the Pacific coast had long been engaged in international trade, while the interior tribes on the Columbia River Plateau had been protected from international visitors by the lay of the land and the rivers. When Meriwether Lewis and William Clark and the Corps of Discovery made their military mission of reconnaissance and diplomacy to the West, they traveled through the homelands of more than 100 tribes — homelands that included revered places on the Missouri and Columbia rivers, such as the White Cliffs of the Missouri, Double Ditch in North Dakota, the Great Falls in Montana, Weippe Prairie in Idaho, the Cayuse Sisters in Washington, and Hat Rock and Celilo Falls in Oregon. For the American Indians who met, challenged, bargained with, and assisted the expedition, the explorers represented change. Since then, treaties, acts of Congress, and federal policies have moved many tribes away from the banks of the Missouri and Columbia rivers; some groups are now in Oklahoma.

The Web site for the Lewis and Clark National Historic Trail (nps.gov/lecl) provides information about the route of the expedition across tribal homelands. The Lewis and Clark National and State Historical Parks, along the Columbia River and the Pacific Ocean, includes Fort Clatsop, the Corps' winter home; the Dismal Nitch, where a winter storm trapped the Corps on the rocky shoreline; Cape Disappointment State Park and Interpretive Center; Fort Stevens State Park, which includes a Clatsop village site; the Salt Works, where the Corps boiled seawater to produce salt for their journey home; Ecola State Park, where Clark, Sacagawea, and others traveled to trade with the Tillamook Indians for whale blubber and oil; and Sunset Beach State Recreation Area, which preserves a significant area of the Oregon Coast.

The United States negotiated nearly a thousand treaties with American Indian nations for the purpose of dispossessing them of lands, hunting and fishing rights, and other resources. Substantial numbers of these treaties were never ratified by Congress, leaving many tribes landless and without formal recognition of their existence. Among many others, the Chinook, Clatsop, Lemhi Shoshone, and Monacan still seek federal recognition.

FURTHER READING: *Lewis and Clark Through Indian Eyes,* edited by Alvin M. Josephy, Jr.

362. Whitman Mission National Historic Site, WA: Homeland of the Waiilatpu

Marjorie Waheneka

Off Rte. 12, west of Walla Walla

Visitor center

Waiilatpu — the place of the rye grass — is the homeland of the Waiilatpu band of Cayuse Indians. Until 1847 they lived comfortably in the lush Walla Walla Valley. They lived in tipis made of tule (bulrush) reeds, which were lightweight and waterproof. The men hunted in the Blue Mountains, fished in the mighty Columbia and Walla Walla rivers, and bred the Cayuse horse. The women gathered a variety of roots in the foothills of the Blue Mountains and berries in the higher elevations. The Waiilatpu were 500 strong in 1836 when Marcus Whitman, a Presbyterian minister and doctor, and his wife, Narcissa, traveled across the continent and established a mission among them.

Immigrants who traveled along the Oregon Trail brought new diseases that caused the death of more than half of the Cayuse, mostly children and elders. Talk circulated that Dr. Whitman was poisoning them so that he could take their fertile land. The misunderstanding erupted into a violent clash of cultures. On November 29, 1847, the Cayuse killed the Whitmans and eleven others at the mission. The killings received nationwide attention, prompting Congress to make Oregon a U.S. territory. The Cayuse became fugitives, pursued by the Oregon Territorial Militia. Two years later, five Cayuse men surrendered in Oregon City, where they were tried for the deaths at Whitman Mission, found guilty, and hanged. To this day, no one knows the location of their graves.

Today the Cayuse, with the Umatilla and Walla Walla people, are the Confederated Tribes of the Umatilla Indian Reservation. The tribes once had a homeland of 6.4 million acres in northeastern Oregon and southeastern Washington.

FURTHER READING: *The Cayuse Indians: Imperial Tribesmen of the Old Oregon,* by Robert H. Ruby and John A. Brown

363. Old Mission State Park, ID

Quanah Matheson

Off I-90 at exit 39, east of Cataldo

The Schi'ntsu'umsh, the Coeur d'Alene Tribe's aboriginal territory, includes more than 4 million acres and extends into three states — Idaho, Montana, and Washington. Our territory is everything to us. This is where God put us and where we will stay to take care of the land that he entrusted to us forever. Our tribe's beautiful way of life was made difficult when we heard about the coming of the white people. The great chief Circling Raven, a holy man, had a vision of a people who would bring a new way to the heaven trails. We invited the Black Robes to our country, and they established the first mission on the St. Joe River. Because of excessive flooding, it was later moved to a place on the Coeur d'Alene River now known as Cataldo. The tribe completed the Mission of the Sacred Heart in 1853, using no nails and using huckleberry juice as paint for the ceiling. Handprints in the dry mud used as insulation are still visible. The mission became a state park in 1975.

Today the tribe is vibrant with opportunity because of our enterprises and programs that fulfill our mission to take care of our people. Our casino is one of the major employers in the state. We continue to have challenges but are making the necessary changes to meet them for the sake of our children and future generations. We look to the future with optimism.

Chief J. Allan, tribal chairman: Reverence for the past. Perseverance in the present. Protection of the Tribe in the future. These three guiding principles, along with respect for all community members, have been a hallmark of the Coeur d'Alene Tribe. Through innovation, motivation, and cooperation, the Coeur d'Alene Tribe will continue to perpetuate a way of life that focuses upon family, community, and protection of the Tribal homelands. We have always called this northern region of Idaho home, and we will endure for the sake of all our children.

FURTHER READING: *Landscape Traveled by Coyote and Crane: The World of the Schitsu'Umsh Coeur D'Alene Indians,* by Rodney Frey

364. Fort Simcoe State Park, WA

Carol Craig

On the Yakima Indian Reservation, west of White Swan

Interpretive center and original buildings

The Yakama Nation's homelands extend from the lowlands along the Columbia River to the Cascade Mountains and our sacred mountain, Páhto (Mount Adams). Our ancestors once moved across these lands seasonally, gathering edible roots in the spring, fishing in the rivers, and gathering berries in the fall. The Yakama lost about 12 million acres in the 1855 treaty. After the discovery of gold north of the Spokane

River, whites invaded the area, crossed Yakama lands, and killed Yakama people. In 1856, during the three-year Yakama War, Fort Simcoe was established on the trail between the Yakima Valley and the tribe's traditional fishing areas on the Columbia River. This enabled the soldiers to protect treaty lands from land-hungry settlers and to watch over travelers crossing tribal lands. The war ended when Colonel George Wright executed Yakama chiefs and warriors.

The fort then became the Yakama Agency, part of the Bureau of Indian Affairs, which established a boarding school. For the next twenty-three years, James Wilbur, the agent, worked to "civilize" the children, which included taking away their Yakama names and giving them new names such as Daniel Boone and Abe Lincoln. Mistreatment of the children increased, and the school was finally closed in 1892. Reservation life was tragic for the Yakama, with high death rates.

Today the Yakama Nation manages more than 1 million acres, including 600,000 acres of timberland. The Yakama people continue the teachings of the elders and honor education. Elders carry on the Washat — the Seven Drums religion — which encourages people to care for each other and for the sacred places and to celebrate First Food Ceremonies held in thanksgiving for the Creator's gifts of salmon, deer, roots, and berries. Children and adults are taught the Yakama dialect of Sahaptin, starting in early childhood and continuing through the Heritage College on the reservation. The Cultural Heritage Center sponsors events and exhibits artwork, beadwork, basketry, feather tying, and traditional regalia.

FURTHER READING: *Empty Nets: Indians, Dams, and the Columbia River,* by Roberta Ulrich

365. Point No Point Treaty Site, WA: Hahdskus

Robert T. Anderson

On Point No Point Rd. near the lighthouse, Hansville

Hahdskus, which means long point in Coast Salish, is a low, sandy spit on the Kitsap Peninsula, which extends more than a quarter of a mile into Puget Sound. In January 1855, more than 1,200 local S'Klallam, Chimacum, and Skokomish congregated here for negotiations that culminated in the signing of the Treaty of Point No Point. It was one in a series of treaties negotiated between the Indians of western Washington and the United States. The federal government needed the treaties to open the region legally to non-Indian settlement and to secure peace with the powerful tribes of the region. The territorial governor, Isaac Stevens, came as the emissary of the United States government and was the leader of the U.S. negotiating team. On the first day of the council, Indian leaders argued against signing the treaty, fearing the loss of their homelands and way of life. Stevens persisted, and by the second day the leaders signed the treaty.

Like the other treaties in Washington and Oregon, the Treaty of Point No Point ceded the territorial lands of the S'Klallam, Chimacum, and Skokomish Indians to the United States. The Indians reserved small homelands (reservations) and received assurances that they would be able to continue their way of life after they moved to these reservations. Recognition of the tribes' sovereignty and ownership of these aboriginal territories established the legal basis for modern claims to governmental power over tribal reservations. In Article IV of the Point No Point Treaty, the tribes reserved "the right of taking fish at usual and accustomed grounds and stations . . . in common with all citizens of the United States." More than a hundred years later, in the landmark decision in *United States v.*

Washington, Federal District Judge George Boldt ruled that by this provision the treaty tribes retained the right to one-half of the salmon available for harvest at usual and accustomed tribal fishing sites. In doing so he recognized, as the United States Supreme Court had in 1905, that the ability of the tribes to fish was "not much less necessary to their existence than the atmosphere they breathed." Because of this decision, the descendants of the S'Klallam, Chimacum, and Skokomish Indians continue to fish in many of the places where their ancestors fished. The Lower Elwha Klallam Tribe, the Jamestown S'Klallam Tribe, the Port Gamble S'Klallam Tribe, the Skokomish Indian Tribe, and other federally recognized tribes in Puget Sound are comanagers with the federal and state governments of the fisheries and have great influence over non-Indian development that might affect treaty resources. The tremendous modern-day importance of the rights reserved at the treaty negotiations stand as a tribute to the Indian leaders who were present at the council in 1855.

FURTHER READING: *Treaties on Trial: The Continuing Controversy over Northwest Indian Fishing Rights,* by Fay G. Cohen

366. Golden Gate National Recreation Area, CA: Alcatraz Island

Susan Secakuku

Ferry service from Fisherman's Wharf, San Francisco

Alcatraz Island was a U.S. Army post until 1934, and then a federal penitentiary until 1963. Among the prisoners held on the island were two Modoc Indians, Barncho and Sloluck. The government sent them to Alcatraz in 1873 because they had fought to stay in their homelands in the lava beds of northern California. Barncho died after two years and was buried on nearby Angel Island. After five years Sloluck was sent to

Fort Leavenworth and, finally, freed to join the Modoc in the Indian Territory.

The largest group of Indians imprisoned at Alcatraz were nineteen Hopi men from the village of Oraibi who had rejected the U.S. government's efforts to "civilize" their families. In 1887 the government had built a boarding school 30 miles from their village. The school's mission was to change the children from their Hopi ways to those of the white man. When parents refused to permit their children to be taken from them, soldiers occupied Oraibi. In November 1894, Constant William, the acting agent of the Navajo Agency at Fort Defiance, Arizona, arrested the Hopi men. They were sent to Alcatraz, where they worked willingly and were well behaved and quiet. They did not communicate with others because they did not speak English. Ten months later the government sent them back to Oraibi.

An initial attempt in 1964 by American Indians to occupy Alcatraz Island led to the nineteen-month-long occupation in 1969 by "Indians of All Tribes," including students and other Indians from around the nation. They protested the poor conditions on reservations and had as a goal establishing an Indian university and a cultural center on the island. When the government cut off power and the source of fresh water, dissension increased, and the number of occupiers decreased; federal marshals forcibly removed them all in June 1971. While they did not get the deed to the island, they did succeed in bringing needed attention to the concerns of American Indians and to changes in government policies that would benefit Indians throughout the United States. In addition, their actions led to the end of the government's termination program and the establishment of self-determination for federally recognized tribes.

FURTHER READING: *Heart of the Rock: The Indian Invasion of Alcatraz,* by Adam Fortunate Eagle

Contemporary American Indian Identity and Place

Duane Champagne

❖ American Indians today are often challenged by non-Indians' perceptions of how Indians should look and act. The public's images are drawn from movies, novels, academic books, and, occasionally, direct contact. There is a tendency to envision Indians as homogeneous or vanished noble savages or, sometimes, as rich casino owners. Often children receive limited information about them from history books or classroom reenactments of the first Thanksgiving dinner embraced by the Wampanoags and the Pilgrims at Plymouth in the early 1620s. Consequently, there is a tendency to view authentic Indians as only those who adhere to the traditional images, which are hard to shake and do not take into account the diversity of cultures and several hundred years of cultural, political, and economic change. American Indian peoples and communities have changed, but not necessarily voluntarily. At the time of Columbus, Indians occupied all of the Americas, but today they have relatively little land left. Many sacred places often recalled in the creation stories are no longer in their control. Hundreds of millions of acres of land have been transferred to American society. It is no longer possible for communities to live in the old ways. The many cultural, political, and economic contacts of the last several centuries have transformed and marginalized American Indian communities to conditions of economic dependence, political subordination, and cultural secrecy. From the 1880s to the 1930s, concentrated government policies worked to transform their communities and suppress their languages, ceremonies, and traditional governments.

Many in the general public expect Indians to act and behave the way people living at the time of the Pilgrims did, despite the many changes in recent history and the government policies designed to transform the people and their communities. This is equivalent to expecting the average American to act like a Pilgrim of the 1620s. Today there are more than 560 federally recognized American Indian tribes and at least 200 Indian communities not formally recognized by the federal government. These communities participate in the contemporary world but, to the extent possible, in their own ways and according to their own teachings. Most American Indians are not traditionalists who want to return to the ways of the first Thanksgiving. They watch TV, listen to contemporary music, watch movies, participate in sports, and speak English. Much of their culture went underground during the early 1900s, but in more recent decades, some ceremonies, such as the Sun Dance and potlatches, are again practiced in the open.

Living in the contemporary world has increased the internal diversity of American Indian communities. In some, a spiritually minded individual may participate in the Sun Dance, lead sessions of the American Indian Church, and take communion on Sunday at Catholic Mass. Scientific knowledge and methods are known by some, many are Christians, many have served in the U.S. armed forces, and many families have lived and worked in large cities for one or more generations. Nevertheless, among most, there persists a commitment to living and preserving American Indian cultural, political, and often religious heritages. The internal cultural diversity of Indian communities has many social and political implications. How are community values, norms, and rules preserved in a world of economic competition, political centralization, and the internationalization of cultural knowledge? Such issues continue to be debated today within many communities.

Place continues to play a central role in American Indian communities, and sacred places continue to live for many. Although sacred places are not always located on the reservation, they are remembered in ceremonies, sometimes secretly, conducted according to creation stories to honor and acknowledge past events, sacred beings, and powers. Bear Butte in South Dakota — known as Devils Tower National Monument — is sacred to the Lakota and the Cheyenne, who go there to pray, to seek visions, and, for the Cheyenne, to honor significant parts of their creation stories. The Hopi have sacred places within the Grand Canyon where the first beings emerged into the present world from underground. The locations are entrusted to spiritual leaders of Hopi clans and religious societies.

American Indian communities or nations retain rights to land through treaties, acts of Congress, and executive orders from the president. These lands are not grants to the Indians; they are the remnants of their original, much larger lands, which have been transferred to U.S. juris-diction. However, for American Indians, the land was given as a gift to the people from the Creator. It is their responsibility to care for and honor the land, the waters, the animals, the heavenly bodies, and the forces of nature that make up the universe. Many ceremonies are about honoring and thanking the Creator for the gifts granted for their sustenance. Places, land, the entire universe, is a gift, and the animate forces of the universe, including plants and animals, are kindred spirits who form significant parts of the Creator's unknowable plan. American Indian communities are working to make their way in the contemporary world while acknowledging themselves as participants and stewards of a world given in a sacred and beneficial way.

FURTHER READING: *The Native North American Almanac: A Reference Work on Native North Americans in the United States and Canada,* edited by Duane Champagne

About the Contributors

Adams, E. Charles, "Homolovi Ruins State Park." E. Charles Adams is curator of archaeology at the Arizona State Museum and the author of *The Origin and Development of the Pueblo Katsina Cult* and *Homol'ovi: An Ancient Hopi Settlement Cluster.* He has directed archaeological research on and in the vicinity of Homol'ovi since 1985.

Agent, Dan (Cherokee/Choctaw), "Sequoyah's Cabin: Monument to the Cherokee Genius." Dan Agent, a Cherokee Nation citizen and former editor of the award-winning *Cherokee Phoenix* newspaper, lives in Tahlequah, the capital of the Cherokee Nation. Now retired from the *Cherokee Phoenix,* he is working on a book about the Cherokee constitutional crisis of 1995–99 and other media projects.

Anderson, David G., and **Paul D. Welch,** "Shiloh National Military Park: Mississippian Mound Group." David G. Anderson is an archaeologist on the faculty of the University of Tennessee, Knoxville. His publications include *The Paleoindian and Early Archaic Southeast* (with K. E. Sassaman) and *The Woodland Southeast* (with R. C. Mainfort, Jr.). His fieldwork spans thirty-five years. Paul D. Welch is an archaeologist at

Southern Illinois University Carbondale. His publications include *Archaeology at Shiloh Indian Mounds, 1899–1999* and *Moundville's Economy.*

Anderson, Fred, "The Seven Years' War." Fred Anderson is professor of history at the University of Colorado and the author of *Crucible of War,* which won the Francis Parkman Prize and the Mark Lynton History Prize. With Andrew Cayton, he is the author of *The Dominion of War: Empire and Liberty in North America, 1500–2000.*

Anderson, Robert T. (Bois Forte Band of Ojibwe), "Point No Point Treaty Site: Hahdskus." Robert T. Anderson is assistant professor of law and director of the Native American Law Center at the University of Washington School of Law. He is a coauthor and member of the board of editors of *Cohen's Handbook of Federal Indian Law.*

Baker, Gerard (Yellow Wolf) (Mandan, Hidatsa, and Arikara Nation), "Knife River Indian Villages National Historic Site" and "The Battle of the Little Bighorn: Mandan, Hidatsa, and Arikara Nation." Gerard Baker, the superintendent of Mount Rushmore National Monument, is an enrolled member of the Mandan, Hidatsa, and Arikara Nation from the Fort Berthold Indian Reservation in North Dakota. He has done extensive research and work on documentaries about Lewis and Clark, American Indians, and the fur trade.

Balenquah, Lyle (Hopi), "Walnut Canyon, Wupatki, and Sunset Crater National Monuments." Lyle Balenquah is a member of the Hopi Tribe from the Greasewood (Dep'wungwa) Clan of Paaqavi (Reed Springs) Village on Third Mesa. Formerly he was an archaeologist in the Hopi Cultural Preservation Office.

Barbour, Jeannie (Chickasaw), "Chickasaw National Recreation Area." Jeannie Barbour is director of the Chickasaw Nation Library, Archives, and Collections Department. She was editor of the *Journal of Chickasaw History* and served on the National Trail of Tears advisory board and the Oklahoma Film Commission. She was an interpreter at the recreation area.

Barnett, Jim, "The Grand Village of the Natchez Indians." Jim Barnett is director of the Historic Properties Division of the Mississippi Department of Archives and History. His publications include *The Natchez Indians: A History to 1735,* published in 2007 by the University Press of Mississippi.

Basso, Keith H., "Wisdom Sits in Places." Keith H. Basso is a rancher in Arizona and the University Regents Professor emeritus and Distinguished Professor of Anthropology emeritus at the University of New Mexico. His most recent book, with Eva Tulene Watt, a White Mountain Apache, is *Don't Let the Sun Step Over You.*

Beebe, Rose Marie, and **Robert M. Senkewicz,** "California Missions." Rose Marie Beebe is professor of Spanish at Santa Clara University. Her publications, with Robert M. Senkewicz, include

Lands of Promise and Despair: Chronicles of Early California, 1535–1846, and *Guide to the Manuscripts Concerning Baja California.* She was president of the California Mission Studies Association (2001–2005). Robert M. Senkewicz is professor of history at Santa Clara University. His publications include *Vigilantes in Gold Rush San Francisco* and, with Rose Marie Beebe, *The History of Alta California by Antonio María Osio,* and *Testimonios: Early California through the Eyes of Women, 1815–1848.*

Bell, Theresa Hayward (Mashantucket Pequot) and **Jack Campisi,** "Mashantucket Pequot Museum and Research Center: Recreated Sixteenth-Century Pequot Village and Site of a Seventeenth-Century Fortified Village." Theresa Hayward Bell was until 2006 the executive director of the Mashantucket Pequot Museum and Research Center, and she headed the team that began planning the facility in 1992. She has played an important role in the cultural resurgence of her tribe for more than a quarter century. Jack Campisi was on the faculty at Wellesley College, is director of museum projects at the Mashantucket Pequot Museum and Research Center, and has worked with more than thirty tribal nations on issues involving federal recognition and land claims. His publications include *The Mashpee Indians: Tribe on Trial.*

Benally, Ailema (Navajo), "Canyon de Chelly National Monument: The Place and the People." Ailema Benally is a National Park Service ranger at Canyon de Chelly National Monument.

Berens, Rose (Bois Forte Band of Ojibwe), "Voyageurs National Park." Rose Berens is the Bois Forte tribal historic preservation officer and the executive director of the Bois Forte Heritage Center and Cultural Museum.

Bernardis, Timothy, "Chief Plenty Coups State Park." Timothy Bernardis, the library director at

Little Big Horn College, also oversees the Little Big Horn College Archives. He is the author of *Crow Social Studies: Baleeisbaalichiwee History* and the coauthor of "Robert Yellowtail," in *The New Warriors, Native American Leaders Since 1900.*

Berryhill, Alfred (Muscogee Creek), and **Blue Clark** (Muscogee Creek), "Ocmulgee National Monument." Alfred Berryhill is the second chief of the Muscogee (Creek) Nation. His tribal town is Vpekv Etalwv (Arbekah Town), and he belongs to the Hvlpvtvlke (Alligator Clan). Blue Clark is a professor at Oklahoma City University School of Law. His tribal town is Kowetv Etalwv (Coweta Town), and he belongs to the Hodulkvlk (Wind Clan).

Birmingham, Robert A., "Effigy Mound Builders." Robert A. Birmingham was the Wisconsin state archaeologist and is on the faculty of the University of Wisconsin — Waukesha. He is the coauthor, with Leslie Eisenberg, of *Indian Mounds of Wisconsin* and the senior editor of *Wisconsin Archaeology,* published by the Wisconsin Archeological Society.

Bissonnette, Linda E. Dick, with **Les James, Suzanne Ramirez, Karen Sargosa,** and **Bernice Williamson** (Miwok), "Wassama Round House State Historic Park." Linda E. Dick Bissonnette is an anthropologist working for California State Parks. She has a Ph.D. from the University of California, Santa Barbara. Her dissertation is titled "Foothill Yokoch, Mono, and Miwok Women." Born and raised in California, she now makes her home in Sonora, 55 miles north of Wassama. Les James, Suzanne Ramirez, Karen Sargosa, and Bernice Williamson are members of the Wassama Association, which provides educational programs.

Blackburn, Bob L., "Constitutional Government Among the Five Civilized Tribes." Bob L. Black-

burn is executive director of the Oklahoma Historical Society and the author of sixteen books, numerous articles, and several screenplays for documentaries dealing with Indian law enforcement from 1803 to 1907, Indian participation in the Civil War, and early explorers in Indian country.

Blythe, Robert W., "Horseshoe Bend National Military Park." Robert W. Blythe is an independent scholar and former chief of history in the Southeast Region of the National Park Service. He is the author of numerous studies for NPS units and an essay on Alabama textile-mill villages in *Constructing Image, Identity, and Place: Perspectives in Vernacular Architecture* 9.

Bowechop, Janine (Makah), "The Makah Reservation." Janine Bowechop, the executive director of the Makah Cultural and Research Center, lives on the Makah Indian Reservation with her husband and four children. Her publications include a chapter, "Contemporary Makah Whaling," in *Coming to Shore: Northwest Coast Ethnology, Traditions, and Visions.*

Brain, Jeffrey P., "Winterville Mounds." Jeffrey P. Brain is associated with the Peabody Essex Museum of Salem, Massachusetts. He is the author of numerous articles and books on the Native people of the southeastern United States, including *Winterville, Lake George, Tunica Treasure,* and *Tunica Archaeology.*

Brooks, Lisa (Abenaki), and **Louise Lampman Larivee** (Abenaki), "Maquam Wildlife Management Area: The Grandma Lampman Site." Lisa Brooks's family comes from the headwaters of the Missisquoi River. As a young woman, she returned to the Abenaki community and worked in the tribal office, where she assisted the Lampman family on the Grandma Lampman case. She currently teaches Native American literature and history at Harvard University. Louise Lampman's family comes from Missisquoi. Her father, Leonard Lampman, was chief of the St. Francis–Sokoki Band of the Abenaki Nation during the 1980s, and Louise has continued his legacy, serving as a community leader. She is currently the training coordinator for the Title IV Abenaki-UVM-SRS Child Welfare Training Project.

Brown, Ian W., "Natchez Trace Parkway: Emerald Mound." Ian W. Brown is professor of anthropology at the University of Alabama and curator of Gulf Coast archaeology at the Alabama Museum of Natural History. His publications include *Natchez Indian Archaeology: Culture Change and Stability in the Lower Mississippi Valley.*

Brown-Eagle III, Jim (Southeastern Elem Pomo), "Anderson Marsh State Historic Park." Jim Brown-Eagle III is a traditional roundhouse leader and the tribal administrator of the Elem Indian Colony. He is a champion of tribal sovereignty, preservation of sacred sites, environmental justice, and cross-cultural educational training.

Bulletts, Angelita S. (Kaibab Band of Paiute Indians), "Pipe Spring National Monument." Angelita Bulletts is the associate district manager of the Arizona Strip District, Bureau of Land Management. The district manages approximately 2.7 million acres of BLM land, including the Vermilion Cliffs and Grand Canyon–Parashant National Monument. She has worked extensively with her tribe, preserving tribal culture and traditions.

Burge, Thomas L., "Sequoia and Kings Canyon National Parks: The Western Mono and the Foothill Yokuts." Tom Burge has been the archaeologist at Sequoia–Kings Canyon since 1994. His interests include prehistoric uses of high-elevation environments. He currently

serves on the Yokuts Archaeological Advisory Team, Tule River Indian Reservation, and consulted with Lawrence Bill of the Sierra Nevada Native American Coalition on this entry.

Butler, Brian M., "Shawnee National Forest: Millstone Bluff." Brian Butler is the director of the Center for Archaeological Investigations at Southern Illinois University, Carbondale. He has conducted archaeological research in southern Illinois and adjacent areas for more than thirty years.

Buvelot, Gene (Federated Indians of Graton Rancheria), **Sylvia Thalman**, and **Nick Tipon** (Federated Indians of Graton Rancheria), "Point Reyes National Seashore: The Coast Miwok." Gene Buvelot is a tribal council member (treasurer) of the tribe and the Tribal Council liaison to the tribe's Sacred Sites Protection Committee. Sylvia Thalman is a coeditor of *Interviews with Tom Smith and Maria Copa*. She is an honorary elder and a cofounder of Kule Loklo and of the Miwok Archeological Preserve of Marin (MAPOM). Nick Tipon is a tribal member and chairman of the tribe's Sacred Sites Protection Committee.

Calloway, Colin G., "The American Revolution in Indian Country." Colin G. Calloway is a professor of history, the Samson Occom Professor of Native American Studies, and chair of the Native American Studies Program at Dartmouth College. He has published widely on American Indian history, including *One Vast Winter Count: The American West Before Lewis and Clark.*

Cameron, Bertha (Shawnee), and **Greg Pitcher** (Shawnee), "Shawnee Indian Mission State Historic Site." Bertha Cameron is a member of the Shawnee Tribe and the founding president of the Monticello Community Historical Society in Johnson County, Kansas. Greg Pitcher is a member of the Shawnee Tribe. He is a former member of the Shawnee Tribal Business Committee and is the chairman of Shawnee Development.

Cameron, Catherine M., "Tools from the Earth." Catherine M. Cameron is an associate professor of anthropology at the University of Colorado. She has published articles on the stone artifacts of Chaco Canyon, on Chacoan and post-Chacoan sites in southeastern Utah, and on sites in northeastern Arizona, and the book *Hopi Dwellings: Architectural Change at Orayvi.*

Carleton, Kenneth H., "Nanih Waiya." Kenneth H. Carleton is the tribal historic preservation officer and tribal archaeologist for the Mississippi Band of Choctaw Indians. His research includes the eighteenth- and nineteenth-century Choctaw, their trail system, and their origins. His publications include "Nanih Waiya (22WI500): An Historical and Archaeological Overview."

Carter, Cecile Elkins (Caddo), "Caddoan Mounds State Historic Site: A Sacred Site." Cecile Carter is a Caddo historian and an enrolled member of the Caddo Nation. She is the author of *Caddo Indians: Where We Come From.*

Champagne, Duane (Turtle Mountain Band of Chippewa), "Contemporary American Indian Identity and Place." Duane Champagne is professor of sociology and American Indian studies at UCLA and a faculty member of the UCLA Native Nations Law and Policy Center. He is the author or editor of more than 100 published works.

Child, Brenda J. (Red Lake Band of Chippewa), "American Indian Boarding Schools." Brenda J. Child is an associate professor of American studies at the University of Minnesota. She was a recipient of the President's Outstanding Award for Community Service in 2003. Her book *Boarding School Seasons: American Indian Fam-*

ilies, 1900–1940 won the North American Indian Prose Award.

Clark, Caven, and **Tim Cochrane,** "Isle Royale National Park: The Minong Mine." Caven Clark is the archaeologist/curator at Buffalo National River. From 1986 to 1991 he conducted extensive archeological surveys on Isle Royale, where he studied prehistoric copper mining and copper-working technology. Tim Cochrane is the superintendent of Grand Portage National Park. He is completing a book on the Ojibwe use of Minong.

Clark, Jeffery J., and **Patrick D. Lyons,** "The Elusive Salado." Jeffery Clark is a preservation archaeologist at the Center for Desert Archaeology, a nonprofit organization in Tucson. His fieldwork during the past fifteen years has been in Arizona, and his research includes migration and architectural analyses. He has also worked extensively in Southwest Asia. Patrick Lyons is the head of collections and associate curator of archaeology at the Arizona State Museum. For the past fifteen years he has conducted fieldwork in Arizona, and his research has focused on migration, ceramics, the use of oral tradition in archaeology, and the dynamics of ancient social identities.

Coates, Julia (Cherokee), "New Echota Historic Site: Early Cherokee Nationalism in the Nineteenth Century." Julia Coates serves on the Tribal Council of the Cherokee Nation, representing the at-large citizens. An assistant professor of Native American Studies at the University of California, Davis, her research interests include the Cherokee diaspora and Cherokee historical criticism. She was formerly the director of the Cherokee Nation history course.

Coleman, Louis, and **Robert Powell West** (Choctaw), "Removal and Recovery." Louis

Coleman is a native Oklahoman and holds a master's degree from the University of Central Oklahoma. He has written extensively on Choctaw history for *The Chronicles of Oklahoma* and is the author of *Cyrus Byington: Missionary and Choctaw Linguist,* about the missionary who developed the written Choctaw language. Robert Powell West has been a newspaper reporter within the area of the Choctaw Nation of Oklahoma for thirty-five years. He is a staff writer for the *McCurtain Daily Gazette* and enjoys researching and writing about the history and resources of the Red River Valley and the Onachita Mountains.

Conner, Roberta (Confederated Tribes of the Umatilla), "Lewis and Clark National and State Historical Parks." Roberta Conner, Sisaawipam, the director of the Confederated Tribes of the Umatilla museum, Tamástslikt Cultural Institute, is vice president of the National Council of the Lewis and Clark Bicentennial and a leader in the council's Circle of Tribal Advisors. She is a contributor to *Lewis and Clark Through Indian Eyes.*

Cooke, Charlie, Dennis Garcia, Ted Garcia, Jr., and **Mati Waiya,** "Santa Monica Mountains National Recreation Area: Satwiwa Native American Indian Culture Center and Natural Area." Charlie Cooke (Tiq Slow) is descended from the Native peoples who occupied the region surrounding the San Fernando Valley. A leader in his tribe and active in site protection, he is one of the founders of Satwiwa and is chairman of Satwiwa's Advisory Board. Dennis Garcia, a traditional dancer, is involved with preserving and transmitting traditional culture. Ted Garcia, Jr., is president of the Friends of Satwiwa. He is a traditional stone carver and storyteller. Mati Waiya was vice president of the Friends of Satwiwa. He is the founder of the Wishtoyo Foundation, and through it he is involved with many heritage and educational projects, as well

as with protecting land from insensitive development.

Coombs, Linda (Aquinnah Wampanoag), "Plimoth Plantation: The Wampanoag Homesite." Linda Coombs is the associate director of the Wampanoag Indigenous Program and has been with the program for twenty-eight years. She began her career as a Native intern at the Boston Children's Museum in 1974.

Cordell, Linda S., "Ancestral Pueblo Peoples." Linda Cordell is Senior Scholar at the School for Advanced Research, former director of the University Museum, and professor of anthropology at the University of Colorado, a member of the National Academy of Sciences, a recipient of the A. V. Kidder Medal, and the author of *Archaeology of the Southwest.*

Cornell, George L. (Sault Ste. Marie Chippewa), "Marquette Mission Park and Mackinac State Historic Parks." George Cornell is professor of history and director of the Native American Institute at Michigan State University. He served as a trustee of the National Museum of the American Indian. He works with Michigan tribal governments and has published extensively on Great Lakes Indian populations and American Indians and conservation.

Craig, Carol (Yakama Nation), "Fort Simcoe State Park." Carol Craig is the public information manager for the Yakama Nation Fisheries Program, the editor of *Sin-Wit-Ki* (All Life on Earth), and an award-winning journalist. She travels through the Pacific Northwest speaking about treaty rights, tradition, culture, and restoration of natural resources in the Columbia Basin.

Crown, Patricia L., "The Hohokam: People of the Desert." Patricia L. Crown is a professor of anthropology at the University of New Mexico. She is the author of many works on the Hohokam, including "The Hohokam of the American Southwest," and is the coeditor with W. James Judge of *Chaco and Hohokam*.

Culpepper, Brian, and **Curlinda Holiday** (Navajo), "Navajo National Monument. People of the Red Rock Canyon." Brian Culpepper, now in his second decade as a professional archaeologist, has participated in archaeological projects in Minnesota, Wyoming, Montana, New Mexico, and Arizona. He is currently employed by the National Park Service at Navajo National Monument, serving as the supervisory archaeologist. Curlinda Holiday is of the Bitterwater Clan, born for the Towering House People Clan of the Diné. In her eighth year with the NPS at Navajo National Monument, she helps people understand and learn about Ancestral Pueblo Peoples' cliff dwellings as a park ranger interpreter.

Damp, Jonathan E., "El Morro National Monument." Jonathan Damp is the director of the Zuni Heritage and Historic Preservation Office and principal investigator for Zuni Cultural Resource Enterprise.

Darrow, Leland Michael (Fort Sill Apache), "Fort Bowie National Historic Site." Leland Michael Darrow has been the designated tribal historian of the Fort Sill Apache Tribe since 1986. He also serves as secretary-treasurer on the Business Committee of the tribe. He works with the Fort Sill Apache tribal cultural program on history, culture, language, and repatriation issues.

Dean, Jeffrey S., "Tree-Ring and Radiocarbon Dating." Jeffrey S. Dean, professor of dendrochronology and anthropology at the University of Arizona, conducts research on archaeological dating theory and method, southwestern dendroarchaeology, paleoenvironmental reconstruction, and cultural ecology. His publications include "Dendrochronology" and "Chronological Analysis of Tsegi Phase Sites in Northeastern Arizona."

deBuys, William, "Valles Caldera National Preserve." William deBuys was the first chairman of the Valles Caldera Trust, serving from 2001 to 2005. His books include *Enchantment and Exploitation, River of Traps, Salt Dreams, Seeing Things Whole, Valles Caldera,* and *The Walk.* He is a professor of documentary studies at the College of Santa Fe.

DeCory, Jace (Lakota/Cheyenne River Sioux), "Bear Butte State Park: Mato Paha — Sacred Sentinel of the Northern Plains." Jace DeCory is a professor of American Indian studies at Black Hills State University in Spearfish, South Dakota. She is the mother of three sons and grandmother of six. Jace credits Lakota elders for guidance, prayers, and support. *Mitakuye Oyasin* (We are all related).

Deloria, Philip J. (Yankton Dakota descent), "People and Place." Philip J. Deloria is a professor of history and American studies at the University of Michigan and the director of the Program in American Culture. He is the author of *Playing Indian* and *Indians in Unexpected Places* and coeditor with Neal Salisbury of *A Companion to American Indian History.*

Deschampe, Norman (Ojibwe), "Grand Portage National Monument." Norman Deschampe is the chairman of the Grand Portage Band of the Minnesota Chippewa Tribe. He was born and raised in Grand Portage and has been on the Tribal Council for more than twenty years. As an avid fisherman and hunter, he respects the beauty of the tribe's traditional territory.

Deur, Douglas E., "Lava Beds National Monument: Modoc Homelands." Douglas Deur is a research coordinator with the University of Washington's Pacific Northwest Cooperative Ecosystem Studies Unit and adjunct professor of environmental studies at the University of Victoria. His recent publications include *Keeping It Living: Traditions of Plant Use and Cultivation on the Northwest Coast of North America.*

Diaz-Granados, Carol, "Thousand Hills State Park: Images on Stone." Carol Diaz-Granados is an archaeologist in the Anthropology Department at Washington University, specializing in American Indian petroglyphs and pictographs and their iconography. Her publications (with James Duncan) include *The Petroglyphs and Pictographs of Missouri* and *The Rock-Art of Eastern North America, Capturing Images and Insight.*

Dikeman, Wes (Red Hawk) (Abenaki), and **Nicholas Westbrook**, "Fort Ticonderoga: Ticonderoga in Indian Eyes." Wes (Red Hawk) Dikeman, a member of the St. Francis–Sokoki Band of the Abenaki Nation at the Missisquoi homeland, was a Native museum educator-interpreter at Fort Ticonderoga for seven years. He has long been a close student of Abenaki and Eastern Woodland material culture in the Champlain Valley. Nicholas Westbrook has been director of Fort Ticonderoga since 1989. Earlier he directed major exhibitions on the fur trade and Dakota, Ojibwe, and Hidatsa history and culture at the Minnesota Historical Society. Under his leadership, Fort Ticonderoga Museum has revitalized its long commitment to interpreting Indian history.

Downum, Christian E., "The Sinagua." Christian E. Downum is an associate professor of anthropology and the director of the Anthropology Laboratories at Northern Arizona University. His publications include "The Sinagua" and, with Glenn Davis Stone, "Non-Boserupian Ecology and Agricultural Risk: Ethnic Politics and Land Control in the Arid Southwest."

Drake, James D., "King Philip's War." James D. Drake is a professor of history at Metropolitan State College of Denver and the author of *King Philip's War: Civil War in New England, 1675–1676.*

Dugan, Joyce Conseen (Eastern Band of Cherokee Indians), "Kituhwa Mound: Return to Kituhwa Conseen." Joyce Dugan is the first woman elected principal chief (1995–1999) of the Eastern Band of Cherokee Indians. She was superintendent of the Cherokee Central School System and is now director of external affairs and communications at Harrah's Cherokee Casino and Hotel, an enterprise of the Eastern Band of the Cherokee Nation.

Duncan, Barbara R., "Nikwasi Mound." Barbara R. Duncan, education director at the Museum of the Cherokee Indian, works on cultural revitalization projects with the Warriors of Ani-Kituhwa dance group and the Cherokee Potters Guild. She holds a Ph.D. in folklore and folk life. Her publications include *Cherokee Heritage Trails Guidebook* (with Brett H. Riggs) and *Living Stories of the Cherokee.*

Dutschke, Dwight (Ione Band of Miwok Indians), "Indian Grinding Rock State Historic Park." Dwight Dutschke is the Native American heritage coordinator in the California Office of Historic Preservation and the chairman of the Sierra Native American Council, the sponsor of Chaw sé Big Time.

Eder, Jeanne Oyawin (Assiniboine and Sioux tribes), "Medicine Wheel National Historic Landmark" and "The Battle of the Little Bighorn: Dakota Sioux." Jeanne Oyawin Eder was born and raised on the Fort Peck Indian Reservation. She is a tenured associate professor of history at the University of Alaska. Her publications include *American Indian Education: A History* (with Jon Reyhner), *The Dakota Sioux*, and *The Makah*.

Edmunds, R. David (Cherokee), "Indian-White Relations in the United States 1776–1900." David Edmunds is the Watson Professor of American History at the University of Texas at Dallas. His books include *The Shawnee Prophet* and *Tecumseh and the Quest for Leadership*. He has served as a consultant to tribal governments and federal agencies and has held Ford Foundation, Newberry, NEH, and Guggenheim fellowships.

Elders of the Yurok Tribe Culture Committee (Yurok Tribe), "Redwood National and State Parks: Rek-woi, Where the Klamath River Meets the Pacific Ocean, Klamath River Overlook." The Elders of the Yurok Tribe Culture Committee are Glenn Moore (chairperson), Elsie Bacon (vice chairperson), Fern Bates, Blanche Blankenship, Lavina Bowers, Kenneth Childs, Sr., Aileen Figueroa, Jimmie James, Katherine Reed Lundy, Fawn Morris, Archie Thompson, and Georgiana Trull.

Ellis, A. D. (Muscogee Creek) and **Ted Isham** (Muscogee Creek), "Creek Council House Museum." A. D. Ellis, the principal chief of the Muscogee (Creek) Nation of Oklahoma, was born in Pawnee to Doolie Ellis and Nellie Bruner Ellis of Ekvncate, Twin Hills Community. He resides on his mother's original allotment and belongs to the Turtle Clan. His tribal town is Locapoka. Ted Isham is the curator of the Creek Council House Museum in Okmulgee. He teaches the Mvskoke language at Oklahoma State University and works as a language preservationist in the community. Ted Isham is of the Wind Clan and born to the Tulmuchusse tribal town.

Esteves, Pauline (Timbisha Shoshone), "Death Valley National Park: Tüpipüh, Our Timbisha Shoshone Homeland." Pauline Esteves is an elder of the Timbisha Shoshone Tribe and coordinator of its Historic Preservation Advisory Council. She was one of the authors of *The Timbisha Shoshone Tribe and Their Living Valley* and the Homeland Act of Timbisha Shoshone.

Evans, Marlon B. (Tohono O'odham and Aikmel O'Odham), "Mission San Xavier del Bac: O'odham *Himdag*." Marlon Evans graduated from Rochester Institute of Technology and is a senior at the University of Arizona, majoring in creative writing — poetry and media arts. After taking Luci Tapahonso's poetry course, he decided to write poetry for the rest of his life.

Fields, Robert (Pawnee/Iowa/Otoe-Missouria), "Pawnee Indian Museum State Historic Site." Robert Fields is an associate professor of anthropology and Native American studies adjunct professor at the University of Oklahoma. His courses include Indian People of Oklahoma, Native American Artistic Tradition, Contemporary Native American Issues, and Plains Indians; he also does fieldwork in ethnology. He previously taught at Iowa State University.

Fixico, Donald L. (Shawnee, Sac and Fox, Muscogee Creek, and Seminole), "Dade Battlefield Historic State Park." Donald Fixico is the Distinguished Foundation Professor of History at Arizona State University. His publications include numerous articles and several books; the most recent are *The American Indian Mind in a Linear World* and *Daily Life of Native Americans in the Twentieth Century*.

Flores, Dan L., "Palo Duro Canyon State Park." Dan Flores is the A. B. Hammond Professor of Western History at the University of Montana. His books on the American West include *Jefferson and Southwestern Exploration* (1984), *Jour-*

nal of an Indian Trader (1985), *Canyon Visions* (1989), *Caprock Canyonlands* (1990), *Horizontal Yellow* (1999), and *The Natural West* (2001).

Forsman, Leonard (Suquamish), "Old Man House Park at D'Suq'Wub: Ancient Suquamish Winter Village Site." Leonard Forsman is chairman of the Suquamish Tribal Council and an anthropologist/historian who has written articles on the importance of American Indian values in historic preservation and archaeology. He is working with the Suquamish Foundation to help replace Old Man House with a new, traditional building to support Suquamish heritage.

Foster, Lance M. (Iowa Tribe of Kansas and Nebraska), "Blood Run National Historic Landmark." Lance Foster is the former director of Native Rights, Land, and Culture for the Office of Hawaiian Affairs. His publications include "A Closing Circle: Musings on the Ioway Indians in Iowa" and "Tanji na Che: Recovering the Landscape of the Ioway."

Fowler, Catherine S., "Great Basin Indigenous Places." Catherine S. Fowler, the Foundation Professor of Anthropology emerita, University of Nevada, Reno, works with Great Basin indigenous peoples on linguistic, cultural, and environmental issues. She is a research associate of the National Museum of Natural History and is on the Board of Trustees, National Museum of the American Indian.

Garate, Donald T., "Tumacácori National Historical Park: The O'odham and the Missions." Donald T. Garate is chief of interpretation and historian at Tumacácori National Historical Park. His publications include *Juan Bautista de Anza: Basque Explorer in the New World*.

Gibson, Jon L., "Poverty Point State Historic Site." Jon L. Gibson is an archaeologist specializing in the study of ancient cultures in the Lower Mississippi Valley and other parts of the southeastern United States. He is the author of *The Ancient Mounds of Poverty Point: Place of Rings* and coeditor, with Philip J. Carr, of *Signs of Power*.

Gilbert, Matthew Sakiestewa (Hopi), "Montezuma Castle National Monument, Montezuma Well, and Tuzigoot National Monument." Matthew Sakiestewa Gilbert received his Ph.D. in Native American history from the University of California, Riverside. He is an enrolled member of the Hopi Tribe from the village of Upper Moencopi, Arizona, and is an assistant professor of American Indian studies and history at the University of Illinois at Urbana-Champaign.

Gray, Jim (Osage), "Osage Tribal Museum." Chief Gray was elected principal chief in 2002 under the tribe's old form of government, one of the biggest upsets in modern tribal history. He was elected principal chief under the new constitution and inaugurated on July 1, 2006. The two elections reflect the electorate's support for his leadership.

Green, Richard, "Chickasaw Council House Museum and Chickasaw Nation Capitol." Richard Green has been the tribal historian since 1994. He founded the *Journal of Chickasaw History* and was the editor of the first five volumes. He is the author of *Te Ata: Chickasaw Storyteller, American Treasure*.

Haefeli, Evan, and **Kevin Sweeney**, "Deerfield." Evan Haefeli is an assistant professor of history at Columbia University. Kevin Sweeney is professor of history and American studies at Amherst College. Haefeli and Sweeney are coauthors of *Captors and Captives: The 1704 French and Indian Raid on Deerfield*.

Harjo, Suzan Shown (Cheyenne and Hodulgee Muscogee), "Sacred Places and Visitor Protocols." Suzan Shown Harjo — the Morning Star Institute's president, a National Museum of the American Indian founding trustee, and an *Indian Country Today* columnist — has developed federal laws for Native sacred places, religious freedom, repatriation, cultural property, and the return of 1 million acres of Native lands.

Harlan, B. Lynne (Eastern Band of Cherokee Indians), and **Tom Hatley**, "Oconaluftee Indian Village: The Eastern Band of Cherokee Indians." B. Lynne Harlan holds a B.A. in history from the University of North Carolina at Asheville. She is the author of "Museum Perspectives from Within," in *Mending the Circle: A Native American Guide to Repatriation,* and coauthor, with Joyce Dugan, of *The Cherokees.* Tom Hatley is the Sequoyah Distinguished Professor at Western Carolina University, where he teaches in the Cherokee Studies Program. His publications include *The Dividing Paths: Cherokees and South Carolinians through the Revolutionary Era.*

Hart, Lawrence (Cheyenne-Arapaho Tribes of Oklahoma), "Washita Battlefield National Historic Site." Lawrence Hart, executive director of the Cheyenne Cultural Center, is one of four principal peace chiefs in the Council of Forty-Four. He replaced his grandfather John P. Hart, son of Afraid of Beavers. Cheyenne warriors who become peace chiefs follow instructions of Sweet Medicine. He was a Marine Corps jet fighter pilot.

Hauptman, Laurence M., "American Indians and the Civil War." Laurence Hauptman is the SUNY Distinguished Professor of History at the State University of New York at New Paltz. His publications include *Between Two Fires: American Indians in the Civil War* and, with L. Gordon McLester, *Chief Daniel Bread and the Oneida Nation of Indians of Wisconsin.*

Haworth, John (Cherokee), "Historic Battery Park and the Smithsonian National Museum of the American Indian's George Gustav Heye Center." John Haworth, director of the George Gustav Heye Center, was a Revson Fellow at Columbia University, from which he received his M.B.A. He was an assistant commissioner of the New York City Department of Cultural Affairs, and he serves on the boards of Americans for the Arts and the Museum Association of New York.

Hobson, Geary (Cherokee-Arkansas Quapaw), "Arkansas Post National Memorial." Geary Hobson is a professor of Native American literature at the University of Oklahoma. He is the author of the novel *The Last of the Ofos* and other books. He grew up in rural Desha County, Arkansas, almost within shouting distance of the Arkansas Post National Memorial.

Hood, J. Edward, "Tantiusques." Edward Hood is director of the Department of Research, Collections, and Library at Old Sturbridge Village. He directed archaeological excavations at the Crowd site and has done extensive research on the site and the nearby graphite mine.

Horse Capture, George (A'aninin Gros Ventre), "Pictograph Cave State Park." George Horse Capture, from the Fort Belknap Indian Reservation, was curator at the Plains Indian Museum for eleven years and senior counselor to the director of the National Museum of the American Indian for six years. He received an honorary doctorate from Montana State University.

Hoxie, Frederick E., "Reformers." Frederick Hoxie is the Swanlund Professor of History at the University of Illinois, Urbana-Champaign. He is the author of *A Final Promise: The Campaign to Assimilate the Indians* and other works and coauthor, with David Edmunds and Neal Salisbury, of *The People: A History of Native America.*

Hunter, Andrea A. (Osage), "Osage Village State Historic Site." Andrea A. Hunter, professor of anthropology at Northern Arizona University, is an archaeologist whose research includes Osage pre/protohistory. Her publications include "Paleoethnobotany of the Osage and Missouri Indians" and the forthcoming *Wa-zhá-zhe (Osage) Culture: Chronicles and Consequences of the European Invasion* and *Wa-zhá-zhe (Osage) Identity? We Came from the Stars.*

Hunter, Wilson, Jr. (Navajo), "Canyon de Chelly National Monument: Telling Its Story." Wilson Hunter, Jr., is the chief of interpretation at Canyon de Chelly National Monument. His clan is the Coyote Pass Clan, and he was born for the Bitter Water Clan. He received the 1991 Freeman Tilden Award and is the author of *Canyon de Chelly: The Continuing Story.*

Ironstrack, George (mihtohseenia — Miami) and **Scott M. Shoemaker** (mihtoseenia — Miami), "Forks of the Wabash Historic Park: *alikalakonci wiipicahkionki* (Beyond the Place of Flint)." George Ironstrack is an enrolled member of the Miami Tribe of Oklahoma. He has been involved in Miami language and culture revitalization efforts since 1996 and helps organize and run children's language programs in Oklahoma. He received an M.A. in U.S. history from Miami University in 2006. Scott Shoemaker is an enrolled member of the Miami Nation of Indiana and is of the Meshingomesia Band. He is a Ph.D. candidate in American studies at the University of Minnesota. He works in revitalizing the Miami language and is chair of the Miami Nation of Indiana Language Committee.

Ivey, James E., "Salinas Pueblo Missions National Monument." James E. Ivey is a research historian with the National Park Service. He is the author of *In the Midst of a Loneliness: The Architectural History of the Salinas Missions* and "Convento Kivas in the Missions of New Mexico."

Jackson, Loretta (Hualapai), "Lake Mead National Recreation Area: Wikame — Spirit Mountain: The Hualapai Perspective on Creation." Loretta Jackson is the tribal historic preservation officer. She is dedicated to cultural resource management and protection, and she advocates for sacred site protection on Hualapai ancestral homelands. Educating the public is part of that process. *Han-kyu* (It is good).

Jemison, G. Peter (Seneca), and **Michael J. Galban** (Washoe Paiute), "Ganondagan State Historic Site: Ganondagan, the Town of Peace." Peter Jemison, a member of the Heron Clan of the Seneca Nation of Indians, is the historic site manager of Ganondagan. He is an artist, a curator, a consultant on Native American history and art, and the coeditor of *Treaty of Canandaigua, 1794.* Michael Galban has worked in the interpretive program at Ganondagan for fifteen years and has dedicated his life to preserving Haudenosaunee history and material culture. He has been a historical consultant and an expert on historic Native clothing and material culture on programs for the History Channel and PBS.

Johnson, John R., "Channel Islands National Park." John R. Johnson is head curator of anthropology at the Santa Barbara Museum of Natural History specializing in the culture and history of California Indians, especially Chumash peoples. His publications include "Ethnohistoric Reflections of Cruzeño Chumash Society."

Jones, Anne Trinkle, "Petrified Forest National Park." Anne Trinkle Jones is the National Park Service cultural resources coordinator for the Colorado Plateau Cooperative Ecosystem Studies Unit. She was the first park archaeologist at Grand Canyon, then conducted research at Petrified Forest National Park for twenty years. Her publications include *Stalking the Past: Discovering Prehistory at Petrified Forest.*

Jones, Matthew (Kiowa/Otoe-Missouria), "Van Meter State Park: Missouria Village." Matthew Jones is a member of the Otoe-Missouria Tribe of Oklahoma. He is a lecturer at the University of Nebraska — Lincoln. He has a master's degree in anthropology and is a published scholar, with articles in *Wicazo Sa Review* and *Native America in the Twentieth Century: An Encyclopedia.*

Judge, W. James, "Chaco Culture National Historical Park: The Place and Its People." W. James Judge is professor emeritus of anthropology at Fort Lewis College and was the director (1977–1985) of the NPS Chaco Project. With Patricia L. Crown, he is the coeditor of *Chaco and Hohokam: Prehistoric Regional Systems in the American Southwest.*

Kantner, John, "Seven Great House Communities of the Chacoan Era." John Kantner is vice president for academic and institutional advancement at the School of Advanced Research and was formerly associate professor of anthropology at Georgia State University. His publications include *Great House Communities across the Chacoan Landscape* (with N. M. Mahoney, coeditor) and *Ancient Puebloan Southwest.*

Kavanagh, Thomas W., "Adobe Walls." Thomas Kavanagh, Ph.D., currently holds a dual appointment at Seton Hall University in the Sociology and Anthropology Department and the Seton Hall University Museum. He has written extensively on Comanche history and ethnology. His book *The Comanches: A History* has been recommended by the Comanche Language and Cultural Preservation Committee.

Kelly, John E., "Cahokia Mounds State Historic Site." John E. Kelly, a senior lecturer in the De-

partment of Anthropology at Washington University in St. Louis, has conducted research at Cahokia and the surrounding region for more than thirty years. His publications include "Redefining Cahokia: Principles and Elements of Community Organization."

Kennedy, Frances H., editor of and principal contributor to *American Indian Places.* Frances Kennedy became interested in American Indian places in New Mexico, where she was born. Her publications include *The Civil War Battlefield Guide* and *Dollar$ and Sense of Battlefield Preservation* (with Douglas R. Porter).

Kessell, John L., "Pecos National Historical Park." John L. Kessell is a professor emeritus, Department of History, and founding editor of the Vargas Project at the University of New Mexico. His publications include *Kiva, Cross, and Crown: The Pecos Indians and New Mexico, 1540–1840* and *Spain in the Southwest.*

Kidwell, Clara Sue (Chippewa/Choctaw), "So Far and Yet So Near." Clara Sue Kidwell is director of the American Indian Center, University of North Carolina at Chapel Hill. She was assistant director of cultural resources at the National Museum of the American Indian. She has published "Ethnoastronomy as the Key to Human Intellectual Development and Social Organization."

King, Adam, "Etowah Indian Mounds Historic Site." Adam King is an archaeologist in the University of South Carolina's Savannah River Archaeological Research Program, a division of the South Carolina Institute of Archaeology and Anthropology. He is the author of *Etowah: The Political History of a Chiefdom Capital.*

King, Duane, "Trail of Tears National Historic Trail: The Forced Removal of the Cherokee." Duane King, the executive director of the Gilcrease Museum in Tulsa, was formerly the executive director of the Southwest Museum of the Autry National Center and the assistant director of the National Museum of the American Indian. He is the author of more than seventy-five publications on Native American subjects.

Kuwanwisiwma, Leigh (Hopi), "Taawa Park: Stories of the Ancient Hopi." Leigh Kuwanwisiwma is the director of the Hopi Cultural Preservation Office and focuses on having the Hopi Tribe conduct its ethnographic research and publish its reports. He works with universities and museums to facilitate interaction between the Hopi Tribe and academics.

LaDuke, Winona (Ojibwe), "*Manoominike: Making Wild Rice.*" Winona LaDuke lives on the White Earth Reservation in northern Minnesota. She is the director of the White Earth Land Recovery Project and the program director for the foundation Honor the Earth. Her publications include *All Our Relations, The Winona LaDuke Reader, Last Standing Woman,* and *In the Sugarbush.*

LaPena, Vince (Nomtipom Wintu), "Ancil Hoffman County Park: Effie Yeaw Nature Center — The Nisenan Maidu Lived Here." Vince LaPena is a Wintu Indian from Northern California and is a park interpretive specialist with the Sacramento County Regional Parks and the cultural programs director at the Effie Yeaw Nature Center. He has spent many years among local tribal people and is active in cultural preservation.

LaPier, Rosalyn (Blackfeet/Little Shell Chippewa), "Buffalo Jumps." Rosalyn LaPier, a Ph.D. candidate in history at the University of Montana, works for the Piegan Institute on the Blackfeet Reservation in northwest Montana. She researches and writes about Blackfeet history, language, and ethnobotany.

LeBeau, Sebastian C. II (Cheyenne River Sioux Tribe), "Agate Fossil Beds National Monument: *A 'bekiya wama 'k'aśk'aŋ s'e* — Animal Bones Brutally Scattered About." Bronco LeBeau is an Itazipco (Without Bow) Lakota of the Tiospaye Nape Luta (Red Hand Band). His CRM company is Pahin Hunkankan (Porcupine Tales). He is a traditional Lakota spiritual leader and oral historian and is a Ph.D. candidate at the University of Minnesota in Minneapolis.

Lee, Georgia, and **William D. Hyder,** "Carrizo Plain National Monument: Painted Rock." Georgia Lee is a Ph.D. archaeologist who has been studying rock art sites for over thirty-five years. Although much of her research has been in the Pacific Islands, her initial field of study was the art of the Chumash Indians. Lee's publications include *The Chumash Cosmos* and, with Edward Stasack, *Spirit of Place.* William Hyder is a graduate-trained archaeologist and photographer with twenty-five years of experience in rock art studies. Along with Georgia Lee, he has recorded rock art sites throughout California for the National Park Service and California State Parks. Hyder's publications include *Rock Art and Archaeology in Santa Barbara County, California.*

Lekson, Stephen H., "The Chaco Meridian." Stephen H. Lekson is curator of anthropology at the University of Colorado Museum in Boulder. He is the author of *Great Pueblo Architecture of Chaco Canyon* and *The Chaco Meridian.*

Lepper, Bradley T., "Early Mound Builders." Bradley T. Lepper is a curator of archaeology at the Ohio Historical Society. His publications include *People of the Mounds: Ohio's Hopewell Culture,* "Tracking Ohio's Great Hopewell Road," and *Ohio Archaeology.*

Leverett, Robert T., "Mohawk Trail State Forest: The Mohawk Trail." Robert Leverett is the cofounder, executive director, and principal forest ecologist for the Friends of the Mohawk Trail State Forest. He is the coauthor, with Bruce Kershner, of *The Sierra Club Guide to the Ancient Forests of the Northeast.*

Lindauer, Owen, "Tonto National Monument." Owen Lindauer is the supervisor of the archaeological studies program at the Texas Department of Transportation. He conducted field investigations in the Tonto Basin while he was a research assistant professor in the Department of Anthropology at Arizona State University.

Lipe, William D., "Mesa Verde National Park." William Lipe is professor emeritus of anthropology at Washington State University and is on the board of the Crow Canyon Archaeological Center. From 1995 to 1997 he was president of the Society for American Archaeology. His publications include "The Mesa Verde Region: Chaco's Northern Neighbor," in *In Search of Chaco.*

Lister, Florence C., "Chacoans Away from Home: Chacoan Outlying Communities." Florence C. Lister, research associate at the Crow Canyon Archaeological Center, is a specialist in the history of southwestern archaeology and Spanish-tradition ceramics in the Americas. Her most recent book is *Troweling Through Time: The First Century of Mesa Verdean Archaeology.*

Littlefield, Daniel F., Jr., "Fort Smith National Historic Site: The Fort Smith Council, 1865." Daniel Littlefield is director of the Sequoyah Research Center, which houses the American Native Press Archives and oversees the J. W. Wiggins Collection of Native American Art. He has published more than twenty books and scores of scholarly articles. Littlefield is a member of the Oklahoma Historians Hall of Fame.

Livermont, Glen H. (Oglala Sioux), "Pipestone National Monument." Glen Livermont is the

chief of visitor services and protection at Pipestone National Monument.

Lone Hill, Karen (Oglala Lakota), "Devils Tower National Monument: Mato Tipila Paha — The Hill of the Bear's Lodge." Karen Lone Hill is the chair of the Lakota Studies Department at Oglala Lakota College. She is the author of *The Sioux* and *Lakota Language,* the coauthor of *The Pine Ridge Indian Reservation: Yesterday and Today* and *Shaping Survival,* and a contributor to the *Encyclopedia of North American Indians.*

Lowery, Malinda Maynor (Lumbee), "Town Creek Indian Mound." Malinda Maynor Lowery is a documentary filmmaker and assistant professor of history at Harvard University. Her films include *In the Light of Reverence* (2001), *Sounds of Faith* (1997), and *Real Indian* (1996). She is writing a book about Lumbee identity and federal recognition in the twentieth century.

Madalena, Joshua (Jemez), "Jemez State Monument." Joshua Madalena was the superintendent at Jemez State Monument and the commissioner of District 5, Sandoval County. For fiscal year 2008 he is the first lieutenant governor of Jemez Pueblo. He specializes in the Native American Graves Protection and Repatriation Act (NAGPRA) and cultural and oral history preservation.

Madsen, David B., "The Fremont." David Madsen is the retired Utah state archaeologist. He is an adjunct research professor at the Texas Archaeological Research Laboratory, the Desert Research Institute, Reno, and the Mercyhurst Archaeological Institute, Erie. He divides his research time between the eastern Great Basin and western China/Tibet. His publications include *Exploring the Fremont.*

Mainfort, Robert C., Jr., "Pinson Mounds State Archaeological Park." Robert C. Mainfort, Jr., is the sponsored research administrator at the Arkansas Archeological Survey and professor of anthropology at the University of Arkansas. He is the coeditor, with David G. Anderson, of *The Woodland Southeast,* and coauthor, with David S. Brose and C. Wesley Cowan, of *Societies in Eclipse.*

Mallickan, Diana (Nez Perce), and **Allen Pinkham** (Nez Perce), "Nez Perce National Historical Park: The Nez Perce Since 1876." Diana Mallickan, an NPS ranger at the park, was a coeditor of *The Nez Perce Nation Divided,* volume 2 of *Voices from Nez Perce Country,* and assisted the Nez Perce Tribe in *Treaties: The Nez Perce Perspective.* She wrote the introduction to *Memorial of the Nez Perce Indians,* a 1911 record of the allotment period. Allen Pinkham, historian and storyteller, recently completed eight years on the National Council of the Lewis and Clark Bicentennial with the Circle of Tribal Advisors. He was coauthor, with Dan Landeen, of *Salmon and His People* and was one of nine authors of *Lewis and Clark Through Indian Eyes.*

Margolin, Malcolm, "Native Californians." Malcolm Margolin is the publisher of Heyday Books in Berkeley, with over twenty books in print on California Indian history and arts. He is the founder and publisher of *News from Native California,* a quarterly magazine about California Indian culture, and author of *The Way We Lived: California Indian Stories, Songs, and Reminiscences.*

Marquardt, William H., "The Calusa." William Marquardt is a curator in archaeology, Florida Museum of Natural History. He has done archaeological research in New Mexico, Kentucky, South Carolina, Georgia, Florida, and Burgundy, France. Since 1985 he has directed the Southwest Florida Project, which focuses on the ancient domain of the Calusa Indians.

Martin, Phillip (Choctaw), "Natchez Trace Parkway: Choctaw Agency." Phillip Martin served as the democratically elected chief of the Mississippi Band of Choctaw Indians from 1980 through 2006. While he was chief, the tribe became a model for economic development in Indian Country. The Mississippi Band of Choctaw today has a tribal population of more than 10,000, with a thriving and prosperous traditional culture.

Masayumptewa, Lloyd (Hopi), "Navajo National Monument: *Hisat'katsi* (Hopi Life in the Past) at Betatakin (Talastima), Keet Seel (Kawestima), and Inscription House (Tsu'ovi)." Lloyd Masayumptewa is a member of the Hopi Tribe from Old Oraibi (Orayvi) village and is of the Coyote Clan. He is the manager of the Vanishing Treasures Ruins Preservation/Archaeology Program at the Flagstaff Area National Monuments. He has worked for the National Park Service for seven years doing ruins preservation work.

Matheson, Quanah (Coeur d'Alene), "Old Mission State Park." Quanah Matheson is the cultural resource manager/tribal historic preservation officer of the Coeur d'Alene Tribe. His Indian name means "He is a good cedar man." He resides on the Coeur d'Alene Reservation and is of the St. Joe Band of the Schi'ntsu'umsh.

McBride, Bunny, and **Harald E. L. Prins,** "Acadia National Park: Asticou's Island Domain." Bunny McBride is an award-winning author and adjunct lecturer in anthropology at Kansas State University. Her books include *Women of the Dawn* and *Molly Spotted Elk: A Penobscot in Paris.* She has worked on a range of issues and projects with Maine tribes since 1981. Harald Prins is Distinguished Professor of Anthropology at Kansas State University. Born in the Netherlands, he did fieldwork among North and South American Indians and has long been active in Native rights issues. His numerous publications include award-winning documentaries and books, including *The Mi'kmaq: Resistance, Accommodation, and Cultural Survival.*

McEwan, Bonnie G., "Mission San Luis." Bonnie G. McEwan is the executive director of Mission San Luis in Tallahassee. Her publications include *The Apalachee Indians and Mission San Luis* (with John H. Hann) and *Indians of the Greater Southeast: Historical Archaeology and Ethnohistory.*

McKay, Neil (Cantemaza) (Spirit Lake Dakota), "Fort Snelling State Park." Neil (Cantemaza) McKay is an enrolled member of the Spirit Lake Dakota Nation. He is the Dakota language instructor at the University of Minnesota and is currently pursuing an M.A. in second languages and cultures with a focus on indigenous language immersion and indigenous language acquisition.

McKenna, Peter J., "Aztec Ruins National Monument." Peter J. McKenna is an archaeologist with the Bureau of Indian Affairs, Department of Interior, and has conducted research at Chaco and Aztec Ruins. He is the coauthor, with John R. Stein, of *An Archeological Reconnaissance of a Late Bonito Phase Occupation Near Aztec Ruins National Monument, New Mexico.*

McManamon, Francis P., "Cape Cod National Seashore: The Nauset Area." Francis P. McManamon is the National Park Service chief archaeologist. His areas of professional expertise include North American archaeology and public archaeology. His publications include "The Indian Neck Ossuary" and *The Antiquities Act: A Century of American Archaeology, Historic Preservation, and Nature Conservation.*

Medicine Crow, Joseph (Crow), "The Battle of the Little Bighorn: Crow." Joseph Medicine Crow was born in Montana in 1913 and raised by grandparents who knew Plains Indian life before the reservation. From them he acquired training in Indian ways and customs of that time. He received an honorary doctorate from the University of Southern California.

Meltzer, David J., "Places of the First Americans." David Meltzer is the Henderson-Morrison Professor at Southern Methodist University and director of the Quest Archaeological Research Program, investigating North America's first inhabitants. Among his more than 125 publications are the books *Search for the First Americans, Folsom,* and a forthcoming volume on the peopling of the Americas.

Milanich, Jerald T., "Florida's Native American Heritage." Jerald T. Milanich is curator in archaeology at the Florida Museum of Natural History. He is the author of books on Florida and southeastern Indians, including *Laboring in the Fields of the Lord — Spanish Missions and Southeastern Indians* and *Florida's Indians from Ancient Times to the Present.*

Miller, James V. (Choctaw), "Sellars Farm State Archaeological Area." James Miller is a member of the Choctaw Nation of Oklahoma, president of the area's Friends group, a retired Lebanon High School teacher, and curator of the Lebanon Museum. He is the coauthor, with Kevin E. Smith, of *Speaking with the Ancestors: Mississippian Stone Statuary of the Tennessee-Cumberland Style.*

Miller, Jay (Delaware), "Schoenbrunn Village." Jay Miller is the American Indian studies coordinator at Ohio State University. He has taught in the Midwest, Northwest (both sides of the U.S.-Canada border), and Southeast, publishing dozens of articles and ten books in anthropology, linguistics, and American Indian studies, including a chapter in *The Native Americans.*

Mitchem, Jeffrey M., "Parkin Archeological State Park." Jeffrey M. Mitchem is the station archaeologist for the Arkansas Archeological Survey at Parkin Archeological State Park. His articles on early Native American/Spanish contact include "Investigations of the Possible Remains of de Soto's Cross at Parkin."

Mohawk, John C. (Seneca), "Fort Stanwix, Oriskany Battlefield, and Newtown Battlefield." John Mohawk (d. 2006) was associate professor of American studies and director of indigenous studies at the State University of New York at Buffalo. A noted Native philosopher, his books include *War Against the Seneca* and *Utopian Legacies: A History of Conquest and Oppression in the Western World.*

Montgomery, John L., "Blackwater Draw, Locality 1 Archaeological Site: People and Water." John Montgomery is the director of the Blackwater Draw Museum and Blackwater Locality No. 1. He also is the chair of the Anthropology and Applied Archaeology Department at Eastern New Mexico University, Portales.

Myers, Larry (Pomo), "Our Final Place." Larry Myers is the executive secretary of the Native American Heritage Commission of the State of California.

Nelson, Margaret C., and **Michael W. Diehl,** "The People of the Mimbres Mogollon Region." Margaret Nelson is a professor of anthropology at Arizona State University. In collaboration with Michelle Hegmon, she directs the Eastern Mimbres Archaeological Research Project. Her publications include *Mimbres During the Twelfth Century: Abandonment, Continuity and Reorganization.* Michael W. Diehl is a research

director at Desert Archaeology. His publications include *Early Pithouse Villages of the Mimbres Valley and Beyond* (with Steven A. LeBlanc), *Hierarchies in Action: Cui Bono?, Archaeological Investigations of the Early Agricultural Period Settlement at the Base of A-Mountain, Tucson,* and journal articles.

Ortiz, Beverly R., with **Carol Bachmann** (Mutsun Ohlone), **T. Michael Bonillas** (Rumsien/Mutsun Ohlone), **Theodore W. Bonillas** (Rumsien Ohlone), **Lisa Carrier** (Mutsun Ohlone), **Mary Carrier** (Mutsun Ohlone), **Roberta Chew** (Mutsun Ohlone), **Ramona Garibay** (Jalquin Ohlone/Bay Miwok), **Sabrina Garibay** (Jalquin Ohlone/Bay Miwok), **Judy Hall** (Mutsun Ohlone), and **Ruth Orta** (Jalquin Ohlone/Bay Miwok), "Coyote Hills Regional Park." Beverly R. Ortiz, the park naturalist, is the coordinator of a program in which Ohlone individuals of varied tribal heritage share their history and cultures with the public. She is an ethnographic consultant and a contributing editor at *News from Native California* and coauthor with Julia F. Parker of *It Will Live Forever: Traditional Yosemite Indian Acorn Preparation.* The Ohlone who work at the park conduct year-round open houses at a Tuibun Ohlone village site, with workshops, demonstrations, lectures, and other special programs. They join with other Ohlone at Coyote Hills for an annual Gathering of Ohlone Peoples, now in its fifteenth year.

Ostler, Jeffrey, "Rosebud Battlefield State Park." Jeffrey Ostler teaches history at the University of Oregon. He is the author of *The Plains Sioux and U.S. Colonialism from Lewis and Clark to Wounded Knee.*

Parkman, E. Breck, "Olompali State Historic Park." E. Breck Parkman is a senior California state archaeologist, a research associate at the

Archaeological Research Facility, University of California at Berkeley, and the director of the UNESCO-sponsored Fort Ross Global Village Project, which connects American and Russian students in the study of archaeology, history, and ecology.

Parrish, Otis (Kashaya Pomo), "Fort Ross State Historic Park." Otis Parrish is a member of the Kashaya Pomo Tribe and the author of "The First People," in *Fort Ross*. He is a consultant to the Native American Health Center in Oakland.

Pauketat, T. R., "The Rise and Fall of the Mississippians." Tim Pauketat is an archaeologist and professor of anthropology at the University of Illinois in Urbana-Champaign. He is the author of, most recently, *Ancient Cahokia and the Mississippians* and, for children, *Cahokia Mounds,* and the coeditor of *North American Archaeology.*

Pepper Henry, James (Kaw/Muscogee), "Allegawaho Memorial Heritage Park." James Pepper Henry, a member of the Kaw Nation of Oklahoma, is the director of the Anchorage Museum at Rasmuson Center. He was previously associate director for community and constituent services at the National Museum of the American Indian. He actively promotes the continuum of traditional and cultural lifeways of indigenous peoples.

Perry, Kirk (Chickasaw), "Natchez Trace Parkway: A Glimpse of Chickasaw Nation History from the Chickasaw Village Site." Kirk Perry is the administrator of the Chickasaw Nation Division of Heritage Preservation. The division, which operates the museums, library, and archives and deals with the Native American Graves Protection and Repatriation Act and historic preservation, is building a new, world-class cultural center.

Peters, John A., Jr. (Mashpee Wampanoag), "Old Indian Meetinghouse." Jim Peters is the ex-

ecutive director of the Massachusetts Commission on Indian Affairs.

Peterson, Dennis Anthony, "Spiro Mounds Archaeological Center." Dennis Peterson has been the manager and resident archaeologist for the Spiro Mounds Archaeological Center since 1985. He was part of the Oklahoma Archeological Survey in 1979. He is an author of *An Archeological Survey of the Spiro Vicinity, LeFlore County, Oklahoma.*

Pinkham, Josiah (Nez Perce), "Nez Perce National Historical Park: The Nez Perce Before 1876." Josiah Pinkham is an ethnographer in the Nez Perce Tribe Cultural Resource Program.

Pitt, Louie, Jr. (Confederated Tribes of Warm Springs), "Columbia Hills State Park." Louie Pitt, Jr., is director of government affairs and planning for the Confederated Tribes of Warm Springs and has served on the Columbia River Gorge Commission. His parents taught that lands relating to our way of life need continued care and protection, including lands off the reservation.

Pluckhahn, Thomas J., "Kolomoki Mounds Historic Park." Thomas J. Pluckhahn is assistant professor of anthropology at the University of South Florida. He is the author of *Kolomoki: Settlement, Ceremony, and Status in the Deep South,* A.D. 350 to 750, and coeditor, with Robbie F. Ethridge, of *Light on the Path: The Anthropology and History of the Southeastern Indians.*

Potter, Tracy, "Fort Abraham Lincoln State Park: On-a-Slant Village." Tracy Potter is the president and executive director of the Fort Abraham Lincoln Foundation and a North Dakota state senator. He is the author of *Sheheke: Mandan Indian Diplomat.*

Powers, Robert P., "Bandelier National Monument." Robert P. Powers, a retired supervisory archaeologist with the National Park Service, was the director of the Bandelier Archeological Survey and a member of the NPS Chaco Canyon research team. He is the editor of *The Peopling of Bandelier: New Insights from the Archaeology of the Pajarito Plateau.*

Pyle, Gregory E. (Choctaw), "Choctaw Nation Tribal Capitol: Tushka Homma." Gregory E. Pyle is chief of the Choctaw Nation of Oklahoma. Under his leadership, accomplishments have been numerous. Newly constructed facilities include a hospital, the Diabetes Wellness Center, two new clinics, Hospitality House, Recovery Center and Women's Treatment Center, homes for elderly, community centers, and child development centers.

Rettig, Donald R., Jr., and **G. Michael Pratt,** "Fallen Timbers Battlefield and Fort Miamis National Historic Site." Donald R. Rettig is the director of cultural and historical programs for the Metropolitan Park District of the Toledo Area, the managing agency of Fallen Timbers Battlefield and Fort Miamis National Historic Site. Michael Pratt is dean of graduate studies at Heidelberg College and professor of anthropology at its Center for Historic and Military Archaeology. His efforts led to the discovery of the battlefield site. His publications include "The Battle of Fallen Timbers: An Eyewitness Perspective."

Richter, Daniel K., "Eastern North America." Daniel K. Richter is the Richard S. Dunn Director of the McNeil Center for Early American Studies and professor of history at the University of Pennsylvania. His books include *Facing East from Indian Country* and *The Ordeal of the Longhouse.*

Riggs, Brett H., "Unicoi Turnpike Trail: Nunna'hi-tsune'ga." Brett Riggs, a staff archaeologist with the Research Laboratories of Archaeology

at the University of North Carolina at Chapel Hill, formerly served as archaeologist for the Eastern Band of Cherokee Indians. His publications include works on Cherokee basketry and pottery and, with Barbara R. Duncan, the *Cherokee Heritage Trails Guidebook.*

Robertson, Paul M., "Badlands National Park: Mako Sica and the Oglala Lakota." Paul Robertson chairs the Humanities and Social Sciences Department at Oglala Lakota College. His publications include *Power of the Land* (2002) and, with Miriam Jorgensen and Carrie Garrow, "Indigenizing Evaluation Research: How Lakota Methodologies Are Helping Raise the Tipi in the Oglala Sioux Nation."

Rountree, Helen C., "Colonial National Historical Park: Jamestowne and the Powhatan Indians." Helen Rountree, professor emerita of anthropology at Old Dominion University, has worked with Virginia Indian tribes and researched their history since 1969. Her books include *The Powhatan Indians of Virginia, Pocahontas's People, John Smith's Chesapeake Voyages, 1607–1609,* and *Eastern Shore Indians of Virginia and Maryland, Before and After Jamestown.*

Salisbury, Neal, "Indian-White Relations in North America Before 1776." Neal Salisbury is a professor of history at Smith College. His publications include *A Companion to American Indian History* (editor, with Philip J. Deloria); *Manitou and Providence: Indians, Europeans, and the Making of New England, 1500–1643*; and, with R. David Edmunds and Frederick E. Hoxie, *The People: A History of Native Americans.*

Sando, Joe S. (Jemez Pueblo), "The History of the Pueblo Indians." Joe S. Sando was born and raised at Jemez Pueblo. He has held teaching and research positions at three universities and was director of the Institute for Pueblo Studies and Research at the Indian Pueblo Cultural

Center. His publications include *Pueblo Nations* and *Nee Hemish: The History of Jemez Pueblo.*

Sandoval, Nicolasa I. (Chumash), "La Purísima Mission State Historic Park." From the Chumash community on the Santa Ynez Indian Reservation in California, Dr. Sandoval has dedicated her personal and professional life to increasing access to artistic, cultural, and educational resources. She is a lecturer at the University of California at Santa Barbara and a consultant.

Saubel, Katherine Siva (Mountain Cahuilla), and Paul Apodaca (Navajo-Mixton), "Founding a Tribal Museum: The Malki Museum." Katherine Siva Saubel is founder/chair of the Malki Museum, tribal chairwoman of Los Coyotes Indian Reservation, and an inductee in the Southern California American Indian Hall of Fame and the National Women's Hall of Fame. She is coauthor with Lowell John Bean of *Temalpakh: Cahuilla Indian Knowledge and Usage of Plants.* Paul Apodaca is a professor at Chapman University, an adjunct professor at UCLA, the former curator of the Bowers Museum, holder of the Mary Smith Lockwood Medal for Education, an inductee in the Southern California American Indian Hall of Fame, and editor of the *Journal of California and Great Basin Anthropology.*

Schaafsma, Polly, "Petroglyph National Monument." Polly Schaafsma is a research associate at the Museum of Indian Arts and Culture/Laboratory of Anthropology in Santa Fe. She is the author of *Rock Art in New Mexico* and *Warrior, Shield, and Star* and the editor of *New Perspectives on Pottery Mound Pueblo.*

Scheffler, Lenor A. (Mdewakanton Dakota, Lower Sioux Indian Community in Minnesota), "The Dakota in Minnesota 1851–1862." Lenor Scheffler grew up in the area of the Dakota Uprising and heard stories about her ancestors.

Through her work as a lawyer representing Indian tribes, she has read treaties and other historic documents and learned about the survival, perseverance, wisdom, and courage of tribal people across the United States.

Scheirbeck, Helen Maynor (Lumbee), "University of North Carolina at Pembroke: A Part of Lumbee Indian Heritage." Helen Scheirbeck was the assistant director for public programs, National Museum of the American Indian. Her work includes Indian education, early childhood development, museum programs, and tribal colleges. She holds an Ed.D. from Virginia Polytechnic Institute.

Schier, Rhonda Buell, "Mount Rushmore National Memorial: Paha Sapa — Ancestral Homeland of the Lakota." Rhonda Buell Schier now serves as assistant chief of interpretation at Mount Rushmore National Memorial, after twenty-five years as a classroom teacher in South Dakota and Colorado. She shares the powerful story of our land of many nations with students, teachers, and visitors from around the country and around the world.

Schwadron, Margo, "De Soto National Memorial." Margo Schwadron is an archaeologist at the National Park Service, Southeast Archeological Center. She has investigated the prehistoric shell mound complex at De Soto National Memorial and prehistoric sites within the Everglades National Park and Big Cypress National Preserve, examining prehistoric settlement patterns along coastal and wetland environments.

Scolari, Paul, and **Linda Yamane,** "Golden Gate National Recreation Area: The Ohlone Village Site and the Restored Tidal Marsh at Crissy Field." Paul Scolari is a historian and American Indian liaison with the National Park Service. He received a Ph.D. from the University of

Pittsburgh in 2005. His dissertation was "Indian Warriors and Pioneer Mothers: American Identity and the Closing of the Frontier in Public Monuments, 1890." Linda Yamane is a basket weaver, singer, and storyteller who traces her heritage to the Rumsien Ohlone, the Native people of the Monterey area. Her publications include *Weaving a California Tradition, When the World Ended, In Full View: Three Ways of Seeing California Plants,* and *A Gathering of Voices.*

Secakuku, Susan (Hopi), "Golden Gate National Recreation Area: Alcatraz Island." Susan Secakuku is the owner of Secakuku Consulting, providing services in museum operations. She worked for the National Museum of the American Indian. She is the author of *Meet Mindy: A Native Girl of the Southwest.* She received a B.S. from Arizona State University and an M.A. from George Washington University.

Sheoships, Susan (Cayuse–Walla Walla), "Tamástslikt Cultural Institute: Naamí Níshaycht — Our Village." Susan Sheoships is a Cayuse–Walla Walla member of the Confederated Tribes of the Umatilla Indian Reservation. As the education coordinator of the Tamástslikt Cultural Institute, she contributed to the chapter "Indians in Oregon Today," in the textbook *Get Oregonized,* published by the Oregon Agriculture in the Classroom Foundation.

Sherfy, Michael, "The Black Hawk War." Michael Sherfy is a visiting assistant professor of history at Ohio State University. He completed his Ph.D. at the University of Illinois in December 2005 and is preparing his dissertation, "Narrating Black Hawk: Indian Wars, Memory, and Midwestern Identity," for publication.

Skelton, Gerald D., Jr. (Klamath Tribes), "Crater Lake National Park: Song of the Lake." Gerald Skelton, an enrolled member of the Klamath Tribes, served as the Klamath Tribes culture and

heritage director for five years. He teaches tribal culture, history, traditional basketry, dugout-canoe making, and bow-and-arrow making. He conducts Native American history presentations for universities, schools, and the National Park Service.

Smith, Chad (Cherokee), "Cherokee National Capitol, Cherokee National Supreme Court Building, and Cherokee National Prison." Chad Smith is the principal chief of the Cherokee Nation and an attorney with a long history of service to Cherokee people. He believes strongly in the concept of *ga-du-gi* (coming together to work for the good of all Cherokees).

Smith, Troy D., "Fort Laramie National Historic Site." Troy D. Smith is a Ph.D. student in the history department at the University of Illinois, Urbana-Champaign, working under the direction of Frederick Hoxie and Vernon Burton. He has published five novels and dozens of magazine articles and was the 2001 winner of Western Writers of America's Spur Award.

Snead, James E., "The Pueblo Diaspora." James Snead is associate professor in the Department of Sociology and Anthropology at George Mason University. His books *Ruins and Rivals* and *Knowing the Country* explore the history of archaeology in the American Southwest as well as the story of its ancient people.

Soctomah, Donald G. (Passamaquoddy First Nation), "St. Croix Island International Historic Site." Donald Soctomah is a citizen of the Passamaquoddy First Nation and has represented the Passamaquoddy people in the Maine State Legislature. He is the tribal historic preservation officer for two Passamaquoddy communities in Maine and one in New Brunswick, Canada.

Spiess, Arthur, Bonnie Newsom (Penobscot), and **Leon Cranmer,** "Colonial Pemaquid State

Historic Site." Arthur Spiess is the senior archaeologist at the Maine Historic Preservation Commission, a position he has held since receiving a Ph.D. in anthropology from Harvard University in 1978. He oversees programs of research, excavation, and archaeological site protection. Bonnie Newsom is the tribal historic preservation officer for the Penobscot Nation. She holds a B.A. in anthropology and an M.S. in quaternary science from the University of Maine. In her position with the tribe, she oversees all programs related to the management of Penobscot sacred sites and historic properties. Leon Cranmer is the historic archaeologist with the Maine Historic Preservation Commission, responsible for maintaining site records and interpreting information from sites of European American origin. He holds an M.A. in history and historical archaeology from the University of Maine, Orono, 1988.

Steponaitis, Vincas P., "Moundville Archaeological Park." Vincas P. Steponaitis, director of the Research Laboratories of Archaeology at the University of North Carolina, was president of the Society for American Archaeology and editor of *Southeastern Archaeology.* He is the coeditor, with Vernon J. Knight, Jr., of *Archaeology of the Moundville Chiefdom.*

Stern, Donna R. (Mescalero Apache), and **Nicole G. Stern** (Mescalero Apache), "Guadalupe Mountains National Park: The Mescalero Apaches and the Guadalupe Mountains." Donna Stern is a cultural anthropologist on the Mescalero Apache Reservation in south-central New Mexico. She works as the operations training specialist for the Inn of the Mountain Gods Resort and Casino. She lives on the reservation with her husband and two sons. Nicole Stern is an internal medicine and sports medicine physician who lives in Tucson, Arizona. She works for the University of Arizona and is a member of the

Association of American Indian Physicians. She has published articles in *Winds of Change* magazine (American Indian Science and Engineering Society).

Strickland, Rennard (Osage/Cherokee), "Under Treaty Oaks: Lingering Shadows of Unfinished Business." Rennard Strickland was dean of the University of Oregon Law School and the Phillip H. Knight Professor of Law. He is the author or editor of more than thirty books, including *Tonto's Revenge, American Indian Spirit Tales, The Indians in Oklahoma,* and *Cohen's Handbook of Federal Indian Law.*

Sundberg, Joy (Yurok), "Patrick's Point State Park: The Yurok Village of Sumeg." Joy Sundberg was born into a traditional dance family and maintains the family's dance regalia. She is the past chairwoman of the Trinidad Rancheria and is on the boards of the Sumeg Patrick's Point Lagoons Interpretive Association and two Indian health organizations.

Swagerty, William R., "The Fur Trade." William Swagerty is professor of history and director of the John Muir Center for Environmental Studies at the University of the Pacific. His former academic posts include Colorado College (1977–1978), the Newberry Library (1978–1981), and the University of Idaho (1982–2001).

Swinehart, Kirk Davis, "Fort Johnson, Johnson Hall, and the Anglo-Mohawk Alliance." Kirk Davis Swinehart, assistant professor of history at Wesleyan University, is writing a book about Sir William Johnson and his Mohawk common-law wife, Molly Brant. He has been a fellow at the Cullman Center for Scholars and Writers at the New York Public Library.

Swisher, Karen Gayton (Standing Rock Sioux), "Haskell Indian Nations University: From Assimilation to Self-Determination." Karen Gayton Swisher was president of Haskell Indian Nations University from 1999 to 2006. Dr. Swisher is an author or coauthor of several articles and books related to American Indian education. Her most recent book is *Next Steps: Research and Practice to Advance Indian Education,* coedited with John W. Tippeconnic, III.

Tabaha, Kathleen (Navajo), "Hubbell Trading Post National Historic Site: Lok'aahnteel." Kathleen Tabaha is a museum technician with the National Park Service and works to preserve the Hubbell collections. She also works with researchers, schools, and other museums. Her maternal clan is Tsénjíkiní (Honey Combed Rock People or the Cliff Dwellers People Clan) and her paternal clan is Tódích'íi'nii (Bitter Water Clan).

Thomas, David Hurst, "Franciscan Designs for the Native People of La Florida." David Hurst Thomas is curator of anthropology at the American Museum of Natural History and a founding trustee of the National Museum of the American Indian. His publications include *Columbian Consequences* (general editor), *Exploring Ancient Native America,* and *Skull Wars: Kennewick Man, Archaeology, and the Battle for Native American Identity.*

Thompson, Ian, "Hovenweep National Monument." Ian Thompson was the executive director of the Crow Canyon Archaeological Center from 1985 to 1991. He lived in Cortez, Colorado, where he wrote about the natural and cultural history of the Four Corners country. His books include *The Towers of Hovenweep* and *People of the Mesa Verde Country.* He died in 1998.

Tilley, Carey L., "Chieftains Museum/Major Ridge Home." Carey Tilley is the executive director of the Cherokee Heritage Center in Tahlequah, Oklahoma. His research interests include the geographical and political landscape of the Cherokee Nation prior to removal. He served as director of the Chieftains Museum/Major Ridge Home in Rome, Georgia, from 2001 to 2006.

Trafzer, Clifford E. (Wyandot ancestry), "Joshua Tree National Park: The People and Their Homeland." Clifford E. Trafzer holds the Rupert Costo Chair in American Indian Affairs at the University of California, Riverside, and is a graduate advisor and the director of public history. His publications include *Native Universe, The People of San Manuel,* and *Chemehuevi People of the Coachella Valley.*

Turpin, Solveig A., "Pictographs and Petroglyphs in Texas." Solveig Turpin, the retired director of the Borderlands Archeological Research Unit, University of Texas, remains a research fellow in Latin American studies. Her publications include *Pecos River Rock Art* and "Archaic North America," in *The Handbook of Rock Art Research.*

Two Bears, Davina (Navajo), "Fort Sumner State Monument." Davina Two Bears is Bitter Water Clan, born for Red Running into the Water Clan, from Bird Springs, Arizona, on the Southwest Navajo reservation. She is the program manager of the Navajo Nation Archaeology Department, Northern Arizona University Branch Office.

Vallo, Brian D. (Pueblo of Acoma), "Pueblo of Acoma: Sky City." Brian Vallo is the director of the Indian Pueblo Cultural Center Museum in Albuquerque. He was the founding director of the Sky City Cultural Center and Haaku Museum on the Acoma Reservation. He is also involved with many national initiatives related to cultural and historic preservation, tourism, and economic development.

Viola, Herman J., "Little Bighorn Battlefield National Monument." Herman J. Viola is a curator emeritus at the Smithsonian Institution. An authority on the history of Indian-white relations, his special interest has been the battle of the Little Bighorn. He is the author of *Little Bighorn Remembered, It is a Good Day to Die,* and *Trail to Wounded Knee.*

Waheneka, Marjorie (Cayuse, Palouse, Warm Springs), "Whitman Mission National Historic Site: Homeland of the Waiilatpu." Marjorie Waheneka is the exhibit manager at the Tamastslikt Cultural Institute on the Umatilla Confederated Tribes Reservation. She was an interpreter at the Whitman Mission National Historic Site for eighteen years.

Walczynski, Mark, "Starved Rock State Park: Starved Rock." Mark Walczynski is employed by the Illinois Department of Natural Resources at Starved Rock State Park. As a historical researcher for the Starved Rock Foundation, he has written on the Franco/Native American period, has been a historical consultant for books and DVDs, and has presented programs across Illinois.

Walks Along, William (Northern Cheyenne), "The Battle of the Little Bighorn: Northern Cheyenne." William Walks Along is the great-grandson of Yellow Robe, a young Northern Cheyenne at the battle of the Little Bighorn. He and Joe Walks Along, Sr., his father, honorably served their people as Northern Cheyenne president and as Tribal Council members. William holds a master's degree in political science.

Walters, Harry (Navajo), "Navajo Pueblitos of the Dinétah." Harry Walters is director of the Hatathli Museum at Diné College in Tsaile, Arizona. He teaches Navajo history and culture at the college and has published *Navajo Bird Tales* (1971), *Navajo Figurines Called Dolls* (1972), and *Anasazi and Anaasazi: Two Words, Two Cultures* (2002).

Warren, Dave (Tewa, Santa Clara Pueblo), "Places and Spaces." Dave Warren was founding deputy director, National Museum of the American Indian. His career as an educator, administrator, and professional historian includes appointments at universities and at the Institute of American Indian Arts. Santa Clara Pueblo recognized his efforts leading to the recovery of Pòpii Khanu, the Santa Clara headwaters.

Warren, Stephen, "Tippecanoe Battlefield and Prophetstown State Park." Stephen Warren is assistant professor of history at Augustana College in Rock Island, Illinois. He is the author of *The Shawnees and Their Neighbors* and has worked as an advisor and consultant for the *American Experience* documentary series *We Shall Remain: A Native History of America.*

Waseta, Jeffery Kevin (Zuni), "El Malpais National Monument: The Zuni-Acoma Trail." Jeffery Waseta is a supervisory archaeologist for Zuni Cultural Resource Enterprise.

Watkins, Joe E. (Choctaw), "Expanding the Dialogue between American Indians and Non-Indian Archaeologists." Joe Watkins, director of Native American studies at the University of Oklahoma, has done archaeology for forty years. His research interests include ethics in anthropology and anthropology's relationships with descendant communities and indigenous populations. His books include *Indigenous Archaeology: American Indian Values and Scientific Practice* and *Sacred Sites and Repatriation.*

Weber, David J., "San Antonio Missions National Historical Park." David J. Weber directs the Clements Center for Southwest Studies at

Southern Methodist University in Dallas. His books include *The Mexican Frontier, 1821–1846: The American Southwest under Mexico, The Spanish Frontier in North America,* and *Bárbaros: Spaniards and Their Savages in the Age of Enlightenment.*

Weisman, Brent Richards, "Tree Tops Park: Pine Island Ridge." Brent Weisman is a professor of anthropology at the University of South Florida. His research specialty is Florida archaeology. In addition to *Unconquered People,* he has written about Seminole history and archaeology in *Like Beads on a String.*

Wesler, Kit W., "Wickliffe Mounds State Historic Site." Kit W. Wesler is professor of archaeology in the Department of Geosciences at Murray State University. His work includes prehistoric and historical archaeology in the mid-South and middle Atlantic regions of the United States, in Nigeria, and in Jamaica. He is the author of *Excavations at Wickliffe Mounds.*

West, W. Richard, Jr. (Southern Cheyenne), "National Museum of the American Indian: A Native Place in Washington, D.C." W. Richard West, Jr., founding director emeritus of the Smithsonian Institution's National Museum of the American Indian, served as its director from 1990 to 2007. West, raised in the state of Oklahoma, is a citizen of the Cheyenne Arapaho Tribes of Oklahoma and a peace chief of the Southern Cheyenne.

White Mountain Apache Tribe Heritage Program: Mark Altaha, Doreen Gatewood, Karl Hoerig, Ramon Riley (White Mountain Apache), and **John R. Welch,** "Fort Apache and Theodore Roosevelt School Historic District: Past Is Present." Mark Altaha, Doreen Gatewood, Karl Hoerig, and Ramon Riley are members of the White Mountain Apache Tribe Heritage Pro-

gram. John R. Welch is a Heritage Program advisor and a faculty member at Simon Fraser University.

White Mountain Apache Tribe Heritage Program: Mark Altaha, Nick Laluk (White Mountain Apache), and **John R. Welch,** "Kinishba Ruins National Historic Landmark: Decolonizing Kinishba." Mark Altaha and Nick Laluk are members of the White Mountain Apache Tribe Heritage Program. John R. Welch is a Heritage Program advisor and a faculty member at Simon Fraser University.

Widdiss, Donald A. (Aquinnah Wampanoag), "The Cliffs of Aquinnah: We Belong Where We Are From." Donald Widdiss is currently chairman of the 1,100-member Wampanoag Tribe of Gay Head (Aquinnah), federally recognized by the Department of the Interior, Bureau of Indian Affairs, in 1987. He uses natural material from the Aquinnah homeland to fashion traditional quahog-shell beads known as wampum.

Wilkins, David E. (Lumbee), "The Myth of Nomadism and Indigenous Lands." David Wilkins is professor of American Indian studies at the University of Minnesota and holds adjunct appointments in political science, law, and American studies. His publications include *American Indian Politics and the American Political System* and, with Richard Grounds and George Tinker (eds.), *Native Voices: American Indian Identity and Resistance.*

Wilkinson, Charles, "American Indians' Spirituality and Land Use." Charles Wilkinson, the Moses Lasky Professor of Law and Distinguished University Professor at the University of Colorado, is the author of thirteen books, including the standard casebooks on Indian law and federal public land law. His most recent book is

Blood Struggle: The Rise of Modern Indian Nations.

Williams, Joe (Sisseton Wahpeton Oyate), "Jeffers Petroglyphs." Joe Williams is an elder from the Sisseton Wahpeton Oyate.

Williams, Stephen, "Mississippian: A Way of Life." Stephen Williams is the Peabody Professor of American Archaeology and Ethnology emeritus and honorary curator of North American archaeology at the Peabody Museum of Harvard University. He is the author of *Fantastic Archaeology: The Wild Side of North American Prehistory.*

Woody, Alanah, and **Angus R. Quinlan,** "Petroglyphs and Pictographs in the Great Basin." Alanah Woody (d. 2007) was the collections manager at the Nevada State Museum and the executive director of the Nevada Rock Art Foundation. She wrote her dissertation, "How to Do Things with Petroglyphs: The Rock Art of Nevada," at the University of Southampton, England, in 2000. Angus R. Quinlan is an archaeological technical editor for Summit Enviro-Solutions, Inc., and the director of the Nevada Rock Art Foundation. He wrote his dissertation,

"Towards an Archaeology of Religion," at the University of Southampton, England, in 1993.

Wray, Jacilee, "Olympic National Park." Jacilee Wray, the anthropologist at Olympic National Park, is the editor of *Native Peoples of the Olympic Peninsula: Who We Are,* written by the nine tribes of the Olympic Peninsula region. The tribes established the Olympic Peninsula Intertribal Cultural Advisory Committee and work together on many research projects.

Ygnacio-De Soto, Ernestine (Chumash), "Chumash Painted Cave State Historic Park." Ernestine Ygnacio-De Soto, the coauthor, with Mary J. Yee, of *The Sugar Bear Story,* is working to bring back the Barbareño Chumash language. Her mother was the last Barbareño Chumash speaker. Ernestine's ancestors lived near the area of Painted Cave.

Zobel, Melissa Tantaquidgeon (Mohegan), "Fort Shantok." Melissa Zobel is the Mohegan tribal historian and the winner of the 1992 North American Native Writers' First Book Award in Creative Nonfiction for *The Lasting of the Mohegans.* She is also the author of *Medicine Trail* and coauthor of *Makiawisug: The Gift of the Little People.*

Bibliography

The bibliography includes publications mentioned in About the Contributors and in the Further Reading sections at the end of most of the essays.

Adams, E. Charles. *The Origin and Development of the Pueblo Katsina Cult.* Tucson: University of Arizona Press, 1991.

———. *Homol'ovi: An Ancient Hopi Settlement Cluster.* Tucson: University of Arizona Press, 2002.

Anderson, David G., and Robert C. Mainfort, Jr., eds. *The Woodland Southeast.* Tuscaloosa: University of Alabama Press, 2002.

Anderson, David G., and Kenneth E. Sassaman, eds. *The Paleoindian and Early Archaic Southeast.* Tuscaloosa: University of Alabama Press, 1996.

Anderson, Fred. *Crucible of War: The Seven Years' War and the Fate of Empire in British North America.* New York: Alfred A. Knopf, 2000.

Anderson, Fred, and Andrew Cayton. *The Dominion of War: Empire and Liberty in North America, 1500–2000.* New York: Viking, 2005.

Anderson, Gary Clayton. *Kinsman of Another Kind: Dakota-White Relations in the Upper Mississippi Valley 1650 to 1862.* St. Paul: Minnesota Historical Society, 1984; reprint, 1997.

Arnold, Morris S. *The Rumble of a Distant Drum.* Fayetteville: University of Arkansas Press, 2000.

Atkinson, James, R. *Splendid Land, Splendid People: The Chickasaw Indians to Removal.* Tuscaloosa: University of Alabama Press, 2003.

Bailey, Garrick A., ed. *The Osage and the Invisible World: From the Works of Francis La Flesche.* 2nd ed. Norman: University of Oklahoma Press, 1999.

Balesi, Charles J. *The Time of the French in the Heart of North America, 1673–1818.* 2nd ed. Chicago: Alliance Française, 1996.

Barnett, Jim. *The Natchez Indians: A History to 1735.* Jackson: University Press of Mississippi, 2007.

Barrett, S. A., and Edward W. Gifford. *Indian Life of the Yosemite Region: Miwok Material Culture.* El Portal, CA: Yosemite Association, 1990 (paperback).

Basso, Keith. *Wisdom Sits in Places: Landscape and Language Among the Western Apache.* Albuquerque: University of New Mexico Press, 1996.

Bayman, James M. "The Hohokam of Southwest North America." *Journal of World Prehistory* 15 (2001): 257.

Bean, Lowell John. *Mukat's People: The Cahuilla Indians of Southern California.* Berkeley: University of California Press, 2001.

———, ed. *The Ohlone Past and Present: Native Americans of the San Francisco Bay Region.* Menlo Park, CA: Ballena Press, 1994.

Bean, Lowell John, and Katherine Siva Saubel. *Temalpakh (From the Earth): Cahuilla Indian Knowledge and Usage of Plants.* Banning, CA: Malki Museum Press, 1972.

Bearss, Edwin C., and Arrell M. Gibson. *Fort Smith: Little Gibraltar on the Arkansas.* Norman: University of Oklahoma Press, 1969.

Beebe, Rose Marie, and Robert M. Senkewicz. *Testimonios: Early California Through the Eyes of Women, 1815–1848.* Berkeley: Heyday Books and the Bancroft Library, 2006.

———, eds. *Lands of Promise and Despair: Chronicles of Early California, 1535–1846.* Berkeley and Santa Clara: Heyday Books and Santa Clara University, 2001.

———. *Guide to the Manuscripts Concerning Baja California in the Collections of the Bancroft Library.* Berkeley: University of California Library, 2002.

Bernardis, Tim. *Crow Social Studies: Baleeisbaalichiwee History.* Crow Agency, MT: Bilingual Materials Development Center, 1986.

Bernardis, Tim, and Frederick E. Hoxie. "Robert Yellowtail." In *The New Warriors: Native American Leaders Since 1900,* ed. R. David Edmunds. Lincoln: University of Nebraska Press, 2001.

Bighorse, Tiana. *Bighorse the Warrior,* ed. Noel Bennett. Tucson: University of Arizona Press, 1990.

Birmingham, Robert A., and Leslie Eisenberg. *Indian Mounds of Wisconsin.* Madison: University of Wisconsin Press, 2000.

Blue, Martha. *Indian Trader: The Life and Times of J. L. Hubbell.* Walnut, CA: Kiva Publishing, 2000.

Blythe, Robert W. "Unraveling the Threads of Community Life: Work, Play, and Place in the Alabama Mill Villages of West Point Manufacturing Company." In *Constructing Image, Identity, and Place. Perspectives in Vernacular Architecture* 9. Knoxville: University of Tennessee Press, 2003.

Bowechop, Janine. "Contemporary Makah Whaling." In *Coming to Shore: Northwest Coast Ethnology, Traditions, and Visions,* ed. Marie Mauzé, Michael E. Harkin, and Sergie Kan. Lincoln: University of Nebraska Press, 2004.

Bowers, Alfred W. *Mandan Social and Ceremonial Organization.* Lincoln: University of Nebraska Press, 2004.

Brain, Jeffrey P. *Tunica Treasure.* Papers of the Peabody Museum, no. 71. Cambridge, MA: Peabody Museum of Archaeology and Ethnology, 1979.

———. *Excavations at the Lake George Site, Yazoo County, Mississippi, 1958–1960.* Papers of the Peabody Museum, no. 74. Cambridge, MA: Peabody Museum of Archaeology and Ethnology, 1983.

———. *Tunica Archaeology.* Papers of the Peabody Museum, no. 78. Cambridge, MA: Peabody Museum of Archaeology and Ethnology, 1988.

———. *Winterville: Late Prehistoric Culture Contact in the Lower Mississippi Valley.* Archaeological Report no. 23. Jackson: Mississippi Department of Archives and History, 1989.

Bray, Kingsley M. *Crazy Horse: A Lakota Life.* Norman: University of Oklahoma Press, 2006.

Brose, David S., C. Wesley Cowan, and Robert C. Mainfort, eds. *Societies in Eclipse: Archaeology of the Eastern Woodlands Indians, A.D. 1400–1700.* Washington, DC: Smithsonian Institution Press, 2001.

Brown, Ian. *Natchez Indian Archaeology: Culture Change and Stability in the Lower Mississippi Valley.* Archaeological Report no. 15. Jackson: Mississippi Department of Archives and History, 1985.

———. "Natchez Indians and the Remains of a Proud Past." In *Natchez Before 1830,* ed. Noel Polk. Jackson: University Press of Mississippi, 1989.

Bryan, Liz. *The Buffalo People: Prehistoric Archaeology on the Canadian Plains.* Edmonton: University of Alberta Press, 1991.

Buan, Carolyn M., and Richard Lewis, eds. *The First Oregonians: An Illustrated Collection of Essays on Traditional Lifeways, Federal-Indian Relations, and the State's Native People Today.* Portland: Oregon Council for the Humanities, 1991.

Burns, Louis F. *A History of the Osage People.* Tuscaloosa: University of Alabama Press, 2004.

Callahan, Kevin. *The Jeffers Petroglyphs: Native American Rock Art on the Midwest Plains.* St. Paul: Prairie Smoke Press, 2004.

Calloway, Colin G. *The Western Abenaki of Vermont.* Norman: University of Oklahoma Press, 1990.

———. *The American Revolution in Indian Country.* Cambridge, UK: Cambridge University Press, 1995.

———. *New Worlds for All: Indians, Europeans, and the Remaking of Early America.* Baltimore: Johns Hopkins University Press, 1997.

———. *One Vast Winter Count: The American West Before Lewis and Clark.* Lincoln: University of Nebraska Press, 2003.

Cameron, Catherine. *Hopi Dwellings: Architectural Change at Orayvi.* Tucson: University of Arizona Press, 1999.

Camp, Helen, and Robert Bradley. *The Forts of Pema-*

quid, Maine: An Archaeological and Historical Study.* Occasional Publications in Maine Archaeology, no. 10. Augusta: Maine Archaeological Society, 1994; CD, 2005.

Campisi, Jack. *The Mashpee Indians: Tribe on Trial.* Syracuse: Syracuse University Press, 1991.

Carleton, Kenneth H. "Nanih Waiya (22WI500): An Historical and Archaeological Overview." *Mississippi Archaeology* 34, no. 2 (1999): 125–55.

Carlson, Pamela McGuire, and E. Breck Parkman. "Camillo Ynitia: The Last Headman of the Olompalis." *California History* 65, no. 4 (1986): 238–47, 309–10.

Carter, Cecile Elkins. *Caddo Indians: Where We Come From.* 2nd ed. Norman: University of Oklahoma Press, 2001.

Champagne, Duane. *Social Order and Political Change: Constitutional Governments Among the Cherokee, the Choctaw, the Chickasaw, and the Creek.* Palo Alto: Stanford University Press, 1992.

——, ed. *The Native North American Almanac: A Reference Work on Native North Americans in the United States and Canada.* Detroit: Gale Group, 2001.

Chapman, Berlin Basil. *The Otoes and Missourias: A Study of Indian Removal and the Legal Aftermath.* Oklahoma City: Times Journal Publishing, 1965.

Chappell, Sally A. Kitt. *Cahokia: Mirror of the Cosmos.* Chicago: University of Chicago Press, 2002.

Child, Brenda J. *Boarding School Seasons: American Indian Families, 1900–1940.* Lincoln: University of Nebraska Press, 1998.

Clark, Caven P., and Susan R. Martin. "A Risky Business: Late Woodland Copper Mining on Lake Superior." In *The Cultural Landscape of Prehistoric Mines,* ed. Peter Topping and Mark Lynott. Oakville, CT: David Brown Book Co., Oxbow Books, 2005.

Clark, Ella E. *Indian Legends of the Pacific Northwest.* Berkeley: University of California Press, 1953.

Coe, Joffre Lanning. *Town Creek Indian Mound: A Native American Legacy.* Chapel Hill: University of North Carolina Press, 1995.

Cohen, Fay G. *Treaties on Trial: The Continuing Controversy over Northwest Indian Fishing Rights.* Seattle: University of Washington Press, 1986.

Cohen's Handbook of Federal Indian Law, ed. Newton et al. Newark, NJ: LexisNexis, 2005.

Cohen, Lucy Kramer, ed. *The Legal Conscience: Selected Papers of Felix S. Cohen.* New Haven: Yale University Press, 1960.

Collier, Mary, and Sylvia B. Thalman, eds. *Interviews with Tom Smith and Maria Copa: Isabel Kelly's Ethnographic Notes of the Coast Miwok Indians of Marin and Southern Sonoma Counties.* Novato, CA: Miwok Archeological Preserve of Marin, 2002.

Conley, Robert J. *The Cherokee Nation: A History.* Albuquerque: University of New Mexico Press, 2005.

Cook, James H. *Fifty Years on the Old Frontier.* Norman: University of Oklahoma Press, 1923; reprint, 1980.

Cordell, Linda S. *Ancestral Pueblo Peoples.* Washington, DC: Smithsonian Institution Press, 1994.

——. *Archaeology of the Southwest.* New York: Academic Press, 1997.

Cornell, G. L., J. A. Clifton, and J. M. McClurken. *People of the Three Fires.* Grand Rapids: Michigan Indian Press, 1986.

Crown, Patricia L. "The Hohokam of the American Southwest." *Journal of World Prehistory* 4, no. 2 (1990).

Crown, Patricia L., and W. James Judge, eds. *Chaco and Hohokam: Prehistoric Regional Systems in the American Southwest.* Santa Fe: School of American Research Press, 1991.

Davisson, Lori. "Fort Apache, Arizona Territory: 1870–1922." *Smoke Signal* no. 78. Tucson: Tucson Corral of the Westerners, 2004.

d'Azevedo, Warren L., ed. *Great Basin.* Vol. 11 of *Handbook of North American Indians,* ed. William C. Sturtevant. Washington, DC: Smithsonian Institution, 1986.

Dean, Jeffrey S. *Chronological Analysis of Tsegi Phase Sites in Northeastern Arizona.* Papers of the Laboratory of Tree-Ring Research, no. 3. Tucson: University of Arizona Press, 1969.

——. "Dendrochronology." In *Chronometric Dating in Archaeology,* pp. 31–64, ed. R. E. Taylor and M. J. Aitken. New York: Plenum Press, 1997.

——, ed. *Salado.* Albuquerque: University of New Mexico Press, 2000.

Debo, Angie. *The Road to Disappearance: A History of the Creek Indians.* Norman: University of Oklahoma Press, 1941.

deBuys, William. *Enchantment and Exploitation: The Life and Times of a New Mexico Mountain Range.*

Albuquerque: University of New Mexico Press, 1985.

———. *Salt Dreams: Land and Water in Low-Down California.* Albuquerque: University of New Mexico Press, 1999.

———. *The Walk.* San Antonio, TX: Trinity University Press, 2007.

———, ed. *Seeing Things Whole: The Essential John Wesley Powell.* Washington, DC: Island Press, 2001.

deBuys, William, and Alex Harris. *River of Traps.* Albuquerque: University of New Mexico Press, 1990.

deBuys, William, and Don J. Usner. *Valles Caldera.* Santa Fe: Museum of New Mexico Press, 2006.

Deloria, Philip J. *Playing Indian.* New Haven: Yale University Press, 1998.

———. *Indians in Unexpected Places.* Lawrence: University Press of Kansas, 2004.

Deloria, Philip J., and Neal Salisbury, eds. *A Companion to American Indian History.* Malden, MA: Blackwell Publishing, 2002.

Deloria, Vine, Jr. *God Is Red: A Native View of Religion.* New York: Grosset and Dunlap, 1973.

Deur, Douglas E., and Nancy J. Turner, eds. *Keeping It Living: Traditions of Plant Use and Cultivation on the Northwest Coast of North America.* Seattle: University of Washington Press; Vancouver: University of British Columbia Press, 2005.

Dial, Adolph L. *The Lumbee.* New York: Chelsea House Publications, 1993.

Diaz-Granados, Carol, and James R. Duncan. *The Petroglyphs and Pictographs of Missouri.* Tuscaloosa: University of Alabama Press, 2000.

———, eds. *The Rock-Art of Eastern North America: Capturing Images and Insight.* Tuscaloosa: University of Alabama Press, 2004.

Diehl, Michael W. *Archaeological Investigations of the Early Agricultural Period Settlement at the Base of A-Mountain, Tucson.* Tucson: Center for Desert Archaeology, 1997.

———, ed. *Hierarchies in Action: Cui Bono?* Occasional Paper no. 27. Carbondale: Center for Archaeological Investigations, Southern Illinois University, 2000.

Diehl, Michael W., and Steven A. LeBlanc. *Early Pithouse Villages of the Mimbres Valley and Beyond: The McAnally and Thompson Sites in their Cultural and Ecological Contexts.* Papers of the Peabody Museum, no. 83. Cambridge, MA: Peabody Museum of Archaeology and Ethnology, 2001.

Dongoske, Kurt, Mark Aldenderfer, and Karen Doehner, eds. *Working Together: Native Americans and Archaeology.* Washington, DC: Society for American Archaeology, 2000.

Downum, Christian. "The Sinagua," *Plateau* 63, no. 1 (1992). Flagstaff: Museum of Northern Arizona.

Drake, James D. *King Philip's War: Civil War in New England, 1675–1676.* Amherst: University of Massachusetts Press, 1999.

Dugan, Joyce, and B. Lynne Harlan. *The Cherokees.* Cherokee, NC: Eastern Band of Cherokee Indians, 2002.

Duncan, Barbara R., ed. *Living Stories of the Cherokee.* Chapel Hill: University of North Carolina Press, 1998.

Duncan, Barbara R., and Brett H. Riggs. *Cherokee Heritage Trails Guidebook.* Chapel Hill: University of North Carolina Press, 2003.

Dupris, Joseph C., Kathleen S. Hill, and William H. Rodgers. *The Si'lailo Way: Indians, Salmon and Law on the Columbia River.* Durham, NC: Carolina Academic Press, 2006.

Edmunds, R. David. *The Shawnee Prophet.* Lincoln: University of Nebraska Press, 1983.

———. *Tecumseh and the Quest for Leadership.* Boston: Little, Brown, 1984.

Edmunds, R. David, Frederick E. Hoxie, and Neal Salisbury. *The People: A History of Native America.* Boston: Houghton Mifflin, 2007.

Erickson, Winston P. *Sharing the Desert: The Tohono O'odham in History.* Tucson: University of Arizona Press, 1994.

Ericson, Jonathon E., and Barbara A. Purdy. *Prehistoric Quarries and Lithic Production.* Cambridge, UK: Cambridge University Press, 1984.

Farris, G., and J. Johnson. *Prominent Indian Families at Mission La Purísima Concepcíon as Identified in Baptismal, Marriage, and Burial Records.* Occasional Paper no. 3. California Mission Studies Association, 1999.

Fawcett, Melissa Jayne. *The Lasting of the Mohegans: The Story of the Wolf People.* Uncasville, CT: Mohegan Tribe, 1995.

———. *Medicine Trail: The Life and Lessons of Gladys Tantaquidgeon.* Tucson: University of Arizona Press, 2000.

Ferguson, T. J., and E. Richard Hart. *A Zuni Atlas.* Norman: University of Oklahoma Press, reprint, 1990.

Finger, John R. *The Eastern Band of Cherokees, 1819–1900.* Knoxville: University of Tennessee Press, 1984.

Five Views: An Ethnic Historic Site Survey for California. California Department of Parks and Recreation, Office of Historic Preservation, December 1988.

Fixico, Donald L. *The American Indian Mind in a Linear World.* New York: Routledge, 2003.

——. *Daily Life of Native Americans in the Twentieth Century.* Westport, CT: Greenwood Press, 2006.

Flores, Dan L. *Caprock Canyonlands: Journeys into the Heart of the Southern Plains.* Austin: University of Texas Press, 1990.

——. *Horizontal Yellow.* Albuquerque: University of New Mexico Press, 1999.

——, ed. *Jefferson and Southwestern Exploration.* Norman: University of Oklahoma Press, 1984.

——, ed. *Journal of an Indian Trader.* College Station: Texas A&M Press, 1985.

——. *The Natural West: Environmental History in the Great Plains and Rocky Mountains.* Norman: University of Oklahoma Press, 2001.

Flores, Dan L., and Amy Gormley Winton. *Canyon Visions.* Lubbock: Texas Tech Press, 1989.

Foreman, Grant. *Indian Removal: The Emigration of the Five Civilized Tribes of Indians.* Norman: University of Oklahoma Press, 1932; reprint, 1976.

Fortunate Eagle, Adam. *Heart of the Rock: The Indian Invasion of Alcatraz.* Norman: University of Oklahoma Press, 2002.

Foster, Lance M. "Tanji na Che: Recovering the Landscape of the Ioway." In *Recovering the Prairie,* ed. Robert Sayre. Madison: University of Wisconsin Press, 1999.

——. "A Closing Circle: Musings on the Ioway Indians in Iowa." In *The Worlds Between Two Rivers: Perspectives on American Indians in Iowa,* ed. Gretchen Bataille, David Gradwohl, and Charles Silet. Iowa City: University of Iowa Press, 2000.

Fowler, Catherine S. "Timbisha Shoshone." In *The Cambridge Encyclopedia of Hunters and Gatherers,* ed. Richard B. Lee and Richard Daly. Cambridge, UK: Cambridge University Press, 1999.

Frey, Rodney. *Landscape Traveled by Coyote and Crane: The World of the Schitsu'Umsh Coeur D'Alene Indians.* Seattle: University of Washington Press, 2001.

Garate, Donald T. *Juan Bautista de Anza: Basque Explorer in the New World, 1693–1740.* Reno: University of Nevada Press, 2003.

Gibson, Arrell M. *The Chickasaws.* Norman: University of Oklahoma Press, 1971.

Gibson, Jon L. *The Ancient Mounds of Poverty Point: Place of Rings.* Gainesville: University Press of Florida, 2000.

Gibson, Jon L., and Philip J. Carr, eds. *Signs of Power: The Rise of Cultural Complexity in the Southeast.* Tuscaloosa: University of Alabama Press, 2004.

Gilbert, Claudette Marie, and Robert L. Brooks. *From Mounds to Mammoths.* Norman: University of Oklahoma Press, 2000.

Gilman, Carolyn. *The Grand Portage Story.* St. Paul: Minnesota Historical Society Press, 1992.

Goodman, Ronald. *Lakota Star Knowledge: Studies in Lakota Stellar Theology.* Rosebud, SD: Sinte Gleska University Press, 1992.

Grant, Campbell. *Rock Paintings of the Chumash: A Study of a California Indian Culture.* Santa Barbara: Santa Barbara Museum of Natural History, 1993.

Green, Richard. *Te Ata: Chickasaw Storyteller, American Treasure.* Norman: University of Oklahoma Press, 2002.

Greene, Jerome A. *Washita: The U.S. Army and the Southern Cheyennes, 1867–1869.* Norman: University of Oklahoma Press, 2004.

Griffith, Thomas D., and Dustin D. Floyd. *Insider's Guide to South Dakota's Black Hills and Badlands.* Guilford, CT: Globe Pequot, 2006.

Grounds, Richard, George Tinker, and David E. Wilkins, eds. *Native Voices: American Indian Identity and Resistance.* Lawrence: University Press of Kansas, 2003.

Haefeli, Evan, and Kevin Sweeney. *Captors and Captives: The 1704 French and Indian Raid on Deerfield.* Amherst: University of Massachusetts Press, 2004.

Hafen, Le Roy R., and Francis M. Young. *Fort Laramie and the Pageant of the West, 1834–1890.* Lincoln: University of Nebraska Press, 1984.

Hally, David J., ed. *Ocmulgee Archaeology, 1936–1986.* Athens: University of Georgia Press, 1994.

Hann, John H., and Bonnie G. McEwan. *The Apalachee Indians and Mission San Luis.* Gainesville: University Press of Florida, 1998.

Harlan, B. Lynne. "Museum Perspectives from Within: A Native View." In *Mending the Circle: A Native American Guide to Repatriation,* ed. Elizabeth Sackler. New York: American Indian Ritual Object Repatriation Foundation, 1994.

Harmon, David, Francis P. McManamon, and Dwight T. Pitcaithley, eds. *The Antiquities Act: A Century of American Archaeology, Historic Preservation, and Nature Conservation.* Tucson: University of Arizona Press, 2006.

Hatley, Tom. *The Dividing Paths: Cherokees and South Carolinians Through the Revolutionary Era.* New York: Oxford University Press, 1993.

Hauptman, Laurence M. *Between Two Fires: American Indians in the Civil War.* New York: Free Press, 1995.

Hauptman, Laurence M., and L. Gordon McLester. *Chief Daniel Bread and the Oneida Nation of Indians of Wisconsin.* Norman: University of Oklahoma Press, 2002.

Hauptman, Laurence M., and James D. Wherry, eds. *The Pequots in Southern New England: The Fall and Rise of an American Indian Nation.* Norman: University of Oklahoma Press, 1990.

Heizer, Robert F., ed. *California.* Vol. 8 of *Handbook of North American Indians,* ed. William C. Sturtevant. Washington, DC: Smithsonian Institution, 1978.

Heizer, R. F., and J. E. Mills. *The Four Ages of Tsurai: A Documentary History of the Indian Village on Trinidad Bay.* Berkeley: University of California Press, 1952; reprint, Trinidad, CA: Trinidad Museum Society, 1991.

Hester, J. J. *Blackwater Locality No. 1: A Stratified Early Man Site in Eastern New Mexico.* Ranchos de Taos, NM: Southern Methodist University and Fort Burgwin Research Center, 1972.

Hinton, Leanne, and Lucille J. Watahomigie, eds. *Spirit Mountain: An Anthology of Yuman Story and Song.* Tucson: Sun Tracks and University of Arizona Press, 1984.

Hobson, Geary. *The Last of the Ofos.* Tucson: University of Arizona Press, 2000.

Hoig, Stan. *Sequoyah: The Cherokee Genius.* Oklahoma City: Oklahoma Historical Society, 1995.

Houk, Rose. *Navajo of Canyon de Chelly.* Tucson: Southwest Parks and Monuments Association, 2000.

Hoxie, Frederick E. *A Final Promise: The Campaign to Assimilate the Indians, 1880–1920.* Lincoln: University of Nebraska Press, 1984.

——, ed. *Encyclopedia of North American Indians.* Boston: Houghton Mifflin, 1996.

Huck, Barbara. *Exploring the Fur Trade Routes of North America.* Winnipeg, MB: Heartland, 2000.

Hudson, Charles. *Knights of Spain, Warriors of the Sun: Hernando de Soto and the South's Ancient Chiefdoms.* Athens: University of Georgia Press, 1997.

Hunter, Andrea A. "Paleoethnobotany of the Osage and Missouri Indians: Analysis of Plant Remains from Historic Village Sites." *Missouri Archaeologist* 47 (1986): 173–96.

Hunter, Wilson. *Canyon de Chelly: The Continuing Story. In Pictures* series. Las Vegas, NV: KC Publications, 1999.

Hyder, William D. *Rock Art and Archaeology in Santa Barbara County, California.* Occasional Paper no. 13. San Luis Obispo County Archaeological Society, 1989.

Ivey, James E. *In the Midst of a Loneliness: The Architectural History of the Salinas Missions.* Santa Fe: National Park Service, 1988.

——. "Convento Kivas in the Missions of New Mexico." *New Mexico Historical Review* 73, no. 2 (1998): 121–52.

Jackson, Donald, ed. *Black Hawk: An Autobiography.* Urbana: University of Illinois Press, 1955.

James, Harry C. *Pages from Hopi History.* Tucson: University of Arizona Press, 1974.

Jemison, G. Peter, and Anna M. Schein, eds. *Treaty of Canandaigua, 1794: 200 Years of Treaty Relations Between the Iroquois Confederacy and the United States.* Santa Fe: Clear Light Publishers, 2000.

Johnson, John R. "Ethnohistoric Reflections of Cruzeño Chumash Society." In *The Origins of a Pacific Coast Chiefdom: The Chumash of the Channel Islands,* pp. 53–70, ed. J. E. Arnold. Salt Lake City: University of Utah Press, 2001.

Jones, Anne Trinkle. *Stalking the Past: Prehistory at Petrified Forest.* Petrified Forest, AZ: Petrified Forest Museum Association, 1993.

Jones, Evan. *Citadel in the Wilderness: The Story of*

Fort Snelling and the Northwest Frontier. Minneapolis: University of Minnesota Press, 2001.

Josephy, Alvin M., Jr. *The Nez Perce Indians and the Opening of the Northwest*. Boston: Houghton Mifflin, 1965.

——, ed. *Lewis and Clark Through Indian Eyes*. New York: Alfred A. Knopf, 2006.

Kantner, John. *Ancient Puebloan Southwest*. New York: Cambridge University Press, 2005.

Kantner, John, and N. M. Mahoney, eds. *Great House Communities across the Chacoan Landscape*. Anthropological Papers no. 64. Tucson: University of Arizona Press, 2000.

Kavanagh, Thomas W. *The Comanches: A History*. Lincoln: University of Nebraska Press, 1999.

Keator, Glenn, and Linda Yamane. *In Full View: Three Ways of Seeing California Plants*. Berkeley: Heyday Books, 1995.

Kelly, Isabel T., and Catherine S. Fowler. "Southern Paiute." In *Great Basin*, ed. William d'Azevedo. Vol. 11 of *Handbook of North American Indians*, ed. William C. Surtevant. Washington, DC: Smithsonian Institution, 1986.

Kelly, John E. "Redefining Cahokia: Principles and Elements of Community Organization." In "The Ancient Skies and Sky Watchers of Cahokia: Woodhenges, Eclipses, and Cahokian Cosmology," ed. Melvin L. Fowler. *Wisconsin Archeologist* 77, nos. 3–4 (1996): 97–119.

Kennedy, Frances H., ed. *The Civil War Battlefield Guide*. Boston: Houghton Mifflin, 1998.

Kershner, Bruce, and Robert T. Leverett. *The Sierra Club Guide to the Ancient Forests of the Northeast*. San Francisco: Sierra Club Books, 2004.

Kessell, John L. *Kiva, Cross, and Crown: The Pecos Indians and New Mexico, 1540–1840*. Washington, DC: National Park Service, 1987.

——. *Spain in the Southwest*. Norman: University of Oklahoma Press, 2002.

Kidwell, Clara Sue. *Choctaws and Missionaries in Mississippi 1818–1918*. Norman: University of Oklahoma Press, 1995.

——. "Ethnoastronomy as the Key to Human Intellectual Development and Social Organization." In *Native Voices: American Indian Identity and Resistance*, ed. Richard Grounds, George Tinker, and David Wilkins. Lawrence: University Press of Kansas, 2003.

King, Adam. *Etowah: The Political History of a Chiefdom Capital*. Tuscaloosa: University of Alabama Press, 2003.

King, Duane. *The Cherokee Trail of Tears*. Portland, OR: Graphics Arts Center Publishing, 2007.

Kirkland, Forrest, and W. W. Newcomb, Jr. *The Rock Art of Texas Indians*. Austin: University of Texas Press, 1967; reprint, 1990.

Knight, Vernon, Jr., and Vincas P. Steponaitis, eds. *Archaeology of the Moundville Chiefdom*. Washington, DC: Smithsonian Institution Press, 1998.

Kroeber, A. L. *Handbook of the Indians of California*. Bulletin no. 78, Bureau of American Ethnology of the Smithsonian Institution. Washington, DC: Government Printing Office, 1925; reprint, New York: Dover Publications, 1976.

LaDuke, Winona. *All Our Relations*. Cambridge, MA: South End Press, 1999.

——. *Last Standing Woman*. Osceola, WI: Voyageur Press, 1999.

——. *The Winona LaDuke Reader*. Osceola, WI: Voyageur Press, 2002.

Lamb, Susan. *Tumácacori National Historical Park*. Tucson: Southwest Parks and Monuments Association, 1993.

Landeen, Dan, and Allen Pinkham. *Salmon and His People: Fish and Fishing in Nez Perce Culture*. Lewiston, ID: Confluence Press, 1999.

Lee, Georgia. *The Chumash Cosmos: Effigies, Ornaments, Incised Stones and Rock Paintings of the Chumash Indians*. Arroyo Grande, CA: Bear Flag Books, 1997.

Lee, Georgia, and Edward Stasack. *Spirit of Place: Petroglyphs of Hawai'i*. Los Osos, CA: Bearsville and Cloud Mountain Presses, 1999.

Lekson, Stephen H. *Great Pueblo Architecture of Chaco Canyon*. Albuquerque: University of New Mexico Press, 1986.

——. *The Chaco Meridian*. Walnut Creek, CA: AltaMira Press, 1999.

Lepper, Bradley T. "Tracking Ohio's Great Hopewell Road." *Archaeology* 48, no. 6 (1995): 52–56.

——. *People of the Mounds: Ohio's Hopewell Culture*. Fort Washington, PA: Eastern National, 1999.

——. *Ohio Archaeology*. Wilmington, OH: Orange Frazer Press, 2005.

Linderman, Frank B. *Plenty-Coups, Chief of the Crows*. Reprint, Lincoln: University of Nebraska Press, 2002.

Lindstrom, Linea. *Indian Rock Art of the Black Hills Country*. Norman: University of Oklahoma Press, 2004.

Lipe, William D. "The Mesa Verde Region: Chaco's Northern Neighbor." In *In Search of Chaco: New Approaches to an Archaeological Enigma*, ed. David Grant Noble. Santa Fe: School of American Research Press, 2004.

Lister, Florence C. *Troweling Through Time: The First Century of Mesa Verdean Archaeology*. Albuquerque: University of New Mexico Press, 2004.

Lister, Robert H., and Florence C. Lister. *Aztec Ruins on the Animas: Excavated, Preserved, and Interpreted*. Albuquerque: University of New Mexico Press, 1987.

MacMahon, Darcie A., and William H. Marquardt. *The Calusa and Their Legacy: South Florida People and Their Environments*. Gainesville: University Press of Florida, 2004.

Madsen, David B. *Exploring the Fremont*. Salt Lake City: University of Utah Press, 2002.

Mails, Thomas. *The People Called Apache*. Englewood Cliffs, NJ: Rutledge Books, Prentice-Hall, 1974.

Margolin, Malcolm. *The Way We Lived: California Indian Stories, Songs, and Reminiscences*. Berkeley: Heyday Books, 1981; rev. ed., 1993.

Martin, Joel W. *Sacred Revolt: The Muskogees' Struggle for a New World*. Boston: Beacon Press, 1991.

Mauzé, Marie, Michael E. Harkin, and Sergie Kan, eds. *Coming to Shore: Northwest Coast Ethnology, Traditions, and Visions*. Lincoln: University of Nebraska Press, 2004.

McBride, Bunny. *Molly Spotted Elk: A Penobscot in Paris*. Norman: University of Oklahoma Press, 1995; paperback, 1997.

———. *Women of the Dawn*. Lincoln: University of Nebraska Press, 1999; paperback, 2001.

McChristian, Douglas C. *Arizona: Combat Post of the Southwest, 1858–1894*. Norman: University of Oklahoma Press, 2005.

McEwan, Bonnie G., ed. *Indians of the Greater Southeast: Historical Archaeology and Ethnohistory*. Gainesville: University Press of Florida, 2000.

McLendon, Sally, and Michael J. Lowy. "Southeastern and Eastern Pomo." In *California*, ed. R. F. Heizer, pp. 308–23. Vol. 8 of *Handbook of North American Indians*, ed. William C. Sturtevant. Washington, DC: Smithsonian Institution, 1978.

McManamon, Francis P., and James W. Bradley. "The Indian Neck Ossuary." *Scientific American* 256, no. 5 (1988): 98–104.

McMaster, Gerald, ed. *New Tribe New York: The Urban Vision Quest*. Washington, DC: National Museum of the American Indian, 2005.

McMaster, Gerald, and Clifford E. Trafzer, eds. *Native Universe: Voices of Indian America*. Washington, DC: National Museum of the American Indian and National Geographic, 2004.

Meltzer, D. J. *Search for the First Americans*. Washington, DC: Smithsonian Books, 1993.

———. *Folsom: New Archaeological Investigations of a Classic Paleoindian Bison Kill*. Berkeley: University of California Press, 2006.

Merrell, James H., and Daniel K. Richter. *Beyond the Covenant Chain: The Iroquois and Their Neighbors in Indian North America, 1600–1800*. Syracuse, NY: Syracuse University Press, 1987; rev. ed. (paperback), University Park: Penn State University Press, 2003.

Milanich, Jerald T. *Florida Indians and the Invasion from Europe*. Gainesville: University Press of Florida, 1995.

———. *Florida's Indians from Ancient Times to the Present*. Gainesville: University Press of Florida, 1998.

———. *Laboring in the Fields of the Lord: Spanish Missions and Southeastern Indians*. Washington, DC: Smithsonian Institution Press, 1999.

Miller, Jay. "Blending Worlds." In *The Native Americans*, ed. Betty Ballantine and Ian Ballantine. Atlanta: Turner Publishing, 1993.

Milligan, James C. *The Choctaw of Oklahoma*. Abilene, TX: H. V. Chapman and Sons, 2003.

Milliken, Randall. *A Time of Little Choice: The Disintegration of Tribal Culture in the San Francisco Bay Area 1769–1810*. Menlo Park, CA: Ballena Press, 1995.

Mills, Earl H., Sr., and Alicja Mann. *Son of Mashpee: Reflections of Chief Flying Eagle, a Wampanoag*. North Falmouth, MA: Word Studio, 1996.

Minge, Ward Allen. *Acoma: Pueblo in the Sky*. Rev. ed. Albuquerque: University of New Mexico Press, 1991.

Missall, John, and Mary Lou Missall. *The Seminole Wars: America's Longest Indian Conflict*. Gainesville: University Press of Florida, 2004.

Mitchem, Jeffrey M. "Investigations of the Possible Remains of de Soto's Cross at Parkin." *Arkansas Archeologist* 35 (1996): 87–95.

——. "Mississippian Research at Parkin Archeological State Park." *Proceedings of the 14th Mid-South Archaeological Conference,* pp. 25–39. Memphis: Panamerican Consultants Special Publication no. 1, 1996.

Mohawk, John. *War Against the Seneca: The French Expedition of 1687.* Victor, NY: Ganondagan State Historic Site, 1986.

——. *Utopian Legacies: A History of Conquest and Oppression in the Western World.* Santa Fe: Clear Light Press, 1999.

Murray, Robert A. *Pipestone: A History.* Pipestone, MN: Pipestone Indian Shrine Association, 1965.

Nabokov, Peter. *Where the Lightning Strikes: The Lives of American Indian Sacred Places.* New York: Viking, 2006.

Neihardt, John G. *Black Elk Speaks.* Lincoln: University of Nebraska Press, 2004.

Nelson, Margaret C. *Mimbres During the Twelfth Century: Abandonment, Continuity and Reorganization.* Tucson: University of Arizona Press, 1999.

Noble, David Grant, ed. *Wupatki and Walnut Canyon: New Perspectives on History, Prehistory, and Rock Art.* Santa Fe: Ancient City Press, 1993.

Ortiz, Beverly R. "Honoring the Dead and the Living: Dedication of the Sonoma Mission Indian Memorial." *News from Native California* 12, no. 4 (1999): 22–24.

Ortiz, Beverly R., and Julia F. Parker. *It Will Live Forever: Traditional Yosemite Indian Acorn Preparation.* Berkeley: Heyday Books, 1996.

Osio, Antonio María. *The History of Alta California: A Memoir of Mexican California.* Trans., ann., and ed. by Rose Marie Beebe and Robert M. Senkewicz. Madison: University of Wisconsin Press, 1996.

Ostler, Jeffrey. *The Plains Sioux and U.S. Colonialism from Lewis and Clark to Wounded Knee.* Cambridge, UK: Cambridge University Press, 2004.

Parrish, Otis, "The First People." In *Fort Ross,* ed. Lyn Kalani, Rudy Lynn, and John Sperry. Fort Ross, CA: Fort Ross Interpretive Association, 2001.

Pauketat, Timothy R. *Ancient Cahokia and the Mississippians.* Cambridge, UK: Cambridge University Press, 2004.

Pauketat, Timothy R., and Nancy Stone Bernard, *Cahokia Mounds.* Oxford, UK: Oxford University Press, 2004.

Pauketat, Timothy R., and Diana DiPaolo Loren, eds. *North American Archaeology.* Oxford, UK: Blackwell Press, 2005.

Perdue, Theda, and Michael D. Green. *The Cherokee Removal: A Brief History with Documents.* 2nd ed. Boston: Bedford/St. Martin's, 2005.

Peters, Virginia. *Women of the Earth Lodges: Tribal Life on the Plains.* Norman: University of Oklahoma Press, 2000.

Peterson, Dennis A., J. Daniel Rogers, Don G. Wyckoff, and Karen Dohm. *An Archeological Survey of the Spiro Vicinity, Le Flore County, Oklahoma.* Oklahoma Archeological Survey, ARSR 37. Norman: University of Oklahoma, 1993.

Pilling, Arnold. "Yurok." In *California,* ed. R. F. Heizer, pp. 137–54. Vol. 8 of *Handbook of North American Indians.* Washington, DC: Smithsonian Institution, 1978.

Pluckhahn, Thomas J. *Kolomoki: Settlement, Ceremony, and Status in the Deep South, A.D. 350 to 750.* Tuscaloosa: University of Alabama Press, 2003.

Pluckhahn, Thomas J., and Robbie F. Ethridge, eds. *Light on the Path: The Anthropology and History of the Southeastern Indians.* Tuscaloosa: University of Alabama Press, 2006.

Potter, Tracy. *Sheheke: Mandan Indian Diplomat.* Helena, MT: Farcountry Press/Fort Mandan Press, 2003.

Powers, Robert P., ed. *The Peopling of Bandelier: New Insights from the Archaeology of the Pajarito Plateau.* Santa Fe: School of American Research, 2005.

Poyo, Gerald E., and Gilberto M. Hinojosa, eds. *Tejano Origins in Eighteenth-Century San Antonio.* Austin: University of Texas Press, 1991.

Pratt, G. Michael. "The Battle of Fallen Timbers: An Eyewitness Perspective." *Northwest Ohio Quarterly* 67, no. 1 (1995): 4–34.

Prins, Harald. *The Mi'kmaq: Resistance, Accommodation and Cultural Survival.* New York: Harcourt Brace College Publishers, 1996.

Prins, Harald E. L., and Bunny McBride. *Asticou's Island Domain: Wabanaki Peoples at Mount Desert Island 1600–2000. An Ethnographic Overview and*

Assessment of Acadia National Park. Washington, DC: National Park Service, 2007.

Prucha, Francis Paul. *The Great Father: The United States Government and the American Indians.* Lincoln: University of Nebraska Press, 1984.

———. *American Indian Treaties: The History of a Political Anomaly.* Berkeley: University of California Press, 1994.

Rathjen, Fred. *The Texas Panhandle Frontier.* Austin: University of Texas Press, 1973.

Reeves, Carolyn Keller, ed. *The Choctaw Before Removal.* Jackson: University Press of Mississippi, 1985.

Reyhner, Jon Allan, and Jeanne M. Oyawin Eder. *American Indian Education: A History.* Norman: University of Oklahoma Press, 2006.

Richter, Daniel K. *Facing East from Indian Country: A Native History of Early America.* Cambridge, MA: Harvard University Press, 2001.

———. *The Ordeal of the Longhouse: The Peoples of the Iroquois League in the Era of European Colonization.* Chapel Hill: University of North Carolina Press, 1992.

Riddle, Jefferson C. Davis. *The Indian History of the Modoc War.* Mechanicsburg, PA: Stackpole Books, 2004.

Roberts, David. *In Search of the Old Ones: Exploring the Anasazi World of the Southwest.* New York: Simon and Schuster, 1997.

Robertson, Paul M. *Power of the Land: Identity, Ethnicity and Class among the Oglala Lakota.* New York: Routledge, 2002.

Robertson, Paul M., Miriam Jorgensen, and Carrie Garrow. "Indigenizing Evaluation Research: How Lakota Methodologies Are Helping Raise the Tipi in the Oglala Sioux Nation." *American Indian Quarterly* 28, nos. 3 and 4 (2004): 499–526.

Rolde, Neil. *Unsettled Past, Unsettled Future: The Story of Maine Indians.* Gardiner, ME: Tilbury House Publishing, 2004.

Rothman, Hal K. *Navajo National Monument: A Place and Its People. An Administrative History.* Washington, DC: National Park Service, 1991. http://www.nps.gov/nava/adhi/adhi.htm

Rountree, Helen C. *The Powhatan Indians of Virginia: Their Traditional Culture.* Norman: University of Oklahoma Press, 1989.

———. *Pocahontas's People: The Powhatan Indians of Virginia Through Four Centuries.* Norman: University of Oklahoma Press, 1990.

———. *Pocahontas, Powhatan, Opechancanough: Three Indian Lives Changed by Jamestown.* Charlottesville: University of Virginia Press, 2005.

Rountree, Helen C., Wayne E. Clark, and Kent Mountford. *John Smith's Chesapeake Voyages, 1607–1609.* Charlottesville: University of Virginia Press, 2007.

Rountree, Helen C., and Thomas E. Davison. *Eastern Shore Indians of Virginia and Maryland.* Charlottesville: University Press of Virginia, 1997.

Rountree, Helen C., and E. Randolph Turner III. *Before and After Jamestown: Virginia's Powhatans and Their Predecessors.* Gainesville: University Press of Florida, 2002.

Ruby, Robert H., and John A. Brown. *The Cayuse Indians: Imperial Tribesmen of the Old Oregon.* Commemorative ed. Norman: University of Oklahoma Press, 2005.

Salisbury, Neal. *Manitou and Providence: Indians, Europeans, and the Making of New England, 1500–1643.* New York: Oxford University Press, 1982.

Sando, Joe S. *Nee Hemish: The History of Jemez Pueblo.* Albuquerque: University of New Mexico Press, 1982.

———. *Pueblo Nations: Eight Centuries of Pueblo Indian History.* Santa Fe: Clear Light Publishers, 1992.

Schaafsma, Polly. "Rock Art." In *Great Basin,* ed. William d'Azevedo, pp. 215–26. Vol. 11 of *Handbook of North American Indians.* Washington, DC: Smithsonian Institution, 1986.

———. *Rock Art in New Mexico.* Santa Fe: Museum of New Mexico Press, 1992.

———. *Warrior, Shield, and Star.* Santa Fe: Western Edge Press, 2000.

———, ed. *New Perspectives on Pottery Mound Pueblo.* Albuquerque: University of New Mexico Press, 2007.

Secakuku, Susan. *Meet Mindy: A Native Girl of the Southwest.* Hillsboro, OR: Beyond Words Publishing, 2003.

Senkewicz, Robert M. *Vigilantes in Gold Rush San Francisco.* Stanford, CA: Stanford University Press, 1985.

Simmons, William S. *Spirit of the New England Tribes:*

Indian History and Folklore, 1620–1984. Hanover, NH: University Press of New England, 1986.

Smith, Kevin E., and James V. Miller. *Speaking with the Ancestors: Mississippian Stone Statuary of the Tennessee-Cumberland Style.* Tuscaloosa: University of Alabama Press, 2007.

Snead, James E. *Ruins and Rivals.* Tucson: University of Arizona Press, 2001.

———. *Knowing the Country.* Tucson: University of Arizona Press, 2007.

Snow, Dean R. *The Archaeology of New England.* New York: Academic Press, 1980.

Spier, Robert F. G. "Monache" and "Foothill Yokuts." In *California,* ed. R. F. Heizer, pp. 426–36, 471–84. Vol. 8 of *Handbook of North American Indians.* Washington, DC: Smithsonian Institution, 1978.

Stein, John R., and Peter J. McKenna. *An Archeological Reconnaissance of a Late Bonito Phase Occupation Near Aztec Ruins National Monument, New Mexico.* Santa Fe: Southwest Cultural Resources Center, National Park Service, 1988.

Stone, Glenn Davis, and Christian E. Downum. "Non-Boserupian Ecology and Agricultural Risk: Ethnic Politics and Land Control in the Arid Southwest." *American Anthropologist* 101, no. 1 (1999): 113–28.

Strickland, Rennard. *The Indians in Oklahoma: Newcomers to a New Land.* Norman: University of Oklahoma Press, 1980.

———. *Tonto's Revenge.* Albuquerque: University of New Mexico Press, 1997.

———, ed. *Felix Cohen's Handbook of Federal Indian Law.* Charlottesville, VA: Bobbs-Merrill, 1982.

Suquamish Museum. *The Eyes of Chief Seattle.* Suquamish, WA, 1983.

Sweet, John W. *Bodies Politic: Negotiating Race in the American North, 1730–1830.* Baltimore: Johns Hopkins University Press, 2003.

Swisher, Karen Gayton, and John W. Tippeconnic III, eds. *Next Steps: Research and Practice to Advance Indian Education.* Charleston, WV: Appalachia Educational Laboratory, 1999.

Sword, Wiley. *President Washington's Indian War: The Struggle for the Old Northwest, 1790–95.* Norman: University of Oklahoma Press, 1995.

Tanner, Helen Hornbeck, ed. *Atlas of Great Lakes Indian History.* Norman: University of Oklahoma Press for the Newberry Library, 1987.

Taylor, Alan. *Divided Ground: Indians, Settlers, and the Northern Borderland of the American Revolution.* New York: Knopf, 2006.

Thomas, David Hurst. "Saints and Soldiers at Santa Catalina: Hispanic Designs for Colonial America." In *The Recovery of Meaning in Historical Archaeology,* ed. Mark P. Leone and Parker B. Potter, Jr., pp. 73–140. Washington, DC: Smithsonian Institution Press, 1988.

———. *Exploring Ancient Native America.* New York: Macmillan, 1994.

———. *Skull Wars: Kennewick Man, Archaeology, and the Battle for Native American Identity.* New York: Basic Books, 2000.

———, ed. *Columbian Consequences.* Washington, DC: Smithsonian Institution Press, 1990–1992.

Thompson, Ian M. *The Towers of Hovenweep.* Mesa Verde National Park, CO: Mesa Verde Museum Association, 1993.

———. *People of the Mesa Verde Country: An Archaeological Remembrance.* Englewood, CO: EarthTales Press, 2002.

Towner, Ronald H. *Defending the Dinétah.* Salt Lake City: University of Utah Press, 2003.

Townsend, R. F., ed. *Hero, Hawk and Open Hand: American Indian Art of the Ancient Midwest and South.* Chicago: Art Institute of Chicago; New Haven: Yale University Press, 2004.

Trafzer, Clifford E. *The People of San Manuel.* Highland, CA: San Manuel Band of Mission Indians, 2002.

Trafzer, Clifford E., Luke Madrigal, and Anthony Madrigal. *Chemehuevi People of the Coachella Valley.* Coachella, CA: Chemehuevi Press, 1997.

Turpin, Solveig A. *Pecos River Rock Art.* San Antonio, TX: Sandy McPherson Publishing, 1990.

———. "Archaic North America." In *The Handbook of Rock Art Research,* ed. David Whitley, pp. 361–413. Walnut Creek, CA: AltaMira Press, 2001.

Ulrich, Roberta. *Empty Nets: Indians, Dams, and the Columbia River.* Corvallis: Oregon State University Press, 1999.

Unrau, William E. *The Kansa Indians: A History of the Wind People, 1673–1873.* Norman: University of Oklahoma Press, 1971.

Vennum, Thomas. *Wild Rice and the Ojibway People.* St. Paul: Minnesota Historical Society, 1988.

Viola, Herman J. *It Is a Good Day to Die: Indian*

Eyewitnesses Tell the Story of the Battle of the Little Bighorn. Norman: University of Oklahoma, 1998.

———. *Little Bighorn Remembered: The Untold Indian Story of Custer's Last Stand.* New York: Crown Publishers, 1999.

———. *Trail to Wounded Knee: The Last Stand of the Plains Indians 1860–1890.* Washington, DC: National Geographic Society, 2004.

Vivian, R. Gwinn. *The Chacoan Prehistory of the San Juan Basin.* San Diego: Academic Press, 1990.

Wagner, Mark J. "Mississippian Cosmology and Rock Art at the Millstone Bluff Site in Southern Illinois." In *The Rock-Art of Eastern North America: Capturing Images and Insight,* ed. Carol Diaz-Granados and James R. Duncan. Tuscaloosa: University of Alabama Press, 2004.

Warren, Stephen. *The Shawnees and Their Neighbors, 1795–1870.* Urbana: University of Illinois Press, 2005.

Warren, William W. *History of the Ojibwe People.* St. Paul: Minnesota Historical Society Press, 1984.

Watkins, Joe E. *Indigenous Archaeology: American Indian Values and Scientific Practice.* Walnut Creek, CA: AltaMira Press, 2000.

———. *Sacred Sites and Repatriation.* Philadelphia: Chelsea House Publishers, 2005.

Watt, Eva Tulene, and Keith H. Basso. *Don't let the Sun Step Over You: A White Mountain Apache Family Life, 1860–1976.* Tucson: University of Arizona Press, 2004.

Weber, David J. *The Mexican Frontier, 1821–1846: The American Southwest under Mexico.* Albuquerque: University of New Mexico Press, 1982.

———. *The Spanish Frontier in North America.* New Haven: Yale University Press, 1992.

———. *Bárbaros: Spaniards and Their Savages in the Age of Enlightenment.* New Haven: Yale University Press, 2005.

Weisman, Brent Richards. *Like Beads on a String: A Culture History of the Seminole Indians in North Peninsular Florida.* Tuscaloosa: University of Alabama Press, 1989.

———. *Unconquered People: Florida's Seminole and Miccosukee Indians.* Gainesville: University Press of Florida, 1999.

Welch, Paul D. *Moundville's Economy,* Tuscaloosa: University of Alabama Press, 1991.

———. *Archaeology at Shiloh Indian Mounds, 1899–1999.* Tuscaloosa: University of Alabama Press, 2005.

Welch, J. R. "A Monument to Native Civilization: Byron Cummings' Still-Unfolding Vision for Kinishba Ruins." *Journal of the Southwest* 49, no. 1 (2007).

Wellenreuther, Herman, and Carola Wessel, eds. *The Moravian Mission Diaries of David Zeisberger 1772–1781.* Trans. by Julie Tomberlin Weber. University Park: Pennsylvania State University Press. 2005.

Weltfish, Gene. *The Lost Universe.* Lincoln: University of Nebraska Press, 1965.

Wesler, Kit W. *Excavations at Wickliffe Mounds.* Tuscaloosa: University of Alabama Press, 2001.

Westbrook, Nicholas. Introduction to *Fort Ticonderoga: Key to the Continent,* by Edward P. Hamilton. Ticonderoga, NY: Fort Ticonderoga Museum, 1995.

Wilkins, David E. *American Indian Politics and the American Political System.* Rev. ed. Lanham, MD: Rowman and Littlefield Publishers, 2006.

Wilkins, Thurman. *Cherokee Tragedy: The Ridge Family and the Decimation of a People.* Norman: University of Oklahoma Press, 1986.

Wilkinson, Charles. "Land Use, Science, and Spirituality: The Search for a True and Lasting Relationship with the Land." *Public Land and Resources Law Review* 20 (2000).

———. *Blood Struggle: The Rise of Modern Indian Nations.* New York: W. W. Norton, 2005.

Williams, Stephen. *Fantastic Archaeology: The Wild Side of North American Prehistory.* Philadelphia: University of Pennsylvania Press, 1991.

Williamson, Ray A., and Claire R. Farrer, eds. *Earth and Sky: Visions of the Cosmos in Native American Folklore.* Albuquerque: University of New Mexico Press, 1992.

Wilson, Roy L. *Medicine Wheels: Ancient Teachings for Modern Times.* New York: Crossroad General Interest, 2001.

Wray, Jacilee, ed. *Native Peoples of the Olympic Peninsula: Who We Are.* Olympic Peninsula Intertribal Cultural Advisory Committee. Norman: University of Oklahoma Press, 2002.

Yamane, Linda. *When the World Ended.* Berkeley: Oyate, 1995.

———. *Weaving a California Tradition.* Minneapolis: Lerner Publishing Group, 1996.

———, ed. *A Gathering of Voices: The Native Peoples of the Central California Coast.* Santa Cruz: Santa Cruz Museum of Art and History, 2002.

Yee, Mary J., and Ernestine Ygnacio-De Soto. *The Sugar Bear Story.* San Diego: Sunbelt Publications, 2005.

Illustration Credits

Index